Feminist Perspectives on Jewish Studies

LYNN DAVIDMAN & SHELLY TENENBAUM, Editors

Feminist Perspectives
on Jewish Studies

Yale University Press   New Haven and London

Published with assistance from the Louis Stern Memorial Fund.

Designed by Sonia L. Scanlon.

Set in Bembo type by Rainsford Type, Danbury, Connecticut.

Printed in the United States of America by Edward Brothers, Ann Arbor, Michigan.

Library of Congress Cataloging-in-Publication Data

Feminist perspectives on Jewish studies / edited by Lynn Davidman and Shelly Tenenbaum.

    p. cm.

    Includes bibliographical references and index.

    ISBN 0-300-06028-9 (cl)

    1. Women in Judaism—Historiography. 2. Feminism—Religious aspects—Judaism. 3. Women's studies. 4. Judaism—Historiography. 5. Jews—Historiography. 6. Jewish learning and scholarship.

    I. Davidman, Lynn, 1955– . II. Tenenbaum, Shelly.

    BM729.W6F45 1994

    296'.082—dc20   94-16445

              CIP

A catalogue record for this book is available from the British Library.

Contents

Introduction

The contributors to *Feminist Perspectives on Jewish Studies* provide a critical evaluation of the impact of feminist scholarship on several of the disciplines encompassed by Jewish studies. Each author addresses the state of knowledge about women and gender in a specific field; whether and how this knowledge has affected the mainstream of the discipline; existing scholarship and new avenues for research that use gender as a central analytic category for the study of Jewish life; and how research that uses gender in its analytic apparatus leads to a reconceptualization of basic concepts and to paradigm shifts in Jewish studies across disciplines.

Although feminist scholars in various fields of Jewish studies have been publishing research on aspects of Jewish women's lives—for example, Paula Hyman's work on kosher meat boycotts as an expression of immigrant women's social protest, and Chava Weissler's study of Jewish women's prayers in Eastern Europe[1]—no one has evaluated the cumulative impact of this new knowledge on any of the disciplines within Jewish studies. This volume presents a new perspective on feminism and Jewish studies. It looks at the disciplines individually and collectively in terms of their level of integration of knowledge about women and their development of new concepts with which to understand Jewish women's lives. The chapters represent the diversity of Jewish studies. They range from the classical—biblical studies, rabbinics, and philosophy—to the innovative, such as film studies and Jewish feminist theology. In selecting subject areas, we sought to balance the perspectives of the humanities and social sciences. We solicited articles on Jewish history and literary studies as well as in anthropology and sociology. Taken together the articles provide the argument that the traditional disciplinary boundaries are an inadequate structure for producing knowledge about women's lives and understanding their textual representations. Each author writes about her own subject within Jewish studies, but each also draws on feminist scholarship—Jewish or otherwise—in several other disciplines.

Before the explosion of feminist scholarship in the past twenty-five years, women were generally invisible in academia, both as producers and as subjects of knowledge. As feminist women applied their analyses of sexism in society to its effects on the construction of knowledge, they began to document how male scholars perpetuated women's invisibility—by basing their conclusions on studies of men, by not asking research questions about women's lives, by assuming that the conventional division of gender roles is correct and natural, and by not including works by women in their course syllabi. Women's studies scholars have reexamined the established wisdom from the standpoint of women. This was the first stage in the development of feminist scholarship—the critique.

The next stage—and these stages are not simply sequential but continuous and perhaps spiraling—was the attempt to fill the gaps in our knowledge of women by studying their lives according to the categories of traditional male scholarship. For example, sociologists studied women's work by defining work as paid tasks performed outside the home; historians attempted to fill the gaps by locating "women worthies," Gerda Lerner's term for women who excelled in traditionally masculine pursuits.[2] The underlying assumption was that conventional categories of analysis would suffice for the elucidation of women's experiences. However, these concepts and theoretical frameworks often missed much of what was distinctive about women's experiences. There are many crucial tasks that women do for which they are not paid or that are performed outside the home, and the history of women's lives reveals different patterns and priorities than those that shaped men's lives.[3] Thus, correcting for this invisibility of women involves not simply "adding women and stirring,"[4] but reconstructing the model of scholarship in each discipline and across disciplines.[5]

This fundamental insight sparked the third stage of feminist knowledge: the development of a scholarship that places women at the center and begins with women's experiences. It is an approach that requires asking new questions, redefining importance from the perspective of women's experience, formulating new or modified research methods, and reconceptualizing conventional categories of thought and analysis. It is based on an understanding of the significance of gender as a crucial analytic tool for understanding social life and cultural products. The new knowledge of the centrality of gender in the organization of society thus produced pushes us to expand our understanding of many human experiences—work, leisure, art, spirituality, re-lations, and the construction of ethnic-religious identities. Paralleling the development of feminist scholarship within each discipline, feminist scholars in Jewish studies have approached their subjects with skepticism toward established knowledge. They have deconstructed classical and contemporary texts to uncover the hidden assumptions about women's roles and place and have shown that the normative status of maleness underlies theological cat-egories (such as the attributes of God) as well as contemporary studies of Jewish history, sociology, and literature. The growing body of feminist scholarship makes it evident that a thorough understanding of Jewish texts, thought, and social life requires a gendered analysis, since the division of society by gender is such a fundamental component in the construction of Jewish culture.

The Integration of Scholarship on Women

Each author evaluates the level of integration of feminist scholarship and perspectives in her discipline. The subjects vary in the amount of feminist scholarship produced, how much it has been read by other scholars in the field and incorporated into their teaching and research, and its impact on the dominant paradigms in the discipline. Most of our authors report that there has been little integration of feminist knowledge. Judith Hauptman on rabbinics (chapter 3), Judith Plaskow on theology (chapter 4), Hava Tirosh-Rothschild on philosophy (chapter 5), and Naomi Sokoloff on Hebrew literature (chapter 10) all describe the paucity of feminist scholarship in their areas—at least until recently. Sonya Michel (chapter 11) writes that a lack of a feminist perspective characterizes Jewish film studies, and Lynn Da-vidman and Shelly Tenenbaum, in reviewing the sociology of American Jews, find a scarcity of scholarship that places women at the center. In con-trast, as Hyman and Joyce Antler write (chapters 6 and 9, respectively), Jewish history and American Jewish literature have recently experienced a growth of feminist studies that has led to the reconceptualization of such basic ideas as community and assimilation. This scholarship, however, has not been addressed by most mainstream scholars.

At the other end of the continuum, Susan Sered (chapter 8) writes that the anthropological study of Jews has incorporated feminist approaches. Over the past two decades anthropologists have produced numerous studies that begin with women's experiences and have analyzed them according to the many factors of social location that shape women's lives—such as age, ethnicity, marital status, and sexual preference. Similarly, Tikva Frymer-Kensky (chapter 2) argues that the impact of feminist scholarship is apparent in the work of mainstream scholars and the choice of research foci in biblical studies.

The differences between these disciplines in the level of integration of women's studies perspectives can be traced to several factors. One is the nature of the skills required to become an established scholar in a discipline. Some disciplines, such as Bible, theology, and rabbinic studies, require sophisticated training in classical texts unavailable to women until recently. The relative lack of training of women is relevant not only to the possibilities for feminist scholarship in these areas but must be understood as a central component in the Jewish cultural construction of gender; women and men had unequal access to the tradition because only men were trained to be literate in classical texts.

The production of feminist knowledge and the spur toward paradigm shifts in any discipline of Jewish studies depend upon the availability of institutional support structures. For example, the sociology of American Jews is a relatively new field, whereas theology and Jewish film studies are generally not even included in academic curricula. These fields tend to be small, with few graduate programs and even fewer feminist scholars to train students. Rabbinics is dominated by yeshiva-trained men who, according to Hauptman, are not usually open-minded enough to view feminist questions with sympathy. In these disciplines, therefore, even the basic foundation of feminist scholarship—the critique of existing knowledge—remains incomplete. In other disciplines, as Hyman tells us in relation to Jewish history, graduate students are encouraged to ignore gender issues in their research until they have safely established themselves in the profession.

How extensively feminist scholarship has been incorporated into mainstream disciplines also shapes its acceptance within the parallel domains of Jewish studies. In some of these disciplines, notably anthropology and literary criticism, the category of gender has been accepted into the mainstream, and this has eased its incorporation into Judaic studies scholarship. In contrast, although sociology has witnessed a profusion of studies that begin with women's experiences and make gender a category of analysis, feminist scholarship has not generally influenced the basic paradigms of the discipline. This factor in part accounts for the relative lack of influence of feminist perspectives on the sociology of Jews. In still other fields, such as philosophy, history, English literature, and film studies, the category of gender has been incorporated into the analytic apparatus of the disciplines, but it has not yet had a similar impact in Judaic studies.

Tirosh-Rothschild, in her analysis of the lack of integration of feminist scholarship in Jewish philosophy, outlines several characteristics of Jewish studies that might account for the lag behind mainstream philosophy and other disciplines. The flowering of Jewish studies as a distinct discipline has made it possible for Jewish scholars to ignore contemporary debates and modes of thought. "The field . . . has become a semi-autarchic scholarly community that provides its members with the illusion of comfort and strength." In addition, Israel is the primary home for Jewish studies. In Israel, because of its geographic distance from the West and because of its struggle for survival and a collective identity, contemporary debates in the Western academy are less immediate. Thus, many of the subfields of Jewish studies have not engaged in such contemporary thought trends as the postmodern critique of established disciplines, with which feminist scholarship is often allied.

Although feminist theory and the category of gender have not been fully integrated in the disciplines of Jewish studies, the contributors to this volume report on a wide variety of scholarship done from a woman-centered perspective. They do not simply document the relative lack of feminist influence in Jewish studies but draw on the larger body of feminist scholarship in several mainstream disciplines in order to raise new research questions, formulate new theoretical frameworks, and rethink key concepts. The authors begin the work that is the goal of feminist scholarship in general: the reconstruction of discourse in the disciplines.

Gender Hierarchies and Their Social Contexts

Feminist scholarship in Jewish studies builds on and contributes to feminist knowledge in the mainstream disciplines. The authors in this volume begin with the basic assumption that gender implies a hierarchy of values in which males have more power, their activities are seen as more important, and their traits are privileged. These differences are socially constructed rather than biologically determined. The authors show that although gender arrangements in Jewish life are rooted in classical sources, they are also shaped by the structures and culture of the larger societies in which Jews live. By specifying how Jewish patriarchy in its various incarnations is linked to the gender hierarchies of the surrounding cultures, they sometimes conclude that Jewish culture is actually less patriarchal than is typically assumed. This assertion is particularly important in light of Christian feminist arguments that the ancient Hebrews are responsible for the death of the Goddess and therefore for the origin of patriarchy.[6]

For example, Frymer-Kensky writes (in chapter 2) that "one of the significant results of feminist studies of the Bible has been the realization that the biblical text itself, read with nonpatriarchal eyes, is much less injurious to women than the traditional readings of Western civilization." Compared to the texts of other cultures in the ancient world, such as Assyria, the Bible was clearly not the worst perpetrator of patriarchy. In chapter 3, Hauptman similarly challenges the feminist notion that the Mishnah is a thoroughly androcentric document. In fact, she claims, the framers of the Mishnah attempted to "abandon the Torah's extreme androcentrism and view women as members of the Jewish community who have the capacity to assume religious responsibilities but who function at a lower level of religious obligation than men." Despite their recognition of the patriarchal nature of these texts, Frymer-Kensky and Hauptman conclude that the texts must be interpreted with an awareness of the factors that shaped them: the religious texts of surrounding cultures, the patriarchal nature of other major historical civilizations at that time, and the intentions of the framers of the texts, which were often to advance women's rights. In contrast, Plaskow's chapter emphasizes that the Torah is "itself in bondage to patriarchy," and argues that the "feminist relation to the Torah begins in suspicion, critique, and the refusal to assign revelatory status to the establishment and reinforcement of patriarchy."

The Question of Objectivity

By its very being, feminist scholarship challenges the idea of objectivity in scholarship. Feminist scholars in all disciplines have demonstrated that although mainstream scholarship has purported to study basic human experiences and to reflect on universal texts, their definition of what is worthy of attention has reflected the standpoint of the male producers of this knowledge. Claims of objectivity and universality serve to reinforce the status quo and provide excuses for ignoring the experiences of groups of people who thereby are defined as marginal (such as people of color and white women) and for not incorporating their writings into literary canons.

The authors in *Feminist Perspectives on Jewish Studies* similarly criticize the false claims of objectivity in their own disciplines by showing that putative scholarship about Jews was actually focused on male Jews. Uncovering this androcentrism led to a questioning of how knowledge was produced—a concern with research methodology that has also been central in feminist discourse for the past fifteen years. Scholars who seek to illuminate women's lives have questioned whether the traditional methods in the disciplines, those that produced conventional scholarship, would suffice to create a new knowledge of women's lives and shape the development of new paradigms.[7]

A prominent methodological and theoretical innovation of feminist scholarship is its interdisciplinary nature: "By asking questions in terms of *women* (and not in terms of a particular framework such as psychology or history, for example) feminists moved beyond some of the limitations which are imposed by 'compartmentalization.'"[8] To discover the realities of Jewish women's lives, about which there are few historical records and limited contemporary studies, the authors in this volume combine insights that emerge from such disciplinary approaches as archaeology, history, political science, literary theory, sociology, anthropology, psychoanalytic theory, and cultural studies. Questions raised by examining gender in any one study inevitably spill over into Jewish studies as a whole. By working across disciplines, feminist students of Jewish life can better understand the complex linkages between gender and Judaism.

Since the classic texts provide only a sketchy portrait of women's lives, feminist scholars engaged in the study of the Bible, rabbinics, Jewish theology, and history must work to uncover hints about women's experiences that may be embedded in unusual sources, such as "narratives, prophecies, or legal texts focused on other matters."[9] The understanding of ancient texts can be supplemented by evidence from archaeological discoveries, the writings of nonrabbinic groups, and any literature by women dealing with religious themes. Where no sources can be found, the tradition supplies its own innovative methodology: the creation of *midrash* (a reinterpretation of Scripture). Plaskow writes that we can draw upon midrash "received" by contemporary women to help us fill in the gaps, and Sokoloff suggests that feminist literary studies can study "how women [writers] have sought out precursors by conjuring foremothers and rewriting biblical tales."[10]

Jewish feminist scholars in the humanities have incorporated postmodern understandings of the dynamics of "reading" and interpretation in order to suggest new methodological approaches in their disciplines. As Michel describes in her chapter on film studies, contemporary scholarship suggests that the meaning of texts does not simply reside within the texts themselves but rather is created through the interaction of texts with their readers (or audiences, in the case of films). Therefore, she, along with the authors of the chapters on Hebrew literature, American Jewish literature, Bible, and theology, suggests that the interpretation of Jewish cultural products and the analysis of their effect on the shaping of ethnic-religious identities cannot be based simply on close textual analysis. Rather, scholars must take into account how the various factors of the social location of audiences—both Jewish and Gentile—shape their reading and interpretation of any cultural product.

In history, anthropology, and sociology, the authors suggest that beginning with women's experiences and focusing on gender as a major analytic category will involve creating new methodologies or refocusing established ones. Techniques of social history that explore the everyday lives of ordinary individuals increase our understanding of Jewish women's lives over time and in various social classes. As Hyman writes, one can discover new sources by asking new questions of old material or by recognizing as historically significant experiences that were previously "not seen," even when they were documented. Oral histories, in-depth interviewing, and ethnographic methods are techniques that often give voice to those who have not been heard and capture the experiences of those who have not been seen as worthy of attention.

New Areas of Thematic Inquiry

To gain knowledge about women's lives, feminist scholars have redefined what is important; this volume reflects the many new areas of thematic inquiry that have emerged from gendered analyses in the disciplines of Jewish studies. Feminist research has explored the implicit assumptions about women that shaped the development of classical Jewish texts, the gendered nature of language, and its impact on philosophical discourse and literary representations, mother-daughter relations, female eroticism, women's struggles for autonomy and the cultural barriers that constrained them, and the public and private activities of Jewish women.

In all the disciplines discussed here, the new research on gendered topics has led to a rethinking of basic assumptions and concepts in the subject. In history, anthropology, and sociology, for example, research that begins with women's experiences leads to expanded conceptions of such central ideas as spirituality, community, and political activism. A new understanding of the institutional roles of ancient Israel is shaped by the gendered analyses of Jewish feminist scholars in theology, the Bible, and rabbinics. In the humanities, the feminist focus on language and the insight that the larger society is "linguistically male" has led feminist scholars of Jewish culture to read texts for clues about the role of language in the creation and perpetuation of gender distinctions.[11]

Insights from the various disciplinary approaches in Jewish studies can together elucidate such key areas of feminist concern as family life. Feminist scholars in the mainstream disciplines have challenged the idea that the family is a natural rather than a social unit. In Jewish studies gendered analyses have similarly debunked stereotypical images of the Jewish family as a divinely inspired, warm and loving haven organized for the protection of women and children. Instead, by analyzing the depiction of the Jewish family in ancient texts, contemporary literature and films, philosophical discussions, and social science research, feminist scholars have revealed that the concept of family is a locus of political struggle. By showing how Jewish families are institutions that change over time and place but are nevertheless always experienced differently by women and men, the work of feminist scholars contributes to the development of a more realistic and nuanced understanding of Jewish social life.

The feminist concern with the impact of social change on gender is a theme that unites many of the chapters in this book. Since Jews have always lived as minorities in other cultures, their ever-changing relations with host societies have continually produced fluctuations in many aspects of Jewish social life, including gender in its many manifestations. Throughout their history Jews have faced a tension between maintaining a cultural distinctiveness and assimilating into the surrounding culture. Since the ethnic-religious identities that are at stake in this struggle are gendered and because gender is fundamental to the organization of Jewish life, feminist scholarship enlarges our understanding of this critical dilemma by showing how women and men have experienced it differently.

Over time and in different cultures, Jewish women and men had different amounts of interaction with the wider society. Feminist theological and biblical studies reveal that women in ancient Israel may have been more resistant than men to giving up the worship of female deities, a finding that has profound implications for our understanding of the development of Israelite monotheism. Historical and sociological studies, in contrast, reveal that women in the modern period, because of their involvement in the family and the local community, may have been slower to adopt the patterns of the surrounding cultures and hence to assimilate. These findings challenge conventional understandings of assimilation, which presume that it was a rapid and sudden process that affected men and women at the same rate. In anthropological studies of ultra-Orthodox women, scholars show still another variation of how gender shapes the involvement of Jews with the secular society. Despite the gender conservatism of the ultra-Orthodox, feminist researchers have found that when men focus their primary energies on Talmudic scholarship, the task of interacting with the wider, secular society devolves upon the women.

The tensions between ethnic-religious distinctiveness and the attraction of the wider culture are often portrayed in literature and film as gender struggles. The media show how the attempt by immigrants to integrate into the wider society was structured by the differences between the gender roles of the wider society and those of the immigrants' culture in Eastern Europe. The struggle to achieve the economic mobility promised by integration was portrayed as a battle between the sexes: in order to fit into the wider society and attain economic mobility, filmic and literary characters—usually male—often married outside their group. Feminist perspectives in Jewish cultural studies highlight the cultural tensions manifest in the permutations of gender and ethnicity in literature and films.

Public and Private in Jewish Life

The division of social life into public and private realms and the assignment of women to the (typically) less valued private sphere have been studied extensively by feminist scholars.[12] Recent feminist scholarship, however, has challenged the idea that these boundaries between public and private—women's and men's—spheres are as fixed and absolute as conventional scholarship had assumed.[13]

Feminist anthropological theory suggests that male dominance depends on the segregation of men and women in everyday activities.[14] Feminist scholars in Jewish studies have therefore inquired into the precise nature of the segregation between women and men and its impact on women's autonomy in different periods and locations in Jewish history. In biblical times, according to Frymer-Kensky, women's activity was confined to the private sphere since women were not part of the public hierarchies as they developed. Although individual women may have had some access to power, women as a group were disadvantaged relative to men. Nevertheless, Hauptman argues that at the time of the Mishnah, women were not totally powerless, since they were not completely sequestered in the family compound. Rather, "they appeared in public regularly—in the marketplace as buyers and sellers, at rabbinic courts as litigants, at weddings, and at funerals—as active participants." Hyman similarly challenges the idea of such absolute boundaries between the public and private in Jewish life, since they clearly vary with time and place. Studies of Jewish women's lives reveal linkages between the home, family, and the public sphere and the ways that Jewish women fluidly combined work and domesticity.

The ever-shifting boundaries between the private and public in Jewish culture have influenced women's writing and its acceptance by the male literary establishment. Hebrew literature, as Sokoloff describes, has most often been concerned with collective matters, such as national cultural rebirth and the struggle for independence, rather than with private matters. Since women were often excluded from public activity, this body of literature often does not recognize experiences particular to women. In addition, women writers who sought acceptance in Hebrew literary circles were often discouraged from broaching personal topics or expressing themselves freely. A feminist analysis of women's writing illustrates a movement away from the personal over the course of their careers.

In depicting women's frequent exclusion from the public centers of power and decision making in various cultures, feminist scholars have resisted portraying women solely as victims of systems outside their control. As the women's movement in the larger culture has brought women a new sense of power and agency, feminist scholarship in the social sciences and the humanities reveals that when women have been excluded from the dominant culture, they have created their own, separate activities and culture.

Thus sexual segregation must be seen as a two-edged sword. As Sered states in her review of anthropology, although sexual segregation cuts women off from important and culturally esteemed spiritual venues, it also means that they have some autonomy in developing their own perspectives, constructing their own value systems, managing their own resources, and forging their own rituals.

The clearest theme to emerge from scholarship that begins with women's experiences is that women see the world from *their* vantage point, which may not mesh with the dominant world view and definition of reality. As several of the authors in this volume describe, feminist scholarship reveals how women in a variety of cultural contexts maneuver and find meaning within and around the patriarchal cultural heritage. Hyman and Plaskow cite the research of Chava Weissler, showing how, despite their exclusion from the synagogue, Jewish women had texts of their own and developed their own contexts for spiritual expression.

Focusing on women's experiences expands the concept of Jewish spirituality. Most definitions of Jewish religious behavior and experience emphasize the public contexts and activities through which men fulfill their ritual obligations. Women's piety, however, has revolved around the concerns of everyday life.[15] Just as women's rituals in other cultures have much to do with family relations,[16] so too do those of Jewish women. Historical, anthropological, sociological, and literary studies show that women have developed rituals that imbue domestic activities with holiness and that they often define moral and religious behavior in terms of interpersonal relations. Women may not seek God and spiritual experience in the synagogue but rather through domestic routines and biological experiences specific to women.

Differences between Women

As feminist scholarship has grown in sophistication, researchers have addressed not only the similarities between women as a class but also the differences between women based on such factors as race, ethnicity, social class, and sexual orientation.[17] Within the disciplines of Jewish studies, feminist scholars have similarly recognized that not all Jewish women have the same experiences. They have therefore sought to develop an analytic apparatus that highlights the intersection of gender, religion, ethnicity, and social class in Jewish life.

Feminist biblical scholars have applied this analytic framework to produce a new reading of texts that illuminates how class, gender, and ethnicity shape the fate of the characters in biblical narratives. Biblical stories reveal that despite the denial of certain rights to all women as a group, women of wealth and status who belonged to the dominant ethnic and religious group were sometimes able to transcend the limitations of gender and act to shape events. For example, the story of Sarah, Abraham's wife, shows how she used her class status and the ethnic privilege of her son to banish her maid, Hagar, and her son Ishmael from the household. Marital status, too, is clearly a significant factor of social location that shapes women's opportunities and status in biblical society.

Current research that compares Jewish immigrant women with women of other ethnic groups, for example, shows how ethnic-religious culture and social class shape women's opportunities, work, and life patterns. Cultural studies illustrate how ethnic and class politics often take the form of gender politics, such as in literary and filmic representations of the dilemmas of intermarriage. In American Jewish film and writing the conflict over ethnic and religious identity in a new culture can be interpreted from a gendered perspective. Important issues, such as the aspirations of women for love, success, and power, are expressed in their struggles to create an appropriate identity as either masculine or feminine in the terms of their new culture.

The relevance of this volume extends beyond Jewish studies; it is aimed at all scholars interested in feminism, cultural diversity, and multiculturalism. Feminist scholarship on Jewish life offers a particular example of the broader question of how ethnic-religious culture interacts with the structures and values of the surrounding society to produce a group's gender arrangements. Just as women of color have pointed out that most feminist scholarship has ignored their distinctive experiences, Jewish women object when they are indiscriminately placed in the category of white middle-class women. Proponents of multiculturalism, in their attempts to clarify the singular experiences of excluded racial and ethnic minorities, too often ignore the experiences of Jews. In this schema, Jewish women are doubly marginal: as women they have been invisible in the disciplines of Jewish studies, and as Jews they have increasingly been seen as part of the dominant white majority. The current challenge to the traditional canon must seek to open it fully so that the experiences of each diverse group of our society are more accurately represented.

Notes

1. Paula E. Hyman, "Immigrant Women and Consumer Protest: The New York City Kosher Meat Boycott of 1902," *American Jewish History* 70(1) (Sept. 1980): 91–105; Chava Weissler, "The Traditional Piety of Ashkenazic Women," in Arthur Green, ed., *Jewish Spirituality from the Sixteenth-Century Revival to the Present* (New York: Crossroad, 1987); " 'For Women and for Men Who Are Like Women': The Construction of Gender in Yiddish Devotional Literature," *Journal of Feminist Studies in Religion* 5(2) (fall 1989): 7–24.
2. Gerda Lerner, "Placing Women in History: A 1975 Perspective," in B. Carroll, ed., *Liberating Women's History* (Urbana: University of Illinois Press, 1976), 357–67.
3. The classic article that established this point is Joan Kelly-Gadol, "Did Women Have a Renaissance?" in Renate Bridenthal and Claudia Koontz, eds., *Becoming Visible: Women in European History* (Boston: Houghton Mifflin, 1977), 137–64. See also Sydney Stahl Weinberg, "The Treatment of Women in Immigration History: A Call for a Change," *Journal of American Ethnic History* 11(4) (summer 1992): 25–46.
4. Charlotte Bunch, *Passionate Politics: Essays 1968–1986—Feminist Theory in Action* (New York: St. Martin's, 1987), 140.

5. Dorothy Smith, "Women's Perspective as a Radical Critique of Sociology," *Sociological Inquiry* 44 (1974): 7–13.

6. Susannah Heschel, "Anti-Judaism in Christian Feminist Theology," *Tikkun* 5(3) (May/June 1990): 25–28, 95–97; see also the several articles in the special section on feminist anti-Judaism in the *Journal of Feminist Studies in Religion* 7(2) (fall 1991).

7. Feminist scholars have produced numerous essays, books, and anthologies that address the methodologies that would best produce knowledge about women's lives. See, e.g., Ruth Bleier, *Science and Gender: A Critique of Biology and Its Theories on Women* (New York: Pergamon, 1984); Gloria Bowles and Renate Duelli Klein, eds., *Theories of Women's Studies* (London: Routledge, 1983); Patricia Hill Collins, "Learning from the Outsider Within: The Sociological Significance of Black Feminist Thought," *Social Problems* 33(6) (1986): 14–32, and *Black Feminist Thought: Knowledge, Consciousness, and the Politics of Empowerment* (Boston, Unwin Hyman, 1990); Sandra Harding and Jean F. O'Barr, eds., *Sex and Scientific Inquiry* (Chicago: University of California Press, 1987); Joyce McCarl Nielsen, ed., *Feminist Research Methods: Exemplary Readings in the Social Sciences* (Boulder: Westview, 1990); Shulamit Reinharz with Lynn Davidman, *Methods in Social Research: Feminist Perspectives* (Oxford: Oxford University Press, 1992); Dorothy Smith, *The Everyday World as Problematic: A Feminist Sociology* (Boston: Northeastern University Press, 1987); Dale Spender, ed., *Men's Studies Modified: The Impact of Feminism on the Academic Disciplines* (New York: Pergamon, 1981).

8. Spender, *Men's Studies Modified,* 2.

9. Judith Plaskow's chapter in this volume.

10. Naomi Sokoloff's chapter in this volume.

11. Hava Tirosh-Rothschild's chapter in this volume.

12. Classic essays on this topic include Sherry Ortner, "Is Male to Female as Nature Is to Culture?" in Michelle Rosaldo and Louise Lamphere, eds., *Woman, Culture, and Society* (Stanford: Stanford University Press, 1974); and Michelle Rosaldo's introduction to that volume, "Woman, Culture, and Society: A Theoretical Overview." See also the essays in Rayna Reiter, ed., *Toward an Anthropology of Women* (New York: Monthly Review Press, 1975).

13. See, e.g., the chapters by Paula Hyman and Susan Sered in this volume; Ellen C. DuBois, Gail P. Kelly, Elizabeth L. Kennedy, Carolyn W. Korsmeyer, and Lillian S. Robinson, *Feminist Scholarship: Kindling in the Groves of Academe* (Urbana: University of Illinois Press, 1987), esp. chap. 3; Karen Hansen, "Feminist Conceptions of Public and Private: A Critical Analysis," *Berkeley Journal of Sociology* 32 (1987): 107–28; and " 'Helped Put in a Quilt': Men's Work and Male Intimacy in Nineteenth-Century New England," *Gender and Society* 3(3) (Sept. 1989): 334–54.

14. Michelle Rosaldo, "Woman Culture and Society: A Theoretical Overview," in Rosaldo and Lamphere, *Woman, Culture, and Society.*

15. See Susan Sered's chapter in this volume.

16. See, e.g., Karen McCarthy Brown, *Mama Lola: A Voudou Priestess in Brooklyn* (Berkeley: University of California Press, 1991).
17. For an excellent anthology of Jewish lesbian women's writings, see Evelyn Torton Beck, *Nice Jewish Girls: A Lesbian Anthology* (Boston: Beacon, 1989).

The Bible and Women's Studies

In the past two decades there has been a tremendous change in biblical studies. The scientistic philosophy that prevailed for more than a century has given way, in biblical studies as in other humanities, to a more sophisticated understanding of the interaction between the now and the then, the reader and the text. Old ideas of history as "what actually happened" and text as having one correct and original meaning have yielded to a current view of the continual interaction of the viewer and what is seen, of the text and its reader. No longer do we believe that there is a truly "value-neutral" way of reading literature or reconstructing history.

Women's studies did not *cause* this paradigm shift, but they are part of an enormous change in our perception of reality. When only European middle-class Protestant men were doing the reading, they were able to see their consensual understandings as objective. When new voices entered the cultural dialogue—the voices of Catholics, Jews, Asians, Afro-Americans, Africans, people speaking from the perspective of poverty, and women—then the presuppositions that underlay the old objective readings increasingly came to the surface, and the context was understood as part of the reading of the text. This new understanding has made it possible to see beyond the traditional readings of biblical texts to reach newer interpretations and insights.

The impact of this paradigm shift in biblical studies can be seen in several ways. There are increasing numbers of new readings of biblical stories from the perspectives of liberation, the third-world, womanism, and feminism. In addition, literary criticism of the Bible has grappled with the ways that stories have multiple codes that signify meanings and the way that reader responses can be shaped by the text as well as by the culture of the reader. This turmoil in biblical studies has brought a general openness in the field studies to women's studies—an expectation that women's studies can provide fresh perspectives on the texts—and an almost eager receptivity to solid feminist scholarship. There are relatively few people actively doing women-centered analyses of the Bible, but there is general awareness of their efforts and a willingness to learn from them.

Recognizing Patriarchy

The first impact of women's studies on biblical studies has been the recognition that the Bible is a patriarchal document from a patriarchal society. Feminism and women's studies have enabled us to see the parameters of this patriarchy. Biblical society was patrilocal: women left their fathers' households and authority at marriage and physically moved to their husbands' domain. If the husband was still under the authority of his father, then the wife would also come under his authority. Women were subordinate to the men of the household, and men exerted control over women's sexuality.

Patriarchy has a strong economic component. In ancient Israel, women did not normally own land, which made them economically dependent on men, first on their fathers, then on their husbands, and ultimately on their sons. The Bible contains repeated injunctions to care for widows and the fatherless. This humanitarian command is nevertheless predicated on the assumption of patriarchy: the widow is dependent on the concern and good will of males only because she herself has no real property.

Women were not part of the great public hierarchies that developed. The central public organizations of court, temple, and army did not include them. They were not judges, courtiers, or diplomats; they were not military leaders; and they were not priests. To a very large extent, their activity was confined to the private sphere. Yet women were not secluded in their homes. They could be seen in public, they could sing and dance, and women of talent could compose and perform victory dances, love songs, and laments.

Surprisingly, women could be prophets. Miriam, the sister of Moses, and Deborah the Judge are both termed prophet in biblical text. Moreover, 2 Kings 22 relates an episode in which the high priest Hilkiah and the scribe Shaphan go to the prophet Huldah, who confirms that the scroll they have found while repairing the temple is significant and, moreover, that God will carry out its predictions of disaster. The text does not comment on the fact that the prophet was a woman. The casual way she is mentioned indicates that her position was not anomalous; women could be expected to be prophets and to have the prophetic authority to declare something a vital part of sacred tradition. Yet women were not priests. The presence of women as prophets but not as priests may be attributed to the fact that prophecy is by its very nature nonbureaucratic. Prophets operate individually, without a hierarchy of command. As a result, their authority is based on personal charisma and believability rather than on an organizational power base. Although women's skill and charisma could help them attain prophetic authority (much as their skills could lead to considerable power in the household), the hierarchical structure of the priesthood was closed to them, as it was to all men not born into priestly families.

In biblical Israel, individual women could become powerful. This should not blind us to the fact that as a group women were not treated the same way as men, and society was structured along gender lines in a way that disadvantaged women. This structure, which we often call patriarchy, was characteristic of ancient Israel. Despite the charged atmosphere in which the Bible's treatment of women is sometimes discussed, however, Israel was neither the creator of patriarchy nor the worst perpetrator in the ancient world. Anthropology shows patriarchy to have been widespread, almost universal, and history shows that all the great historical civilizations were patriarchal, including the civilizations that preceded and surrounded ancient Israel. The patriarchy of Israel was part of an inherited social structure from the ancient world. A comparison of biblical laws with those of Assyria readily shows that the Bible did not rival Assyria in the extent to which it subordinated women.

Nevertheless, we make a profound statement when we acknowledge that the Bible is patriarchal. We are brought to the realization that the Bible contains a fundamental moral flaw: it does not treat all humans as equals. We in the modern world are learning that respect for the equality of all human beings and their common dignity is a moral imperative. Our perception of a moral imperative that does not derive from biblical teaching indicates that the Bible is no longer our only or even our *final* arbiter of morality. This has enormous religious implications. The authority of the Bible must be tempered with the authority of our experiences as human beings and our principles of morality. It is true that many of our moral ideas ultimately come from the Bible, but it is also true that they have been inspired by our continued reflection on the Bible during the millennia since it was written. The Bible did not eradicate slavery; it was up to people to do so. The Bible did not eradicate patriarchy; that is a task for current generations. The Bible did not eradicate economic oppression, and we do not have a clue as to how to do so.

Because of their implications for our own time, feminist studies of the Bible (and I would argue, all biblical studies) cannot remain isolated from the political implications of their research, nor from their impact on the lives of people. There is no value-neutrality with regard to oppression: if one does not consciously address a problem, one becomes part of the problem. Therefore, there is no absolute cleavage between feminism, feminist theology, feminist hermeneutics, and the study of women in the Bible or in the biblical world.[1] Precisely because of the intersection between politics and biblical study, feminist scholars such as Elisabeth Schüssler-Fiorenza have urged all biblical scholars to take an active part in the moral and theological discussions of our time.[2]

The Women

The study of women in the Bible is hindered by the public nature and androcentricity of the text itself. The Bible concerns itself with the communal history of Israel. Women did not play a great role in the public institutions of the ancient world, and the Bible focuses on the movers and shakers. As a result, women are rarely the major actors in biblical stories, and the stories themselves never deal with the lives of women-among-women, to which men had little access. Finding out about the history of women in biblical times often means ferreting out information that the androcentric biblical authors were either not interested in or were not interested in communicating to their audiences.

Uncovering the lives of biblical women poses serious methodological problems that are shared by all attempts to reconstruct biblical history. To fill in the gaps in the biblical record other than by mere speculation, we must turn to such disciplines as archaeology, ancient Near Eastern studies, anthropology, and sociology. Archaeology and ancient Near Eastern studies provide data, written and unwritten, that are independent of the Bible. They can provide details about the size of families, the nature of subsistence, the laws of the surrounding world, and other information. Anthropology and sociology shed light on cross-cultural patterns and provide models that can help reconstruct life in ancient Israel. The most successful attempt to use such social science data to understand women's history was made by Carol Meyers.[3] Basing her work on information and models from peasant societies to supplement our knowledge of Israel in the period of the judges (about 1200–1000 B.C.E.), Meyers points out that when the most important arena of life was the household, where women had an active role and an important

economic function, they had greater access to power than in later state societies in which the public arena developed and women were excluded. For
Meyers, as for others, the period of the judges was a high point in the
prominence of women in Israel.[4]

The Bible is more than the record of ancient Israelite civilization, and the
woman-centered study of the Bible is more than a reclamation of the history
of women in ancient Israel. The Bible is also a work of art. It is a literary
text that presents people and ideas in an artistic fashion. There has been a
great renewed interest in studying the Bible's major female characters; stories
of the Bible's great women and extensive bibliographies are developing on
such characters as the matriarchs,[5] Hagar,[6] Tamar,[7] Miriam,[8] Rahab,[9] and
Deborah and Yael.[10] From these and other studies it has become clear that
the Bible often portrays women as heroines who possess the characteristics
that Israel needs to emulate. Women were the saviors of Israel at the beginning and at the end of the biblical period. The savior figure at the beginning
is Yael, a marginal woman, wife of the Kenite Heber. Yael took advantage
of the fact that the Canaanite general Sisera fled from battle into her tent.
She agreed to guard him, gave him warm milk, and lulled him to sleep; then
she pounded a tent-peg into his temple to kill him and thus save Israel. The
savior figure at the end of biblical history is Esther, another marginal figure.
She was a Jew living in exile who became queen of Persia and used her royal
connections to foil the villain Haman's plot to destroy Persia's Jews. These
women, who conquered mighty enemies by their wits and daring, were
symbolic representations of the people and pointed to the salvation of Israel.

Her Story

The Bible has many stories in which women play secondary roles. One of
the aims of women's studies and a technique of feminist literary criticism is
to recover minor characters (and women were always minor) by ignoring
the biblical narrators' concentration on heroes, focusing instead on *"her
story."* The biblical scholar Burke Long has focused on the role of the "great
woman" of Shunnem, who appears in the narratives about the prophet
Elisha.

At the beginning of the story, the Shunnemite acknowledges the prophet
Elisha's privileged position and shows her support by feeding and housing
him. At the end of the story, she proclaims his holiness. Nevertheless, at the
heart of the story, she is a determined mover and shaper of events who insists
that Elisha come to the aid of her son. Long points out that our reading of

this story as an Elisha tale is socially formed: the story was written to glorify Elisha as prophet and miracle worker; it was preserved as part of a cycle of tales about the prophets Elijah and Elisha and has been read by generations interested almost exclusively in the heroized prophet. When we read it this way, we may not notice that the story is also the story of a great woman.[11]

Focus on the women in such tales can also yield important insights into ancient social structures. In my own study of biblical gender,[12] the Shunnemite was noteworthy, first as an independent woman who extends patronage to Elisha and then as a determined petitioner willing to confront everyone—husband, prophet, and king—in her pursuit of the physical and economic well-being of her household.[13] Moreover, read closely, this story indicates how gender intersects with class. The Elijah and Elisha stories take place against a backdrop of great poverty among the rural poor. Most of the miracles that Elijah and Elisha perform involve providing food for a starving peasantry. In contrast to all the poor women found in these stories, the Shunnemite is wealthy. This factor gives her striking boldness in her dealings with the prophet; after all, she is his patron and benefactor, the one who provides food and hospitality on his journeys. Wealthy women have greater freedom of action than poor women do, and sometimes even more than poor men.[14]

It is possible to go deeper into the story. The Shunnemite stands out among the women of Israel in being independent of her husband. She does not ask his permission when she entertains Elisha, bringing him into the picture only when she wishes to make an addition to her house. Later, when she seeks Elisha, she does not inform her husband why she is leaving. Though she is wealthy, does her economic well-being not depend on her husband's good will? Is she not in danger of divorce? A clue to the answer lies in her puzzling reply to Elisha when the prophet wants to reward her for her beneficence: "I live among my own kin" (2 Kings 4:13). This odd statement seems to contradict what we know about ancient marriage. We expect her to be living among her husband's kinfolk, not among her own.

The puzzle deepens. When Elisha saves her son, he warns her of famine, and she and her family leave for seven years. When she comes back, she goes to the king to reclaim her property. The king gives instructions to "restore all her property and all the revenue from her farm from the time she left the country until now!" (2 Kings 8:6). The pronouns used are striking: *her* property? *her* farm? This is not the language we expect from the Bible, for the laws indicate that women did not own land. Surely, the land is her husband's, if he is still alive, or her son's. Either there is a greater gap

between the laws and the narratives than we have assumed, or there is something special about the position of the Shunnemite. Her statement to the
prophet, "I live among my own kin," suggests that the Shunnemite might
have the status of a daughter of Zelophehad. The five daughters of Zelophehad appear in the Book of Numbers; they petition to inherit the portion
of their father, who died without sons. Their petition is granted and it is
decreed that if a father dies without sons, the daughters are the rightful
heirs.[15] Later, a provision is added that the daughters who inherit are to
marry their own tribesmen in order to keep the land in the family.[16] A
daughter of Zelophehad *owns* her land for her lifetime. She is not as dependent for her livelihood on men as other women are. If her husband
divorces her, she stays on her land. This is probably why the woman of
Shunnem, singular among the barren women in the Bible, does not actively
seek a child before Elisha announces that she will have one. Because she is
economically secure, the Shunnemite has no need to ask her husband's permission either to seek or entertain Elisha. The same economic security makes
it possible for her to enjoy both status and a secure old age even without
ever having had a child. The story of the Shunnemite can be understood as
a biblical example of how women act when the *economic* constraints of patriarchy are removed.

A similar study can be done of another minor character, Abigail.[17] Abigail
appears as the wife of a wealthy landowner, Nabal ("the boor"), during the
time when the future king David is an outlaw leader. David appears before
Nabal to ask for payment for the protection that David has given Nabal's
shepherds during the year. Nabal refuses to pay, reasoning that he has not
hired David to protect him. David leaves angry and vows to bring his men
back to destroy Nabal's household. The book of Samuel is focused on how
David became king, and the story of Abigail is told because she preserved
David's chances to be king. When, however, we focus attention on Abigail
rather than on David, we see interesting things. Like the Shunnemite, Abigail is both wealthy and noted for her bold initiative. She is not present at
her husband Nabal's negotiations with David, perhaps indicating that she is
less important and less active in her household than the Shunnemite is in
hers; after all, we have no reason to suspect that she owns her own land.
But she is no less decisive. Realizing that David must be angry at her husband
because of his refusal to pay David, Abigail acts immediately. She deduces
correctly that David might attack her household and quickly intercepts him
while bearing him gifts. Her insight saves both Nabal and David from ca-
tastrophe, her brilliant rhetoric convinces David not to kill every male in

Nabal's house, and David blesses her and God, who sent her to him. Once again, an intelligent, determined woman is influential far beyond the formal confines of patriarchy.[18] Just as anthropology has come to a more sophisticated understanding of the various types of power and the access of women to informal power, so too in biblical studies it has become apparent that biblical women had considerable influence on their world.[19]

By focusing on the women in biblical stories, feminist biblical scholarship has also illuminated the institutions of ancient Israel. In Israel there existed the position of *gebirah,* or queen mother.[20] That it was an actual position rather than an honorific title is indicated by the fact that Asa removed his mother from this position because she had made an *asherah* (a sacred grove, tree, or tree-sculpture) (1 Kings 15:13). The existence of the position of queen opens the possibility that the gebirah might have been well situated for harem intrigue, maneuvering to ensure the high status of her sons. In this way, the gebirah may have helped determine policy and succession. Bathsheba was certainly active on behalf of her son Solomon. The other queen mothers whose names are known to us (Maacah, mother of Asa; Hamutal, mother of Jehoiahaz and Zedekiah; and Nehushta, mother of Jehoiachin) were, like Bathsheba, the mothers of younger sons who helped put their sons into the kingship. As a result, these women influenced biblical history and attained a particular prominence during their sons' reigns.

The Bible on Gender

The study of individual women in the Bible has led to several unexpected discoveries. A major example is that even though women were subordinate in the socioeconomic and legal systems, the Bible does not attempt to justify this subordination by portraying women as subhuman or as *other* in any way. The biblical stories portray women as having the same set of goals, the same abilities, and the same strategies as biblical men.[21] To use modern terminology, the Bible is not *essentialist* on gender; it does not consider differences between the sexes to be innate. The same is true of other social divisions in Israel: the Bible has no social Darwinism and does not depict either slaves or poor people as essentially different from "standard" Israelites. The Bible inherited its social structure from antiquity and did not radically transform it.[22] At the same time, the Bible did not justify social inequality by an ideology of superiority or otherness. On the contrary, the Bible's explicit ideology presents a unified vision of humankind wherein women and men were created in the image of God and no negative stereotypes are attached to women, the poor, slaves, or foreigners.

There is a strange dissonance here. The social structure, with its cleavages and oppressions, is not in harmony with the Bible's ideology of equality. Only the Garden of Eden story (Gen. 3–4) seems to note this contradiction, announcing simply that gender inequality is the norm of the imperfect universe. The rest of the Bible does not consider the relation of hierarchical structures to equal worth at all. Of course, the tension between the Bible's ideology and social structure could not endure forever.[23] Postexilic writings pay more attention to gender, and ultimately Israel is greatly influenced by Hellenistic thinking, which treats women as categorically "other." Nevertheless, this later development should not obscure the fact that preexilic Israel had no ideology of gender differences. In the first Temple period, the dualist axes along which the cosmos was perceptually divided were divine-human, holy-profane, pure-tame and Israel-nations. Male-female was not such a category. One of the intriguing questions remaining in biblical scholarship is the place of *woman,* both foreign and Israelite, at the two intersections of Israel-nations and divine-human.

Reading with Nonpatriarchal Eyes

The gender blindness of the Bible's view of humanity prevents the Bible from being a completely patriarchal text, and, indeed, one of the significant results of feminist studies in the Bible has been the realization that the biblical text itself, read with nonpatriarchal eyes, is much less injurious to women than the traditional readings of Western civilization. There is much to recover in the Bible that is not patriarchal, even beyond hitherto neglected stories of strong heroines. The enterprise of liberating biblical text from its patriarchal overlay, called *depatriarchalizing* and first advocated by Phyllis Trible, has revealed important aspects of biblical literature.[24]

The most discussed example of depatriarchalization is the Adam-and-Eve story, long notorious for its denigration of women. A new reading was provided by Trible, who pointed out that the creation of Eve implied no inferiority; the word *ezer* (helpmate), used to describe Eve, connotes a mentor-superior in the Bible rather than an assistant and is used frequently for the relation of God to Israel (and not for the relation of Israel to God). Moreover, in mythology the creation order traditionally indicates that the last-created is the culmination of creation, which is certainly the implication of the structure of Genesis 1, in which humans are created after the rest of creation. In Genesis 2, one might argue that the use of *ezer* for Eve and her last-created position was intended to suggest the woman's superiority over the man. At the very least, the text indicates that humans were destined to be equal partners. Eve shows no inferiority to Adam anywhere in the Garden story, and the subordination of women after the expulsion from the garden is part of the consequences of sin.[25]

Trible's explanation has had widespread acceptance. Some later readings of the story, however, most notably that of Susan Lanser, have pointed out that biblical authors could have expected their readers to respond in certain culturally conditioned ways and that therefore the story relies on patriarchal attitudes to form an indictment of Eve.[26] The truth is that the meaning of the story depends precisely on the assumptions that readers make while reading it. The Adam-and-Eve story is extremely laconic and cannot be retold without the reteller or reader adding additional information. This is true of many other tales in the Bible; they are constructed so that much is left to the reader to fill in and interpret. What one adds to the story determines whether the stories will be liberating or oppressive. In a way, biblical stories may be considered a moral challenge, and it is for the reading community to read them for a blessing rather than a curse.

Biblical stories are often ambiguous. One way, used in the garden story, is by *gapping*: leaving out important details of the story. An additional way is by self-contradiction: the Bible sometimes gives two different readings in the text itself. Judith Plaskow has made the passage in Exodus 19:15 infamous on this point.[27] Moses is preparing the people for the Revelation when he says, "Make ready for the third day—do not go near a woman." Moses looks at the people and sees only men.[28] A similar blindness appears in the tenth commandment with the injunction against coveting your neighbor's wife. Is it all right to covet your neighbor's husband? Women are clearly included in the other commandments and are always considered bound by the covenant of Sinai. Their sudden transformation from subjects of the law ("Do not") to the objects of coveting is startling. The answer may be that women are normally thought of as full persons and legal agents, but the thought of sexual relations transforms women into objects upon whom one acts, or rather, in these cases, into objects upon whom one avoids acting.

A closer look at Exodus 19 reveals that Moses is supposed to be the intermediator between God and Israel, relaying God's words to the people. Yet the narrative has God tell Moses to go to the people and tell them to sanctify themselves for two days, wash their clothes, and be prepared for the third day, when God will come (Exod. 19:10–12). The narrator, who quotes

God, does not quote *God* as saying, "Do not go near a woman." God is not blind; God sees that the people are male and female.[29] It is Moses, with the shortsightedness of a human male, who suddenly addresses only the males. The narrated text contains complex layers of voices. Is there a critique of Moses implied here? Is the text implying that the patriarchal blindness toward women is certainly *not* from God? This is not the only instance in which we hear the voice of patriarchy and the voice of patriarchy's critic in the same story. In the dialogue between God and Abraham in Genesis 17: 18–19, there are also two voices and, once more, the less patriarchal voice, which I call a countervoice, is divine. In this scene, God reiterates the promise to provide Abraham with children, and Abraham remarks that this promise has been fulfilled with the birth of Ishmael. At that point, it is *God* who replies that Ishmael will have his own covenant, but that the promise to Abraham must be fulfilled through Sarah, and announces that Isaac will be born to Abraham and Sarah the following season. By relating this interchange, the narrator of the story warns both ancient and modern readers that we should not be too quick to accept Abraham's androcentric view of the nature of the covenant.

The Bible that subtly warns its readers not to focus solely on the men in its text does not sound like the same Bible that has been quoted throughout history as a way of keeping women in their place. Much of the patriarchy that we associate with the Bible and all of its misogyny has been introduced into the Bible by later generations of readers. One of the impacts of women's studies has been to focus attention on this phenomenon and on the question, "How did we get from there to here?" Once we divorce the text from its patriarchal message we must attempt to delineate some of the influences that began to transform, or rather deform, the Bible into a more patriarchal text. Many of these first become visible in the Hellenistic period and grow more intense as Western history continues.[30]

The Texts of Terror

Another goal of women-centered Bible studies is to focus on the stories in the Bible that look patriarchal, seem to have no possibility of reinterpretation, and clearly read like *texts of terror*.[31] These are the tales of victims, of women abused beyond the structural norm of patriarchy, of women who are physically and emotionally destroyed by others. One such story, the story of Hagar, is well known. Hagar, Sarah's personal slave and Abraham's concubine-wife has no protectors. The text states that Sarah abused Hagar—

that she treated her improperly. Hagar runs away, but God tells her to return and submit, and she does so until Sarah finally sends her and her child away.[32] This story starkly illuminates the relations between women in a patriarchy. Relative to Hagar, Sarah has all the power. Gender intersects with class: Sarah is of the dominant class and therefore in a far better position than Hagar. Moreover, Sarah's actions are perfectly legal. She acts entirely according to customary law when she makes Hagar the surrogate birthgiver. Then, when she feels threatened, she abuses Hagar and finally sends her away. Sarah has a perfect right to do so;[33] she is, after all, only freeing her slave and allowing her to take her son with her. Yet, no one would say that Sarah (or Abraham) has acted with compassion. Sarah's motives are clear: she herself is vulnerable and dependent on Abraham's good will toward her. Ultimately, Sarah lacks both economic security and autonomy, and this makes her incapable of acting well toward her social inferior. The modern reader may be horrified by her actions and yet sympathetic to both her and Hagar.

There is no reason to think that an ancient reader would have reacted differently than the modern reader. As is usual in these biblical stories, the narrator seems neutral and shows no sympathy for Hagar, nor, for that matter, for Sarah. Where would the sympathies of the reader be expected to lie? On the one hand, Sarah is the ancestress of the people reading the story; Hagar is not. There is the matter of race involved here, or at least ethnic consciousness: Hagar starts as a foreigner (an Egyptian) and ends as a foreigner (the mother of the Ishmaelite peoples). Sarah enables Isaac, Israel's ancestor, to be his father's successor. Would not the ancient reader root for the home team? Still, such treatment of foreigners is not supposed to happen in Israel. Over and over again the Israelites are told to be kind to the foreigner, for they too were once foreigners. Israel is also admonished always to be sympathetic to slaves, for they too were once slaves. Sarah and Abraham did not go through the slavery experience of Egypt, but their readers have and should remember these injunctions. The story continues to sound stranger: after Hagar runs away, God tells her to return; Israel's law demands that Israelites *help* fugitive slaves; why does God not help? Furthermore, Sarai mistreats Hagar *before* she herself becomes a captive concubine in the court of Egypt.[34] Afterward (perhaps because she understands what slavery is), Sarah sets her free and allows her to keep her son, but at that point Hagar becomes a freed slave—the very model of what Israel will later become. Hagar, the newly emancipated Egyptian slave, then goes into the wilderness, whereupon she receives a revelation from God and a promise of nationhood.

An ancient Israelite audience could not have missed the many allusions to their own salvation history. Hagar is the prototype of Israel, whose people will be slaves in Egypt, mistreated, and later freed; who will escape to the wilderness and receive God's revelation on Mount Sinai; and who will become the people of Israel. In this story, Sarah who is the progenitress of Israel, and Hagar, the prototype of Israel, are compelled by their situation to be at odds. Israelite readers not only recognize the tragedy of the two women in patriarchy, but they understand how much this tragedy is magnified by the fact that the future Israel is here at odds with itself. The story thereby stands as testimony to the serious problems of a present-day social situation rather than to the personal characteristics of the biblical characters.

Such considerations reveal the great complexity of the tales of terror. They assail the reader's emotions from all directions and make readers distinctly uncomfortable with what is going on. The same play of negative factors is prominent in the tale of Jephthah's daughter (Judg. 11).[35] The narrator is ostensibly telling the tale of one of the judges of Israel, Jephthah. The story begins with Jephthah's birth; immediately the readers' sympathies are with him. He is the son of a prostitute whose half-brothers turned him out when their father died. A disinherited fugitive, he (like David after him) forms a private army and becomes known as a warrior. When his town, Gilead, is in trouble, the elders ask him to save them. He agrees to rescue them if afterward they will make him their head.[36] So far, so good: the underdog has made good, the low has become high, the biblical dream has come true. But something terrible happens. The pious Jephthah makes an oath to sacrifice to God whatever comes to greet him first after his victory. Did he expect an animal? Why not specify? In the tragic event, it is Jephthah's daughter who comes rejoicing. She is his only child; besides her, according to the text, he has neither son nor daughter. The problem is clear. If he sacrifices his daughter, he will have no progeny; his name will die. In Israel, this fate, called *karet,* is considered the worst fate that can happen to a man, and the threat of it is reserved as a sanction for serious offenses against divinity.[37] The daughters of Zelophehad use this Israelite attitude to acquire the right to inherit their father's estate, arguing that otherwise he would lose his future name without having done anything to deserve that penalty. The wise woman of Tekoa uses this Israelite attitude to manipulate David.[38] The narrator knows that the audience will react with great horror at the prospect of his killing his only child, and that this horror will be *on behalf of Jephthah.*

But what about Jephthah's daughter? Although nameless (at least to us), she too is known to ancient Israel, for as the narrator reminds us, every year the Israelite daughters go to the hills to lament her passing. Furthermore, the narrator makes the audience respect and admire her, for it is she who declares that vows must be honored and that God must be our primary consideration. Jephthah's daughter is a pious and faithful woman who is remembered in cult and story: surely nobody in Israel viewed her death lightly. Moreover, the Bible does not condone child sacrifice. The idea of a great savior of Israel offering his daughter in sacrifice would have been as horrible to the ancient Israelite as it is to the modern reader.

Once again, the reader is left disquieted: something is very wrong. No character acts with malice, and yet the most vulnerable character is horribly abused. The reader waits for salvation. Why does somebody not stop the sacrifice? In the world of the reader (ancient and modern), such events do not pass. What reader could kill another with impunity? Fathers do not have the right to kill their children. The story of Jephthah and his daughter points to something seriously lacking in the days of the judges: no one can control the fathers. Abraham, too, had the right to sacrifice his son; no human court would have sought him. The family is its own world, and the father is its ultimate authority. Moreover, a careless vow in this instance compels the father to act against his own self-interest. There is no priesthood to help him undo his vow. There is no authority higher than the family. In the binding of Isaac (Gen. 22), God intervenes to save the son, but God does not intervene to save Jephthah's daughter. The story of Jephthah's daughter, like all the stories in the Book of Judges, tells us that God will no longer intervene to save people who are in danger or who are being abused.

The story of the concubine in Gibeah with which the Book of Judges ends brings these issues into focus.[39] The girl is vulnerable; she is a minor wife, a concubine. When she is unhappy, she runs home. But her father gives her back to her husband-master. The father has already given her to another; now he gives her away again. She is solely under the authority of this new man, a Levite. Levites are a dignified class in Israel, but this Levite is suddenly vulnerable. When they stop in a town of strangers, the strangers attack. A stranger is vulnerable, for he travels without his family to protect him. Since he is alone, there is no one to rescue him. His host offers his daughter to assuage the mob; the Levite sends out his concubine. We are shocked: surely, no one can be gracious to another man by sacrificing his daughter to a mob. The story makes us realize that, in those days, men had ultimate powers of disposal over their women. Abraham could give Sarah to Pharaoh; any man could give his daughter to another as a wife or concubine; Jephthah could sacrifice his daughter to God. The scene in Gibeah is parallel to the story of Sodom and Gomorrah in Genesis 18–19. There, Lot, the only righteous man in town, sent his virginal daughters to the mob that had assembled to abuse his visitors. There is a great difference between Genesis and Judges: when Lot sends out his daughters, the angels of God save them. In the Book of Judges, God no longer intervenes to save individuals, and the concubine is raped to the point of death.

The terror of this story continues. The Levite takes revenge by butchering her body to muster the tribes against the tribe of Benjamin. The civil war that follows nearly wipes out a tribe of Israel; to resuscitate it, hundreds of women are captured into rape-marriages. Horror follows horror, and the narrator caps it with the message: in those days there was no king in Israel, and each man did as he wanted.

This story sets us up to await the kingship as an end to such abuse, and indeed the story has many parallels to the first stories about Saul, the first king of Israel. Nonetheless, kingship does not stop the problems that are caused by society's unequal power alignments. The king may act as a force of control over ordinary men, but who can control the king? King Saul tries to kill David; no one can stop him, and David has to flee. David himself is no guarantee to the end of dominance and oppression. After David becomes king, he sees Bathsheba bathing, covets her, and sleeps with her. Later, when Bathsheba tells David that she is pregnant, and Uriah will not sleep with her because he is engaged in battle, David arranges for Uriah to die in battle. David disposes of people as he wants; there is no one to stop him.[40] Yet, when David's daughter Tamar is raped by her half-brother Amnon, David does not protect her or avenge her by killing his son, Amnon the rapist. The reader of the story, who expects that the state will provide protection for the vulnerable,[41] now sees that the state cannot control itself.

These biblical tales of terror portray the horrible things that happen to women under patriarchy; they serve as a warning to us to prevent such happenings, and they were probably included in the Bible to show how things went wrong in Israel. Neither the lack of polity of the Genesis ancestors nor the localized sporadic government of the period of the judges could prevent such outrages. But neither could kingship, as the stories of Bathsheba and Tamar clearly show. The Bible, after all, was written as the sky was falling, in the shadow of the disastrous conquests by the Assyrians and the Babylonians.[42] The historical books maintain their faith in the ultimate justice of God and the Cosmos by blaming Israel for its own destruction: because such things happened, Israel was destroyed. This is not misogynist storytelling but something far more complex, in which the treatment of women becomes the clue to the morality of the social order.

Woman as Symbol

The literary treatment of women illuminates other symbolic uses of women and of the female. Just as women are relatively small and powerless in society, so is Israel small and powerless among the nations. Some of the heroines in the Bible symbolize Israel rising and subduing its enemies. This is particularly true of Yael, the Kenite woman who killed the Canaanite general Sisera at the beginning of the period of the judges, and Esther, the "diaspora Jew," who married the king of Persia and prevented the extermination of the Jews of Persia. *Woman* is also the personification of Israel in the marital metaphor of Israel as the wife of God. This well-known and much-beloved image is not as simple as it first appears. It captures well the intimacy between God and Israel, but it captures equally well the terror that such intimacy can hold with a more powerful force. This is not the equal love affair of the Song of Songs, interpreted either as human love or as the love of God and Israel. This is a patriarchal marriage: the husband has all the power. In today's view the marriage is also abusive, for the husband gets angry, punishes, and then proclaims his love and wants reconciliation.[43] The beloved wife is also a victim, and the woman symbol captures both love and vulnerability.

The marital metaphor has another problem: it codifies the gender of God as male. Monotheism has a potential advantage over polytheism, for it can create a divine world in which there is no gender division, no division of powers or attributes between male and female. This advantage, however, is only a potential advantage. In ancient Israel the gender of God was usually thought of as male because males were predominant in the social order. If the gender of God is *frozen* as male, then the danger is present that males will become the earthly representatives of divinity, and females will be frozen out of what is sacred. This does not fully happen in biblical Israel, which preserves images of God as mother. Nevertheless, the marital metaphor is one example of the dangers of this process.

In postexilic Israel another danger of using woman as symbol becomes clear. The images of Zion as daughter and Zion as mother become combined in an eschatological vision with the idea of the wife of God. In many ways this is a beautiful vision of wholeness: the madonna (mother Zion) and the virgin (daughter Zion) are fused with the whore. Moreover, Zion is seen as the wife of Israel as well as the wife of God (Isa. 62:5). She becomes a symbol and means of union for God and Israel—they both love her, and their love for her unites them. If Israel is the lover of the woman Zion, however, then there is a danger that Israel will be seen as totally *male* and the women of Israel will become invisible. This is the danger of all the female divine symbols that begin to multiply in the postexilic and second Temple periods. In these periods, the portrayal of wisdom as a lover-woman develops into the depiction of the divine Sophia as the wife of her devotees, and the Torah as the beloved of her sages. Rabbinic writings also have an image of the Sabbath as a bride. In all these metaphors, the human is *male,* his partner is an unearthly female, and flesh and blood women are not part of the image at all.[44] The use of the feminine as a symbol can serve highly patriarchal purposes when human women are left out.

There are many other questions raised by feminist scholarship. Some are questions about sexuality. When the Bible addresses the subject of sexuality and its control, men are seen as agents and women as objects. What does this say about biblical ideas of sexuality, and in turn, how does that interact with our current attempts to construct a nonpatriarchal theology of sexuality? The Bible is not antisex, but it does not develop a clear understanding of sexuality, and postbiblical religion, particularly Christianity, has developed a distinct antisex bias.

There are still other questions being addressed today. Some questions concern the ancient Israelite religion and the role of the Asherah: Was the Asherah the feminine part of God? Was it a case of idolatry? Why was it ultimately exorcised from biblical religion, and did this contribute to or reflect the emergence of God-as-husband?[45] Beyond these are two interlinked questions: Were women better served by polytheism, which created a symbolic straightjacket of what a female and a male can be, and which nevertheless afforded women an undeniable and unremovable part of the sacred, or were women better served by monotheism, which does not *necessarily* limit the roles and characters of women, but which was clearly used for patriarchal purposes? Can the Bible be the inspiration for a truly liberated monotheism, free of patriarchy and all other forms of oppression? In the past twenty years, as we have come increasingly to appreciate the intricacies, ambiguities, and multiple meanings of biblical texts, it has become evermore apparent that the answer is truly up to us.

Notes

1. None of the notes in this article is meant to be exhaustive. A complete annotated bibliography of women in the Bible is being prepared by Mayer Gruber and should be published soon. For the many issues involved in feminist studies and the Bible, see the articles in two pioneering anthologies: Adela Yarbro Collins, ed., *Feminist Perspectives on Biblical Scholarship*, Society of Biblical Literature Centennial Publications (Chico: Scholars Press, 1985); and Letty M. Russell, ed., *Feminist Interpretation of the Bible* (Philadelphia: Westminster, 1985); Nancy Fuchs-Kreimer, "Feminism and Scriptural Interpretation: A Contemporary Jewish Critique," *Journal of Ecumenical Studies* 20 (1983): 534–48; Katharine Doob Sakenfeld, "Feminist Perspectives on Bible and Theology: An Introduction to Selected Issues and Literature," *Interpretation* 42 (1988): 5–18; and Phyllis Trible, "Five Loaves and Two Fishes: Feminist Hermeneutics and Biblical Theology," *Theological Studies* 50 (1989): 279–95.
2. See Elisabeth Schüssler-Fiorenza, "The Ethics of Biblical Interpretation: Decentering Biblical Scholarship," presidential address to the Society of Biblical Literature, *Journal of Biblical Literature* 107(88): 3–17.
3. Carol Meyers, *Discovering Eve: Ancient Israelite Women in Context* (New York: Oxford, 1988).
4. In addition to Meyers, see Jo Ann Hackett, "In the Days of Jael: Reclaiming the History of Women in Ancient Israel," in Clarissa W. Atkinson, Constance H. Buchanan, and Margaret R. Miles, eds., *Immaculate and Powerful: The Female in Sacred Image and Social Reality*, pp. 15–38 (Boston: Beacon, 1985); and Claudia V. Camp, "The Wise Women of 2 Samuel: A Role Model for Women in Early Israel?" *Catholic Biblical Quarterly* 43 (1981): 14–29. My own, somewhat different, view is expressed later in this chapter.
5. See, among others, Christine G. Allen, "Who Was Rebekah: 'On Me Be the Curse, My Son,'" in Rita M. Gross, ed., *Beyond Androcentrism: New Essays on Women and Religion*, pp. 183–216 (Missoula: Scholars Press, 1977); Kathleen M. Ashley, "Interrogating Biblical Deception and Trickster Theories: Narratives of Patriarchy or Possibility?" *Semeia* 42 (1988): 103–16; Samuel Dresner, "Rachel and Leah," *Judaism* 38:151–50; Irmtraud Fischer, "Sara: Frauen unter der Verheißung," in Karin Walter, ed., *Zwischen Ohnmacht und Befreiung, Biblische Frauengestalten*, pp. 23–31 (Freiburg: Herder, 1988); Nelly Furman, "His Story versus Her Story: Male Genealogy and Female Strategy in the Jacob Cycle," in Collins, *Feminist Perspectives*, 107–16, Society of Biblical Literature, Biblical Scholarship in North America 10 (Chico, Calif.: Scholars Press, 1985; rep. in *Semeia* 46 [1989]: 141–49); Eva Renate Schmidt, "1. Mose 29–31: Vom Schwesternstreit zür Frauensolidarität," in Eva Renate Schmidt, Mieke Korenhof, and Renate Jost, eds., *Feministisch gelesen*, vol. 2, pp. 29–39 (Stuttgart: Kreuz, 1989); Phyllis Trible, "Genesis 22: The Sacrifice of Sarah," Gross Memorial Lecture, Valparaiso University, 1989; Marie-Theres Wacker, "1. Mose 16 und 21: Hagar-die Befreite," in Schmidt, Korenhof, and Jost, *Feministisch gelesen*, vol. 1 (1988), 25–32; Mary K. Wakeman, "Feminist Revision of the Matriarchal Hypothesis," *Anima* 7 (1981): 83–96.

6. Phyllis Trible, "The Other Woman: A Literary and Theological Study of the Hagar Narratives," in James T. Butler, Edgar W. Conrad, and Ben C. Ollenburger, eds., *Understanding the Word: Essays in Honor of Bernhard W. Anderson*, pp. 221–46 (*Journal for the Study of the Old Testament*/Sheffield: Almond, 1985); and Phyllis Trible, "Hagar: The Desolation of Rejection," in idem, *Texts of Terror: Literary-Feminist Readings of Biblical Narratives* 9–35, *Overtures to Biblical Theology* 13 (Philadelphia: Fortress, 1984); and Jo Ann Hackett, "Rehabilitating Hagar: Fragments of an Epic Pattern," in Peggy L. Day, *Gender and Difference in Ancient Israel*, pp. 12–27 (Minneapolis: Fortress, 1989).

7. Johanna W. H. Bos, "Out of the Shadows: Genesis 38; Judges 4:17–22; Ruth 3," *Semeia* 42 (1988): 37–67; Calum Carmichael, "Forbidden Mixtures," *Vetus Testamentum* 32 (1982): 394–415 (on Tamar and Judah); Fokkelien van Dijk-Hemmes, "Tamar and the Limits of Patriarchy: Between Rape and Seduction," in Mieke Bal, ed., *Anti-Covenant: Counter-Reading Women's Lives in the Hebrew Bible*, pp. 135–56, *Journal for the Study of the Old Testament* (SS) 81, Bible and Literature Series, 22 (Sheffield: Almond, 1989); J. Emerton, "Some Problems in Genesis 38," *Vetus Testamentum* 25 (1975): 338–61; idem, "Judah and Tamar," *Vetus Testamentum* 29 (1979): 403–15; idem, "An Examination of a Recent Structuralist Interpretation of Genesis 38," *Vetus Testamentum* 26 (1976): 79–98; Angelika Engelmann, "2. Samuel 13, 1–22: Tamar, eine schöne und deshalb geschandete Frau," in Schmidt, Korenhof, and Jost, *Feministisch gelesen*, vol. 2, pp. 120–26; Barbara Georgi and Renate Jost, "1. Mose 38: Tamar, eine Frau kämpft für ihr Recht," in Schmidt, Korenhof, and Jost, *Feministisch gelesen*, vol. 2, pp. 40–46; Randy L. Maddox, "Damned If You Do and Damned If You Don't: Tamar, A Feminist Foremother," *Daughters of Sarah* 13 (1987): 14–17; Susan Niditch, "The Wronged Woman Righted: An Analysis of Genesis 38," *Harvard Theological Review* 72 (1979): 143–49; Helen Schungel-Straumann, "Tamar: Eine Frau verschafft sich ihr Recht," *BiKi* 39 (1984): 148–57; Joan Goodnick Westenholz, "Tamar, *Qedesa, Qadistu*, and Sacred Prostitution in Mesopotamia," *Harvard Theological Review* 82 (1989).

8. Rita Burns, *Has the Lord Spoken Only through Moses? A Study of the Biblical Portrait of Miriam* (Atlanta: Scholars Press, 1987); Carol Meyers, "Of Drums and Damsels: Women's Performance in Ancient Israel," *Biblical Archaeologist* 54 (1991): 16–27; Annette Rembold, "Und Mirjam nahm die Pauke in die Hand, eine Frau prophezeit und tanzt einem anderen Leben voran: Das Alte Testament feministisch gelesen," in Christine Schaumberger and Monika Maaβen, eds., *Handbuch Feministische Theologie*, pp. 285–98 (Münster: Morgana, 1986); Phyllis Trible, "Bringing Miriam out of the Shadows," *Bible Review* 5(1) (1989): 14–25, 34; idem, "Subversive Justice: Tracing the Miriamic Traditions," in Douglas A. Knight and Peter J. Paris, eds., *Justice and the Holy: Essays in Honor of Walter Harrelson*, pp. 99–109 (Atlanta: Scholars Press, 1989); Marie-Theres Wacker, "Mirjam: Kritischer Mut einer Prophetin," in Karin Walter, ed., *Zwischen Ohnmacht und Befreiung, Biblische Frauengestalten*, pp. 44–52 (Freiburg: Herder, 1988).

9. Elinor Artman, "Between Two Gods," *Journal of Women and Religion* 1 (1981): 8–12; Phyllis A. Bird, "The Harlot as a Heroine: Narrative Art and Social Presupposition in Three Old Testament Texts," *Semeia* 46 (1989): 119–39; Yair Zakovitch, "Humor and

Theology or the Successful Failure of Israelite Intelligence: A Literary-Folkloric Approach to Joshua 2," in S. Niditch, ed., *Text and Tradition: The Hebrew Bible and Folklore,* Society of Biblical Literature Semeia Studies (Atlanta: Scholars Press, 1990), 75–98; and "Reply to Zakovitch," Niditch, *Text and Tradition* (1990): 99–106.

10. For Deborah: Peter C. Craigie, "Deborah and Anat: A Study of Poetic Imagery (Judges 5)," *Zeitschrift für die alttestamentliche Wissenschaft* 90(3) (1978): 374–81; Stephen G. Dempster, "Mythology and History in the Song of Deborah," *Westminster Theological Journal* 41 (1978): 33–53; Katharina Elliger, "Debora: 'Mutter in Israel,'" in Karin Walter, ed., *Zwischen Ohnmacht und Befreiung, Biblische Frauengestalten,* pp. 53–61 (Freiburg: Herder, 1988); J. Cheryl Exum, "Mother in Israel': A Familiar Story Reconsidered," in Letty M. Russell, ed., *Feminist Interpretation of the Bible,* pp. 73–85 (Philadelphia: Westminster, 1985); Jürgen Kegler, "Debora: Erwagungen zür politischen Funktion einer Frau in einer patriarchalischen Gesellschaft," in Willy Schottroff and Wolfgang Stegemann, *Traditionen der Befreiung 2: Frauen in der Bibel,* pp. 37–59 (Munich: Kaiser, 1980); Barnabas Lindars, "Deborah's Song: Women in the Old Testament," *Bulletin of the John Rylands University Library of Manchester* 65(2) (1983): 158–75; Rachel C. Rasmussen, "Deborah the Woman Warrior," in Bal, *Anti-Covenant,* 79–93; for Yael, see esp. Yair Zakovitch, "Sisseras Tod," *Zeitschrift für die alttestamentliche Wissenschaft* 93 (1981): 364–74; and Mieke Bal, *Murder and Difference: Gender, Genre, and Scholarship on Sisera's Death* (Bloomington: Indiana University Press, 1988).

11. Burke O. Long, "The Shunammite Woman: In the Shadow of the Prophet?" *Bible Review* 7 (1991): 12–19, 42.

12. Tikva Frymer-Kensky, *In the Wake of the Goddesses: Women, Culture, and the Biblical Transformation of Pagan Myth* (New York: Free Press, 1992), 118–43.

13. Ibid.

14. On the other hand, a parallel story about Elijah and a widow-woman indicates that even poor women could have considerable freedom of action. Elijah could live in the widow's house without causing a local scandal. Cf. I Kings 17:7–24.

15. Kings 27:1–11.

16. Kings 36.

17. Jon Levenson, "1 Samuel 25 as Literature and as History," *Catholic Biblical Quarterly* 40 (1978): 11–28; Moshe Garsiel, "Wit, Words, and a Woman: 1 Samuel 25," in Y. Radday and Athalya Brenner, eds., *On Humour and the Comic in the Hebrew Bible,* pp. 161–68 (Sheffield, England: Almond Press, 1990); and Frymer-Kensky, *In the Wake of the Goddesses,* 133–34.

18. Jon Levenson, "1 Samuel 25 as Literature and as History," *Catholic Biblical Quarterly* 40 (1978): 11–28; and Frymer-Kensky, op. cit; Garsiel, "Wit, Words, and a Woman," 161–68.

19. For a discussion of some of the newer anthropological approaches to power, see the editor's introduction to Jill Dubisch, ed., *Gender and Power in Rural Greece* (Princeton: Princeton University Press, 1986), 3–41.

20. For recent studies of this role, see Niels Erik A. Andreason, "The Role of the Queen

Mother in Israelite Society," *Catholic Biblical Quarterly* 35 (1983): 179–94; Zafrira Ben-Barak, "The Status and Right of the Gebira," *Journal of Biblical Literature* 110 (1991): 23–34, with an extensive bibliography; and Zafrira Ben-Barak, "The Queen Consort and the Struggle for Succession to the Throne," in Jean-Marie Durand, ed., *La Femme dans le Proche-Orient Antique, Comptes Rendu de la rêconte assyrologique* 33 Paris 1986 (Paris: Editions Recherche sur les Civilisations, 1987), 33–40.

21. For details see Frymer-Kensky, *In the Wake of the Goddesses,* 118–43.

22. Note that even the prophets sought to ameliorate the condition of the poor and blamed the wealthy for taking advantage of them. They did not advocate uprooting the social order and eliminating economic classes.

23. In our own time we have two major examples of societies whose social structure does not match their ideology. In the former Soviet Union, where the proclaimed Marxist classlessness and economic equality were totally at variance with the reality of life, the ideology and the state that proclaimed it totally collapsed. In the United States we proclaim democratic classlessness and economic equality of opportunity, but the rich are getting richer, the poor are multiplying, and there is a large underclass. How this tension will be resolved remains to be seen.

24. Phyllis Trible, "Depatriarchalizing in Biblical Interpretation," *Journal of the American Academy of Religion* 41 (1973): 30–48; and idem, *God and the Rhetoric of Sexuality, Overtures to Biblical Theology* 2 (Philadelphia: Fortress, 1978). More recently, see idem, "Feminist Hermeneutics and Biblical Studies," *Christian Century* (Feb. 1982): 116–18; and idem, "Five Loaves and Two Fishes: Feminist Hermeneutics and Biblical Theology," *Theological Studies* 50 (1989): 279–95. Other such approaches are by J. Cheryl Exum, "'You Shall Let Every Daughter Live': A Study of Exodus 1:8–2:10," *Semeia* 28 (1983): 63–82; idem, " 'Mother in Israel': A Familiar Story Reconsidered," in Letty M. Russell, ed., *Feminist Interpretation of the Bible,* pp. 73–85 (Philadelphia: Westminster, 1985); and Toni Craven, "Women Who Lied for the Faith," in Douglas A. Knight and Peter J. Paris, ed., *Justice and the Holy: Essays in Honor of Walter Harrelson,* pp. 35–49 (Atlanta: Scholars Press, 1989). Some scholars are more interested in indicting the Bible, such as Esther Fuchs, "For I Have the Way of Women: Deception, Gender, and Ideology in Biblical Narrative," *Semeia* 42 (1988): 68–83; idem, "Marginalization, Ambiguity, Silencing: The Story of Jephthah's Daughter," *Journal of Feminist Studies in Religion* 5(1) (1989): 35–45; idem, "The Literary Characterization of Mothers and Sexual Politics in the Hebrew Bible," in Collins, *Feminist Perspectives,* 117–36. So, too, see Pamela Milne, "Eve and Adam: Is a Feminist Reading Possible?" *Bible Review* 4(3) (1988): 12–21, 39; and idem, "The Patriarchal Stamp of Scripture: The Implications of Structuralist Analyses for Feminist Hermeneutics," *Journal of Feminist Studies in Religion* 5(1) (1989): 17–34.

25. See Trible, *The Rhetoric of Sexuality.*

26. Susan S. Lanser, "(Feminist) Criticism in the Garden: Inferring Genesis 2–3," *Semeia* 41 (1988): 67–84. For an overview of the negative argument, see Milne, "Eve and Adam." For a newer depatriarchalizing reading of the actions of Eve, see Frymer-Kensky, *In the Wake of the Goddesses,* 108–17.

27. See Judith Plaskow, *Standing Again at Sinai* (San Francisco: Harper and Row, 1990), 25–27.

28. Note that later rabbinic commentators were careful to read women back into this chapter, but Moses was not.

29. Rabbinic Judaism clearly put women back into the picture at Sinai. God's commanding Moses to speak to the "House of Jacob" and the "Sons of Israel" was understood to mean the women (the "house") and the men (the "sons"), and interpreters commented on the reasons that the women were mentioned before the men.

30. See Frymer-Kensky, *In the Wake of the Goddesses*, 203–12. There is a considerable body of literature emerging on the Bible in the Hellenistic period. See, e.g., Betsy Halpern Amaru, "Portraits of Biblical Women in Josephus' Antiquities," *Journal of Jewish Studies* 39 (1988): 143–70; Leonie Archer, "The 'Evil Women' in Apocryphal and Pseudepigraphical Writings," in R. Givenon, M. Anbar, et al., Proceedings of the Ninth World Congress of Jewish Studies, 1986, pp. 239–45; James L. Bailey, "Josephus' Portrayal of the Matriarchs," in L. Feldman and G. Hata, eds., *Josephus, Judaism, and Christianity* (Detroit: Wayne State University Press, 1987), 154–79; Cynthia Baker, "Pseudo-Philo and the Transformation of Jephthah's Daughter," in Bal, *Anti-Covenant*, 195–209; Leila L. Bronner, "Biblical Prophetesses through Rabbinic Lenses," *Judaism: A Quarterly Journal of Jewish Life and Thought* 40 (1991): 171–83; Sharon Cohen, "Reclaiming the Hammer: Toward a Feminist Midrash," *Tikkun* 3:55–57, 93–95; Louis H. Feldman, "Josephus' Portrait of Deborah," in A. Caquot, M. Hadas-Lebel, and J. Riaud, *Hellenica et Judaica*, 1986, pp. 115–28.

31. This felicitous term was coined by Phyllis Trible in *Texts of Terror*.

32. For readings on Hagar, see Cynthia Gordon, "Hagar: A Throw-Away Character among the Matriarchs," Society of Biblical Literature Papers 24 (1985): 271–77; Jo Ann Hackett, "Rehabilitating Hagar: Fragments of an Epic Pattern," in Peggy L. Day, ed., *Gender and Difference in Ancient Israel*, pp. 12–27 (Minneapolis: Fortress, 1989); Sean E. McEvenue, "Comparison of Narrative Styles in the Hagar Stories," *Semeia: An Experimental Journal for Biblical Criticism* 3 (1975): 64–80; Trible, "Hagar: The Desolation of Rejection," 9–35.

33. Near Eastern contracts differ on whether the wife can *sell* the slave woman even after she has born the master's children. For details see Tikva Frymer-Kensky, "Near Eastern Law and the Patriarchal Family," *Biblical Archaeologist* 44 (1981).

34. The alternation of names may be confusing to someone not familiar with these biblical stories. When God announces that Sarai will give birth to Isaac, God also renames her Sarah, a name that means "princess." Similarly, Avraham (Abraham) is a renaming of Abram to indicate that he is the father (Av) of many.

35. Peggy L. Day, "From the Child Is Born the Woman: The Story of Jephthah's Daughter," in Peggy L. Day, ed., *Gender and Difference in Ancient Israel*, 58–74 (Minneapolis: Fortress, 1989); J. Cheryl Exum, "The Tragic Vision and Biblical Narrative: The Case of Jephthah," in J. Cheryl Exum, ed., *Signs and Wonders: Biblical Texts in Literary Focus*, pp. 59–83, Society of Biblical Literature Semeia Studies, 1989; Esther Fuchs, "Marginalization,

Ambiguity, Silencing: The Story of Jephthah's Daughter." *Journal of Feminist Studies in Religion* 5(1) (1989): 35–45; Beth Gerstein, "A Ritual Processed: A Look at Judges 11.40," in *Anti-Covenant: Counter-Reading Women's lives in the Hebrew Bible,* ed. Mieke Bal, pp. 175–93, *Journal for the Study of the Old Testament* (SS): 81, Bible and Literature Series, 22 (Sheffield: Almond, 1989); W. Lee Humphreys, "The Story of Jephthah and the Tragic Vision: A Response to J. Cheryl Exum," in *Signs and Wonders: Biblical Texts in Literary Focus,* ed. J. Cheryl Exum, 85–96, Society of Biblical Literature Semeia Studies (1989); Michael O'Connor, "The Women in the Book of Judges," *Hebrew Annual Review* 10 (1987): 277–93; Anne Michele Tapp, "An Ideology of Expendability: Virgin Daughter Sacrifice in Genesis 19.1–11, Judges 11.30–39 and 19.22–26," in *Anti-Covenant: Counter-Reading Women's Lives in the Hebrew Bible,* ed. Mieke Bal, 157–74, *Journal for the Study of the Old Testament* (SS): 81, Bible and Literature Series, 22 (Sheffield: Almond, 1989); Phyllis Trible, "A Meditation in Mourning: The Sacrifice of the Daughter of Jephthah," *Union Seminary Quarterly Review* 36 (1981): 59–73; idem, "The Daughter of Jephthah: An Inhuman Sacrifice," in *Texts of Terror: Literary-Feminist Readings of Biblical Narratives,* 93–116.

36. This pattern of the warrior becoming king is well known in both history and mythology. Marduk became king of the gods in this way, as did the Greek tyrants.

37. For the penalty, see Donald Wold, "The *Kareth* Penalty in P: Rationale and Cases," in P. J. Achtemeir, ed., *Society of Biblical Literature 1979 Seminar Papers* (Missoula, Mont.: Scholars Press, 1979), vol. 1, 1–46. For its uses, see Tikva Frymer-Kensky, "Pollution, Purification, and Purgation," in ed. Carol Meyers, *And the Word of the Lord Will Go Forth* (Winona Lake, Ind.: Eisenbraun's, 1983), 399–414.

38. See the story in 2 Samuel 14. The wise woman pretends to be a widow, one of whose two sons has killed the other in a fight. If she delivers the killer to the family for execution (as Israelite law demands), then, she declares, her husband, a good man, would be left without a name or remnant. David responds by placing the killer's son under his own protection, and the wise woman then makes David realize that it is his own son, Absalom, who needs pardon for having killed his brother.

39. For this story see Susan Niditch, "The 'Sodomite' Theme in Judges 19–20: Family, Community, and Social Disintegration," *Catholic Biblical Quarterly* 44 (1982): 365–78, and Trible, *Texts of Terror.* The conclusions expressed here, however, are my own.

40. For the story, see 2 Samuel 11.

41. Deuteronomy reflects the transfer of much power over the family from the father to the community. See Tikva Frymer-Kensky "Deuteronomy," in Carol A. Newsom and Sharon H. Ringe, *Women's Bible Commentary* (Louisville, Ky.: Westminster / John Knox Press, 1992), 52–62.

42. The Assyrian conquest of the Northern Kingdom of Israel and decimation of the Southern Kingdom of Judah was in 722 B.C.E.; Judah survived until it was conquered by the Babylonians in 589 B.C.E..

43. See Renita Weems, "Gomer: Victim of Violence or Victim of Metaphor," *Semeia* 47 (1989): 87–104; and Frymer-Kensky, *In the Wake of the Goddesses,* 144–152.

44. See Carol A. Newsom, "Woman and the Discourse of Patriarchal Wisdom: A Study of Proverbs 1–9," in Peggy L. Day, ed., *Gender and Difference in Ancient Israel*, pp. 142–60 (Minneapolis: Fortress, 1989); and Frymer-Kensky, *In the Wake of the Goddesses*, 175–183.

45. See Frymer-Kensky, *In the Wake of the Goddesses*, for discussions of sex and of the asherah. The questions I am asking here, however, remain unanswered.

Feminist Perspectives
on Rabbinic Texts

Feminists and Talmudists, one might say, are working side by side, examining the same texts. Yet, like parallel lines in a Euclidean plane, they do not seem destined to meet. The reason Talmudists ignore feminists, I think, is that critical Talmudic studies are still in their infancy. Even though the Talmud and associated rabbinic works have been studied in a religious setting for hundreds of years and countless volumes of commentary have been produced, many basic questions remain unanswered. No one yet knows, for example, how the hundreds of statements by and about sages living during a period of several centuries in a variety of locales in Babylonia and Israel coalesced into a single text, the Talmud. Until these and other issues are resolved, feminist studies will not beckon.

One reason that the critical study of the Talmud is still in its early stages is that, although unquestionably and self-admittedly man-made, it is viewed by many as divinely imbued or inspired. According to this outlook, the sages were engaged in expanding and developing God's holy writ or, in more extreme terms, restoring the rules and regulations that God had dictated to Moses on the mountain but that had been forgotten over time. The impact of such a characterization of the Talmudic corpus has been to inhibit freedom of inquiry, which seems to imply that the text is fully explicable on purely human terms. Even after the dawn of the critical era, religious Jews, who made up most of Talmud devotees the world over, rejected the validity of all but the traditional approach to the study of the text. Their scholarly contributions, although many and important, are therefore

I acknowledge the invaluable assistance of Prof. Baruch M. Bokser, of blessed memory, and Prof. Richard Kalmin.

limited to a narrow sphere, that of adding levels of supercommentary to the text.

Significant changes in the study of rabbinics occurred in the nineteenth and twentieth centuries when individuals trained to think critically about broad literary and historical issues began to ask new questions about the text. Over the years, traditional scholarship—although barely countenancing questions about contrived or forced explanations of passages—either generously tolerated interpretations that deviated from the simple definition of the words or read meaning into the text rather than elicit meaning from it. Unhappy with such practices, many twentieth-century Talmudists began to focus on one issue in particular: How were the words of the ancient sages intended to be understood, what was their original meaning, once stripped of subsequent overlay? This quest, spurred by a number of important discoveries—for example, that embedded in the text itself is its own first commentary, that later Talmudic rabbis provided an anonymous interpretive framework for the statements of the earlier ones, and that Talmudic materials underwent continuous redaction over time—has revolutionized the study of Talmud.[1]

Other vistas of inquiry have been opened recently by Jacob Neusner, an eminent and prolific historian and text critic. His holistic approach to the examination of rabbinic texts dictates looking at each work as a whole, evaluating its worldview, program, and religious, social, and political agenda. New research directions generated by this perspective include searching a text for the editor's imprint, trying to understand how he reworked earlier materials in order to fashion a message of his own; and comparing two works from the same period, noting their similarities and differences in order to appreciate the variety of approaches to life and law that existed at the time. In particular, Neusner warns against forcing the entire mass of rabbinic material into a seamless whole, as has been the case for so long.

At the same time, there have been parallel developments in manuscript studies. In the middle of the nineteenth century, R. Rabbinovicz, recognizing the importance of manuscript variants for the study of the Talmud, began collecting and publishing collations of such variants under the title *Diqduqei Soferim*.[2] He died before completing this project. To this day no critical edition of the entire Talmud has been published; many tractates, including several in the Division of Women, still lack an accompanying volume of manuscript variants. In the years since Rabbinovicz's death, many more partial manuscripts and fragments have been located, so that his work is now in serious need of revision. Following in his footsteps, later scholars have produced critical editions of other major rabbinic texts, the outstanding exemplars being Saul Lieberman's edition of the Tosefta (a companion volume to the Mishnah) and his supplementary volumes of commentary, *Tosefta Kifshuta*.[3]

Given this research agenda, it should not be surprising that rabbinics scholars assign a low priority to feminist studies. It is not that Talmudists are repudiating feminism. Rather, they do not view feminist studies as essential to the development of the discipline as are the kinds of critical and textual studies mentioned above. Feminist studies, in this case, would include an examination of the rabbinic view of women and their social and legal status; a search for the nascent protofeminist views held by individual rabbis; and an exploration of the impact of the gender construction of society on rabbinic thinking and legislation. Unlike the fields of literary theory and history, which have been transformed because of a feminist challenge of basic methodologies, the reigning forms of Talmudic analysis, which are text- and not issue-oriented, do not submit to such a critique. For now, determining the best possible reading of the text and the simple meaning of its words is the highest priority.

These reasonable goals notwithstanding, there are several formidable barriers to the infiltration of feminist methodologies into the field of rabbinics. To begin with, many Talmudists are prejudiced against thematic studies. In their opinion, only textual lightweights would investigate such a topic as the status of women (or any other group) in rabbinic literature. Serious, acceptable research at present means studies like those I have described.[4]

Second, rabbinics, particularly in the Israeli universities, is dominated by yeshiva-trained men. True, the decision of these individuals to abandon the yeshiva world and enter the arena of critical thinking suggests that they are open-minded—but, it turns out, they are usually not open-minded enough to view feminist questions with sympathy. It may be that what inhibits them is that feminism is not just a new perspective on ancient texts but a movement for social and religious change.

Third, although the field is not closed to them, only a small number of women are engaged in the academic study of rabbinics. One reason is that few women arrive in graduate school with the ability to read rabbinic texts. Again, most men in the discipline have spent years in a yeshiva learning how to read and interpret Talmudic texts and commentaries, while few women have been able to undertake such intensive Talmud study because yeshivas are closed to them. To prepare for a career in rabbinics, a woman would need to spend years trying to make up for the background deficit.

Even so, some women as well as men have begun to conduct feminist studies of rabbinic texts.[5] Their approaches to the material range from the historical to the anthropological to the literary. Of particular value are two books of feminist research on rabbinic texts published in the past fifteen years: one is Neusner's, the other is by Judith Wegner, a former student of his with training in jurisprudence as well as the Talmud.[6]

Although in most disciplines engaging in feminist research is no longer viewed as rebellious or even unusual, in the area of rabbinics a feminist researcher still risks being ignored or dismissed by colleagues. It should not be surprising, therefore, that though rabbinics researchers have paid Neusner and Wegner little heed, feminist scholars in related fields have given their work a warm reception. Scholars of religion, particularly those investigating early Christianity, are thirsting for knowledge about the status of women in the parallel period in Judaism. Neusner has established a language of discourse with them, and Wegner has developed it even further.

Both of these writers examine the Mishnah—the first edited code of law to follow the Torah—and attempt to extrapolate from it the rabbinic conception of women and their status in Jewish law. As different as their conclusions may be, the two works are similar in approach: both authors apply well-defined analytic techniques to an entire corpus of material in order to test their hypotheses and find answers to their questions.

Before summarizing and assessing the importance of these two studies, I would like to point out that at the same time that feminist scholarship in rabbinics is progressing slowly, there has been an explosion in the number of recently published popular works on feminism and Judaism. These writings are often polemical in nature, either attacking the sexism found to be rampant in synagogue ritual and marital law, or apologetically defending a system that treats women differently from men.[7] But these are not works of critical scholarship. The authors rarely conduct a comprehensive and analytic study of the topic, but simply select sources to support their preconceived notions.

Jacob Neusner

There is no question that the individual who laid the foundation for feminist readings of rabbinic texts is Jacob Neusner. Not only has he systematically analyzed all of the Mishnah, tracing the development of the worldview and religious philosophy of the framers in their specific social-historical context, he has also examined this corpus from a feminist perspective and in the context of general feminist writings.[8]

Neusner's main thesis can be summarized in a few paragraphs. He opens his study by noting that Mishnah's data on women (a series of seven tractates called Seder Nashim [the Division of Women]) form a system within a larger system. By subjecting this subsystem to taxonomical analysis—that is, attempting to understand why the framers chose to discuss some issues and leave out others—he claims that one can get to the center of its worldview (82). After listing briefly the contents of each tractate, Neusner observes that the Division pays much attention to women's entry into and exit from marriage but little to their life within marriage. He concludes that the framers' selection of topics for consideration, together with the Division's patriarchal stance that only men may form and dissolve marital bonds, suggests that in their view women may set the stage for the processes of the sacred, but may not activate them (86).

He goes on to say that the reason the framers worked out a division on the subject of women is that they viewed them as abnormal, anomalous, dangerous, dirty, and polluting (97). And since the source of this abnormality, in the framers' opinion, was a woman's sexuality and its potential for disturbing the social order, they found it necessary to regulate the transfer of women from one man to another, thereby effecting the sanctification of that which could disrupt and disorder the orderly world.

Finally, Neusner places Mishnah's system of women in the context of other ancient systems. Citing Michelle Rosaldo's observation that women's status will be lowest in societies in which there is a firm differentiation between domestic and public spheres of activity,[9] he comments that Mishnah's system seems to follow this pattern with only slight exceptions, such as granting women the right to own property (94).

I find Neusner's grand theories intriguing, his methodological approach novel, and most of his general observations convincing. But I am troubled by several of his specific assertions. First, by including "polluting" in his list of the negative attributes of women, he implies that this quality is characteristic of females only. The Division of Purities, however, contains not one but two tractates on the topic of human beings as sources of pollution:[10] Niddah (Menstruants), about women who pollute by virtue of their menstrual blood, and Zavim, about men who pollute by virtue of genital discharge. If the Mishnah sees both men and women as possible sources of pollution, even though men pollute to a lesser extent, it is misleading to suggest that it was woman's capacity to pollute (among other things) that led the framers to treat her differently from man.

Second, I think Neusner has incorrectly characterized Mishnaic society as one in which Rosaldo would predict the lowest status for women. He fails to note that for a society to fall into this category, in addition to differentiating between spheres, it also has to be one in which "women are isolated from one another and placed under a single man's authority in the home."[11] But in the Mishnah we often find women in one another's company—baking bread together, lending each other pots and pans, and gossiping (Gittin 5:9; Pesahim 3:4; Sotah 6:1). In addition, women were not sequestered in the family compound; peddlers, barbers, and other tradespeople and craftspeople conducted business with women in their homes (Qiddushin 4:13; Baba Qama 10:9). Women appeared in public regularly—in the marketplace as buyers and sellers, at rabbinic courts as litigants, and at weddings and funerals as active participants. In fact, there does not seem to have been a sharp delineation between the public and private spheres. According to Rosaldo, then, in such a society women would have had a relatively high status, although not necessarily equal to that of men.

As for Neusner's assertion that the Mishnah's conception of woman as Other derives from the framers' belief that women's unruly sexual potential is always there, just below the surface, a careful reading of the Mishnah suggests that it is men's sexuality—that is, men's easily aroused and then hard-to-control sexual lust—that lies, not below, but on the surface of some of the Mishnah's statements, such as those concerning the segregation of the sexes in semiprivate settings, like inns or schoolhouses (Qiddushin 4:12–14; Gittin 7:4; 8:9). In the Mishnah, men's uncontrollable sexuality plays a key role in shaping behavioral guidelines for casual social relations between the sexes. However, since the Mishnah is silent on the topic of both men's and women's unruly sexuality in reference to marital transfers, it follows that it is not of critical concern in this area.

Furthermore, according to Neusner, the consequence of viewing woman as disorderly is that man must sanctify her to restore the system to stasis. What this implies is that women on their own cannot actively engage in the process of sanctification, that they can only be acted upon by men.[12] It is true that women cannot effect sanctification in reference to marriage, for the marital bond can only be formed or dissolved by man: in the entire process woman remains totally passive (except, perhaps, for her opportunity to withhold consent to marry). Nonetheless, women have the identical capacity to men's to sanctify the fruit of the herd and of the field, the bed, chair, table, and hearth, as stated in Niddah 5:6 and elsewhere (Shabbat 2: 6,7; Hallah 2:3, 3:1; Bikkurim 1:5). Even more noteworthy, as indicated in the Division of Women, women can also sanctify themselves. Like a man, a woman can declare herself to be a Nazirite (Nazir 3:6; 4:1–6; 9:1). Chapter 4 of the tractate Nazir discusses in detail the rules pertaining to women who assume this vow in the context of marriage.[13] In short, I find Neusner's assertion that the framers viewed women as dangerous and disorderly not only lacking support from within the system but actually conflicting with explicit statements appearing in this division and elsewhere. Being Other is not the same as being odious.

I would therefore modify Neusner's suggestion that Seder Nashim is the Mishnah's Division of Women. First, the name Seder Nashim is nowhere used in the Mishnah itself and hence is extrinsic to the system.[14] Second, if we examine the various tractates of the division, we see that, as Neusner claims, they focus on the formation and dissolution of the marital bond. This means that what we have before us is not a Division of Women but a Division of Marriage or Married Women, because *nashim* also means wives. What the text of this Division seems to be saying about women in marriage is that they are subject to men's control—not absolute control by any means, but that husbands dominate in the marital relationship: it is the husband who forms and dissolves the bond and controls his wife within the confines of marriage.

As for the Mishnah's abiding interest in moments of transfer, this can be explained in another way. An issue of prime concern to the framers is to whom do the financial benefits of a woman's estate accrue during the period of transfer and which of the two men, father or husband, is responsible for providing her with food and the other necessities of life during this time.[15] These questions arise because a woman is not "picked up" as soon as she is "paid for." The need to determine the precise limits of financial responsibility and privilege is what generates the excessive attention paid to moments of transfer and not the framers' fear that the transfer of a woman is like that of a caged tiger.

Using Neusner's own taxonomy, I find that the Division of Marriage is to be paired with the Division of Damages, which follows it, and that as Neusner himself claims, the two together show, within the larger framework of order, "the congruence . . . of human concerns of family and farm, politics and workaday transactions."[16] Just as the Division of Damages strives to maintain social order and stasis in commercial transactions, so the Division of Marriage, which deals with the transfer of women from one man to another, seeks to maintain order in social relations by carefully regulating the formation and dissolution of marriage bonds so that situations do not arise in which two men lay claim to the same woman. Just as in commercial transactions the item that changes hands is not viewed as a source of disorder, so women in marriage are not viewed as a source of disorder. And just as the commercial transaction itself, if not secured by properly prepared documentation, can lead to disorder and strife, so marriage, if not accompanied by proper declarations and documents, can lead to disorder and strife.

If the critical issue of the Division of (Married) Women is how to maintain social stasis through the proper transfer of women, then it is not necessary to import from outside the system a view of woman as a source of disorder and danger. Instead, it is possible to frame a different basic conception of woman, one that does not see her as a source of pollution any more than it sees the male Zab as one, and that does not view her as a source of disorder any more than it views real estate or a slave as such a source. I cannot yet suggest what the reformulated basic conception would be, but it must at least take into consideration the fact that the Mishnah gives woman the power to sanctify and assigns her a variety of religious obligations, such as prayer, although it draws distinctions between men's and women's ritual obligations.

Furthermore, for these purposes one must consider not just what the Mishnah says about women but also, as Neusner comments, Mishnah's mode of expression. Unlike the Torah, which seems in many instances to be addressed only to men (as is evident in such verses as "do not covet your neighbor's wife" [Exod. 20:18]), the statements in the Mishnah are formulated as if they apply to all equally ("Three who join together for a meal must recite Grace together" [Berakhot 7:1]) and then lists the exclusions ("Women, slaves, and minors do not count in the communal quorum for Grace" [7:2]).[17] That is, in those instances when the Mishnah does not explicitly exempt or exclude women, they remain obligated.[18] Mishnah's framers thus abandon Torah's extreme androcentrism and view women as members of the Jewish community who have the capacity to assume religious responsibilities but who function at a lower level of religious obligation than men, possibly because they are subordinate to them and hence have lower social status, like slaves and minors.[19] In fact, the reason that some mishnahs group women, slaves, and minors together is that each of these cohorts is subordinate to and financially dependent on the head of the household: women to their husbands, children to their fathers, and slaves to their masters.

Another question that arises in reference to Neusner's analysis of the Mishnah is whether his formulation of such a negative basic conception of women prevents him from seeing some of the progressive social ideas in the Mishnah. On occasion he points out the framers' enlightened social thinking, saying, for instance, that the *ketubah* (marriage document) is "one of the single most powerful documents in the Israelite system as the Mishnah knows it,"[20] or, "So far as the Mishnaic system moves from the pure patriarchal world of Scripture, it moves toward, but does not completely approximate, the Romans' modified system, in which the woman enjoys a considerable measure of freedom and independence."[21] But when it comes to examining institutions rooted in Scripture that the Mishnah appears on the surface not to develop, Neusner ignores evidence of the framers' departure from patriarchy.

A striking example of this is his comment: "Sotah . . . shows us what a Mishnah tractate looks like when the Mishnah has nothing important to say about a chosen topic."[22] Perhaps he is referring only to new religious concepts and not to social concepts. But to my mind, Sotah is probably the most revolutionary tractate in the Division of Women.

A cursory reading of the verses about a wayward wife (Num. 5:11–31) reveals that according to Scripture, if a husband merely suspects his wife of infidelity ("v'qinaei et ishto," v. 14), he may take her to the temple (in Jerusalem) and submit her to the ordeal of the bitter waters. He needs no corroborating evidence. It is therefore remarkable that tractate Sotah opens with a law that uses the same verb as Scripture (QN', as in the scriptural *v'qinaei* above) but assigns it a radically different interpretation, changing it from an essentially intransitive to a transitive verb. The framers of the Mishnah say (1:1) that only if a man "m'qanei l'ishto," warns his wife publicly and in the presence of two witnesses against conversing or closeting herself with a particular man, and only if at least one man (even if he be the husband himself) notices that she did not heed the warning, may her husband take her to the temple for the ordeal.[23] That is, if a husband suspects his wife of infidelity but does not warn her properly, he may not force her to submit to the ordeal. The framers have thus subverted the meaning of Scripture by taking a ritual designed to deal with uncorroborated accusations and limiting it to corroborated accusations. By subjecting to the ordeal only women about whom witnesses are ready to testify (as to their highly suspicious behavior), the framers display their profound dissatisfaction with the Torah's deviation from due process for women. They also seem to be struck by the injustice of punishing only one of two equally culpable parties and hence state later in the tractate (5:1), "Just as the waters test her, so they test him"—namely, the paramour.

I mention these Mishnaic statements not because I have conclusive proof that the framers are presenting a radical reconstruction of the scriptural institution, but because these few remarks suggest that Neusner underestimates the independent thought expressed in tractate Sotah. Not that there is evidence of an attempt to overthrow patriarchy in this tractate, with its full-blown description of the ordeal and its endorsement of a husband's right to control his wife's social contacts, but within the patriarchy there seems to be a growing sympathy for women who are treated unfairly.

In general, Neusner's analysis of Mishnaic thinking is penetrating, and his holistic methodological approach is innovative. Yet in his attempt to show that the Mishnah is not the logical outcome of Scripture, as interpreters claim it is, he pays close attention to those parts of Mishnah that do not derive from Scripture—because they serve his purpose well—but not enough attention to those parts of the Mishnah that are a fresh reworking of Scripture. In other words, significant residual patriarchy prevents Neusner from noting that the Mishnah itself, in comparison to the system upon which it is based, is moving away from patriarchy.

A serious consequence of this shortcoming in Neusner's work is that, given his extensive literary output and wide audience, many scholars have come to think that the Mishnah is far more committed to the maintenance of patriarchy than it actually is. For example, Elisabeth Schüssler-Fiorenza comments that Neusner has shown conclusively that Mishnah "is produced in and can only imagine a patriarchal society."[24]

What Schüssler-Fiorenza sets out to do, openly admitting her passionate attachment to Christianity, is to develop a feminist critical hermeneutics that "allows women to move beyond the androcentric biblical text to its social-historical context" (35). At the same time, she says, such a hermeneutics must search for theoretical models of historical reconstruction that will take women from the periphery and place them at the center of Christian life.

In the course of applying this analytic method to texts from the Christian Bible, she develops the theory that the historical Jesus movement was a "discipleship of equals" in which women could assume positions of leadership. But since this model stood in conflict with the patriarchal ethos of the Greco-Roman world, Paul, in his missionizing activity, later introduced rules that made women subordinate to men and denied them leadership roles in the developing church. That is, many patriarchal developments were later accretions and were not part of the original Christian message (35, 100).

She goes on to say that the Jesus movement may have been not an op-
positional movement but an alternative, feminist Jewish movement within
the dominant patriarchal religion (107).[25] By this she means that Jesus' feminism is understandable only if Judaism in his time already had within it
elements of a critical feminist impulse. This point goes beyond Neusner's
findings of patriarchy.

Schüssler-Fiorenza's proposition is fascinating, but if she is positing the
existence of a feminist impulse within Judaism as a necessary part of a radical
reconstruction of Christian beginnings, then the feminist reading I suggest
for tractate Sotah, in particular, and for the Mishnah in general, may lend
support to her theory.[26] It is troubling, however, that she pays no attention
to the unfolding developments and direction of change in Jewish law. By
saying that feminist elements "came to the fore in the vision and ministry
of Jesus" (106), she suggests that Jesus was the first to synthesize these ideas
and produce a feminist ideology. Still, many of these notions had already
found expression in the Mishnah's legislative enactments, which, although
not egalitarian, were certainly aimed at improving women's lives.[27]

Judith Wegner

An important recent addition to feminist scholarship is Judith Romney
Wegner's *Chattel or Person? The Status of Women in the Mishnah.* Unlike
Neusner, who describes the framers' basic conception of women in predominantly negative terms, Wegner lucidly analyzes a vast array of Mishnaic
sources, mainly culled from the Division of Women, and extrapolates from
them a more balanced view of women. Also unlike Neusner, who views
the Mishnah as a philosophical treatise, Wegner views it as a book of legal
rules and hence subjects it to a jurisprudential analysis.[28]

In building her analytic framework, Wegner uses Neusner's observation
that the framers had a penchant for analogical-contrastive exegesis, holding
that if a thing is like something else it must possess the same characteristics,
but if not, it must be like its opposite and possess the opposite characteristics.
She argues that there are thus only two choices for the legal status of women,
either chattel or person. No other choices are possible because the framers
routinely exclude a third category that might lie between the two poles.
However, she continues, since the Mishnah treats a woman sometimes like
chattel and sometimes like a person, the question to ask is not whether the
Mishnah sees woman either as one or the other, but when and why it treats
her like chattel and when and why like a person (6).

Wegner further notes that the framers, like Scripture, divide women into three sets of matched pairs—minor and emancipated daughters, married and divorced women, normal and levirate widows. She organizes her material around these categories and comes to the surprising conclusion that whenever the law relates to a man's proprietary interest in a woman's sexuality—his exclusive marital right to her sexual and reproductive function—it treats her like chattel. But whenever the law addresses any other topic, such as the ownership of property, it treats a woman like a person. Noting that the exclusion of married and even autonomous women from the synagogue and house of study does not conform to this paradigm, Wegner suggests that these limitations flow from the framers' fear of cultic pollution by the menstruant (18).

Finally, like Neusner, Wegner places her feminist study of rabbinic texts in the context of general feminist theory. She finds that the Mishnah's view of woman accords well with Simone de Beauvoir's concept of woman as Other,[29] as well as with Mary O'Brien's "men's club hypothesis." Nevertheless, since these theories do not explain why the Mishnah exempts emancipated minors, widows, and divorcees from men's control, Wegner additionally suggests that what virtually compelled the framers to grant these women autonomy is that Scripture gives them control of their own vows, and the framers considered themselves bound by the authority of Scripture (196).

The most attractive feature of Wegner's book is her systematic feminist analysis of one of the critical layers of Jewish law. Her conclusions derive from the texts themselves, each of which Wegner has painstakingly translated, annotated, and then examined from the perspective of her hypothesis. She convincingly argues that in many areas the Mishnah accords women lower status and fewer rights than men, yet in many others it confers upon them rights and responsibilities not consonant with patriarchy as it is generally understood and practiced. This is a finding of major importance, which in part substantiates and in part repudiates Neusner's theories.

These positive comments notwithstanding, I have reservations about Wegner's methodology and conclusions. First, in assuming that Scripture has such a tight grip on the framers' minds, Wegner neglects their more progressive thinking about women. Her theory of the Mishnah's taxonomy of women rests in part on her identification of the three pairs of women in Scripture. Although it is easy to find scriptural mention of wives, divorcees, widows, levirate widows, and daughters, there is no reference in Scripture to an emancipated minor. Wegner admits as much but asserts that one can find implicit reference to this category: when Scripture, concluding its discussion of a father's right to nullify his daughter's vows, says that these rules apply "bin' ureiha bet aviha" (in her youth in her father's house [Num. 30: 17]), it implies that when a daughter has attained majority in her father's house she becomes an emancipated minor. I do not accept this reading. Scripture speaks of no girl attaining emancipated status in her father's house, for it speaks only of a "betrothed maiden" who passes, upon marriage, from the authority of her father to the authority of her husband, with no autonomous in-between stage.[30] I therefore question Wegner's assertion that Scripture demonstrates an affinity for binary opposition. More important, if the category of emancipated minor does not exist in Scripture, then the clear emergence of such a category in the Mishnah is all the more significant. I suspect that a major advance of the Mishnaic treatment of women in comparison to Scripture is the creation of the category of *bogeret,* which means giving a girl the rights of personhood when she reaches the age of twelve and a half.

Second, I am troubled by Wegner's principal thesis that a woman is treated like chattel in all matters affecting a man's proprietary interest in her sexuality, but like a person in all other matters. To prove this claim, she would have to show that all instances of chattellike treatment involve only a man's stake in a woman's sexuality and that all instances of personlike treatment apply only to nonsexual matters. However, this is impossible, since all tractates in the Division of Women deal with marriage— clearly an example of male proprietary interest in a woman's sexuality—and yet all tractates treat women sometimes as chattel and sometimes as person. For instance, Wegner claims that the first chapter of Qiddushin presents espousal as the acquisition of chattel (42–45), noting that espousal is unilateral, that the term used in the Mishnah (1:1) for acquiring a wife is QNY, which means to purchase, and that the methods of espousal are virtually identical to those listed for the acquisition of slaves and animals, which are listed immediately after.

These arguments are substantial, but what the Mishnah describes here is only the procedure for acquisition, not the wife's status in the acquisition itself. With the procedure of acquisition are stipulations, such as the wife's right to financial support (which may be viewed as payment for sexual and other services rendered) and to conjugal satisfaction. As Wegner herself indicates, within marriage a woman has a long series of rights and responsibilities. These rights and responsibilities by definition make it impossible to claim that marriage treats woman as chattel. If this is so, it is logically untenable to disassociate the acquisition of a wife from the other rules of marriage (as Wegner does), thereby suggesting that only in establishing the marriage does a man have a stake in his wife's sexuality, *not* for the duration of the marriage, during which she is treated like a person.

In a more profound way what troubles me about Wegner's poles of chattel and person is that the binary opposition in this case is illusory, for when a woman is treated like chattel, she is treated better than other chattel, and when she is treated like a person, she is treated less like a person than a man is. Therefore I find the categories of person and chattel to be so broad and inclusive as to leave no room for the excluded middle range of the framers' analogical-contrastive mode of reasoning. The question of woman as either chattel or person is rendered meaningless.

Third, I question Wegner's theories on women's exclusion from full participation in the religious life of the community. Wegner views the potential for cultic pollution as the underlying rationale for excluding women from the public domain, yet she devotes just three pages to an analysis of tractate Niddah (Menstruants) (162–65). I find it strange that a topic viewed to hold the key to rabbinic thinking about women in the public domain is given so little attention. I find even stranger Wegner's comments that although Scripture prohibits menstruants from entering the temple, no Mishnaic law forbids them from setting foot in the synagogue. Yet, she continues, "Menstruation played a psychological role . . . in keeping women out of the public domain and reinforcing their inability to function as religious leaders" (162). Is she reading something out or reading something into the text?

Even a brief reading of tractate Niddah reveals that the framers were primarily interested in how the onset of a menstrual period retroactively affected the cultic cleanness of the food a woman prepared and the permissibility of sexual relations with her husband. That is, tractate Niddah in no way suggests that the trajectory of a menstruant's uncleanness extends beyond the private domain. Why would a system like the Mishnah, which openly discusses the topic of menstruants in the private domain, have a second, underlying agenda for the public domain to which one can appeal to explain other ritual restrictions?[31]

In general, as seminal a study as Wegner's is, it is marred by her attempt to impose on the material a chattel-sexuality link that is too rigid. She herself notes the points at which the fit is bad, but rather than discard the unifying theory, she adds explanations for each conflicting datum. For instance, she wonders whether it was Genesis 1:27, "Male and female He created them," that led the framers to see woman as sharing a common humanity with man and as a result accord her more rights (197). Yet just the opposite may be the case: what the framers began with was a set of Pentateuchal rules that treat married women almost like chattel with respect to vows, bride-price, premium on virginity, levirate claims, and the ordeal of bitter waters. What they accomplished in the course of their deliberations was a movement away from levirate ties and water ordeals toward standardizing *ketubot, gittin* (bills of divorce), and betrothal declarations. Although one cannot overlook that all their rules presuppose patriarchal institutions, at the same time the framers did attempt to infuse the biblical legacy with a more sympathetic attitude toward women.

A Feminist Research Agenda: A Proposal

I propose that feminists build—through an expanded agenda—on what others have done. Stated succinctly: it is important to apply the same high-powered analytic techniques currently being used in rabbinics research to texts dealing with women and marriage. In this way a rabbinics researcher can achieve two goals at the same time: new insight into rabbinic texts and a deeper understanding of rabbinic attitudes toward women.

Rather than evaluate individual rabbinic texts by contemporary feminist standards, it is essential that each rabbinic work—for example, the Mishnah—be considered on its own terms and evaluated from the perspective of what its framers set out to accomplish in their own day. The key question is, In what direction was the rabbinic system as a whole headed? Given the entrenched patriarchy of the Bible, was the Mishnah moving in the direction of protecting women, affording them greater social and economic independence and control over their own lives, or was it issuing ever-harsher decrees that fortified patriarchal ordinances?

To answer this question it is necessary to study the relevant tractates, the seven tractates of the Division of Women and tractate Niddah—not atomistically, but holistically—as Neusner has suggested. That is, we need to engage in an analysis of each tractate as a literary and legal whole in order to find out what aspects of the topic its framer selects for discussion; the relative amount of attention that is devoted to each topic; the ordering principle for materials within the tractate; how the order affects meaning; and the extent to which the Mishnah departs from the simple meaning of Scripture. With this information in hand it should be possible to reach general conclusions about the social and religious thrust of the document and a sense of its feminist stance.

My own work on the tractate Gittin shows that it focuses to a great extent on preserving the validity of bills of divorce sent by a husband living abroad to his wife back in Israel but spends little time discussing bills of divorce prepared and delivered by a husband in residence. This suggests that to the framers the safeguarding of a woman's ability to remarry without the risk of the first husband returning and challenging the validity of her *get* is of paramount importance. In addition, that the tractate repeatedly links bills of divorce to writs of manumission suggests that if the latter are given in reward for loyal service upon a master's death or following his decision not to return home from abroad, then the same may be true for bills of divorce: that is, they are not only delivered when a marriage fails but also when a husband wishes to express concern for his wife's welfare after his death,[32] or in the event that he does not return home from afar. Holistic observations like these suggest that the Mishnaic system, although not concerned with equality for women under divorce law, was interested in protecting women from abuse by men's shrewd manipulation of patriarchal legal instruments.[33]

A second important task is to read the Mishnah in the context of the Tosefta, assuming either that the Tosefta is the Mishnah's earliest commentary or that it is a collection of materials from the same time as the Mishnah. In either case it should be possible, by carefully comparing the two documents, to define the parameters of rabbinic thinking on the subjects of the Division of Women and then to determine whether the Mishnah's approach or attitude can be characterized as more or less feminist than the Tosefta's. That is, did the redactor of the Mishnah include in his collection the most or least liberal point of view of the many expressed at that time? If it turns out that the Mishnah's rulings with respect to divorce are consistently more strict than those of the Tosefta, then it may be true that the document that assumed ascendancy and became canon for later generations was more pietistic and less feminist than others that existed at roughly the same time.[34]

But even if what appear to be the Tosefta's more liberal stands did not become hegemonic, they should not be forgotten. A central item on the feminist agenda is to search the text for protofeminists and the outer limits of leniency. In locating these voices it would be possible to render more accurately the range of attitudes toward women in Judaism's formative period and then to propose a multifaceted model of rabbinic Judaism. If many sympathetic voices are found, it may be necessary to revise the regnant view of rabbinic Judaism as unrelievedly patriarchal.[35]

Furthermore, the subsequent history of lenient or profeminist positions needs to be traced. For example, if a minority of early rabbis held that women deserved an equal share of their mothers' estates (as opposed to the majority view that all of a woman's property should be awarded to her sons), how was this minority view received by later rabbis in Babylonia? In Palestine? This information will help us to trace the evolution or devolution of rabbinic sympathies for women.[36]

The same kinds of questions need to be raised about Midrash Halakhah and Midrash Aggadah. Given that Midrash Halakhah is an extensive legal commentary on Scripture, which, unlike the Mishnah, preserves scriptural links, does it appear that Midrash chooses to diminish or uphold the patriarchy of Scripture? Do the different collections of tannaitic midrash, which are believed to come from one or the other of two schools, differ in their approach to women? How does the Midrashic treatment of women compare to the Mishnah's and the Tosefta's treatment of women? Do the biblical commentaries and homilies of Midrash Aggadah present biblical women in a positive or negative light?

It is then necessary to read the Mishnah in light of the Babylonian and Palestinian Talmuds to see whether these documents, which clearly represent a statement *on* the Mishnah's meaning and not *of* the Mishnah's meaning, move away from the Mishnah's patriarchy or attempt to strengthen it. To find out, one must answer such questions as: Do the spokespersons for the Babylonian Talmud interpret the Mishnah literally or in light of parallel Midrashic or Toseftan material that expresses a different, possibly more feminist, viewpoint? If the Mishnah presents a dispute, do the amoraim (later Talmudic rabbis) rule according to the more lenient or more stringent point of view found in the Mishnah? Regarding the new topics raised by the amoraim: Do these fresh initiatives reflect a feminist outlook or not? How do the approaches of the two Talmuds compare?

A significant caveat must be issued about the analysis of Talmudic texts. As I have noted, a major discovery of contemporary Talmud criticism is that the Talmud contains not only a tannaitic and amoraic stratum, but also a third distinct layer, an extensive set of unattributed editorial statements. The importance of this discovery for feminist interpretation is that in appraising the patriarchal content of tannaitic or amoraic statements, they must be read apart from the anonymous interpretive framework, which, because of assumptions about the rules of logical argument, sometimes imputes new meaning to old statements that may differ from the author's intent. That is, the anonymous spokesman may interpret tannaitic and amoraic statements that were favorable (or unfavorable) to women in ways that significantly alter their original content.[37]

Another promising avenue of inquiry is attendance to the historical sources embedded in the legal texts. There is a wealth of anecdotal material in the Talmud and the Midrash in which women figure as litigants in a courtroom, as petitioners who come before rabbis with questions about religious ritual, as wives, daughters, and mothers of rabbis who recount fascinating personal vignettes (which often prove to be instructive), as inn-keepers, bailors, and occasionally as sources of knowledge. If this material were studied systematically, it might serve to correct rabbinic pronouncements on many issues. For instance, I strongly suspect that women had more freedom of action in social contexts than the legal dicta suggest.

In addition, studying these materials may help to fill a gap in the history of Jewish women by shedding light on their participation in life-cycle rituals, such as dressing the bride and bewailing the dead. A serious difficulty in working with these materials, however, is that the sources have often been deliberately tampered with; many stories have been embellished for didactic or dramatic purposes. Even so, an analytic methodology can be developed that would peel away later accretions to uncover the kernel of historical truth.

Yet another area of inquiry should be cross-cultural comparisons. It is important to know whether rabbinic patriarchy was more or less benign than Roman or Persian patriarchy. Did the rabbis establish a system of marriage, divorce, inheritance, and religious ritual that was more inclusive or less inclusive of women than those of the surrounding cultures? Although some attempts have been made to conduct such studies, no systematic work has been published.

Another virtually untapped area of feminist inquiry is the search for and evaluation of extratextual evidence that may shed light on the life and status of women. Perhaps such evidence would support or contradict the view of women emerging from the pages of the Talmud.[38]

The agenda I have proposed, together with my survey and evaluation of Neusner's and Wegner's books on feminist interpretation, should indicate both the potential fruitfulness of this research and the enormity of the challenge that lies ahead. The increasing numbers of women and open-minded men entering rabbinics and attaining positions of prominence will bring about a rapid increase in feminist studies in the not-so-distant future and an explosion of knowledge about the lives of women and attitudes toward them in the period of formative Judaism.

Notes

1. On the theory and practice of Talmud criticism, see Hyman Klein, "Gemara and Sebara," *Jewish Quarterly Review* 38 (1947); Y. N. Epstein, *Mavo Lenusach Hamishnah* (Jerusalem: Magnes, 1964); David Halivni, *Mekorot Umesorot* (Moed, Nashim, Jerusalem: Jewish Theological Seminary of America, 1975); Shamma Friedman, "A Critical Study of Yevamot X with a Methodological Introduction," *Texts and Studies,* vol. 1 (New York: Jewish Theological Seminary of America, 1977). See in particular David Goodblatt, "The Babylonian Talmud," in *The Study of Ancient Judaism,* ed. Jacob Neusner (New York: Ktav, 1981), for a full account of the various forms of Talmud criticism, as well as an extensive bibliography. See also Baruch M. Bokser, "Talmudic Studies," in *The State of Jewish Studies,* ed. Shaye J. D. Cohen and Edward L. Greenstein (Detroit: Wayne Sate University Press, 1990), 80–112.

2. Rabbinovicz published manuscript collations for Tractate Berakhot, the entire Divisions of Moed and Neziqin, and several tractates in the Division of Qodashim (New York, [1867–86] 1960). Efforts to complete his work are now under way. Volumes of manuscript collations and notes for tractates in the Division of Women have been published in the past thirty years.

3. Lieberman, *Tosefta Kifshuta* (New York: Jewish Theological Seminary, 1955–88).

4. Talmudists are currently working on preparing critical editions of rabbinic texts and commentaries; exploring the relation between tannaitic and amoraic material; understanding the technical terminology; tracing the history of the text, the rabbinical academy and collegial relations within it and the development of modes of argumentation; and lexical studies.

5. In May 1991, the Annenberg Research Institute in Philadelphia held the conference "Women in Religion and Society." Five feminist studies of rabbinic texts were read: Daniel Boyarin, "Eve, Pandora, and Lilith: Gynophobic Beginnings and the Beginnings of Gynophobia"; Howard Eilberg-Schwartz, "The Nakedness of a Woman's Voice, the Pleasure of a Man's Mouth"; Mordechai A. Friedman, "Levirate, Temporary Marriage, and Veils: On the Meaning of Change in Jewish Law"; Judith Baskin, "Images of Wives in Rabbinic Literature"; Judith Hauptman, "Women and Inheritance in Rabbinic Texts: Identifying Elements of a Critical Feminist Impulse." Other recent feminist articles and books by Talmudic scholars are: Judith Baskin, "The Separation of Women in Rabbinic Judaism," in *Women, Religion, and Social Change,* ed. Yvonne Y. Haddad and Ellison B. Findly (Albany: SUNY Press, 1985), 3–18; "Rabbinic Reflections on the Barren Wife," *Harvard Theological Review* 82(1) (1989): 101–14; "The Rabbinic Transformation of Rahab the Harlot," *Notre Dame English Journal: A Journal of Religion in Literature* 9(2) (1979): 141–57; Eilberg-Schwartz, *The Savage in Judaism* (Indianapolis: Indiana University Press, 1990); Judith Romney Wegner, "The Image and Status of Women in Classical Rabbinic Judaism," in *Jewish Women in Historical Perspective,* ed. Judith Baskin (Detroit: Wayne State University Press, 1991), 68–93; Devora Steinmetz, "A Portrait of Miriam in Rabbinic Midrash," *Prooftexts* 8 (1988): 35–65; David Goodblatt, "The Beruriah Traditions,"

Journal of Jewish Studies 26(1–2) (spring–autumn 1975): 68–85. See also references in later notes to studies by Shaye J. D. Cohen and Daniel Boyarin.

6. Jacob Neusner, *Judaism: The Evidence of the Mishnah* (Chicago: University of Chicago Press, 1982); and Judith Wegner, *Chattel or Person? The Status of Women in the Mishnah* (New York: Oxford University Press, 1988).

7. Two examples of popular feminist studies: Eliezer Berkovits, *Jewish Women in Time and Torah* (Hoboken, N.J.: Ktav, 1990); Leonard Swidler, *Women in Judaism* (Metuchen, N.J.: Scarecrow, 1976).

8. Jacob Neusner, *Method and Meaning in Ancient Judaism,* Brown Judaica Studies, no. 10 (Missoula, Mont.: Scholars Press, 1979), 79–100. (In the discussion that follows, numbers in parentheses refer to pages in Neusner's book.)

9. Michelle Zimbalist Rosaldo and Louise Lamphere, eds., *Woman, Culture, and Society* (Stanford: Stanford University Press, 1974).

10. A third tractate, called Tevul Yom, discusses people—both men and women (see, e.g., 4:2)—who are in the process of becoming ritually clean.

11. Rosaldo and Lamphere, 36.

12. Neusner notes that in the context of the Division of Women that only men have the power to effect sanctification. He admits that he does not know whether according to Mishnah women, too, have the power to effect sanctification (p. 84).

13. See Elisabeth Schüssler-Fiorenza, *In Memory of Her* (New York: Crossroad, 1985), 35.

14. Y. N. Epstein (*Mavo Lenusach Hamishnah,* 980) writes that the earliest reference to the divisions of Mishnah is found in *Avot d'Rabbi Natan* 29. The first explicit reference to the Division of Women is found in the Babylonian Talmud, Shabbat 31a.

15. See, e.g., Ketubot 4:4–6; 8; Gittin 6:4; Yevamot 6:3.

16. *Judaism: The Evidence of the Mishnah* (Chicago: University of Chicago Press, 1981), 232.

17. Note that these same groups are obligated to say grace after eating (Berakhot 3:3). See Wegner, 156–57.

18. One cannot rely on Qiddushin 1:7 alone for a survey of women's obligations and exemptions, because of the numerous exceptions to the rule, already noted in the Talmud (Qiddushin 34a).

19. That is, I find Mishnah far more advanced than Torah in its conception of women as religious personalities.

20. Neusner, *Judaism,* 191.

21. Neusner, *A History of the Mishnaic Law of Women* (Leiden: Brill, 1980), 265.

22. Neusner, *Judaism,* 194.

23. Neusner (*History,* 93) concurs with this interpretation, translating: "If the husband forms the opinion that his wife is unfaithful, he may require her to submit to the ordeal of the bitter waters only if he provides suitable warning in advance."

24. Schüssler-Fiorenza, *In Memory of Her,* 59. Drawing on Neusner, Schüssler-Fiorenza concludes that according to Mishnah, women can enter the sacred space only by being acted upon by man. This is incorrect. Another feminist scholar of Christianity who relies on Neusner's analysis of Mishnah is Jane Schaberg; see *The Illegitimacy of Jesus* (New York:

Crossroad, 1990), 36. (In the discussion that follows, numbers in parentheses refer to pages in Schüssler-Fiorenza's book.)

25. Later in the book, in her comments on women in Judaism before 70 C.E., she suggests that Christian feminists consistently denigrate Rabbinic Judaism in order to depict Jesus as radical and feminist. They need to do this, she says, because there is no positive evidence that Jesus sought to overthrow patriarchy, and they buttress his feminist image by making the Jewish context in which he operated look worse (106–8).

26. If one can identify a feminist impulse in Mishnaic texts, it may ease Ross Kraemer's acute discomfort with Schüssler-Fiorenza's implicit anti-Jewish suggestion that many Jewish women were not attracted to Jesus because of their "stubborn refusal to acknowledge the truth" (review of *In Memory of Her, Religious Studies Review* 2[1] [Jan. 1985]: 7). Shaye J. D. Cohen, in "The Modern Study of Judaism," discusses the "anti-Jewish animus" of much Christian feminist liberation theology, in Shaye J. D. Cohen and Edward L. Greenstein, eds. *The State of Judaism* (Detroit: Wayne State University Press, 1990).

27. Both Schüssler-Fiorenza and I are making the assumption that the Mishnah, even though its publication in the year 200 C.E. postdates the period of Jesus, accurately reflects societal values and outlook at the time of Jesus. See Schüssler-Fiorenza, *In Memory of Her,* 115.

28. All numbers in parentheses refer to pages in Wegner's book.

29. See Wegner, 192–95.

30. For example, Deut. 22:23.

31. Shaye Cohen (in *Women's History and Ancient History,* ed. Sarah B. Pomeroy [Chapel Hill: University of North Carolina Press, 1991], 282–84) demonstrates that in the rabbinic period menstruants were not barred from entering the synagogue, nor were they isolated from society.

32. If a childless husband divorces his wife before he dies, she is not subject to the requirements of levirate marriage and may marry any man she pleases.

33. I reported on these results in "The Relative Impact of Mishnah Gittin's Enactments on Husbands and Wives," delivered at the Twentieth Annual Conference of the Association for Jewish Studies (Boston, 18–20 Dec. 1988).

34. See my article, "Pesiqah L'humra B'mishnat Gittin," in *Proceedings of the Tenth World Congress of Jewish Studies,* Jerusalem, August 1990.

35. See chapter 6, "Studying Women," in Daniel Boyarin, *Carnal Israel: Reading Sex in Talmudic Culture* (Berkeley: University of California Press, 1993), for an excellent example of how to tease profeminist voices out of a text that tried to suppress them. See also my article "Women and Procreation," in *Tikkun* (Nov./Dec. 1991).

36. In studying the laws of inheritance I discovered that unlike the Mishnah, which awards a mother's estate to her sons only, two sages whose views appear in the Tosefta advocate equality for daughters and sons in the disposition of a mother's estate. Although the Mishnah makes no mention of this dissenting opinion, both the Babylonian and Palestinian Talmuds cite it and then go on to say that a number of early amoraim invoked this rule in cases they adjudicated. Regrettably, later amoraim in each of the two Talmuds suppressed this egalitarian point of view and made the Mishnah's male-biased rule dominant.

37. These anonymous comments may shed light on the attitudes of their own authors but not on the authors of the statements under scrutiny.

38. Bernadette Brooten, *Women Leaders in the Ancient Synagogue: Inscriptional Evidence and Background Issues,* Brown Judaica Series (Chico, Calif.: Scholars Press, 1982). A set of synagogue inscriptions analyzed by Brooten indicates that women functioned in leadership roles that the texts suggest were not open to them.

Jewish Theology in
Feminist Perspective

Jewish feminist theology is not an academic field in the same
sense that feminist history or literature is. Rather, it is a triple
outsider to Jewish studies: first, because the place of theology
in the academy is complex and controversial; second, because theology has never had an esteemed role within Judaism; and third, because it is feminist. In this chapter, I
explore the implications of each of these aspects of marginality, the first two for the sake of laying to rest shibboleths
that might otherwise get in the way of discussion, the third
as my central concern. What *is* Jewish feminist theology,
and what are its implications for Jewish studies?

Theology and the Academy

The place of theology within Jewish studies is part of a
larger debate concerning the place of theology in the academy, a debate that emerged with the rapid growth of religious studies in the 1950s and 1960s. The founders of new
religious studies programs, especially in state universities,
were anxious to locate and justify these programs in the
context of a religiously pluralistic culture. Arguing that they
held no brief for any particular religion but were simply
exploring religion as a human phenomenon according to
accepted norms of university scholarship, many departments
named themselves religious studies specifically in contradis-
tinction to theology. The point of the distinction was that
religious studies is serious, objective, and scholarly—concerned with a significant dimension of human thought and
experience, with a clear impact on many aspects of life—
while theology is particularistic, engaged, and unscholarly.
Theology not only comes out of distinct communities of
faith and is done from a stance of commitment, but it deals

with an object—God—that can be discerned only by faith, using warrants—revelation—that are not publicly discernible or testable.[1] Although this dichotomy has been repeatedly questioned, it still shapes many responses to the incorporation of theology into the university curriculum.[2]

Since Jewish studies is itself particularistic according to these same criteria, it cannot hold that fault specifically against theology. Yet Jewish studies can still object to theology on the ground of its engaged stance or lack of scholarly neutrality. To the extent that Jewish studies is influenced by a *Wissenschaft des Judentums* (the science of Judaism) approach that sees the history, literature, sociology, and religious life of the Jewish people as data to be studied objectively and critically,[3] Jewish studies—like religious studies—must be skeptical about the academic legitimacy of theology. From a science of Judaism perspective, theology can be of interest only insofar as it is studied historically or viewed as so much material on the thought of some important figure, rather than as a living and constructive art. I do not mean to deny that in practice many Jewish studies programs encourage or at least tolerate constructive questions. But given the vulnerability of Jewish studies in the university, it is tempting to assert its respectability by emphasizing its adherence to canons of disinterested scholarship and critical research. When one adds to the committed stance of theology the double commitment of feminist theology, the possible place of such a subject within Jewish studies becomes even more problematic.

Theology and Judaism

The actual or potential tension between the nature of theology and the nature of Jewish studies is just one issue confronting would-be Jewish feminist theologians. Often this tension is never articulated because of a different and prior claim that theology is not Jewish or that Jewish theology simply does not exist. The history of Jewish religious reflection from Philo on is named philosophy or religious thought. Theology is defined narrowly as the systematization of doctrines or the systematization of communal beliefs about the nature of God. Christianity, it is then asserted, rests on a common faith that makes one a Christian, a faith that theology appropriately defines and refines. What most centrally defines Judaism, however, is not beliefs but *behaviors,* and these are elaborated through *halakhah* (Jewish law). The energy that Christianity has poured into theology Judaism has poured into elaborating a legal system that encompasses every aspect of life. Insofar as Jews have reflected on the foundations or presuppositions of this system, this reflection has been more narrative or midrashic than systematic, so that, again, the term *theology* would be misplaced.[4]

It is not surprising, given these widely held assumptions, that all of us who do Jewish theology, feminist or not, find ourselves in an odd and somewhat defensive position. Many recent works on Jewish theology begin with a justification of the enterprise or describe as a goal putting theology back on the Jewish map.[5] Although a full-scale defense of Jewish theology is out of place in this context, some discussion of the importance of theology and its relation to Jewish studies seems necessary, or there is little point in discussing the feminist transformation of theology at all.

As Arthur A. Cohen and Paul Mendes-Flohr point out in the introduction to their *Contemporary Jewish Religious Thought,* "Theology is the discipline that Jews eschew while nonetheless pursuing it with covert avidity."[6] Provided that theology is not defined too narrowly, their comment makes perfect sense. If theology is understood as *sustained and coherent reflection on the experiences and categories of a particular religious tradition,* and as *reflection on the world in light of that tradition,* then how can Jews not be at least closet theologians? The practices that are supposedly central to Judaism are grounded in a series of theological claims: that God gave the law to Moses on Sinai, that revealed law is both written and oral, that the law constitutes part of the obligation of the covenant, that there is a special covenantal relation between God and Israel, and so forth. All Jewish observance rests on some sort of theological preunderstanding, some relation to these fundamental claims, however they are interpreted, modified, or even rejected. What would be the meaning of a Jewish identity that had no relation to any set of beliefs about the nature of Jewishness?

Feminist Theology

Jewish feminists have considerable experience of the extent to which the boundaries of Jewish identity are guarded by theology. I know of no Jew, for example, who would agree that "Jews for Jesus" are Jewish. Belief in the messianic significance of Jesus seems to constitute a universally agreed-upon end-point in the great spectrum of Jewishness. Jewish feminists are discovering that another such point is the belief in a Goddess. Advocacy of Goddess rituals—indeed, even mention of the Goddess—is enough in the eyes of many Jews to place one outside the Jewish pale. No one has ever asked me, when I speak on Jewish feminism, whether I keep kosher or observe the Sabbath. But I have been asked again and again whether my understanding of God is really Jewish, whether I think one can have Judaism without monotheism, and how far I am willing to go in expanding the boundaries of Jewish belief. Jewishness is being defined, in other words, by theological criteria. And if this is happening covertly, surely these criteria must be subject to public examination and criticism.

It is not simply because they already operate on a hidden level, however, that theological assumptions need to be discussed openly. Jewish lack of interest in theology is itself a separate and significant problem. Observance of the law, I have suggested, is rooted in certain theological claims about the origins of the law. But it is also true that over time, the law becomes self-justifying and the legal system self-perpetuating. In applying the law to ever-changing situations, one does not need to return to the original situation of standing at Sinai. It is enough to study the sources, to know one's precedents, to quote text—as in any legal system. And so it can happen that over time the relation to God that was expressed through and animated the law—that was its foundation and purpose—is lost. A similar process takes place in non-Orthodox Judaism, with social action, eclectic forms of observance, or simply a sense of community with other Jews replacing some deeper religious understanding and purpose. In either case, a profound spiritual void lies at the heart of American Judaism. American Jews do not know how to talk about God; they are embarrassed to do so. Such spiritual experiences as they have often seem to take place outside the realm of Judaism, and they do not know how to reconnect these experiences with prayer or other forms of observance. At the same time, many Jews are turning to other spiritual traditions for answers to questions that Judaism seems not to address.

Theology, and in practice especially feminist theology, can help reanimate the connection between practice and larger questions of meaning. Theology's purpose is to reflect on the experiences and events that lie at the heart of Judaism, to reformulate or transform central Jewish ideas in response to contemporary needs, and to articulate a Jewish framework for understanding basic human questions. Jewish feminist theology approaches the tradition with both a profound critique of its sexism *and* a vision of the religious meaning of women's full participation in Jewish life. It is rooted in the experience of a larger and richer way of being, which it seeks to express within and against the terms of the tradition. It approaches theology not as an intellectual exercise but with a deep stake in the outcome of theologizing, challenging other Jews to examine their religious assumptions and the way they find expression in religious practice and institutions.

All this is to acknowledge that Jewish theology is not a strictly academic enterprise, that it is rooted in and comes out of the Jewish community, and, in the case of feminist theology, that it is concerned with concrete issues of communal practice, liturgy, and experience. It does not, however, follow that theology has no place in an academic program. On the contrary, theology can expose the notion of the detached, disinterested scholar as a dangerous myth. Feminist theology in particular, but other theologies as well, make it amply clear that all thinkers have special interests and that claims to objectivity serve only to disguise the interests of scholars who are generally involved in serving the status quo. Thus, those who teach Jewish studies as historical or literary "science" take an implicit stand in a theological debate about the meaning of Jewish history. Those who teach Jewish studies using the many sources that make no reference to women perpetuate the ideological contention that women have made no significant contribution to the shaping of Judaism and implicitly support a particular theological understanding of women's proper role. Such assumptions can be examined and criticized only when the theological presuppositions of different Jewish frameworks become the subject of classroom discussion.

Jewish Feminist Theology as Critique and Recovery

If Jewish theology not only exists but is central to the Jewish studies enterprise, where does Jewish feminist theology fit into this larger context? On the one hand, it provides one instantiation of theology. It deals with all the questions of the meaning and purpose of Jewish and human existence that any Jewish theology is called on to deal with. On the other hand, Jewish feminist theology is particularly important to the process of critical reflection, for it subjects other Jewish theology—indeed, all Jewish studies—to searching criticism. It comes at religious questions with a passion that reanimates theological discussion, but it also asks fundamental questions about the origins, nature, and function of theological discourse. It is concerned with the foundations of central Jewish ideas, the groups that generated them, and the interests they serve. It is a thoroughly *critical theology,* a theology as appropriate to the university as it is necessary to the reconstitution of Jewish community.[7]

Jewish feminist theology, although it has its roots in the Jewish community, is also part of the larger context of feminist scholarship as a critical and constructive enterprise. Feminist scholarship in many disciplines has gone through a number of stages that began with a critique of male scholarship and moved to a thoroughgoing redefinition or transformation of many fields. The first feminist works in many areas were criticisms of canonical male texts, theories, presuppositions, and images. They attempted to show the particularity of what have been accepted as universal perspectives, to expose the androcentrism of traditional scholarship, and to highlight the absence of the voices of women and other oppressed groups. This critique of male sources was often followed by an emphasis on the recovery of lost women, by efforts to show that certain disciplines, movements, and historical periods were not defined solely by men, but that women made important contributions that had been forgotten or passed over. Often in this second phase, feminist scholars accepted prevailing definitions of historical importance and sought to locate women in contexts deemed important by reigning norms. The third or constructive phase of feminist scholarship is characterized by a radical questioning of such norms, by redefinitions of "importance" from the perspective of women's experience, and by the creation of theory from a feminist point of view. These phases were consecutive in terms of a shift in emphasis over the past twenty years, but they are also concurrent in that no stage has disappeared to make way for the other. Feminist scholarship remains critical scholarship and continues to insist on the ubiquity of women's historical agency.

These stages provide a useful structure for discussing Jewish feminist theology, and for seeing how its development has been affected by the subordinate role of theology within Judaism. It is striking, especially in contrast to Christian feminist theology, that virtually no work has been done by Jewish feminists that criticizes earlier Jewish theologians. Although Christian (and non-Christian) feminists have analyzed the thought of Augustine, Aquinas, Paul Tillich, Reinhold Niebuhr, and numerous other thinkers, no parallel body of work exists that discusses Saadia, Maimonides, Franz Rosenzweig, Martin Buber, or other Jewish figures.[8] There is no specifically intratheological dialogue within Jewish feminism. This is probably owing in part to the absence of an institutional base for such studies. The paucity of graduate programs in Jewish theology means that there are few places that might generate or encourage such work. Perhaps Jewish feminists, however, also have the sense that theology is not sufficiently central to Judaism to be worth criticizing. If one has attacked Anders Nygren's or Niebuhr's view of grace, one has deconstructed and unsettled a whole trend within modern Protestantism. But supposing that one could demonstrate Rosenzweig's androcentrism, what would be the effects of that knowledge? What would it change in the nature or practice of Judaism?

The transformative and communal bent of Jewish feminist theology makes it unlikely that such theological critiques will ever constitute a major part of Jewish feminist discourse. Yet there is interesting scholarly work to be done in this area. Lauren Granite has pointed out, for example, that the centrality of relation in Martin Buber's work has led feminists uncritically to adopt aspects of his thought without thinking to analyze it from the perspective of gender.[9] Buber's I-You theology, however, rests on the assumption that we human beings spend most of our lives in the It-world, only occasionally experiencing moments of I-You connection. Granite suggests that "while relation is key both to Buber's philosophy and feminist theory, it seems that it enters their experience from opposite ends: Buber works toward relation, while feminists begin with relation."[10] The relevance of a gender analysis to Buber's work becomes especially clear in connection with his discussion of the emergence of the two modes of I-You and I-It relation. Here Buber focuses on the experience of the child and its gradual acquisition of self-consciousness without ever naming the mother as the one with whom the child is in relation or looking at the mother-child relationship from the mother's side.[11] Were the child's development seen from the perspective of the mother, a third mode of relation might be required to capture her experience. The child is not characteristically an object to the mother—as in the I-It mode—but neither does she necessarily experience a perpetual reciprocity of relation. Her experience of care and connection even when mutuality is absent may constitute a third sort of relation insufficiently accounted for in Buber's theology.[12]

If theological criticism in the narrow sense awaits the attention of a new generation of Jewish feminist thinkers, criticism on a broader scale is absolutely central to Jewish feminist theology. Starting from Jewish religious practice and the communal exclusion of women, Jewish feminists have examined the theological presuppositions embedded in the Bible, halakhah, and liturgical texts and have called into question a range of basic assumptions from the normative character of maleness to the holiness of separation.

This wide-ranging critique of the theological presuppositions of Jewish religious and institutional practice presupposes the broad definition of theology I discussed earlier. Once theology is understood, not just as teachings about God, but as sustained reflection on all the fundamental categories and experiences of Judaism, the normative character of maleness emerges clearly as the basic principle of Jewish theological anthropology.[13] As I argued in my article "The Right Question Is Theological"—the first sustained theological critique of Jewish women's situation—women's otherness is not simply a sociological fact but a fundamental assumption that underlies both the details of halakhah and a larger discourse about the nature of Israel as a people.[14] Israel, in both the narrative and legislative portions of the Bible and in the basic categories of the Mishnah, is defined as male heads of households. If one asks within Judaism: What is a Jew? What is a person? What are the responsibilities of a Jew? the questions are impossible to answer in any but the most abstract way without recourse to gender differentiation and hierarchy. This is the starting point of the feminist critique of Judaism: that a woman is not simply a Jew but always a female Jew (as in "a *woman* rabbi")—always the one perceived as Other in relation to a male norm.

Drorah Setel makes the further point that maleness–femaleness is not the only hierarchy within Judaism, but rather one of a host of dualistic separations that together are taken to constitute holiness.[15] From the very beginnings of its history, Israel saw itself as called on to separate or differentiate itself from the nations of surrounding peoples. This differentiation was made manifest both in the theological claim to chosenness and in many internal separations that were to mark the life of a holy nation: Shabbat and week, kosher and trafe, male and female.[16] Since a critique of hierarchical dualisms has been central to the entire feminist project from its beginnings, Setel locates the central tension between Judaism and feminism at this point: in separative versus relational modes of understanding. Her critique raises a series of fascinating questions for Jewish theology: Why the centrality of separation as a mark of holiness, especially in those cases where separation seems to have no moral significance (as in the separation of linen and wool or different kinds of cattle)? How closely identified are separation and holiness within Judaism? Is separation itself problematic for feminism, or only hierarchical modes of separation?[17]

Seen in the context of these other issues, the image of God as male in Judaism is not the only locus of feminist theological criticism but one important aspect of a larger pattern. Jewish feminists have pointed out that the overwhelming preponderance of male images for God in biblical and rabbinic texts and in the traditional liturgy correlates with the normative status of maleness. Since God in the fullness of God's reality is ultimately unknowable, our images tell us more about our social arrangements—in this case the subordinate status of women—than they do about God.[18] Moreover, the image of God as a being outside ourselves ruling over and controlling the world fits into the pattern of hierarchical dualisms that Setel identifies as central to Judaism. God as the locus of holiness, meaning, and value is infinitely more than the world "he" created. The idea that this God has chosen Israel supports the dualistic separation between Israel and other people. The idea that this God is male supports the normative character of maleness.[19]

These points do not exhaust the feminist theological critique of Judaism. The fundamental nature of women's otherness, of hierarchical dualisms, and of the male image of God has implications for the concepts of revelation and Torah as well as for other issues. What is the source of Jewish understandings of self, world, and God? Why is it that these understandings seem so clearly to reflect a patriarchal social order? What is the source of Torah, and what are its parameters? If women's voices and experiences are excluded from Torah as it has been handed down, does it need to be expanded? Is there a "woman's Torah"? How do we recognize it, and what would it include? A full theological critique of Judaism is beyond my scope here, but even a brief outline of feminist criticism serves to suggest the range and significance of a feminist probing of Jewish theological foundations and its importance for the critical study of Judaism.

If we turn to the second stage of feminist scholarship, the recovery of women's history, we find that it has been similarly affected by the status of theology within Judaism. Although it may well be that time will turn up medieval or other women theologians whose names are as yet unknown to us, there is no dense history of theologizing among Jews in whose twists and tangles women can be easily lost. What feminists have attempted to recover, therefore, is not necessarily full-blown theologies, but the history of women's *spirituality*—understandings of God and Jewish life embedded in ritual and prayer, memoirs and sermons—that may at some point be incorporated into theologies by contemporary Jewish women.

In seeking out the history of women's spirituality, feminist theologians are dependent on the work of women in other areas of Jewish studies who have examined ancient sources, studied archaeological remains, and searched for new documents in modern women's history. Since, particularly for the early periods of Jewish history, few sources are interested in the religious lives of women, hints concerning women's experiences must be carefully ferreted out from narratives, prophecies, and legal texts focused on other matters. Biblical scholars, for example, have argued that the scant sources concerning Miriam suggest that she was probably an important cultic leader in early Israel.[20] What exactly was the nature of her contribution and role? Or, in a different vein, Genesis tells us (34:1), "Dinah . . . went out to visit the women of the land." Does this bespeak some kind of connection on the part of Israelite women to Canaanite religion? Prophetic texts accusing women of worshiping the Queen of Heaven (Jer. 44) or bewailing Tammuz

(Ezek. 8:14), son of the Goddess Ishtar, imply that women may have been more resistant than men to giving up the worship of female deities. What are the implications of this resistance for our understanding of both paganism and Israelite monotheism? From the rabbinic period, the stories about Beruriah in the Talmud suggest that a small number of women found pleasure and religious purpose in the study of rabbinic texts, in the same way that an elite group of men has.[21] Jewish women's spirituality apparently has both diverged from *and* flowed into the mainstream of Jewish spirituality.

As we get into the modern period, texts written by women provide evidence of both a distinct religious outlook and one shaped by the role of women within patriarchal Judaism. Chava Weissler, for example, has discussed the *tkhines,* or petitionary prayers of early modern Eastern European Jewish women. These prayers, written for women and some by women, reflect a spirituality structured by private events and experiences. Unlike the public liturgy of the *siddur,* the content of the tkhines revolves largely around women's special commandments (lighting the Sabbath candles, taking the hallah dough, and ritual immersion), women's biological experiences, and personal and intimate moments (a visit to the graves of the dead, the illness of a child, the desire to raise children well). Although these prayers connect women to the larger tradition and occasionally even subtly transform it, they most strikingly convey the emotionality and intimacy of women's piety and its relation to ordinary life. If the God of Jewish women was the "God of our fathers" and of Jewish history, God was also the God of the matriarchs, domestic routines, and biological experiences particular to women.[22]

Interestingly, these same themes of the importance of religious feeling and the presence of God in everyday life also come through in the work of those modern women who have most claim to the title theologian, in that they developed a coherent religious vision, which they shared with others. Ellen Umansky has examined the sermons and addresses of Lily Montagu, founder of liberal Judaism in England, and Tehilla Lichtenstein, cofounder and leader of the Society of Jewish Science, to see whether and how the religious visions of these women differed from those of the men they saw as their mentors and teachers. Umansky finds that although the women understood themselves as simply promulgating the teachings of their mentors, in fact both saw religion as emotional and personal and grounded their sermons in their own life experience, feelings, and perceptions. Thus, although Claude Montefiore, Montagu's inspiration, preached about abstract concepts like beauty, truth, and justice, Montagu rooted her sermons in specific plays, movies, poems, books, and people that to her embodied the principles of liberal

Judaism and allowed the discovery of these principles in everyday life. Similarly, although Lichtenstein's husband, Morris, spoke in general terms about human character and the capacities of the mind, she always tied her discussions of Jewish science to concrete examples, most drawn from her experiences of motherhood, marriage, and the home.[23] Whether this focus on the concrete comes from a specifically women's perspective or is simply the product of the restricted role of women in Judaism, there is an interesting continuity between the work of these modern women and the spirituality of more traditional women.

The search for the gaps and silences in traditional texts and for devotional and sermonic material by women suggests a broadening of the definition of Jewish spirituality. Spirituality is found not simply in the products of a male elite but in the experiences and testimonies of women and ordinary men whose religious lives and theological presuppositions have generally been neglected. One could even argue that to understand the range of women's spiritual expression in the modern era, it is necessary to move beyond the realm of texts altogether. The female social reformers of the late nineteenth century, the founders of religious schools, settlement houses, and Jewish women's organizations, as well as participants in Zionist and Bundist activities saw themselves as serving God through moral and social action. Sharing the wider nineteenth-century belief in the innate piety of women, they believed that this piety placed a special obligation on them to worship God by helping others.[24] Their activism came from a clear theological understanding that prefigured the insight of feminist liberation theology: that theological reflection must always be rooted and expressed in concrete actions.

Jewish Feminist Theology as Construction

The need to expand the definition of spirituality to incorporate women's experience begins to suggest the constructive and transformative nature of Jewish feminist theology. A repetition or contemporary restatement of traditional ideas is impossible for such a theology because it begins with the critical moment in which all Jewish texts and ideas are viewed with suspicion for their possible collusion with patriarchy in silencing women's voices. Louis Jacobs, in the first chapter of his Jewish theology, suggests that theological ideas are to be embraced or rejected according to their "consistency with the tradition and coherence with the rest of our knowledge. Where there are contradictions in the traditional sources the contemporary Jewish theologian must try to decide which of the views is closest to the spirit of the tradition."[25] But if all the sources on which the theologian can draw take for granted the normative character of maleness, then it is impossible for the feminist theologian to root herself in the tradition without at the same time questioning some of its most fundamental assumptions. This is why the stage of criticism is never left behind in the move to construction. Rather, the transformative character of Jewish feminist theology is revealed in the back-and-forth movement between these stages.

Insistence on the value of women's experience and its integration into the tradition has ramifications for every theological question. In the rest of this chapter, I look at some of the implications of women's experience for the concepts of God and Torah, but a similar dialectic of critique and reconstruction would characterize a feminist discussion of any theological issue. Feminist analysis, moreover, often lays bare important dynamics in the nature of Judaism as a religion, so that specifically theological questions open up into "religious studies" questions concerning the function of religious language, symbols, and rituals and the origins and consolidation of religious traditions.

A Jewish feminist approach to Jewish God-language and Jewish concepts of God begins with the critique and process of recovery of women's spirituality I described earlier. The correlation between dominant images of God as male and Jewish social and institutional arrangements raises basic questions about the nature and purpose of God-language. What are Jews saying when we attribute particular qualities or characteristics to God? Are we describing God in words that God has revealed to us? Are we projecting our own wishes or social systems onto the cosmos? Are we responding to some special dimension of our experience using the concepts and vocabulary at our disposal? Although a theory of God-language is often more implicit than explicit in feminist theological constructions, by and large Jewish feminists insist on the socially shaped and created nature of religious language, but without reducing language about God to purely social projection. On the one hand, language about God is precisely that, *language* about God. Everything we say about God represents a human attempt to recapture or evoke experiences sustained within linguistic and cultural frameworks that already color our experience and interpretation.[26] On the other hand, language about God, if it is to move people and provide a sense of meaning, must come from a genuine individual or communal experience. It cannot be a product of individual fiat or scholarly consensus, nor can it be a mechanical response to a diagnosed ailment in Jewish God-language of the past.

For an increasing number of Jewish women and men, images of God as a male Other no longer work. This is the communal, nonacademic basis of the feminist theological quest. The search for the God of Jewish feminism is a search for a God experienced in women's new sense of empowerment and presence within the context of the Jewish tradition. Although feminist images of God draw on many sources, I see a fundamental experience out of which the new naming of God arises as the discovery of women's agency in the Jewish past and present in relation to a greater power that grounds and sustains it. Women's sense of coming to full selfhood in community—which to me is the fundamental feminist experience—is not simply self-referential but leads to a sense of participation in a reality and energy that finally enfold the cosmos and that both the individual and community can and must respond to.

The sense of women's power and agency that has propelled the Jewish feminist movement and its attempts at new God-language constitutes a new Jewish situation in discontinuity with much of the spirituality of Jewish women of the past. Gluckel of Hameln, whose memoir captures a segment of Jewish life and faith in seventeenth-century northern Germany,[27] the women who wrote or recited the tkhines, even as bold a figure as Montagu, were all trying to define their own religious lives within the context of a male-defined Judaism, be it traditional or Reform. Where they departed from tradition—or in Montagu's case, the Reform theology of Monte-fiore—they did so unselfconsciously. Contemporary Jewish feminists, by way of contrast, are deliberately claiming power as women to criticize the oppressive aspects of tradition and to reshape our relation to it. This means that although the history of women's spirituality is an important resource in that it reminds us that women always have been agents within Judaism and that Jewish religious belief and practice have always been broader than male elite texts would have us believe, women's history cannot simply be taken over whole. The relation between a self-consciously *feminist* spirituality and traditional *women's* spirituality remains an open question that feminist the-ology needs to explore.

Thus, although earlier generations of Jewish women spoke to the God of Jewish tradition as a God present in the details of their daily lives, for the most part they spoke to "him" using traditional images. Contemporary Jew-ish feminists also seek God in messy, embodied, everyday reality, but they have tried to translate this sense of God's immanence into the very language of metaphors for God. Feminist God-language, moreover, seeks to give expression not simply to God's presence in ordinary events and situations, but more specifically to the amazing discovery of God's presence moving in and among women. Rita Gross's article on female God-language, the first to raise the issue in a Jewish context, argued that if we want to reflect and affirm the "becoming" of women within the Jewish community, then everything we say about "God-He" we must be equally willing to say about "God-She."[28] Although on one level Gross's text reads like a simple political prescription for the disease of Jewish sexism, it also clearly represents an attempt to give concreteness to the image of God as present in women. At the time Gross wrote her article, Naomi Janowitz and Maggie Wenig were compiling a Sabbath prayerbook for women that not only used female pronouns for God but also experimented with female metaphors. God was not simply the traditional deity in female form, but a mother birthing the world and protecting it with her womb. The accumulation of female pronouns and images in both their prayers and those of later innovators provides a wonderful celebration of women's sexuality and power rare in the culture and still rarer in a religious context.[29]

Important as such language was and is as an affirmation of female selfhood in relation to the sacred, there is also a certain naïveté in the assumption that the insertion of female pronouns or images into traditional prayers provides a solution to women's invisibility. Rather, insofar as male images of God are part of a larger pattern of hierarchical dualisms, female language introduces a contradiction into the pattern that begins to reveal and disrupt it but does not in itself dislodge the larger system of dualisms. God-She can also be the supreme Other in a hierarchical system. Jewish feminist God-language has therefore also tried to address the notion of God as wholly Other, a notion that persists even in female imagery, by more radically challenging traditional metaphors and blessing formulas.

Lynn Gottlieb, for example, has drawn on images from various religious traditions to create a litany of names and metaphors for God that evoke the infinite, changing, and flowing depths of God's nature. Gottlieb is much interested in female metaphors, which she borrows from ancient Goddess traditions and develops from the feminine resonances and associations of many Hebrew terms. What characterizes her use of God-language above all, however, is not just its female imagery but its fluidity, movement, and multiplicity, its evocation of a God within and without, in women and all that lives.[30] Marcia Falk works in a different way to dislodge the traditional conception of God and male images. Focusing on the blessing formula that is so central in Jewish life, she challenges not simply its maleness but its anthropocentrism. Her blessing over bread, for example, changes "Blessed art thou Lord our God king of the universe," to "Let us bless the source or wellspring of life" that "brings forth bread from the earth." The Hebrew word for source *(ayin)* is feminine, adding an "ah" *(ha-motziah)* ending to the word for bread that displaces the ubiquitous masculine. Beyond this, the image of wellspring or source is both natural and nonhierarchical, shifting our sense of direction from a God in the high heavens ruling over us to a God present in the very ground beneath our feet, nourishing and sustaining us.[31]

In some ways, it is easier to articulate the new conception of God that lurks behind this abundance of imagery than it is to find the images that express the conception. The effort to create new metaphors for God bespeaks an understanding of monotheism that rejects the worship of a single image of God in favor of a new and inclusive notion of unity. Many Jewish feminists have pointed out that the inability of most Jews to imagine God as anything but male is a form of idolatry in that it identifies a finite image with the reality of God. Jews are used to thinking of idols as stones and carved figures, but verbal images can be equally idolatrous in their fixedness—indeed, can actually be more dangerous for being invisible.[32] Underlying feminist metaphors, by way of contrast, is a conception of monotheism, not as a single image of God, but, in Falk's phrase, as "an embracing *unity of a multiplicity of images.*"[33] Since the divine totality is all-embracing, every aspect of creation provides a clue to some dimension of God's reality. Every image of God is part of the divine reality that includes the diversity of an infinite community of human and nonhuman life. A true monotheism is able to discern the One in and through the changing forms of the many, to glimpse the whole in and through its infinite images.[34]

The nature of this divine totality is developed in feminist discourse through both what is denied and what is affirmed. God is not male. God is not a lord and king. God is not a being outside us, over against us, who manipulates and controls us and raises some people over others. God is not the dualistic Other who authorizes all other dualisms. God is the source and wellspring of life in its infinite diversity. God—as our foremothers seem to have known—is present in all aspects of life, but present not just as father and protector but as one who empowers us to act creatively ourselves. God, to use Nelle Morton's image, is the great hearing one at the center of the universe, the one who hears us to speech and is altered by the hearing.[35] God is inside and outside us. God is transcendent in the way that community transcends the individuals within it. God is the God known in community, encountered by the Jewish people at Sinai at the same time they became a community. But God embraces the inexhaustible particularities of all communities and is named fully by none.

The difficulties of translating this conception of God into metaphor—or better, many metaphors—is related to the nature of religious symbols. Since new symbols cannot simply be invented as a response to some diagnosed problem in the tradition, but rather emerge from new experiences, it takes time for experience to crystallize into imagery. Moreover, language is just one vehicle—and in many ways a poor vehicle—for expressing the nature of divine reality. The experiences that language tries to pin down are many times undergone in silence, and the making of metaphor represents but a halting attempt to translate that silence into a language that can be shared with others. Ritual, because it involves the whole self, is potentially a more effective vehicle for communicating a total conception of the sacred. Both the communal roots of Jewish feminist theology and the nature of religion make it important to look at feminist ritual as an expression of Jewish feminist understandings of God. The rejection of hierarchical leadership in feminist ritual, its preference for circles, its participatory style of prayer that seeks to empower all present, offer testimony to a feminist conception of God that is as powerful as any new metaphor.

A second important focus of feminist theological discussion is the nature and meaning of Torah. Obviously, there is a connection between the concept of Torah and the concept of God, for the assertion that God is the giver of Torah is central to Jewish theology and, like many important theological assertions, justifies itself through its circularity. Because God is the giver of Torah, it reliably testifies to the nature of God, and the faithfulness of God is warrant for the believability of Torah. But if feminists are suspicious of traditional metaphors for God because they reinforce larger patterns of male domination, this suspicion in turn implies a critique of Torah as itself in bondage to patriarchy.

Feminist suspicion of Torah does not stem specifically from its male God-language, but as I suggested earlier, from the normative character of maleness Torah assumes. Whether understood in the narrow sense as the five books of Moses or the wider sense as all Jewish teaching and learning, Torah defines the male as the normative Jew and perceives women as Other in relation to men. Torah is male texts—not simply in the sense of authorship, but in the sense that its concerns are defined and are circumscribed from a male perspective. Women are often absent—"You shall not covet your neighbor's wife" (Exod. 20:14)—or nameless—Jephthah's daughter (Judg. 11) and Samson's mother (Judg. 13). Women's religious experiences are passed over in silence. (What was Miriam's true role in the Exodus community?) Women's sexuality is strictly controlled in the interests of male heads of household.[36]

Torah constructs a world that orders and makes sense of Jewish experience, but the world it constructs places men at the center. It is the written record of those with the power to keep records and to interpret and define the meaning of Jewish existence. In creating a particular vision of reality, it disguises alternative Jewish realities that may have coexisted alongside it. It understands the imperatives of Jewish life from the perspective of those at the center: the prophets rather than the common people, who for centuries "whored after false gods," and the rabbis who said that only men could write a bill of divorce, rather than the individual women who gave themselves that power.[37] The feminist relation to Torah thus begins in suspicion, critique, and the refusal to assign revelatory status to the establishment and reinforcement of patriarchy.

This insistence on suspicion does not mean, however, that Jewish feminists view Torah as just a series of historical texts, interesting for what they reveal about the past but of no enduring significance. The decisions to struggle with Torah, to criticize it, to remain in relation to it, all presuppose a more complex attitude. Elsewhere, I have called Torah a "partial record of the 'Godwrestling' of part of the Jewish people."[38] In using the term *Godwrestling,* I am trying to encapsulate several assumptions about the theological status of Torah. First, I suggest that Torah is, at least in part, a record of response to some genuine encounter. To be sure, it is an interpretation of encounter encoded in patriarchal language, but still, it tries to remember and to actualize in the life of a concrete historical community the workings of a God understood to be guiding and calling a particular people to their destiny. It testifies to moments of profound experience, illumination, and also mystery, when the curtain was pulled back from the endless chain of historical circumstance and some underlying meaning and presence were traced and read from the events of Jewish history.

The word suggests that Torah is incomplete because it is the nature of religious experience that no oral or written record can either exhaust it or spring entirely free from historical context. "Revelation" can challenge those who receive it and open up perspectives that are genuinely new, but Israel reached its understanding of God and its own destiny at a time when patriarchy was being consolidated throughout the ancient Near East. Its self-understanding helped to institute, support, and reinforce this historical development; it rarely disputed it. My characterization of Torah suggests, moreover, that it is the record of only part of the Jewish people because we do not know how women experienced the large and small events of Jewish history. We do not have Sinai seen through their eyes, their double enslavement, or their wanderings in the desert. We have the names of some of their prophets but not their prophecies. We do not know how women wrestled with God, or even whether, like Jacob, they would have named their experience wrestling.

Although some feminists would argue that reading the traditional Torah from a new angle of vision can provide women with the history we need, others seek to expand Torah, to redefine what Jews consider revelatory and normative.[39] On the one hand, there is no question that Torah as traditionally understood can be sifted and mined for more information about women. Read through feminist lenses, it can provide fragmentary evidence of women's religious leadership, of changing patterns of family and gender relations, of women's lives in and outside normative religious institutions. On the other hand, if we begin with the assumption that Judaism is constituted by women and men, then we must be open to finding Torah far outside the traditional canon. Archaeological evidence that challenges written sources, the writings of nonrabbinic groups, the history of women's spirituality, literature by Jewish women dealing with religious themes, midrash "received" by contemporary women—all these become Torah in that they are parts of the record of the Jewish religious experience, of what Jews have found holy and meaningful in their lives, and of the Jewish attempt to give order to existence.[40]

This new content of Torah is discovered and created in a number of ways. In part, the findings of feminist historiography, when appropriated as normative, themselves come to have the status of Torah. If the tkhines, for example, were taught or recited alongside other Jewish liturgy as equally valid forms of Jewish liturgical expression, their understanding of God would eventually become part of the Jewish imagination much like the God of the synagogue service. If divorce documents written by women had the same status in Jewish legal history as the Mishnah's view that women cannot initiate divorce, the halakhic precedents for contemporary divorce law would be greatly expanded and thereby transformed. If ancient inscriptions describing women as presidents and leaders of synagogues were taken as seriously as is the absence of women from the rabbinate, discussion of the ordination of women in the Orthodox community might take on a much different complexion.[41] In each of these cases, historical evidence is given *theological* weight that serves to shift and enlarge the meaning of Torah.

Yet historiography is not the only nor the best source for the feminist expansion of Torah. Jews have traditionally used midrash to broaden or alter the meanings of texts. The midrashic process of bringing contemporary questions to traditional sources and elaborating on the sources in response to questions easily lends itself to feminist use. Lacking adequate information on Miriam's role in Israelite religion, we can fill in the gaps with midrash; lacking texts on what women experienced at Sinai, we can recreate them through midrash. Such midrash can then become part of the content of Torah, both through study and through incorporation into liturgy. Indeed, just as the structure of feminist liturgy conveys something of the feminist understanding of God, so the content of feminist liturgy is an important vehicle for communicating an expanded Torah.

Such extension of the content of Torah necessarily opens and challenges traditionally normative texts *and* the theological conclusions we might draw from them. Insofar as traditional texts become part of a larger Torah, their authority is relativized and their claims to normativeness are shaken. Including and valuing women's religious experience as Torah precipitates a new critical moment in feminist theology. It leads us to examine the process by which particular texts become normative, the interests they represent, and the kind of social order they support and undergird. What is more important from a theological perspective, broadening Torah broadens the historical and textual basis of Jewish theological discourse. Highlighting aspects of Jewish experience that had previously been obscured and neglected, and valuing these as Torah, offer a richer and more diverse Judaism on which to reflect theologically. The Jewish God is not simply the God of the patriarchs and rabbis, but the God of the matriarchs, the tkhines, and women who interpret and create Torah today. Any attempt to articulate a Jewish understanding of God must take account of all these sources, exploring the concepts and images of God in the women's Torah as part of the heritage that a contemporary theology reworks or transforms. The same must be said of any theological concept. It must be grounded in a history and present that is wholly Jewish, one that represents the Jewishness of the whole community rather than the religious experience of a male elite.

The challenge of Jewish feminist theology to Jewish studies should by now be obvious. What part of the tradition does Jewish studies set out to study? Who defines what is worth studying, what is centrally and normatively Jewish? Whose interests does a supposedly objective and historically accurate Jewish studies support and share? Do theological judgments concerning normativeness creep in under the guise of objectivity? When and to what extent is Jewish studies *male* Jewish studies parading in the cloak of universality? Jewish feminist theology calls into question our basic understanding of Jewishness, the texts, the history, and the literature that Jewish studies examines. It also moves beyond critical questions to ask what Judaism looks like when we take seriously the perspectives and experiences of women as they try to understand and construct their own visions of the world. It pursues the task of shaping meaning, of making sense of being a Jewish woman and human being in the world today. In this sense, precisely as theology, it serves the central tasks of a liberal education: inviting students to encounter and reflect on difference, fostering critical self-consciousness, and encouraging the development of a personal worldview accountable to the needs of a larger community.[42]

Notes

1. Edward Farley, "The Place of Theology in the Study of Religion," *Religious Studies and Theology* 5 (Sept. 1985): 10; William F. May, "Why Theology and Religious Studies Need Each Other," *Journal of the American Academy of Religion* 52 (Dec. 1984): 748.

2. For recent rethinking of the theology–religious studies polarity, see, e.g., the discussion "Religious Studies/Theological Studies: The St. Louis Project," *Journal of the American Academy of Religion* 52 (Dec. 1984): 727–57, which includes papers by Walter Capps, Laurence O'Connell, Jacob Neusner, P. Joseph Cahill, and William F. May; Wilfred Cantwell Smith, "Theology and the Academic Study of Religion," *Iliff Review* 44 (fall 1987): 9–18; and Farley, "The Place of Theology," 9–29.

3. Joseph L. Blau, *Modern Varieties of Judaism* (New York: Columbia University Press, 1964), 34–35.

4. These sentiments are more often expressed orally—or even institutionally—than in writing. For example, when I was a graduate student at Yale, Judah Golden frequently insisted that there was no Jewish theology, so there was no possibility of our having a course on the subject. More revealing, when I began graduate work in theology in 1968, I had to study Christian theology because there was simply no place in the country to study Jewish theology. Other Jews before me had found themselves in the same situation.

5. Arthur Cohen and Paul Mendes-Flohr, *Contemporary Jewish Religious Thought* (New York: Scribner, 1987), xiii–xvii; Neil Gillman, *Sacred Fragments: Recovering Theology for the Modern Jew* (Philadelphia: Jewish Publication Society, 1990), xviii; Louis Jacobs, *A Jewish Theology* (West Orange, N.J.: Behrman House, 1973), 10–12; Judith Plaskow, *Standing Again at Sinai: Judaism from a Feminist Perspective* (San Francisco: Harper and Row, 1990), 21–24; Michael Wyschogrod, *The Body of Faith: Judaism as Corporeal Election* (San Francisco: Harper and Row, 1983), xiii.

6. Cohen and Mendes-Flohr, *Jewish Religious Thought,* xiii.

7. For the notion of feminist theology as a critical theology, see Elisabeth Schüssler-Fiorenza, "Feminist Theology as a Critical Theology of Liberation," *Theological Studies* 36 (1975): 605–26.

8. For examples of a larger body of feminist work on Christian theologians, see Rosemary Radford Ruether, "Misogynism and Virginal Feminism in the Fathers of the Church," and Eleanor Commo McLaughlin, "Equality of Souls, Inequality of Sexes: Woman in Medieval Theology," both in Rosemary Radford Ruether, ed., *Religion and Sexism: Images of Woman in the Jewish and Christian Traditions,* pp. 150–83, 213–66 (New York: Simon and Schuster, 1974); Valerie Saiving Goldstein, "The Human Situation: A Feminine View," *Journal of Religion* 40 (April 1960): 100–12; Judith Plaskow, *Sex, Sin, and Grace: Women's Experience and the Theologies of Reinhold Niebuhr and Paul Tillich* (Lanham, Md.: University Press of America, 1980).

9. This paragraph is based on a conversation I had in May 1990 with Lauren Granite and also on her reflections, "Some Notes toward a Feminist Critique of Buber's Work" (June 1990, available from L. Granite). Granite is a graduate student at Drew University, who, when she sat down to prepare a comprehensive exam on Buber, was startled to find that there was no feminist criticism of his work.

10. Granite, "Some Notes," 1–2, 10–11.

11. Martin Buber, *I and Thou,* trans. Walter Kaufmann (New York: Scribner, 1970), 76–80.

12. Granite, "Some Notes," 10f.

13. Judith Wegner completely misses this point when she reduces the theological status of women's Otherness to the "male patriarchal image of God"; *Chattel or Person? The Status of Women in the Mishnah* (New York: Oxford University Press, 1988), 186.

14. Judith Plaskow, "The Right Question Is Theological," in Susannah Heschel, ed., *On Being a Jewish Feminist: A Reader* (New York: Schocken, 1983), 224–27.

15. T. Drorah Setel, "Feminist Reflections on Separation and Unity in Jewish Theology," *Journal of Feminist Studies in Religion* 2 (spring 1986): 113–18.

16. Plaskow, *Standing Again,* 96; Setel, "Feminist Reflections," 116.

17. See Marcia Falk's response to Setel in the same issue of the *Journal of Feminist Studies in Religion* 15:121–25.

18. Rita Gross, "Female God Language in a Jewish Context," in Carol P. Christ and Judith Plaskow, eds., *Womanspirit Rising: A Feminist Reader in Religion* (San Francisco: Harper and Row, 1979), 168–71.

19. Setel, "Feminist Reflections," 117; Plaskow, *Standing Again,* 123–35.

20. For example, Rita J. Burns, *Has the Lord Indeed Spoken Only through Moses? A Study of the Biblical Portrait of Miriam,* Society of Biblical Literature Dissertation Series 84 (Atlanta: Scholars Press, 1987), chap. 2, esp. p. 40. For development of these themes, see my *Standing Again,* 36–51.

21. David Goodblatt, "The Beruriah Traditions," *Journal of Jewish Studies* 26 (spring–autumn 1975): 68–85; but for the "bad end" assigned this uppity woman by the rabbis, see Rachel Adler, "The Virgin in the Brothel and Other Anomalies: Character and Context in the Legend of Beruriah," *Tikkun* 3 (Nov. 1988): 28–32, 101–6.

22. Chava Weissler, "The Traditional Piety of Ashkenazic Women," in Arthur Green, ed., *Jewish Spirituality from the Sixteenth Century Revival to the Present* (New York: Crossroad, 1987), 247–49, 266–67; "The Religion of Traditional Ashkenazic Women: Some Methodological Issues," *AJS Review* (June/July 1987): 87–88; "Voices from the Heart: Women's Devotional Prayers," *Jewish Almanac,* ed. Richard Siegel and Carl Rheins (New York: Bantam, 1980), 544; "Women in Paradise," *Tikkun* 2 (1987): 43–46, 117–20.

23. Ellen M. Umansky, "Piety, Persuasion, and Friendship: Female Jewish Leadership in Modern Times," in Paula Cooey, Sharon Farmer, and Mary Ellen Ross, eds., *Embodied Love: Sensuality and Relationship as Feminist Values* (San Francisco: Harper and Row, 1987), 189–206; and *Lily Montagu and the Advancement of Liberal Judaism: From Vision to Vocation,* Studies in Women and Religion 12 (New York: Edward Mellen, 1983), 205–6.

24. Ellen M. Umansky, "Matriarchs and Monotheism: A History of Jewish Women's Spirituality," in Ellen Umansky and Dianne Ashton, eds., *Piety, Persuasion, and Friendship: A Sourcebook of Modern Jewish Women's Spirituality* (Boston: Beacon, 1992), 15–18.

25. Jacobs, *A Jewish Theology,* 14.

26. Plaskow, *Standing Again,* 134–36.

27. *The Memoirs of Gluckel of Hameln,* trans. Marvin Lowenthal (New York: Schocken, [1932] 1977).

28. Gross, "Female God Language," 165–73, esp. 172–73.

29. Naomi Janowitz and Maggie Wenig, *Siddur Nashim: A Sabbath Prayer Book for Women* (Providence: Privately published, 1976); short sections are reprinted in *Womanspirit Rising,* pp. 174–78. Since Janowitz and Wenig, there have been many other prayer services using female language, many privately circulating for use in small groups. *Vetaher Libenu* (Sudbury, Mass.: Congregation Beth El, 1980) and *Or Chadash* (Philadelphia: P'nai Or Religious Fellowship, 1989) are two generally available prayerbooks that use female language, the latter in Hebrew as well as English.

30. Much of Lynn Gottlieb's work is unpublished, but see "Speaking into the Silence," *Response* 41–42 (fall–winter 1982): 19–32, esp. 21–22, 32.

31. Marcia Falk, "Notes on Composing New Blessings: Toward a Feminist Jewish Reconstruction of Prayer," *Journal of Feminist Studies in Religion* 3 (spring 1987): 39–49. I discuss the new Jewish feminist God-language in *Standing Again,* 136–43.

32. Gross, "Female God Language," 169; Falk, "Notes on Composing New Blessings," 44–45.

33. Falk, "Notes on Composing New Blessings," 41 (emphasis in original).

34. Plaskow, *Standing Again,* 150–53.

35. Nelle Morton, *The Journey Is Home* (Boston: Beacon, 1985), 54–55.

36. See Wegner, *Chattel or Person?* for a thorough exploration of this theme in relation to the Mishnah.

37. Carol P. Christ, "Heretics and Outsiders," in her *Laughter of Aphrodite: Reflections on a Journey to the Goddess* (San Francisco: Harper and Row, 1987), 35–40; Bernadette Brooten, "Could Women Initiate Divorce in Ancient Judaism? The Implications for Mark

10:11–12 and 1 Corinthians 7:10–11'' (Ernest Cadwell Colman Lecture, School of Theology at Claremont, 14 April 1981).

38. Plaskow, *Standing Again,* 33. My explication of the phrase here depends on my discussion in the book, pp. 32–34.

39. Compare, e.g., Tamar Frankiel, *The Voice of Sarah: Feminine Spirituality and Traditional Judaism* (San Francisco: Harper and Row, 1990), with Sue Levi Elwell, *Texts and Transformation: Towards a Theology of Integrity* (Rabbinic thesis, Hebrew Union College-Jewish Institute of Religion, 1986).

40. I have in mind such things as the ancient inscriptions testifying to women's religious leadership studied by Bernadette Brooten (*Women Leaders in the Ancient Synagogue: Inscriptional Evidence and Background Issues,* Brown Judaic Studies 36 [Chico, Calif.: Scholars Press, 1982]); the New Testament as evidence for the right of Jewish women to initiate divorce (see n.37); the *tkhines;* novels like E. M. Broner's *A Weave of Women* (New York: Bantam, 1978); and midrash like Ellen Umansky's "Creating a Jewish Feminist Theology," in Judith Plaskow and Carol P. Christ, eds., *Weaving the Visions: New Patterns in Feminist Spirituality* (San Francisco: Harper and Row, 1989), 195–97.

41. See nn.37 and 40.

42. Neusner, "Religious Studies/Theological Studies: The St. Louis Project," *Journal of the American Academy of Religion* 52 (Dec. 1984): 740; Farley, "The Place of Theology," 12.

"Dare to Know": Feminism and the Discipline of Jewish Philosophy

"Dare to Know *(Sapere aude).* **Have the courage to use your own understanding, is therefore the motto of the Enlightenment." —Kant, "What Is Enlightenment?"**

To date, feminism has made no impact on the discipline of Jewish philosophy. Scholars of Jewish philosophy have virtually ignored the presence of feminism in the academy, the feminist critique of Western philosophy, and the feminist attempt to articulate an alternative to traditional philosophy. The discipline thus lags behind other subfields of Jewish studies—history, sociology, anthropology, and literature— that have begun to respond to and be enriched by the feminist challenge. By not keeping pace, the field of Jewish philosophy has excluded itself from a major theoretical discourse in contemporary Western culture.

In this chapter, I lay the ground for a three-way conversation between feminist philosophy, Jewish philosophy, and Jewish feminism. Since scholars in Jewish studies are perhaps unfamiliar with feminist scholarship in philosophy, I first summarize its critical and constructive aspects. Second, I attempt to account for the failure of feminism to influence Jewish philosophy, by looking at the nature of Jewish philosophy and how feminism has presented its case. Third and last, I call on both disciplines to dare to know about each other and to engage in a critical dialogue both to broaden the scope of Jewish philosophy and to help feminism (especially Jewish feminism) avoid the trap of militant dogmatism.

Feminist Philosophy

Feminism is a social movement that seeks equality and justice for women. During the past two decades feminism has become a major critical voice within Western culture, especially in North America. As women committed to feminism have entered the academy in significant numbers, they have demanded its transformation.[1] They have questioned the way scholars define their subject matter, gather and interpret data, and draw and apply conclusions. They have also demanded a broadening of the scope of academic disciplines by recognizing women's experiences and outlook as objects of academic research. Feminists have introduced the distinction between *sex* (that is, biological, anatomical features that differentiate men and women) and *gender* (social, behavioral expectations for men and women), thereby raising a new set of questions and formulating new theories. Feminists have created a new academic field—women's studies—to examine a wide array of women's experiences across disciplinary boundaries. Finally, feminists have attempted to change the politics of the academy by demanding equality in hiring, promotions, allocations of resources, and professional representation.

The social and political nature of feminism dictated that feminist scholars devote their attention first to the social sciences, especially anthropology, sociology, and history. Feminist scholars placed at the forefront of their academic concerns the following questions: "What about women? What are the women's lives like in such a society? How is their work assessed and valued? What are the prevailing attitudes about women? What notions are there of "women's nature?"[2] Feminist inquiries in the social sciences soon showed that gender differences could not be understood apart from theories about human nature or the purpose of human life—issues that belong to the domain of philosophy. To liberate women from all forms of oppression, feminists had to turn their attention to philosophy.

The Feminist Critique

The field of philosophy presented feminists with a particularly difficult challenge. First, women were conspicuously absent from the list of great Western philosophers, and most of the practitioners of philosophy have been, and still are, male. Second, male philosophers have explicitly devalued women, believed them to be inferior, or held them in contempt. For example, Aristotle proclaimed: "As between male and female, the former is by nature superior and ruler, the latter inferior and subject."[3] Similarly, Immanuel Kant held that women are incapable of certain intellectual pursuits: "Women will avoid the wicked not because it is unright, but because it is ugly. . . . Nothing of duty, nothing of compulsion, nothing of obligation! They do something only because it pleases them, and the art consists in making only that please which is good. I hardly believe that the fair sex is capable of principles."[4] Arthur Schopenhauer was no less condescending to women when he pronounced, "She may, in fact, be described as intellectually shortsighted, because while she has an intuitive understanding of what lies close to her, her field of vision is narrow and does not reach to what is remote: so that things which are absent or past or to come have much less effect upon women than upon men."[5]

Third, and most important, the very self-understanding of Western philosophy has excluded women from its purview. By that I mean to suggest that until recently, the Western philosophical tradition has understood itself as a discipline that seeks universally valid knowledge about objective reality.[6] The subject of philosophy has been that which is essential and timeless, not that which is accidental and time or space bound. To the extent that philosophy reflects on humans, it focuses on the human condition per se and not on the specific concerns and aspirations of one segment of humanity. Seeking universality, philosophers have disregarded the particular circumstances of the knower, such as religion, ethnicity, political affiliation, and, of course, sex and gender. The philosophical enterprise has no room for women's (or anyone else's) particular experiences, emotions, needs, and aspirations—those concerns that constitute the core of feminism.

Feminist philosophy has attempted to dismantle this lofty self-perception of traditional philosophy produced exclusively by men.[7] By exposing the misogynist bias of Western rationalism, feminist philosophers have argued that what Western male philosophers have presented as "essentially human" is no more than a composite of those traits that have historically been associated with the male. Theories about human nature were found to be theories about the male of the species, which explicitly or implicitly conceived of the female as a deviation from the norm and excluded her from full participation in all that was considered human.[8] By regarding the woman as the Other, Western philosophy has diminished her self-worth, excluded her from mainstream—or rather *malestream*—society and culture, and supplied reasons for her oppression.[9]

Moreover, feminist philosophers have charged that the ideal of rationality is genderized. In Western patriarchal society, philosophy (like other forms of culture) reflects the perspective of those who produce it, namely, men. Not surprisingly, even though the ideals of reason in Western culture have changed, their gender inflection remained the same. Reason has been exclusively associated with maleness, and its practice reflects the male trait of aggression. Socrates notwithstanding, traditional philosophy is based on the aggressive confrontation between opponents that both limits philosophy and serves to exclude the nonaggressive—notably women.[10] Moreover, feminist thinkers have charged that the Western conception of reason not only incorporates values that have been defined as masculine, it is defined in terms of them. Whereas reason is associated with maleness, "the feminine has been associated with what rational knowledge transcends, dominates or simply leaves behind."[11]

Probing into the foundations of philosophy, feminist philosophers have argued that a masculinist bias pervades the models of knowledge and the scientific method itself. They have shared the "growing uncertainty within Western intellectual circles about the appropriate grounding and method for explaining and/or interpreting human experience."[12] The feminist critique of the philosophical method was inspired by the works of postmodern male philosophers who attacked Western logocentrism, transcendental grounding, epistemological foundationalism, authority, hegemony, and grand narratives. Philosophers such as Jean-François Lyotard, Jacques Derrida, Michel Foucault, and Richard Rorty have expressed radical doubts about the most cherished assumptions of modern culture derived from the Enlightenment, namely, that reason and its science—philosophy—provide an objective, reliable, and universal foundation for knowledge. They have argued that philosophy as traditionally practiced has reached an end; it cannot go on doing business as usual. After Friedrich Nietzsche and Sigmund Freud, it is no longer possible to deny the influence of the unconscious on the conscious, the role of the preconceptual or nonconceptual in the conceptual, and the presence of the irrational. After Karl Marx, it is no longer possible to ignore the intrinsically social character of "structures of consciousness" and the interdependence of thought and changing forms of material production. And after Martin Heidegger, it is no longer possible to ignore the linguisticality and embodiment of all human knowledge. For postmodern thinkers the traditional dichotomies between subject-object, self-other, knower-known, language-world, will-intellect, and so on, have all crumbled under the weight of their own internal self-contradictions. Philosophy can no longer claim to aspire to, let alone attain, objective, universal truths: all knowledge is subjective, historically situated, linguistically bound, and politically motivated.

The feminist assault on rationalism exemplifies the current identity crisis of philosophy.[13] Along with Rorty,[14] for example, feminists have claimed that the seeds for the demise of traditional Western philosophy were sown by the greatest thinker of the Enlightenment—Kant. As Lorraine Code put it, "Kant posited ahistorical, universal categories of understanding and conditions of knowability. Yet for him, the mind does not read off what it is given, what is there in the world. The intellect is no passive recording instrument, but an active creator—constructor—of knowledge. Hence, Kant prepared the way for analyses of knowledge as construct and for contextualizing epistemic activity so that the knower, and not just the known, comes under epistemological scrutiny."[15] If the human mind constructs knowledge, then the identity of the knower (including the knower's sexual identity) becomes cognitively significant. It was Kant's own theory of knowledge that made it possible for us to ask, "Whose knowledge are we talking about?" Philosophical knowledge that purports to be universal, atemporal, and objective is thus no more than a knowledge claim predicated on the identity of the knower and the circumstances of knowledge production.

Second, feminists have charged that the Enlightenment ideal of detached, impartial knowledge is oppressive to women because it confuses men's experience of themselves as knowers with the definition of knowledge and science. Feminists have claimed that the subjective-objective dichotomy has traditionally been linked to a series of such dichotomies as theory-practice, reason-emotion, universal-particular, mind-body, abstract-concrete, in which the first member of each pair is associated with the male and the second with the female. The relation between the members of each dichotomy is hierarchical: the first member of each pair is deemed superior to and thus dominant over the second.[16] Grounded in dichotomous thinking, the ideal of objectivity is not only distorted and partial (reflecting only the male perspective), it also provides reasons for the exclusion and oppression of women.[17] Women are purported to be unable to rise above "the practical, sensuous and emotional preoccupations of everyday life. Hence they are judged unfit for the abstract life of pure reason in which true knowers must engage."[18]

Third, feminist philosophers have criticized the radical split between reason and emotion and, more broadly, the mind-body dichotomy. Since Plato, and particularly after René Descartes, Western philosophy has regarded emotions as distractions that clutter and impede the attainment of certainty in knowledge.[19] To ensure the purity of knowledge, emotions and other subjective factors located in the body had to be strictly controlled. Feminist critics have charged that the suppression of emotions characteristic of Western philosophy is itself male-biased, because the tradition associates emotions exclusively with femaleness. Some feminists see the negation of emotions to be causally linked to the ascendance of mechanistic explanations of nature in the seventeenth century. Viewed in their historical context, these theories reflect the self-interest of the men who constructed them or the "flight from the feminine" inherent in the masculine attempt to tame "the female universe."[20] Though the epistemological stance of detached objectivity was necessary for the completion of that task, such a stance is false.

Fourth, feminists criticize the notion of the autonomous self and the ideology of autonomy and self-sufficiency that has prevailed in modern philosophy and inspired political and philosophical liberalism. In particular, feminist moral theorists direct their critique of autonomy against Kantian morality, arguing that not only did Kant exclude women from the community of ideal knowers and moral agents, but his notion of autonomous moral agents is anomalous, irrelevant, and threatening to moral integrity.[21] This critique might appear to be at odds with the women's liberation movement, which urged women to take charge of their own lives and become totally independent. Feminists who drew on psychoanalytic theories found the notion of autonomous self to reflect the specific manner in which a male child differentiates himself from his mother.[22] The process of individuation for girls is more complex and subtle and is never fully complete. Yet there is no good reason why male individuation should provide a paradigm for understanding the self. In fact, there is more evidence to suggest that personhood (or selfhood) is relational; the self is intrinsically social and the boundaries between the self and the world are extremely porous.

The Feminist Alternative

The feminist alternative to allegedly masculinist philosophy places the concept of gender at the center of philosophical reflections in order to transform the method and substance of philosophy. In Kuhnian terms,[23] feminist philosophy attempts to introduce a new paradigm for human understanding by including historicity, materiality, emotions, and values as fundamental epistemological categories. Feminist philosophy takes into consideration the actual experiences of women, the constructive nature of knowledge claims and of human language, the embodiment of the human mind, and the relationality of the self.

Recognizing the limitations of radical subjectivism and not wishing to be identified with the forces of irrationality,[24] feminist philosophers advanced the *feminist standpoint epistemology*,[25] which grants objective status to truth-claims grounded in subjective factors.[26] Feminist standpoint epistemology is based on the premise that the identity of the knower is essential to the production of knowledge. Because all knowledge is socially situated, women do think differently from men in a genderized society; these differences are rooted not in a feminine essence but in socially constructed circumstances. The feminist standpoint assigns a positive cognitive value to how women think and claims that its incorporation into philosophy and science can correct traditional (masculinist) distortions. A feminist standpoint epistemology means thinking that comes from women's lives or, more specifically, from the lives of oppressed, exploited, and marginalized women. Such thinking is cognitively advantageous precisely because women are strangers within the social order.[27] Furthermore, the experience of oppression enables women to reveal aspects of social reality that lie beyond the perspective of the oppressor. In telling the story from the other side, so to speak, feminist scholarship offers a corrective to "normal" scholarship in all fields, including the natural sciences and philosophy.

The feminist reclamation of subjectivity manifested itself in the claim that feelings and emotions are valid sources of knowledge. Feminist philosophers have argued that truth and knowledge become distorted when feelings and emotions are not acknowledged. To take these factors into account means to consider the history of the individual, the time and place in which she lives, and her human body—all as sources of knowledge. Feelings must be accepted as "a route to truth" and must not be controlled by the rational mind. As Caroline Whitbeck put it, "the rational agent is required to attend and reflect on feelings, and not to attempt to control them."[28]

Recognizing that all human thinking—as well as feelings, passions, and emotions—takes place within a human body, feminist philosophers have argued that sexual differences between males and females must exhibit themselves in the way men and women think. To counteract traditional philosophy, which reflects the distinct features of the male body, the French feminist philosophers—Hélène Cixous, Luce Irigaray, and Julia Kristeva—have recommended "embodied thinking."[29] Crossing the boundaries between philosophy, literary theory, and psychoanalysis, they criticize not only the dominant order (in particular its patriarchal aspect) and valorize the feminine, they go further, striving to dissolve any form of binary thinking, any ism, including feminism. Female sexuality itself should provide the model for a nonbinary thinking since it is, as Irigaray put it, "not one" but multiple and plural.[30]

By thinking from the female body, feminists expose the phallocentric nature of traditional philosophy, with its false dichotomies and hierarchies, thereby liberating women from oppressive patterns of thought. Cixous has objected to masculinist writing and thinking on the ground that its binary opposition has (allegedly) reflected men's genital and libidinal economy, symbolically represented in the phallus.[31] For her, phallocentrism is but another form of logocentrism. She challenges women to write themselves out of that male world by "developing a way of writing which is not limited by the rules that currently govern language. Thereby women will change the way the Western world thinks and writes and with it women's place in that world."[32]

Irigaray too regards female sexuality and the female body as sources of feminine writing. As a psychoanalyst she wants to liberate the feminine from all philosophical thought, including the thought of such postmodern philosophers and psychoanalysts as Derrida and Jacques Lacan. For her, Western philosophy is preoccupied with sameness.[33] Wherever the woman is not like the man, she does not exist. Irigaray searches for psychoanalytic ways to reconceptualize the feminine female. Women must avoid the gender-neutral voice and instead find the courage to speak in an active, authentic, and feminine voice. They must recognize the multiple nature of female sexuality, and they must extend the plural, circular, aimless, vaginal/clitoral, libidinal economy of women to all forms of human expression, including social structures.

Kristeva goes further than even Cixous and Irigaray, resisting the notion of identifying biological women with "feminine" and biological men with "masculine." Such identification is itself the product of patriarchy, which tends to operate in essentialist terms. "Women as such does not exist" as a philosophical entity. She is viable only politically. For Kristeva, the fact that "the woman cannot be—she is always becoming and never being—allies her with other groups excluded from the dominant: homosexuals, Jews, racial and ethnic minorities and other assorted misfits."[34] In her psychoanalytic theory, women's marginalization reflects society's fundamental problem with the irrational sense of disgust traceable to the infant's preoedipal experiences with its own body and that of the mother. The oedipal castration complex links the "feminine" with the "abject." Using Lacan's framework, Kristeva contrasts the "semiotic," or preoedipal, stage with the symbolic, or postoedipal, stage and charges that phallo-logocentric thought is founded on a repression of the semiotic and the maternal body. The two orders also differ from one another in their sense of time; whereas the semiotic order is cyclical and eternal, the symbolic order represents linear and sequential time.[35] The two orders lead to two kinds of writing: masculine writing, which is linear, rational, objective, and is governed by the rules of normal syntax, and feminine writing, which emphasizes rhythm, sound, and color and permits breaks in syntax to express what horrifies and disgusts us.

The writings of the French postmodern feminists began to influence the Anglo-American academic scene in the mid-1980s as more of their work became available in English. Yet their major impact has been on feminists in literary theory and comparative literature. Most feminist philosophers in the English-speaking world have remained committed to presumably masculinist styles of writing and standards of clarity, even though they have shared the postmodern claim that all knowledge is linguistically constructed. Language itself is neither transparent nor innocent. It does not merely mirror reality but shapes it. All speech acts involve interpretation and understanding, and all linguistic communications consist of translation. But in patriarchal society, language itself is not only man-made; it is also male.[36] In a world that is linguistically male, where the woman's role is maintained by man-made language, women are required to translate twice. Excluded from the public arena and dominated by male speech in the private domain, women's speech patterns have evolved remarkably differently from those of men. Feminists have thus urged women to discover and express their marginalized, repressed voice as well as to challenge public speech patterns that diminish women's stature and worth. But the more women have discovered their own voice, the more it has become evident that even when they use the same words, men and women do not mean the same thing.[37] If language shapes meaning, then no knowledge is pure.

All knowledge claims are embodied, socially situated, and ultimately relational. The relational nature of the self means that human needs and interests arise in a context of relationships with other people. Feminist philosophy, therefore, highlights interdependence and cooperation as human ideals at the expense of the autonomy and self-sufficiency emphasized by traditional philosophy. Some feminists have even claimed that a "feminist ontology" would replace traditional dichotomies (nature-culture, theory-practice, spirit-matter, mind-body, human-divine, public-private, knower-known) with nonoppositional and nondualistic views of these subjects. The feminist relational ontology was combined with a view of person and ethics that is based on "responsibilities arising out of a relationship."[38] In contrast to morality based on abstract general rules and principles, feminist moral theorists argue that female moral reasoning is contextualized and grounded in the notion of responsibility rather than rights.[39]

One type of relationship in particular provides feminist thinkers with alternative models for authoritative knowledge and ideal morality—mothering. "Maternal thinking" was posited as the feminist alternative to traditional epistemology and ethics. The mother's knowledge of and caring for others (the young, the sick, and the aging) serve as a model for the relations of human subjects to their natural and social environment, which can be redirected away from domination and exploitation and toward preservation and nurturing.[40] Maternal thinking has political ramifications: it serves as a foundation for a new political order—"the politics of peace."[41] Thus feminist philosophy emphasizes the close nexus between epistemology and ethics, between theory and praxis, and between truth-claims and normative values.

Feminist Philosophy in Perspective

In sum, for the past fifteen years feminist philosophers have raised serious, theoretical questions that challenge several philosophical conventions. Yet it is difficult to assess the actual strength of feminist thought within the discipline of philosophy. In terms of volume, the literature that is defined as feminist thought or feminist theory is substantial, even though not all of it would be taken to be strictly philosophical by nonfeminist practitioners. Given the interdisciplinary nature of women's studies, feminist philosophers do not abide by traditional disciplinary boundaries and freely draw on scholarship in political science, literary theory, psychoanalysis, sociology, and anthropology, thus going beyond the conventional boundaries of the discipline. The sheer volume of feminist literary output makes the feminist discourse highly visible and vocal, but it is not sufficient to determine its relative strength within the discipline. It seems to me that feminist philosophical literature is still read primarily by scholars who define themselves as feminists, most of whom are women. The feminist attempt to revolutionize the field has succeeded in questioning male domination in philosophy (and in Western culture), but it has failed to transform the way philosophy is produced, written, and studied. In fact, since feminism opened the door of academe to women, many now practice traditional (presumably masculinist) philosophy, apparently believing that gender need not, nay should not, affect their philosophical activity.

More problematic is that the feminist alternative to the alleged masculinist traditional thinking has come dangerously close to embracing that essentialist view of women that feminist theory set out to repudiate. If women think differently from men because they alone can mother, then the differences between the sexes are not merely social constructs but are biologically determined. We have thus come full circle. The more feminist theorists have attempted to articulate a distinct feminist philosophy, the more they have affirmed the essentialist conception of the feminine as well as the traditional male stereotypes of women's thinking: women do think concretely rather than abstractly; they are overwhelmingly concerned with their own body and emotions rather than with pure thought; they are unable to achieve full autonomy and tend to define themselves in relation to others. The only difference is that what the traditional conceptions of women denigrate, feminist thought praises as ideal. By substituting one exclusivist (or absolutist) model for another, feminists also risk the danger of binary thinking and oppressive dogmatism.

As feminist thinkers dared to know, feminist philosophy itself became more self-critical, pluralistic, and theoretical. Today feminist philosophers acknowledge that feminism, as well as feminist philosophy, does not, and indeed cannot, speak in one voice. Precisely because all knowledge claims are contextualized, feminists cannot propose a global, totalizing theory. The postmodern suspicion against global theories, which feminist philosophy shares, is thus directed against feminism itself. And feminism's own commitment to equality and freedom for all women dictates that it will not become oppressively dogmatic. Even the sex-gender dichotomy—the cornerstone of early feminist theory—has now become problematic.[42] If dichotomous thinking is masculinist and hence oppressive, then the sex-gender dichotomy should not be employed in feminist theory. Furthermore, feminist theorists realized that the analytic category of gender does not fully account for real differences between women attributable to class, race, ethnicity, religion, or sexual orientation. The proliferation of Afro-American feminism, Jewish feminism, third-world feminism, and lesbian feminism—each of which aspires to be both equal and different—led to the understanding of gender as a relation that is never independent of social systems. Gender relations have no fixed essence, or as de Lauretis put it: "The female subject is en-gendered across multiple representations of class, race, language, and social relations."[43]

As feminist philosophy (at least in England, Australia, and North America) has more systematically considered gender differences, it has also begun to exhibit some of the characteristics of traditional philosophy. Feminist philosophers are no longer content to speak only for and about women but rather aspire to make assertions that are universally valid.[44] Thus feminist philosophers join their male counterparts in the attempt to understand the human condition per se, even though they do so on the basis of women's experiences. Similarly, as feminist philosophers have exercised the freedom to think philosophically, they have not shied away from using what is known as the "Adversary Method." Despite the feminist preference for collective research and the sharing of ideas, feminist philosophers have taken themselves to task and have employed sharp arguments to buttress their case against opponents from without and from within. The theoretical refinement of feminist theory has also meant that feminist philosophers now focus less on the actual problems of women's lives and more on thinking about how one thinks about women. Finally, the freedom to philosophize has led feminist theorists to question the most cherished assumptions of feminism itself: the oppression of women and the repudiation of sex differences. Recent scholarship has urged women to go beyond the consciousness of victimization, not to be afraid of natural sex differences, and to realize that difference does not necessarily imply inferiority.[45]

So, is there a feminist philosophy? In terms of content, the answer is no. There is no monolithic body of thought that can be defined as feminist philosophy. Rather, there are multiple voices, theories, and perspectives that interpret gender differences in diverse and even conflicting ways. Among them are liberal feminism, Marxist feminism, radical feminism, existentialist feminism, psychoanalytic feminism, and postmodern feminism. Nonetheless, there are certain tendencies that characterize the feminist approach to philosophy. Feminist philosophy is necessarily critical; it focuses on women's experiences, whether actual or potential; it retrieves elements about women that have been neglected, repressed, and suppressed; it is suspicious of essentialist interpretations of the differences between men and women; it focuses on how we think (or avoid thinking) about gender and how gender shapes social reality; it is sensitive to the contextualized nature of thinking; it attempts to avoid dualistic hierarchies; and it affirms the nexus between philosophy and social responsibility. The feminist philosophical method begins with raising consciousness about the oppression of women and proceeds to know about women and their social context. It reflects on issues that are of political concern to women: abortion, pornography, mothering, sexist language, female sexuality, rape, lesbianism, and affirmative action. To philosophize in a feminist way is to do philosophy in a critical, personally engaged, and politically oriented way.

Feminism and Jewish Philosophy

Regardless of one's opinions of feminism and feminist scholarship, it is difficult to ignore their presence in Western culture, especially in the academy.

Yet this is precisely what scholars of Jewish philosophy have done. They have not cited feminist scholarship; they have not acknowledged the existence of the "woman's problem" either within Judaism or within philosophy. They have not responded to the feminist charge that Western philosophy is a male-centered, misogynist, and oppressive tradition. They have not incorporated the category of gender into their writings, and they have remained indifferent to attempts to interpret the human condition from a feminist standpoint.

A lack of interest in feminism and feminist philosophy has not been limited to the male practitioners of the discipline. The most accomplished female scholars who have entered the study of Jewish philosophy since the 1950s—Sarah Heller-Willensky, Rivkah Horowitz, Rivkah Schatz-Uffenheimer, Ruth Salinger-Hyman, Colette Sirat, Sarah Klein-Braslavy, Edith Wischogrod, Brachah Sack, Ada Albert-Rapoport, Rachel Elior, Hanna Kasher, Tamar Ross, Tamar Rudavsky, Idit Dobbs-Weinstein, and Yudit Greenberg—have contributed significantly to the field, but they have done so neither as women nor as feminists. Writing as historians of Jewish philosophy or Jewish religious thought, these women have conformed to the scholarly conventions of the field articulated by its male practitioners. If female scholars of Jewish philosophy have identified with feminism in any way, they have done so in private. To my knowledge, the only scholar of Jewish philosophy who has publicly urged the discipline's practitioners to respond to feminist philosophy is a man.[46] How can we explain this state of affairs?

Defining Jewish Philosophy

To answer this question we must first realize that defining the field of Jewish philosophy is by no means easy. How can there be a Jewish philosophy if philosophy seeks universal truths about human nature and the world in which it is deployed?[47] Is Jewish philosophy simply a philosophy written by Jews, or is it rather a philosophy written for Jews and about Jews? Is Jewish philosophy the systematic reflection about Judaism? Is there one Jewish philosophy or are there several? How could there be Jewish philosophy if Jews have never agreed on the nature of Judaism? Is Jewish philosophy a certain way of doing philosophy, a philosophy with a Jewish twist? How is Jewish philosophy to be distinguished from Jewish theology? These questions are still debated by scholars of Jewish philosophy, and no consensus has emerged concerning the nature, method, and purpose of Jewish philosophy.[48]

I differentiate between Jewish philosophy as a first-order activity and Jewish philosophy as a second-order activity. The former is a systematic reflection about Judaism by means of philosophical categories and in light of philosophical questions. Written exclusively by Jews but not only for Jews, Jewish philosophy emerged in the tenth century as a response to the external challenge of Muslim culture;[49] thereafter it became a self-conscious program of expounding the beliefs of Rabbinic Judaism. The main concern of Jewish philosophy has been to articulate the desired relation between the Jewish religious tradition (believed to be grounded in a historical, divine revelation) and the secular, universal truth-claims of philosophy (grounded in the natural capacity of humans to reason). Among the major Jewish philosophers are Saadia Gaon, Bahya Ibn Pakuda, Judah Halevi, Moses Maimonides, Levi ben Gershon (Gersonides), Hasdai Crescas, Joseph Albo, Moses Mendelssohn, Solomon Maimon, Nachman Krochmal, Solomon Formstecher, Samuel Hirsch, Solomon L. Steinheim, Hermann Cohen, Franz Rosenzweig, Martin Buber, Mordecai Kaplan, Abraham Joshua Heschel, Emmanuel Levinas, and Emil Fackenheim.

The absence of women from this list speaks for itself. There were no female Jewish philosophers. In traditional Jewish society (which existed intact well into the nineteenth century and in some places still exists), women were excluded from formal education (Torah study broadly defined) and were largely ignorant of the intellectual treasures of their own tradition. The uneducated Jewish female could no more create philosophy than she could engage in halakhah, biblical exegesis, poetry, science, or Kabbalah. Neither did the breakdown of traditional Jewish society produce female Jewish philosophers. Modernity offered the Jewish female access to secular education and entry into the liberal professions and the sciences. Jewish women who remained within the confines of traditional society were constrained by its strictures on female education, and Jewish women who embraced secularism lost the ability and the desire to create within the parameters of Judaism. They could become philosophers or scholars of philosophy, but not Jewish philosophers in the sense I have defined here. Indeed, modern Jewish women directed their passions, talents, and intellectual powers to the professions, the sciences, and to modern ideologies such as socialism, anarchism, Zionism, psychoanalysis, and, finally, feminism. The emergence of Jewish feminism in the 1970s, which demanded and achieved the admission of women to the rabbinic seminaries of the Reform, Conservative, and Reconstructionist movements; the inclusion of women in the leadership of Jewish organizations; and the liberalization of female education in modern Orthodoxy signal the beginning of the synthesis of Judaism and modernity for women. Whether these changes will produce Jewish female philosophers remains to be seen.

The works of the male scholars I listed above created a certain discourse, a distinct intellectual tradition, that evolved over time in accordance with the changing historical conditions of the Jews and the dominant intellectual current of the time. Thus, the history of Jewish philosophy can be viewed as a series of conversations (or encounters) with changing partners (for example, Kalam, Neoplatonism, Aristotelianism, deism, Kantianism, Hegelianism, existentialism, and pragmatism). As the partners changed, so did the nature of the conversation, the issues deemed problematic, and the solutions found satisfactory.

The discourse of Jewish philosophy has been philosophically uneven. Some Jewish philosophers were (and are) more committed to, or are more fluent in, philosophy than others, and some who were (and are) highly conversant with philosophy have used it to expose its intrinsic limitations in comparison to revealed religion. Yet the discourse of Jewish philosophy is philosophical because it looks at Judaism through the prism of philosophy, and it is Jewish because the Jewish tradition itself (its beliefs, canonic texts, exegetical modes, legal norms, and ethical ideals) provides the subject matter for reflection. When a Jewish thinker engages in philosophy without any concern for the Jewish religious tradition, his literary output does not belong to the discourse of Jewish philosophy, and when a Jewish thinker reflects about Judaism without any interest in accommodating the way philosophy formulates questions, his reflection does not belong to the discourse of Jewish philosophy.[50]

As a second-order activity, Jewish philosophy is an academic field that studies the discourse of Jewish philosophy as I have defined it. The academic field of Jewish philosophy emerged in the nineteenth century as part of the program of *Wissenschaft des Judentums* (the science of Judaism) to study Judaism from a historical and scientific perspective. Even though the academic study of Jewish philosophy concerns religious matters (for example, the existence of God, divine attributes, providence, and miracles), it is a secular, professional endeavor devoted to interpreting Jewish culture rather than to shaping Jewish beliefs. Among the contributors to the academic study of Jewish philosophy, one could mention Julius Guttmann, Isaac Husik, Harry A. Wolfson, Leo Strauss, Shlomo Pines, Alexander Altmann, Hugo Bergman, Steven Schwarzschild, Isadore Twersky, Marvin Fox, Arthur Hyman, Joseph Sermonetta, Georges Vajda, David Hartman, David Blumenthal, Eliezer Schweid, Lawrence V. Berman, Herbert A. Davidson, Alfred Ivry, Seymour Feldman, Aryeh L. Motzkin, Norbert Samuelson, Barry Kogan, Steven Katz, David Novak, Paul Mendes-Flohr, Warren Z. Harvey, Lenn Goodman, Kenneth Seeskin, Michael Morgan, Richard Cohen, Menachem Kellner, Alan Udoff, and the female scholars mentioned earlier.[51]

The Explanation

When I speak about the failure of feminism to influence Jewish philosophy, I refer to Jewish philosophy as an academic field (that is, a second-order activity). It goes without saying that feminist thought could not have influenced the discourse of Jewish philosophy as a first-order activity since almost all of it came into being long before the emergence of feminism. The feminist perspective, of course, can problematize the exclusion of women from philosophical activity and can interpret its significance, but it cannot change the fact that Jewish philosophy was created only by men. What requires an explanation is the refusal of Jewish scholars today (men and women) to heed feminism and feminist thought. I propose the following hypotheses to account for the absence of conversation between Jewish philosophy and feminism.

Scholars of Jewish philosophy have not responded to feminism, because they have yet to respond to contemporary currents in philosophy.

The discipline of Jewish philosophy has been slow to interact with the major currents in twentieth-century philosophy—the Anglo-American analytic tradition, phenomenology, hermeneutics, critical theory, poststructuralism, and deconstructionism. Ironically, the discipline whose existence depends on interaction between Jewish and contemporary non-Jewish culture has been slow to engage contemporary schools of thought in a serious conversation. Steven Katz acknowledged this situation and called on his colleagues "to stop ignoring what modern linguistic philosophy has to teach us and become its students just as much as we must learn what there is to learn from continental philosophy."[52] Katz also argued that Jewish philosophers have an obligation to respond to modern philosophers—Heidegger, for example—in the name of Jewish values.[53] The interaction between Western philosophy and Jewish philosophy should thus transform both. So far only a few scholars have heeded Katz's plea.[54]

Several factors have contributed to the failure of Jewish philosophy to converse with recent intellectual trends, among them feminist thought. One factor is the extremely reactive nature of Jewish philosophy (as a first-order activity). Precisely because the impetus to philosophize comes from outside Judaism and because the manner of philosophizing changes in accordance with prevailing philosophical currents, there has always been a time lag between the stimulus and the response. It has taken Jewish philosophers several decades (and at times more than a century) to familiarize themselves with a given philosophical school in order to formulate a Jewish response to it, be it critical or positive.[55] The slow response time characteristic of Jewish philosophy is evident in the fact that (with the notable exceptions of Fackenheim and Levinas) there has been little creativity in Jewish philosophy since the 1940s. Justifiably, most scholars of Jewish philosophy write on the more creative epochs in Jewish philosophical activity—the Middle Ages and the turn of the twentieth century.

Another factor is the blossoming of Jewish studies as a distinct discipline within the Western academy, especially in America. The growth of the field in terms of members, academic programs, professional forums, and publications has made it possible for Jewish scholars to ignore contemporary intellectual debates and modes of thought. Not unlike women's studies, the field of Jewish studies has become a semiautarchic scholarly community that provides its members with an illusion of comfort and strength.[56] The creation of an academic home for Jewish philosophy has obscured the fact that scholarship in Jewish philosophy remains marginal within the field of philosophy, notwithstanding that a few Jewish philosophers (such as Buber and Levinas) have been influential in Western philosophy.[57]

A third factor is the renaissance of Jewish studies in the state of Israel, viewed by some scholars as the real home of the discipline. Understandably, Israel's relative geographic isolation from the West, its overwhelming preoccupation with survival, and its ongoing struggle to define its collective identity render contemporary debates in the Western academy irrelevant or, at least, less acute. In Israel it is easy to ignore Western intellectual trends or to dismiss them as passing intellectual fads. Furthermore, the very manner in which Western trends are introduced and interpreted in Israel determines the kind of response they receive.

For example, feminism was imported into Israel in the early 1970s by American Jewish female immigrants. They shaped the movement in accordance with American political models and the religious and cultural sensibilities of American Jewry. But to their chagrin, feminists soon discovered that Israeli society and culture were not receptive to the problematics of American Jewry. On the one hand, the socialist heritage of Israel had created the illusion of equality and blunted feminist social demands; on the other hand, the political power of Israeli Orthodoxy had obstructed the spread of the three progressive branches of modern Judaism that are mindful of feminism. The traditional and patriarchal orientations of Sephardic Israelites further curbed receptiveness to feminist ideas. Organizing itself as a political party, the Israeli feminist movement soon became marginalized and rendered insignificant in Israeli culture.[58] It is not surprising that Israeli scholars of Jewish philosophy (men and women) have remained either uninformed of or uninterested in feminist theories.

Scholars of Jewish philosophy do not perceive feminist scholarship in philosophy to be a serious philosophical discourse.

Although none of them has said so publicly, scholars of Jewish philosophy (along with those of other disciplines) do not regard feminist thought (and perhaps feminist scholarship in general) to be a credible academic discourse. Feminist scholarship is perceived to be too personal, too polemical, and too political. In short, it is not seen as philosophy but as political ideology for the social advancement of women. The dismissive attitude toward feminist philosophy and feminist scholarship in general may be a reflection not only of the perception that it is intellectually lightweight but also the fear that it is academically subversive. Because feminist scholarship challenges the traditional methodology of academic scholarship, nonfeminists see it as a threat to the integrity of the academy.

The conversation between feminist theory and Jewish philosophy has not begun because the players have not yet agreed on the rules of the game. Underlying the refusal to enter a conversation with feminism is a clash (still unarticulated) about the nature and purpose of academic scholarship. Jewish philosophy is largely informed by and still committed to the scholarly ideals of the *Wissenschaft des Judentums* movement. Hence, scholars focus their energies on publishing critical editions of primary sources, solving bibliographical puzzles, describing the history of ideas, and deciphering the original intent of past Jewish philosophers. In line with the nineteenth-century ideal of disinterested, objective scholarship, scholars of Jewish philosophy have been cautious not to confuse descriptive and analytic scholarship *about* Jewish philosophy with prescriptive recommendations for what Jews must think or believe—in other words, not to cross the boundary between scholarship and advocacy. Yet these are just those methodological assumptions that feminist scholars challenge as they seek to transform the academy. "The personal is political" was the motto of the women's liberation movement in the 1960s, a motto that receives its theoretical justification from the feminist appropriation of Foucault's theory of knowledge. Feminists demand that all scientific scholarship be engaged and informed by political ideals—that it must not, and indeed cannot, pretend to be detached, disinterested, and objective. To cite Liz Stanley and Sue Wise: "Accounts of the personal constitute not only a realm for examination and discussion, but also the subject matter of feminist theory and thus the basis of feminist political activity."[59]

The feminists' principled refusal to separate the personal, the scholarly, and the political, as well as their critique of rationality, has challenged the self-understanding of Jewish philosophy. By obliterating the boundary between scholarship and advocacy, feminists have opened themselves to the charges that they have politicized the academy, turned scholarship into a vehicle for consciousness raising, and made women's studies the arena for the empowerment of women.[60] Furthermore, the feminist disregard for traditional disciplinary boundaries has created unconventional scholarship that can easily be rejected without being understood, simply because it is unfamiliar.

Whereas some opponents of academic feminism view it as a misguided, mischievous strategy for the dismantling of the academy, it is instead a serious reflection about what it means to be human, whose methodology is based on certain theoretical premises concerning human knowledge. Scholars of Jewish philosophy (and scholars of other disciplines) need not agree with feminist methodology, but they should at least try to understand it—they must dare to know its theoretical underpinning. In turn, feminist philosophers need not accept the methodology of Jewish philosophy, but they have an obligation to articulate their own methodological premises rationally and intelligibly. Only a rational discourse between the practitioners of both fields can clarify their disagreements.

To date, no feminist scholar in Jewish studies has engaged the practitioners of Jewish philosophy on a philosophical level.

Understandably, Jewish feminists have devoted their efforts to proving Judaism's androcentrism and calling for internal reforms in order to enable Jewish women to become full participants in the·ongoing interpretation of Judaism. Jewish feminists have marshaled substantial evidence to prove the exclusion, marginalization, and denigration of women in traditional Jewish society and culture. They have argued convincingly that patriarchy has shaped the Jewish conception of God in a distinctly masculine way and that Jewish religious worship has been dominated by masculinist sensibilities, to the detriment of female spirituality. With considerable creativity, Jewish feminists have composed feminist homilies, devised new rituals for women, and articulated systematic feminist Jewish theology.[61]

Nonetheless, unless Jewish feminists learn to speak philosophically (both as historians of Jewish philosophy and as philosophers) rather than merely theologically, they cannot expect Jewish philosophy to pay attention to their concerns. To get this attention, Jewish feminists must prove (rather than assert) that because Jewish philosophy attempts to reconcile Judaism and philosophy, it is doubly androcentric and oppressive to women—namely, that Jewish philosophy is a philosophy written by Jewish men, for Jewish men, about androcentric Judaism, by means of masculinist philosophy. Jewish feminists must show that within the binary analytic scheme of Jewish philosophy, the Jewish woman has no room; she was (and still is) "the other within" who cannot be reduced to either of the two analytic categories of Jewish philosophy: Jewish or human.

Jewish feminists need to demonstrate that the academic field of Jewish philosophy is wanting if it does not acknowledge the negative perception of women in Jewish philosophical literature and the exclusion of women from philosophical activity. In line with feminist methodology, they must also expose the myth of objectivity by showing that scholarship in Jewish philosophy is far from objective but rather reflects the androcentric biases of its practitioners (because they are traditional Jews, philosophers, or males). As much as the religious identity of the practitioners is relevant to their (Jewish) philosophy, so is their gender identity relevant to their philosophy.[62] Until Jewish feminists engage the scholars of Jewish philosophy on their own turf, the practitioners will continue to insist that gender is not a valid philosophical category within the parameters of Jewish philosophy, or they will explain gender differences in accordance with the Jewish tradition itself. If Jewish feminism is to reform Jewish philosophy, it must do so from within the philosophical discipline itself by employing the tools of philosophy. Notwithstanding the creativity of Jewish feminism, we are still waiting for a feminist Jewish philosopher capable of doing so.

The Liberating Power of Philosophy

That feminism has failed to influence the discipline of Jewish philosophy is a fact. What is true of the past and the present, however, need not be true of the future. Because feminist philosophy and Jewish philosophy are philosophical, critical enterprises, they must both dare to know about each other.

Scholars cannot seek refuge behind the veils of ignorance, humorless dogmatism, and political correctness. By holding a mirror to each other, these intellectual endeavors could examine themselves more honestly and openly.

If feminist thinkers dared to know about Jewish philosophy, they would recognize the inadequacy of lumping Jews indiscriminately with other groups that have been excluded from Western philosophy.[63] Indeed, Jews have been an oppressed and persecuted group in Western society, but they have had a philosophical tradition that shares some of the premises of Western philosophy. Since that philosophical tradition was produced only by men, it is susceptible to feminist critique. A marginalized, oppressed group is not necessarily less male-centered or less philosophically inclined than the dominant culture. At the same time, familiarity with Jewish philosophy will show feminist scholars that it is possible for a male-centered philosophical tradition to engage Western philosophy critically. Indeed, having emerged from the Jewish religious experience, Jewish philosophy has been critical of the dominant (secular or Christian) philosophy in the West. Thus, feminist philosophers will find that some of their cherished ideas—the primacy of the ethical, the historicality and linguisticality of human existence, and the relationality of humans—have been featured in the philosophical works of male Jewish philosophers, both medieval and modern. That does not mean that Jewish philosophy is feminist or that feminist philosophy is Jewish, but it does suggest that there are limits to the efficacy of gender as an explanatory category. Gender differences clearly need to be taken into consideration in reflecting on the human condition, but they are only a partial explanation of complex human reality. If feminist scholars were to reflect on the Jewish experience more seriously, they might also realize the egalitarian potential of reason itself and rethink their critique of Enlightenment rationality. After all, it is reason—or the admission that women and Jews are endowed with reason—that facilitated the liberation of women and the emancipation of the Jews.

Feminism could not have been possible without the Enlightenment and its ideal of rationality. The first feminist thinker was Mary Wollstonecraft (1759–99), who understood the implications of the principles of the Enlightenment and demanded their extension to women. She argued that "if rationality is the capacity that distinguishes brute animals from human persons, then unless girls are brute animals (a description that most men will probably resist when it comes to their mothers, wives and daughters), women as well as men have this capacity. Thus society owes girls the same education as boys simply because all persons deserve an equal chance to develop their rational and moral capacities so that they can achieve person-hood."[64] Wollstonecraft insisted that because women share the same rational human nature as men, they must be given equal education and must be allowed to become fully autonomous. They could no longer be regarded as mere instruments of someone else's happiness or perfection, but as rational agents whose dignity consisted of having the capacity for self-determination. Wollstonecraft's vision inspired the liberal feminism of the nineteenth century and still informs modern-day liberal feminism.

Enlightenment rationalism was also the force that made possible the emancipation of the Jews. Centuries of hatred, exclusion, hostility, and the abuse of Jews could end (at least in theory if not in practice) only after European society acknowledged that Jews were rational human beings, and as such, they were endowed with human rights to equal treatment under the law. In other words, only an appeal to human rationality that transcends historical boundaries and religious convictions could enable Jews to enter mainstream society as equal citizens. The emancipation of both women and Jews illustrates the link between rationalism and democracy, between the freedom to think and the concept of inalienable human rights, and between the European Enlightenment and liberalism.[65]

Jewish philosophers could thus remind feminist philosophers that an attempt to debunk the ideal of rationality would be self-defeating for both Jews and women. Such an assault (if at all coherent) demolishes the principle of human rights that facilitated the emancipation of women and Jews in the first place. So long as Jews and women (or any other group, for that matter) aspire to equality over separateness, they cannot afford to give up rational discourse, which presupposes the ideal of rationality and the ability of the human mind to know objective reality, however imperfectly. The ideal of rationality is fundamentally democratic because it assumes that each and every human being has access to the truth. The road to truth lies not in social status or political privilege but in the unrelenting pursuit of knowledge. The ideal of rationality, therefore, protects individuals and social groups from the abuses of power and even assures their survival. Without it, unavoidable tensions and disputes between individuals and groups would have to be resolved by brute force rather than by rational discourse, a chilling prospect for both Jews and women.

If scholars of Jewish philosophy dared to know about feminist philosophy, they would realize that, although feminist philosophy has political goals, it is not merely a political ideology for the liberation of women. The leading feminist philosophers are well-trained philosophers who struggle with important philosophical questions to which philosophers and historians of philosophy (including the Jewish philosophers and historians of Jewish philosophy) all seek answers. In ethics, political philosophy, philosophy of mind, epistemology, and metaphysics, feminist philosophers have raised pertinent challenges that need to be answered from the perspective of philosophy as well as from the perspective of Judaism. In particular, Jewish philosophers will have to address the antifoundationalist tendencies of feminist thought, which negate Jewish religious beliefs no less than traditional philosophy.

Familiarity with feminist philosophy would show intriguing similarities between the two projects: both attempt to generalize about humanity on the basis of the historical experience of one group of people (Jews or women); both attempt to resolve the tension between universalism and particularism, between sameness and otherness; both are the work of marginal groups that seek to be included in the mainstream culture without losing their distinctiveness; both encounter Western philosophy as an alien, or hostile, intellectual endeavor and seek either to overcome it (as Jewish philosophy does when it "domesticates" philosophy) or transform it (as feminist philosophy does when it demands the inclusion of the female point of view); both have prephilosophical, axiomatic commitments (religious or ideological) that set the limits for their philosophizing. In short, for both Jewish philosophy and feminist philosophy, experience dictates reflection. These similarities do not mean that each program shares the same goals but rather that each confronts similar problems upon which they can reflect together.

Incorporating the feminist perspective into the study of Jewish history could open new avenues for historical research. In the case of medieval Jewish philosophy, for example, beginning with Maimonides, medieval Jewish philosophers followed Aristotle in equating the metaphysical dualism of Form and Matter with maleness and femaleness, respectively, and in regarding the first member of each pair as superior to the second. Medieval Jewish philosophers not only accepted this scheme as axiomatic but routinely evoked it in their allegorical interpretations of the Bible, identifying the patriarch Abraham with Form and the matriarch Sarah with Matter. Modern scholars of Jewish philosophy have often alluded to these facts but have not paused to ponder their meaning.[66] Only one scholar, Raphael Jospe, understood the link between rationalism, the negative perception of women, and radical asceticism in the writings of the thirteenth-century philosopher Shem Tov Falaquera.[67] Yet the subject should be explored on a much larger scale throughout the entire Jewish Aristotelian tradition.

Historians of medieval Jewish philosophy should ask: What was the perception of women in medieval Jewish Aristotelianism? Did the Jewish Aristotelians simply incorporate Aristotle's view of women as imperfect males, or did they offer a critical response from the standpoint of Judaism? Did medieval Jewish Aristotelians share the views of their Muslim and Christian contemporaries about women? Could women (as a class) embark on the study of philosophy? If not, what did their exclusion mean within the parameters of philosophy? Could women attain the rewards of philosophy, that is, happiness and personal immortality? If, in principle, women were excluded from the pursuit of wisdom, how did the exclusion affect their status in Jewish society? Did Aristotelian philosophy exacerbate the marginalization of women (beyond the limits imposed on them in traditional Jewish society), or did philosophy (and the secular sciences in general) provide an avenue for female learning not available within the confines of rabbinic education? Did Jewish philosophical reflections on love (for example, in philosophical commentaries on the Song of Songs) highlight domination and hierarchy or reciprocity and mutuality? To what extent did the Jewish philosophical critique of Aristotelianism (for example, as set forth by Halevi and Crescas) create a basis for a nonhierarchical (though functionally distinct) relation between the sexes? How did the perception of women in philosophical literature shape their images in other forms of Jewish self-expression, such as secular poetry and prose? How did Aristotelian philosophy differ from Kabbalah in regard to women? Was Kabbalah more accommodating to women because of its theosophy of the androgynous God, or did it contribute to the marginalization of Jewish women from spiritual life?[68] Similar questions apply to other trends in Jewish philosophy, such as Kantianism and existentialism.[69]

To answer these questions, scholars of Jewish philosophy will have to go beyond preoccupation with the canon of Jewish philosophy to study Jewish philosophy in its broad cultural setting.[70] Future research will have to be interdisciplinary, crossing the boundaries between philosophy, history, mysticism, and law; it will have to highlight the nexus between the various dimensions of philosophy (metaphysics, epistemology, ethics, and political theory), and it will have to take into consideration not only the luminaries of Jewish philosophy but also the so-called minor thinkers. Although a contextualized approach to Jewish philosophy is consistent with feminist tendencies, it need not compromise the ideals of rigorous scholarship as articulated by its founders in the *Wissenschaft des Judentums*.

Jewish feminists themselves are the most natural conversation partners of scholars of Jewish philosophy since they are committed to both Judaism and feminism. Yet the Jewish feminists too must dare to know and examine their own feminist convictions in light of Jewish philosophy. For example, feminists view hierarchical dualism as one of the gravest sins of traditional philosophy and Western culture in general. They argue (as I have discussed earlier) that it is oppressive to women because of the gender inflection of all hierarchical dichotomies. Jewish philosophy could offer a critical vantage point from which to examine this assertion. Is hierarchical dualism necessarily masculinist? Does binary thinking necessarily lead to exploitation and oppression? Is it at all possible for humans to avoid binary thinking? Can human society exist without a functional hierarchy or a hierarchy of values? Can there be a moral system that does not presuppose a hierarchy of the good and the bad, of the permitted and the forbidden, of what we ought to do and what we actually do? Does feminist theory itself not presuppose such a hierarchy of values when it demands that modern society substitute one (presumably more just) value system for another (presumably oppressive) one?

It is particularly important that Jewish feminists answer these questions because feminist Jewish theology has taken the attack on hierarchical dualism as its point of departure. With their non-Jewish sisters (such as Carol Christ, Mary Daly, Sally McFague, and Rosemary Reuther), Jewish theologians (such as Judith Plaskow) have regarded hierarchical thinking (and hence transcendence) as oppressive to women; they have sought to articulate religious language that minimizes (if not totally obliterates) divine transcendence. Instead of the abstract conceptualization of the divine, they have highlighted the immanence and closeness of God, articulated God-language that employs metaphors of sensuality and intimacy with God, and emphasized the body as a medium of relating to God.

The feminist critique of hierarchical dualism is problematic from the perspective of Jewish philosophy. Steven Schwarzschild and Kenneth Seeskin, for example, have convincingly argued that Judaism posits the transcendence of the rational: "The transcendence of the Rational, which might also be called 'anti-incarnationism,' asserts that it is impossible for the ideal to be realized in a sensuous medium. This principle is the philosophic equivalent of the basic Jewish conviction that God is separate from the world and cannot be depicted with images of things found in the world. . . . God is never *in* heavenly bodies or earthly phenomena, but is a moral will who stands *above* them. In philosophic terms, this means that everything in the world is fallible and subject to critique."[71]

In other words, the transcendence of the rational in Judaism challenges the feminist "flight toward immanentism" evident in both feminist philosophy and Jewish feminist theology. As Schwarzschild has shown, the immanentist interpretation of the divine-human nexus "conceives transcendence as being, as it were, physically above immanence ('the God out there'). If there is to be a connecting link between two physical places, this link itself will have to be physical."[72] It is this "spatial model" of transcendence that underlies both the incarnationist theology of Christianity and the theory of intermediaries characteristic of medieval Neoplatonism and Neoplatonized Aristotelianism. In Judaism, however, God's otherness is understood in volitional rather than spatial terms.[73] The dialectics of transcendence and immanence revolve around the communication of God's will in revealed Law and the human volitional response through the performance of the commandments. The main question of the Jewish philosophical tradition, therefore, is to what extent revealed Law is philosophically possible. Formulating the problem of transcendence in this manner might lead feminist thinkers to reconsider the problem of hierarchical dualism, the spatial model of transcendence, and the connection between epistemology and ethics. When it is correctly understood, the spatial model is either secular or Christian; it does not fit the understanding of the divine-human nexus within the Jewish tradition itself.

The conversation between scholars of Jewish philosophy, feminist philosophers, and Jewish feminists will not, cannot, and need not reach consensus. Philosophical examinations rarely end in an agreement, because philosophy is an open-ended enterprise that always dares to know about reality and about itself. After each identity crisis and seemingly final threat to its existence, philosophy summons the courage to know and forever regenerate itself. It is this special capacity of philosophy to dare to know that has made it a democratic, liberating endeavor.

To those who seek truth, Kant's motto of the Enlightenment must still ring true. Only when people dare to know can they liberate themselves from erroneous prejudices, harmful superstitions, oppressive social institutions, and unjust human exploitation. Only when people dare to know can they acknowledge their shared humanity, which transcends cultural differences, historical conditioning, and social conventions. Only when people dare to know can they become self-reflective and self-critical and challenge themselves to overcome internal, psychological barriers and to conquer everhigher summits of self-knowledge. If women and Jews were to admit their indebtedness to Enlightenment rationalism, they could begin to explore rationally their shared ideals of human freedom, dignity, and equality. Feminists and philosophers, both Jews and non-Jews, must recognize that the freedom to think expresses the depth of our humanity as much as it makes us aware of our cognitive limitations.

Notes

1. The following discussion of the impact of feminism on the academy glosses over the internal debate within the feminist movement between integrationist and separatist trends. For a general review of this debate see Marian Lowe and Margaret Lowe Benston, "The Uneasy Alliance of Feminism and Academia," in Sneja Gunew, ed., *A Reader in Feminist Knowledge*, pp. 48–60 (London: Routledge, 1991); and Susan Sheridan, "From Margin to Mainstream: Situating Women's Studies," ibid., pp. 61–73. For a general overview of feminism's impact on the Academy see Christie Farnham, ed., *The Impact of Feminist Research in the Academy* (Bloomington: Indiana University Press).

2. Elizabeth V. Spelman, *Inessential Woman: Problem of Exclusion in Feminist Thought* (Boston: Beacon, 1988), 47.

3. Aristotle, *Politics* (1252a, 25–32).

4. Immanuel Kant, *Observations on the Feelings of the Beautiful and the Sublime,* trans. John T. Goldwait (Berkeley: University of California Press, 1960), 81.

5. Arthur Schopenhauer, "On Women," excerpted in *Philosophy of Woman: An Anthology of Classic and Current Concepts,* ed. Mary Briody Mahowald (Indianapolis: Hackett, 1978), 230.

6. Any attempt to define philosophy is futile given the disagreement between philosophers concerning the nature of their pursuit. In this chapter I follow Avner Cohen in talking about philosophy as the ethos of the attempts to capture the essence of the true, the good, and the rational. See Avner Cohen, "The 'End of Philosophy': An Anatomy of A Cross-Purpose Debate," in Avner Cohen and Marcelo Dascal, eds., *The Institution of Philosophy: A Discipline in Crisis,* pp. 111–39 (La Salle, Ill.: Open Court, 1989).

7. When feminists confronted the discipline of philosophy, they regarded the discipline as a stable, continuous tradition that was hostile to women. Since feminists attempted to reform the discipline as a whole, it is not surprising that their critique was based on sweeping generalizations about the nature of "philosophy"—disregarding more nuanced positions of individual philosophers. For a summary of feminist scholarship in philosophy until 1985 see Ellen C. DuBois et al., *Feminist Scholarship: Kindling in the Groves of Academe* (Urbana: University of Illinois Press, 1987), 28–34.

8. Early feminist scholarship focused on exposing misogynist assumptions of Western philosophy. Among the most influential works of this genre are Susan Moller Okin, *Women in Western Political Thought* (London: Virago, 1980); Jean Bethke Elshtain, *Public Man, Private Woman: Women in Social and Political Thought* (Oxford: Martin Robertson, 1981); Sheila Ruth, "Methodocracy, Misogyny, and Bad Faith: Sexism in the Philosophic Establishment," *Metaphilosophy* 10 (1979): 46–61; and Spelman, *Inessential Woman.*

9. The term *malestream* was coined by Mary O'Brien, *The Politics of Reproduction* (London: Routledge, 1980), and has become common in feminist scholarship.

10. Janice Moulton, "A Paradigm of Philosophy: The Adversary Method," in Sandra Harding and Merrill B. Hintikka, eds., *Discovering Reality*, pp. 149–64 (Dordrecht: D. Reidel, 1983), reprinted in Ann Garry and Marilyn Pearsall, eds., *Women, Knowledge, and Reality: Explorations in Feminist Philosophy*, pp. 5–20 (Boston: Unwin Hyman, 1989). Feminists have challenged the notion that philosophy has to be done in a certain way. Mary Daly, for example, charged that such a notion reflects the oppressive male prerogative of naming. She therefore called on women to disregard the traditional conception of philosophy and begin to philosophize in a different way, one that is grounded in a renaming of the relation between passions and reason. See Daly, *Pure Lust: Elemental Feminist Philosophy* (Boston: Beacon, 1984). To substitute for the Adversary Method feminists have called women to philosophize in a collective, nonconfrontational, and egalitarian way. See Susan Sherwin, "Philosophical Methodology and Feminist Methodology: Are They Compatible?" in Lorraine Code, Christine Overall, and Sheila Mullet, eds., *Feminist Perspectives: Philosophical Essays on Method and Morals* (Toronto: University of Toronto Press, 1988), rep. in *Women, Knowledge, and Reality*, pp. 21–35.

11. Genevieve Lloyd, *The Man of Reason: "Male" and "Female" in Western Philosophy* (Minneapolis: University of Minnesota Press, 1984), 2.

12. Jane Flax, "Post Modernism and Gender Relations in Feminist Theory," *Signs* 12 (1987): 624.

13. The literature about the so-called end-of-philosophy debate is too extensive to be cited here in full. For a summary of the major points of the debate see Cohen and Dascal, *Philosophy,* and Kenneth Baynes, James Bohman, and Thomas McCarthy, eds., *After Philosophy: End or Transformation* (Cambridge: MIT Press, 1988).

14. Richard Rorty, *Consequences of Pragmatism* (Minneapolis: University of Minnesota Press, 1982).

15. See Lorraine Code, *What Can She Know? Feminist Theory and the Construction of Knowledge* (Ithaca: Cornell University Press, 1991), 114. The critique of Kant's ahistorical philosophy is not uniquely feminist. It had already been expressed in the nineteenth century by male, neo-Kantian philosophers. Perhaps it is no coincidence that the greatest of them was the Jewish philosopher Hermann Cohen.

16. Hierarchical dualism was among the first features of Western philosophy to be attacked by feminist philosophers. See Sherry B. Ortner, "Is Female to Male as Nature Is to Culture?" in Michelle Zimbalist Rosaldo and Louise Lamphere, eds., *Woman, Culture, and Society* (Stanford: Stanford University Press, 1974), 67–87; Rosemary Ruether, "Motherearth and Megamachine: A Theology of Liberation in a Feminine, Somatic, and Ecological Perspective," in Carol P. Christ and Judith Plaskow, eds., *Womanspirit Rising: A Feminist Reader in Religion* (San Francisco: Harper and Row, 1979).

17. See Elizabeth Fee, "Women's Nature and Scientific Objectivity," in Marian Lowe and Ruth Hubbard, eds., *Women's Nature: Rationalizations of Inequality* (New York: Pergamon, 1983); Evelyn Fox Keller, "Gender and Science," in *Discovering Reality*, 187–205; idem, *Reflections on Gender and Science* (New Haven: Yale University Press, 1985).

18. Code, *What Can She Know*, 29.

19. For this aspect of feminist critique see Allison M. Jaggar, "Love and Knowledge: Emotion in Feminist Epistemology," in Alison M. Jaggar and Susan R. Bordo, eds., *Gender/Body/ Knowledge: Feminist Reconstructions of Being and Knowing* (New Brunswick, N.J.: Rutgers University Press, 1989), rep. in *Women, Knowledge, and Reality*, 129–55.

20. See Lynda Birke, *Women, Feminism, and Biology: The Feminist Challenge* (New York: Methuen, 1986); Susan Bordo, "The Cartesian Masculinization of Thought," *Signs: Journal of Women in Culture and Society* 11 (1986): 439–56; idem, *The Flight to Objectivity: Essays in Cartesianism and Culture* (Albany: SUNY Press, 1987).

21. Feminist ethicists find Kant particularly distasteful not only because he excluded women from the community of ideal moral agents, but also because he privileged duty over love. For Kant, the difference between moral acts and loving acts corresponded to the difference between men and women—women being incapable of moral acts. For a feminist critique of Kantian morality see Jean Grimshaw, *Feminist Philosophers: Women's Perspectives on Philosophical Traditions* (Brighton: Wheatsheaf Books, 1986); Lorraine Code, "Experience, Knowledge, and Responsibility," in Morwenna Griffiths and Margaret Whitford, eds., *Feminist Perspectives in Philosophy*, 187–204 (London: Macmillan, 1988); Nel Noddings, "Ethics from the Standpoint of Women," in *Theoretical Perspectives on Sexual Difference*, 160–73 (New Haven: Yale University Press, 1990).

22. See Nancy Chodorow, *The Reproduction of Mothering: Psychoanalysis and the Sociology of Gender* (Berkeley: University of California Press, 1978); Jane Flax, "The Conflict between Nurturance and Autonomy in Mother-Daughter Relationships and within Feminism," in E. Howel and M. Bayes, eds., *Women and Mental Health* (New York: Basic, 1981); Naomi Scheman, "Individualism and the Objects of Psychology," in Harding and Hintikka, eds., *Discovering Reality*, pp. 225–44; Annette Baier, *Postures of the Mind: Essays on Mind and Morals* (Minneapolis: University of Minnesota Press, 1985).

23. Feminist theorists have made much of Thomas S. Kuhn's celebrated theory of paradigm shifts in science in his *Structure of Scientific Revolutions* (Chicago: University of Chicago Press, 1962). For a summary of the feminist critique of the philosophy of science see Sandra Harding, *Whose Science? Whose Knowledge? Thinking from Women's Lives* (Ithaca: Cornell University Press, 1991), 53–76.

24. Initially, some feminist thinkers embraced radical subjectivism. They argued that in point of fact there is no objective social reality, but only subjective reality—mine, yours, and ours. Only the owner of a given experience has the unique authority to determine what that reality is, and she cannot get it wrong. See, e.g., Liz Stanley and Sue Wise, *Breaking Out: Feminist Consciousness and Feminist Research* (London: Routledge, 1983). Yet, like many relativists beforehand, feminists came to realize that relativism is not only self-contradictory, but also politically counterproductive. If there is no objective social reality, how can feminists claim that women's oppression is real?

25. In acknowledging the intrinsic link between patterns of thought and historical conditions, feminist standpoint epistemology owes much to Marxist epistemology. Not surprisingly, feminist standpoint epistemology is articulated by and appeals to scholars trained in

sociology, history, and political science. For an explicit attempt to reconstruct Marxist philosophy from a feminist perspective see Nancy Hartsock, "The Feminist Standpoint: Developing the Ground for a Specifically Feminist Historical Materialism," in Harding and Hinkikka, eds., *Discovering Reality*, pp. 283–310. For a survey of Marxist feminism and socialist feminism—two distinct strands within feminist theory—see Rosemarie Tong, *Feminist Thought: A Comprehensive Introduction* (Boulder: Westview, 1989), 51–69, 173–93, and the bibliography cited there.

26. For a summary of feminist standpoint epistemology and a list of its major contributors see Harding, *Whose Science? Whose Knowledge? Thinking from Women's Lives*, 119–33.

27. On the "stranger within," see Patricia Hill Collins, "Learning from the Outsider Within: The Sociological Significance of Black Feminist Thought," *Social Problems* 33 (1986), rep. in Mary Margaret Fonow and Judith A. Cook, eds., *Beyond Methodology* (Bloomington: Indiana University Press, 1991), 35–59.

28. Morwenna Griffiths, "Feminism, Feelings, and Philosophy," in Griffiths and Whitford, *Feminist Perspectives*, 148.

29. For a summary of French postmodern feminism, see Andrea Nye, "The Voice of the Serpent: French Feminism and Philosophy of Language," in *Women, Knowledge, and Reality*, 233–49.

30. Luce Irigaray, *The Sex Which Is Not One*, trans. Catherine Porter (Ithaca: Cornell University Press, 1985).

31. Hélène Cixous, "The Laugh of the Medusa," in Elaine Marks and Isabelle de Courtivron, eds., *New French Feminism*, 245–64 (New York: Schocken, 1981); ed. and rep. in Gunew, *A Reader in Feminist Knowledge*, 224–30.

32. Tong, *Feminist Thought*, 225.

33. See Luce Irigaray, *Speculum of the Other Woman*, trans. Gillian C. Gill (Ithaca: Cornell University Press, 1985).

34. Tong, *Feminist Thought*, 230.

35. Julia Kristeva, "Women's Time," trans. Alice Jardine and Harry Blake, *Signs* 7 (1) (1981): 13–35.

36. Opposition to oppressive speech patterns characterized early feminist literature. See, e.g., Janice Moulton, "The Myth of the Neutral Man," in Mary Vetterling-Braggin, Frederic Elliston, and Jane English, eds., *Feminism and Philosophy* (Towota, N.J.: Littlefield, Adams, 1977); rep. in *Women, Knowledge, and Reality*, pp. 219–32; Mary Daly, *Gyn/Ecology: The Metaethics of Radical Feminism* (Boston: Beacon, 1978); Dale Spender, *Man Made Language* (London: Routledge, 1980).

37. Deborah Tannen, *You Just Don't Understand: Women and Men in Conversation* (New York: Morrow, 1990).

38. See Caroline Whitbeck, "A Different Reality: Feminist Ontology," in Carol C. Gould, ed., *Beyond Domination: New Perspectives on Women and Philosophy* (Towota, N.J.: Rowman and Allanheld), 79. Whitbeck and other feminist ethicists tend to ignore the growing number of men who care for children and the fact that as primary breadwinners men have been responsible for the welfare of other members of the family. That contemporary

Western men are more actively involved in parenting, however, is itself the result of the feminist critique of the traditional division of labor within the family.

39. The psychologist Carol Gilligan broke new ground when she challenged the reigning psychological theory concerning human moral development, suggesting that the existing male model does not fit the experiences of most women's lives. She criticized a rights-based ethics and called for the formulation of an alternative view of morality to include the typically feminine way of conceptualizing the relationship between self and other. See Carol Gilligan, *In a Different Voice: Psychological Theory and Women's Development* (Cambridge: Harvard University Press, 1982). Though Gilligan's work drew its own share of feminist critique, it inspired feminists to articulate a "female ethics: [one] that is grounded in women's experience, especially mothering and caring for others." On the critique of Gilligan see Barbara Houston, "Gilligan and the Politics of a Distinctive Women's Morality," in Code, Overall, and Mullet, eds., *Feminist Perspectives,* 168–89.

    As advocates of women's civil and political rights, feminist ethicists cannot give up the discourse of rights. What they oppose is the grounding of rights in abstract reasoning that excludes the way women approach moral dilemmas.

40. See Sara Ruddick, "Maternal Thinking," *Feminist Studies* 6 (1980): 342–67; Nel Noddings, *Caring: A Feminine Approach to Ethics and Moral Education* (Berkeley: University of California Press, 1984); Eva Kittay and Diana Meyers, *Women and Morality* (Towota, N.J.: Rowman and Allanheld, 1987).

41. See Sara Ruddick, *Maternal Thinking: Toward a Politics of Peace* (Boston: Beacon, 1989).

42. See Micheline R. Malson, Jean F. O'Barr, Sarah Westfal-Wihl, and Mary Wyer, *Feminist Theory in Practice and Process* (Chicago: University of Chicago Press, 1989), 4–5; and Sandra Harding, "The Instability of the Analytical Categories of Feminist Theory," *Signs* 11 (1986), rep. in ibid., 15–34.

43. Teresa de Lauretis, *Feminist Studies/Critical Studies* (Bloomington: Indiana University Press, 1986), 14.

44. See, e.g., the editors' introduction to Griffiths and Whitford, *Feminist Perspectives,* 8.

45. See Mary Midgley, "On Not Being Afraid of Natural Sex Differences," in Griffiths and Whitford, *Feminist Perspectives,* 29–41.

46. See Kenneth Seeskin, "Jewish Philosophy in the 1980s," *Modern Judaism* 11 (1991): 160.

47. It is evident that the question, "How can there be a Jewish philosophy?" is equivalent to the question, "How can there be a feminist philosophy?" The answer to both questions depends on how one understands the nature of philosophy. If philosophy is like logic or mathematics, then there can be neither Jewish philosophy nor feminist philosophy. Yet if philosophy is a systematic reflection on any aspect of the human experience, then the existence of either Jewish philosophy and feminist philosophy does not require an explanation.

48. In a recent symposium about Jewish philosophy, participants articulated three major approaches to the nature of Jewish philosophy. Echoing Isaac Husic, Menachem Kellner argued that there can be Jews who do philosophy, and there can even be philosophically trained Jews who employ their knowledge of philosophy to advance the claims of a

specific trend within Judaism, but there cannot be Jewish philosophy as such. Jews may reflect on universal philosophical questions from the perspective of the Jewish tradition, but their philosophic reflection is not Jewish per se. Other scholars (e.g., Norbert Samuelson, Barry Kogan, and Steven Katz) have taken issue with Kellner. They argued that philosophy is a type of analytic procedure that can be applied to the examination of any intellectual discipline or discourse. These scholars defined Jewish philosophy as the critical, systematic reflection about Judaism, its beliefs, rituals, ethical ideals, and legal norms. Such reflection has never been monolithic and has varied according to the prevalent mode of thought in a given period. A third approach was articulated by Steven Schwarzschild, who argued that Jewish philosophy is a certain way of doing philosophy, i.e., a philosophy with a "Jewish twist." Philosophy done in a Jewish way is a philosophy that emphasizes the category of conduct, of that which must be done, and a philosophy that rejects incarnationism or immanentism. The proceedings of the conference were published in Norbert Samuelson, ed., *Studies in Jewish Philosophy* (Lanham, Md.: University Press of America, 1987).

49. I begin the history of Jewish philosophy with Saadia Gaon rather than with Philo (d. 50 C.E.) because the latter's writings were hardly known by Rabbinic Jews and did not affect the discourse of Jewish philosophy. Philo's writings were preserved by the church and exercised profound influence on the history of Christian philosophy.

50. Between these two poles there is the loosely defined area of Jewish religious thought, or Jewish theology. Under Jewish theology fall Kabbalah, Hasidism, and the denominational theologies of modern Judaism—Reform, Conservative Judaism, neo-Orthodoxy, and Reconstructionism. Although some of the contributors to these intellectual traditions have had extensive training in philosophy and have employed philosophical categories in their exposition of Judaism (e.g., Joseph Soloveitchik, Eugene Borowitz, Neil Gillman, David Hartman, and Michael Wyschogrod), their major interest is hermeneutical rather than philosophical. They are interested not in explaining Judaism to philosophy but rather in interpreting the Jewish religious tradition for the sake of enriching Jewish religious life.

51. In reality, of course, the boundary between these two orders of Jewish philosophy is not as rigid as this description suggests. Some academic practitioners of Jewish philosophy are also engaged in the creative enterprise of constructing Jewish philosophy or Jewish theology (e.g., Eliezer Berkovits, Borowitz, Hartman, and Wyschogrod). Yet most would agree that the constructive enterprise belongs in Jewish religious seminaries, the various academies of Jewish learning, or one's own study—but not in the secular university. At the very least, scholars of Jewish philosophy are careful not to turn the classroom of the secular university into a pulpit for their own views about what Jews must think or do. As I explain later in the chapter, this is one of the reasons for the failure of feminist philosophy to influence Jewish philosophy.

52. Katz, "Jewish Philosophy in the 1980s: A Diagnosis and Prescription," *Studies in Jewish Philosophy,* 40.

53. Katz does not mention one (rather cursory) example of a Jewish response to Heidegger:

Emil L. Fackenheim, *Encounters between Judaism and Modern Philosophy: A Preface to Future Jewish Thought* (New York: Schocken, 1973), 213–29.

54. The most notable example is Kenneth Seeskin, *Jewish Philosophy in a Secular Age* (Albany: SUNY Press, 1990). It is not a coincidence that it is this scholar who has urged a serious dialogue with feminist theory. Another scholar who has taken feminists seriously and has attempted to answer them is Eugene B. Borowitz in his recent work *Renewing the Covenant: A Theology of the Post-Modern Jew* (Philadelphia: Jewish Publication Society, 1991). However, Borowitz, who writes as a theologian, engages such feminist Jewish theologians as Plaskow rather than the non-Jewish feminist philosophers I have cited earlier. By the same token, although the adjective *postmodern* is part of the title of the book, the work does not include a systematic, philosophic exchange with postmodern philosophers. Borowitz's case proves my point: Jewish thinkers have been slow to engage contemporary intellectual currents on a philosophical level.

55. For example, Saadia Gaon in the tenth century responded to the Muatazilite Kalam of the ninth century; Moses Maimonides in the twelfth century responded to the philosophies of Alfarabi (d. 970), Ibn Sina [Avicenna] (d. 1037), and Ibn Bajja (d. 1026). Hasdai Crescas in the early fifteenth century responded to theories and debates between the Christian scholastics of the thirteenth and fourteenth centuries (Thomas Aquinas and Johannes Duns Scotus, respectively). The time lag is evident in the modern period as well. Moses Mendelssohn in the late eighteenth century articulated his distinct Jewish philosophy in response to the political theories of seventeenth-century philosophers Thomas Hobbes and Benedict de Spinoza, and nineteenth-century Jewish philosophy is largely a response to the philosophies of Kant (d. 1804) and Georg Hegel (d. 1827). It is this reactive quality that justifies the preoccupation of scholars of Jewish philosophy with identifying the literary sources that have influenced the philosophy of a given Jewish thinker.

56. The proliferation of Jewish studies programs in the 1970s and 1980s was indebted to the rise of both black studies and women studies and their challenge to traditional disciplinary conceptions. That women's studies and Jewish studies are parallel programs is obvious if we bring to mind the questions that feminists put at the forefront of their research. One need only replace the word *women* with the word *Jews* to formulate the parallel agenda of Jewish studies. By the same token, Jewish philosophy and feminist philosophy should be viewed as parallel programs. I spell out this point later in the chapter.

57. Here I am referring to philosophers who have engaged Western philosophy from the perspective of Judaism, rather than philosophers of Jewish descent (e.g., Henri Bergson and Edmund Husserl) or Jews who philosophized without reference to their Judaism (e.g., Ibn Gabirol) or Jews whose philosophy debunked their allegiance to traditional Judaism (e.g., Spinoza).

58. For an overview of the status of women in Israel see Ellen Boneparth, "In the Land of the Patriarchs: Public Policy on Women in Israel," in Lynne B. Iglitzin and Ruth Ross, eds., *Women in the World 1975–1985,* 125–52 (Santa Barbara: Clio Books, 1986). The past election suggests the beginning of a change toward the greater participation of women in Israeli politics.

59. Liz Stanley and Sue Wise, "Feminist Research, Feminist Consciousness, and Experiences of Sexism," in Mary Margaret Fonow and Judith A. Cook, eds., *Beyond Methodology: Feminist Scholarship as Lived Research,* p. 266 (Bloomington: Indiana University Press, 1991).

60. Though these charges are not without merit, scholars of Jewish studies must realize that the same objections can be raised against their own discipline. Jewish studies could also be viewed as a program serving the nonacademic concerns of Jewish survival, as an arena for raising the Jewish consciousness of students and faculty, and as a vehicle for the political empowerment of Jews. Other recently established academic programs—such as Afro-American studies, Asian studies, Near Eastern studies, and Gay and Lesbian studies—are also vulnerable to these accusations. The only way to rebut them is to show that while these programs focus on a single segment of humanity (women, Jews, Afro-Americans, etc.), they also shed light on humanity in general. An overt particularism does not necessarily limit their universal significance. Yet precisely because these disciplines aspire to universality, it is impossible to hold that the pursuit of universality characterizes masculine thinking.

61. See in particular Judith Plaskow, *Standing Again in Sinai: Judaism from a Feminist Perspective* (New York: Harper and Row, 1990), and my review in *Hadoar* 70(32) (1991): 114–19.

62. Jewish feminists still have to explain why the few female scholars of Jewish philosophy have not pressed the feminist agenda. This fact alone can be used by male scholars as evidence that gender is irrelevant to the discipline of Jewish philosophy. Here are some possible explanations for the absence of feminist consciousness among the female scholars of Jewish philosophy: (a) the female scholar is a traditional Jewish woman who is either not aware of the blatant contradiction between her own scholarly work and the exclusion of women from scholarly activity in traditional Judaism, or manages to rationalize that contradiction without endorsing feminism; (b) the female scholar is a secular Israeli woman who is unimpressed by, or unfamiliar with, feminism (for reasons already discussed); (c) the female scholar accepts feminism as a political program for the social and political equality of women but does not believe that feminism belongs in the academy. She holds that it is possible to engage in scholarship without paying attention to the gender issue. Several combinations of these options are also possible.

63. For example, Nancy Holland, *Is Woman's Philosophy Possible?* (London: Rowman and Littlefield, 1990), 121, and Kristeva, "Women's Time," 13-35.

64. Tong, *Feminist Thought,* 15.

65. I am fully aware of the heavy price that Jews have paid for emancipation: the breakdown of corporate structure, ideological fragmentation, alienation from tradition, and assimilation and the loss of Jewish identity. Yet, given that this price was inevitable, few modern Jews would willingly forswear it and return to a ghettoized existence. The modern challenge, of course, is to redefine the balance between Jewishness and modernity, between communal existence and individuality, between the religious tradition and secular sensibilities. But the challenge can be addressed only on the basis of human equality and individual dignity advocated by the Enlightenment project that feminist and other postmodern critics attempt to debunk.

66. See, e.g., Frank Talmage, "Apples of Gold: The Inner Meaning of Sacred Texts in Medieval Judaism," in Arthur Green, ed., *Jewish Spirituality from the Bible through the Middle Ages,* p. 330 (New York: Crossroad, 1986); Colete Sirat, *A History of Jewish Philosophy in the Middle Ages* (Cambridge: Cambridge University Press, 1985), 228.

67. Raphael Jospe, "Rejecting Moral Virtue as the Ultimate Human End," in William M. Brinner and Stephen D. Ricks, eds., *Studies in Islamic and Judaic Traditions,* Brown Judaic 110, pp. 185–204 (Atlanta: Scholars Press).

68. I am working on these questions in ongoing research on the pursuit of happiness in medieval Judaism.

69. For example, if Kant excluded women from the community of ideal knowers and moral agents because of their inherent inability to act in a self-legislating manner, did Jewish neo-Kantian philosophers, such as Hermann Cohen, share the same view? Did Cohen's modification of Kantianism take into consideration the Jewish woman, or was it yet another masculine abstraction on universal principles? To what extent do the Jewish sources of Cohen's philosophy exclude the possibility of considering women as autonomous moral agents? The list can go on, but the point is simple: rereading the philosophic sources from the feminist perspective is not an idle exercise.

70. See my "Response" in *The State of Jewish Studies* (New York: Jewish Theological Seminary, 1986), 128–42.

71. Seeskin, *Jewish Philosophy in a Secular Age,* 5.

72. Menachem Kellner, ed., *The Pursuit of the Ideal: Jewish Writings of Steven Schwarzschild* (Albany: SUNY Press, 1990), 63.

73. Transcendence itself is a spatial category. Interestingly, there is no Hebrew word for "transcendence" in biblical, Rabbinic, or medieval Hebrew.

Feminist Studies and
Modern Jewish History

Feminist historical scholarship is almost twenty years old, yet its impact on the writing of modern Jewish history has been remarkably limited. This is so not because of male malevolence, but because of the very conceptualization of the field of Jewish history. History is a conservative discipline, and Jewish history especially so. Grounded in intellectual history, the field has defined its boundaries narrowly, in a sense secularizing traditional Jewish learning. Just as the task of the *talmid hakham* (the traditional Jewish scholar) was the sacred study and interpretation of classical Jewish texts, so the primary task of the Jewish historian has been the secular study and elucidation of those same texts. The historian might include philosophical and literary texts within an expanded canon, but the texts deemed most worthy of study were the products of the rabbinic class. Even when historians considered the changing political status of Jews and the activities of Jewish communal institutions, they still analyzed those documents created and preserved by a male elite, although one no longer limited to the rabbinic class. Of course, rabbinic, philosophical, and literary texts, as well as communal records, contain important information on the normative role and status of women, but those issues were deemed marginal, at best, by Jewish historians. The issues that Jewish historians considered to be of historical significance were defined by the parameters of male experience. Either women were subsumed within that experience, which was seen as universal, or they were ignored because by definition their experience was particular and of no great interest.

A younger generation of Jewish historians is challenging this paradigm. Trained largely over the past two decades and influenced by the new currents of social history as well as feminist theory, they have begun to enlarge the definition of the historically significant. Furthermore, at least in the United States, with the proliferation of graduate programs in Judaic studies, considerable numbers of women have entered the field of Jewish history, which was once virtually closed to them because the requisite skills were most readily acquired in the exclusively male yeshivot (schools of advanced Talmud study) and rabbinical schools. Most of these women work in the modern period, where their lack of a traditional yeshiva or rabbinic education is not a major obstacle to historical scholarship. Not surprisingly, these women scholars have pioneered in the investigation of Jewish women's history.

Women's history has evolved rapidly in the past fifteen years. In its early stages its aim was compensatory: arguing that the academy had defined history in such a way as to ignore fully half of human experience, feminist scholars pressed for a redress of the imbalance, for the inclusion of prominent women along with their male counterparts in works of history. They also focused their attention on the treatment of women in past societies and on the evolution of movements for women's rights in the course of the past two centuries.[1] For the most part, however, they did not challenge the basic conceptualization of the field. Within a few years, however, feminist historians recognized the significance of the concept of gender, borrowed from anthropology, as a crucial analytic tool for exploring the historical experience of women in different societies and cultures.

Defined as the social and cultural construction of the differences between the sexes, the category of gender enabled historians to organize women's experience and to distinguish it from the experience of men. By focusing on gender, historians like Joan Kelly asked such questions as whether the commonly accepted periodization of history still made sense once women were included. In a now-classic article, "Did Women Have a Renaissance?" Kelly demonstrated that the liberating elements associated with the Renaissance did not apply to women. If women had a renaissance, it was not during the Renaissance period.[2] Kelly's article was a contribution to historiography in general as well as to women's history, for it revealed a social and intellectual complexity in the Renaissance that had previously been overlooked.

As feminist anthropologists and historians have explored the social uses of gender concepts, they have realized that gender always implies a clearly defined hierarchy of values. Gender is a relational category. Concepts of gender presume paired opposites of characteristics divided according to sex. I offer three familiar examples: strong-weak; spiritual-material; public-private. Although the specific pairs vary depending on the culture in question and are modified in accordance with differences in class and ethnicity, the traits associated with masculinity—whatever they are in a particular society—are privileged. There has been a lively debate among feminist theorists as to the central social division that accounts for the universal subordination of women in recorded history. Some anthropologists argue that the appropriation by men of the public sphere and the relegation of women, at least as a social ideal, to the domestic sphere is the single most important social division between the sexes.[3]

Whether or not they accept the public-private division as key, most feminist scholars I think would agree with Joan Wallach Scott's definition of gender in her recent book *Gender and the Politics of History.* Scott bases her definition on two propositions: that "gender is a constitutive element of social relationships based on perceived differences between the sexes, *and* gender is a primary way of signifying relationships of power."[4] These theoretical considerations have led feminist historians both to expand the domain of their research—to explore the private domain and its relation to the public domain, for example, for they are related—and to decode power relations in the use of gendered language. Feminist scholars are aware that the boundaries between public and private spheres have varied with time and place; new forms of female public activity are legitimated by denying their innovative character and blurring their public nature. Looking at women's actual roles and the normative social expectations of their "place," then, provides a vehicle for examining the shift in boundaries between the public and the private. Feminist scholars are also aware that all knowledge is constructed and that the claim that traditional historiography is objective (while feminist studies are subjective) has served as a rationale for continuing to ignore groups and issues neglected in the traditional canon.[5]

As a discipline, modern Jewish history has scarcely begun to grapple with these issues. Most Jewish historians do not regularly incorporate gender into their analyses (as they do class), though they are now less likely to ignore it when they come across appropriate data in their research. The first collection of scholarly articles on the historical experience of Jewish women, Judith Baskin's *Jewish Women in Historical Perspective,* was not published until 1991.[6] Even the particular subfield of Jewish women's history has only begun to advance beyond compensatory history to raise issues that challenge the parameters of the study of Jewish history as a whole. What I do here, then, is first to describe and explore the implications of the contributions that feminist scholarship has made to the historiography of modern Jewry and then to suggest areas where feminist history is likely to prove most fruitful in reshaping our construction of the recent past.

Contributions of Feminist Scholarship

The feminist movement has stimulated scholars to reclaim the historical experience of Jewish women. We now have available serious accounts of such public figures as Henrietta Szold, the writer Anzia Yezierska, American labor activists Rose Schneiderman and Pauline Newman, and Lily Montagu, the leader of Liberal Judaism in England.[7] Jewish women's organizations are no longer dismissed as trivial subjects of historical research. Studies of the Jüdischer Frauenbund (the largest Jewish women's organization in Germany, 1904–38) and the American National Council of Jewish Women have illuminated their important role in Jewish social work and their struggle for recognition within the Jewish community.[8] Linda Kuzmack's *Woman's Cause* (1990), a comparative historical study of the Jewish women's movement in the United States and England at the turn of the century, explores the interaction of feminists in general and Jewish feminists in particular and enriches our understanding of how culture and social context have promoted different versions of female social activism.[9] The records of Jewish women's groups, whether explicitly feminist or not (as in most cases), have provided new sources for investigating the values of middle-class Jews in the first part of this century.

The Public-Private Dichotomy

Several historians have ably demonstrated how gender, ethnic-religious culture, and class have intersected to produce a female vision of philanthropy and social welfare and to challenge the public-private dichotomy. Participants in Jewish women's organizations eroded the boundaries of private and public space as they socialized issues originally seen to be of domestic concern.[10] For example, William Toll has found in his study of Portland Jewry that the involvement of female Jewish philanthropists in what was considered their natural constituency—that is, women and children—seems to have promoted the particular interest in political issues among female-led Jewish social welfare institutions that came into being during the Progressive era. That interest was sustained through the interwar years, when Jewish men active in communal affairs ceased to involve themselves in the politics of social reform. In Portland, then, it was the local chapter of the National Council of Jewish Women that took a stand on such issues as child labor, divorce, and birth control and maintained a committee to monitor governmental regulation of these matters.[11] In her history of the National Council of Jewish Women, Faith Rogow posits, from an analysis of the council's social welfare activity, that a specifically female version of philanthropy emerged within the organization. Indeed, she asserts that "Council members were among the first American Jews to define social reform work as an expression of Judaism rather than merely a civic obligation."[12] To give yet another example, in both the United States and Germany, Jewish women's organizations went public and actively combated Jewish participation in international white slave traffic at a time when Jewish men's organizations preferred to deal with the issue quietly, keeping it, as it were, in the family.[13]

Feminist historiography has also pointed to the impact of women's philanthropic and social welfare organizations on the self-definition of their members and on the normative roles of Jewish women as participants in Jewish communal life and in the larger society. By engaging in the Jewish education of their members, women's organizations have asserted the need for women to be fully prepared for serious involvement in the cultural, religious, *and* philanthropic dimensions of Jewish life. Both philanthropic and social welfare organizations expressed and reinforced the stance of middle-class Western Jews that women were by nature moral arbiters and the source of religiosity—initially in the home and ultimately in civic society. In her major new book, *The Making of the Jewish Middle Class,* Marion Kaplan demonstrates that in imperial Germany of the late nineteenth and early twentieth centuries, Jewish women's philanthropic activity in their own associations not only expanded the functions of the traditional female *chevra* (charitable association) but also served to integrate Jewish women into German society.[14] Finally, Beth Wenger has argued persuasively that American Jewish women's organizations did not simply expand the sphere of acceptable female activity, but renegotiated gender norms along with the division of public and private spheres. By defining their social welfare activity in terms of social housekeeping, they effectively masked the profound social change in the role of women and their civic responsibilities.[15]

The Family

Recognizing the importance of the public-domestic split and that women and men throughout much of history have functioned less as individuals than as family members, Jewish feminist historians, like other feminist historians, have addressed the study of the family as the central locus of most women's lives and a key arena for the articulation of gender relations and the interaction of private and public life. Although the traditional Jewish family has long been mythologized in communal literature as one of the sources of strength of Jewish culture, until recently it has been subject to little scholarly investigation.[16] In the past decade, feminist scholars and those influenced by their work have raised questions about the impact of the culture of Jewish family life on individual Jews and the Jewish community; about the division of labor, both paid and unpaid, among family members; and about the relation between women's roles in the family and their representation and self-definition.

Much of this recent scholarship has concentrated on immigrant Jewish women and their families in America, with American historians making important contributions to our understanding of immigrant Jewish women's lives. In *The World of Our Mothers,* for example, Sydney Stahl Weinberg is particularly successful in illuminating the texture of parent-daughter and sibling relations in the immigrant Jewish family and in demonstrating the embeddedness of immigrants and their children in the family network. Using sources as diverse as manuscript censuses, memoirs, and interviews, these studies have explored such topics as the place of work in Jewish women's lives and the differentials of female and male patterns of education and mobility.[17]

The focus on immigrant Jewish women and their families provides an opportunity to explore the intersection of three historical variables—class, gender, and ethnic culture.[18] Because Eastern European Jews and Italians migrated to America at the same time and settled in similar immigrant neighborhoods, sometimes side by side, several recent books have offered comparisons of the two ethnic groups. Both Elizabeth Ewen's *Immigrant Women in the Land of Dollars* and Judith Smith's *Family Connections* present new information on immigrant women's lives and demonstrate how families developed strategies for economic survival.[19] Both are sensitive to the connection between the domestic and public spheres. Yet both also display the pitfalls of cross-cultural gender comparisons. Although the authors are well versed in the current historiographic arguments about the relations between class and gender, they are more concerned with illustrating the shared experiences of working-class immigrants than delineating the cultural specificity of the two groups. This stance reflects an ideological presupposition that class and gender are more important than ethnicity and religion. It also reflects the relative ignorance of the two authors of the language and particularist culture of immigrant Jews.

Susan Glenn's book on immigrant Jewish women in America, *Daughters of the Shtetl,* takes the relation of class, gender, and ethnic culture more seriously than any previous work.[20] Linking home and family with the public sphere, Glenn demonstrates the fluidity and importance of the combination of work, political activism, and domesticity in the lives of immigrant Jewish women, even though wage work was a temporary stage and activism a transient phenomenon for most individuals. She also analyzes the cultural factors—some a legacy of shtetl life at the turn of the century—that accounted for the political activism of Jewish women through unions and in their neighborhoods. Finally, she describes the emergence of a Jewish version of the *new woman,* born of the immigrant Jewish woman's distinctive encounter with the possibilities of political self-expression and mobility and the greater gender equality offered by the New World. Despite its many strengths, this book, too, would have benefited from a thorough mining of available Yiddish sources.

The works of Ewen, Smith, Weinberg, and Glenn all make splendid use of oral history documentation to give voice to the experiences of Jewish women of Eastern European origin in America. Yet, in depicting the shtetl culture of the immigrants and their adaptation of traditional Jewish ways to the new environment of America, the authors are virtually dependent on a single book, Mark Zborowski's and Elizabeth Herzog's *Life Is with People,* a nostalgic, static depiction of shtetl culture based on interviews with immigrants just coming to the realization that the world of their childhood was destroyed in the Holocaust.[21] Any evaluation of how Jewish culture and the position of Jewish women changed as a result of migration must remain tentative until scholarly investigations are available of the development of Eastern European Jewish society, with particular attention to issues of gender and patterns of accommodation to modernity.[22]

Assimilation

In directing our attention to the family and its interaction with the world of work and politics, feminist scholarship has challenged how Jewish historians have treated what is perhaps the central issue of the modern period—assimilation. Much of modern Jewish historiography deals with the acculturation of Jews and their integration in the larger society. Because Jewish historians have conceptualized assimilation by investigating the public behavior of an urban male elite, they have described the processes of adaptation as being rapid and disruptive, as a traumatic break with the past. When women were included in discussions of assimilation, the female salon Jews of Germany at the turn of the nineteenth century—some two dozen, most of whom had converted to Christianity—were frequently the only ones specifically mentioned.[23] Deborah Hertz's monograph on this group shows just how unusual they were and how specific and rarefied was the social context in which they functioned.[24]

Kaplan's studies of middle-class Jewish women in the *Kaiserreich* have demonstrated the inadequacy of the prevailing view.[25] Her research has shown that women experienced assimilation differently than men, in part because they had to confront neither the workplace nor the university (from which women in Germany were excluded until 1908). She also discovered a surprisingly high level of "domestic Judaism" among acculturated Jewish women who were the wives and sisters of men portrayed as completely assimilated. For a variety of reasons, including the fact that German bourgeois culture expected women to be moderately religious and linked religious expression to familial sentiment, Jewish women served a conservative function in the German Jewish family. Their domestic and social activities were crucial to the maintenance and reshaping of ethnic-religious culture and their adaptation to a bourgeois life. In choosing the title *The Making of the Jewish Middle Class* for her book on women and the family, Kaplan implicitly asserted that placing women at the center of the story would illuminate general social processes, such as assimilation, that have been discussed without taking women into account.

Whether Kaplan's discoveries will be duplicated in other social contexts is not the central issue here. What is crucial is a recognition of the need to refine our definition of assimilation to allow for the experience of women and to include as a matter of course the private along with the public sphere. We particularly need to investigate how the private sphere prepared Jews in the modern period to function in the public sphere, what impact the public sphere had upon the private sphere, and how the boundaries between the two were negotiated at different times and places.

In expanding the parameters of assimilation to consider the role of women, historians have begun to explore the particular areas in which women functioned as agents of adaptation to the standards of the general society. Given their pivotal position as consumers and domestic managers, women assumed responsibility for changes in the aesthetic realm in terms of clothing, cuisine, and home decor. Patterns of consumption, therefore, offer an instrument for evaluating the gendered nature of acculturation. As the title of the book indicates, Andrew Heinze's *Adapting to Abundance* argues that the abundance of consumer goods in America, assumed to be characteristic of America, made it possible for immigrant Jews to acquire concrete symbols of the American way of life—including a piano in the parlor and a vacation in the country—even before they mastered English. They did so more quickly and passionately than other new immigrants. Advertising messages in the Yiddish press led to the transformation, the Americanization, of Jewish patterns of consumption. Immigrant Jewish women, drawing on their commercial experience in Eastern Europe, proved particularly adept at enhancing consumption by driving a hard bargain.[26] Similarly, Barbara Kirshenblatt-Gimblett's analysis of Jewish cookbooks published in America demonstrates both the adoption of middle- and upper-class American styles of cooking and entertaining by acculturated American Jewish women of German origin by the turn of the century and the introduction of an Americanized traditional cuisine to immigrant Jewish women from Eastern Europe.[27] Given the importance of food as a marker of ethnic (and for Jews, religious) identity, the incorporation of "kitchen Judaism" into studies of Jewish assimilation offers an opportunity to understand Jewish cultural transmission, adaptation, and the role of popular culture—much of it in the female domain—in the shaping of modern Jewish identities.

In considering the relation of family and assimilation, feminist historians, myself included, have demonstrated how Jewish communal leaders constructed a gendered vision of assimilation that itself reflected the acceptance of the values of the larger society and presented new expectations of women's roles. In America and in the countries of Western and Central Europe, the home was recast as the primary site for Jewish cultural transmission, and the Jewish mother was deemed the primary agent of the survival of Jewish culture and identity.[28] Consequently, postemancipation Jewish leaders, both lay and rabbinic, blamed Jewish women for the increasing assimilation they witnessed in the nineteenth and twentieth centuries. Despite the fact that men predominated among those who radically assimilated by intermarrying or converting to Christianity, the behavior of these Jewish men was attributed to the failure of their mothers to instill in them a commitment to Judaism. This communal criticism of the Jewish mother articulates a change in the normative role of Jewish parents in the socialization of their children. In traditional Jewish societies, after all, religious socialization was not a task conferred only upon mothers, even though the impact of mothers was recognized and respected; fathers and communal institutions also assumed major responsibility. The criticism of Jewish mothers thus reflects a transformation in prescribed gender roles; it may also reflect a change in the actual social function of women within the family. Additionally, the changed representations of Jewish mothers in twentieth-century American Jewish popular culture—from revered center of the family, responsible for its spiritual and physical welfare, to the controlling and guilt-inducing Sophie Portnoy— illuminate the growing tension felt by third-generation sons regarding assimilation and their own Jewish identity and responsibilities.[29] Certainly, the issue of familial roles deserves additional study if we are to understand the transmission and transformation of Jewish identity in the modern period. The implications of the transferal to women of virtually the total responsibility for the socialization of Jewish children must also be examined.

Community and Political Activism

In addition to challenging how assimilation has been conceptualized and studied, feminist scholarship has suggested, albeit tentatively, that conventional approaches to the study of Jewish communities and Jewish political activism are also inadequate. The recognition of Jewish women's organizations as an integral part of the Jewish community was simply the first step. Feminist historians have also come to recognize that the absence of women from so much of the organized, or "official," Jewish community may indicate that Jewish women have experienced community and implicitly defined it differently than men. Once this question is raised, the historian confronts a double challenge: first, to find and identify female forms of community, when formal institutions do not suffice; and second, to read women's behavior, both within organizations and in informal social networks, for signs of group self-definition and communal solidarity.

In these matters, once again the most substantial work has involved the immigrant Jewish community in America. My own investigation of the kosher meat boycott of 1902,[30] a female-initiated and led political action, brought me to the realization that women found community in informal neighborhood networks that provided personal and political support. Meat boycotts, rent strikes, and women's political campaigns (such as the mobilization of opinion in favor of female suffrage) all drew upon female solidarity and a sense of community rooted in the neighborhood. The stoops and sidewalks of immigrant areas of settlement provided women with a community where interpersonal relations were more important bonds than institutional affiliations and where political activism, spurred by shared needs and collective power, was expressed neither in political parties nor in unions (where unmarried Jewish women were prominent among female activists) but in the streets. In the kosher meat boycott, middle-aged married women were able to enforce it through a combination of moral and physical persuasion. They felt no inhibition, for example, in opening their neighbors' cholent pots as they brought them to the bakery on Friday afternoon to make sure that they were vegetarian. Just as anthropologist Barbara Myerhoff in *Number Our Days* investigated the communities that developed around the men's and women's benches outside the Jewish Senior Citizens Center in Venice, California,[31] and the activities of the center, so historians should learn to recognize all community forms, even though they lack bylaws and membership rolls.

When women did affiliate with formal Jewish communal and political institutions, they may have brought gender-linked concerns to their communal activity. I have already alluded to the specific social welfare agendas of the National Council of Jewish Women and the Jüdischer Frauenbund. It is no accident that Hadassah assumed responsibility within the framework of Zionist institutions in Palestine for the health of women and children. Alice Kessler-Harris has found that it was female activists within the predominantly Jewish garment-workers unions who took the lead in pressing for the educational and recreational programs that became the pride of those unions.[32] Within their labor organizations they expressed a vision of community that saw workers and their families as persons concerned with meaningful leisure-time activity as well as wages and good working conditions.

These few examples suggest that historians attuned to gender must continue to ask what concepts of community and civic welfare women have brought to the institutions they have joined and the informal associations that seem to have characterized much of their experience. Such a research agenda will doubtless bring more nonelite Jews, men as well as women, within the purview of historical scholarship and may yield new insight into those factors that sustain or undermine Jewish communal solidarity.

In looking at the Jewish community as broadly conceived, one sees that the extent of its support for political activism by women and on women's issues calls for more investigation. Within the immigrant Jewish community there was widespread support for female political initiatives. In the New York state elections of 1915 and 1917, which considered the issue of women's suffrage, immigrant Jewish neighborhoods in New York City had the highest percentage of affirmative votes of any electoral district in the city.[33] Although both Elinor Lerner and Susan Glenn have tried with some success to account for this striking show of support, a full explanation will be possible only when we know more about gender norms and practices among different classes of Jews in Poland and Russia.

Spirituality

Although feminist scholarship has explored women's spirituality in settings as diverse as twelfth-century medieval Europe, nineteenth-century America, and contemporary times, its impact has yet to be felt in the study of modern Judaism. Chava Weissler's important work on the spirituality of Ashkenazi women in seventeenth- and eighteenth-century Central and Eastern Europe demonstrates that women in traditional Jewish societies had their own texts and developed their own contexts for spiritual expression. It also suggests that women, who were clearly subordinate to men in traditional Judaism, found the means to empower themselves through liturgical texts that subverted their subordination.[34] As yet we do not have an equivalent exploration of Jewish women's spirituality in the generations that witnessed the decline of traditional Jewish learning, practice and belief, and the adaptation of Judaism to the philosophical and social currents of the modern world. Ellen Umansky's work on Montagu and on Tehilla Lichtenstein, one of the founders of Jewish science, provides us with models of the female religious leader but does not treat the religious self-definition of the masses of Jewish women.[35] Although her collection of women's writings about their spiritual concerns, *Four Centuries of Jewish Women's Spirituality: A Sourcebook* (edited with Dianne Ashton), is a valuable resource, its emphasis is on the contemporary, and its contents await further interpretation.[36]

The analysis of the religious lives of Jewish women in the modern period is all the more important because in western societies since at least the mid-nineteenth century, religion was increasingly perceived as falling within the domain of women. Several books have pointed to the feminization of Christianity among the middle classes in both nineteenth-century America and France, for example; a parallel phenomenon was observed in Reform Jewish congregations at the same time.[37] (Of course, positions of religious leadership remained in the hands of men.)

It is important that Jewish scholarship explore the extent to which Judaism in the modern world has been "feminized" and to consider the implications of whatever feminization has occurred, as well as the representation of Judaism as feminized. In their investigations of the early years of the National Council of Jewish Women, both Sue Elwell and Faith Rogow have highlighted the strong impulse toward Jewish religious education that animated the leaders of the young Council. These educational efforts seem to have been nourished by the enormous spiritual hunger of Jewish women to understand Judaism and to incorporate it in their lives. The religious functions of women's philanthropic societies and synagogue sisterhoods also deserve sustained attention, perhaps using the methods of social anthropology. The recent work of Pamela Nadell on Conservative and Reform sisterhoods and of Jenna Weissman Joselit on Orthodox sisterhoods suggests the need to take these organizations seriously in considering the relation of women to the modern synagogue and the gendered division of religious life in Judaism.[38] The relatively high level of gender segregation in traditional Judaism and even in modern Judaism (though to a lesser extent) necessitates the explicit study of the Jewish religious and social experience of women.

The task of reclaiming the history of Jewish women's religious experience is not an easy one. Unfortunately, unlike anthropologists who study contemporary communities, we cannot be participant-observers of the past. Yet, if we are to comprehend the full scope of Jewish religious experience, we must labor to reconstruct the "popular Judaism" of women with the fragmentary sources available to us, just as historians like Natalie Zemon Davis have explored the popular religion of late medieval and early modern Christians through the creative interpretation of scattered archival references. The Judaism that we study, even in the university, is not the whole of Judaism but an elite religious tradition that informs the popular religion of the masses but is not identical with it. In turning our attention to the religious experience of Jewish women, then, we are broadening our conception of Jewish religious experience as a whole.

Future Research

The excuse of insufficient sources no longer explains the failure to include women and gender concerns in the study of modern Jewish history. Several decades of social history have demonstrated that one can discover new sources by asking new questions of old material or by recognizing as historically significant experiences that were previously unseen even when documented. The kosher meat boycott I analyzed, for example, was front-page news in all the Yiddish newspapers in New York for three weeks and was covered in the mainstream English press as well. The leaders of the boycott were even listed by name and address, enabling me to trace them in the New York state manuscript census of 1905. Several American historians had mentioned this incident only in passing; virtually all Jewish historians turned the page looking elsewhere for the important business of history. Moreover, as the books on immigrant Jewish women I have mentioned and other books on social history have demonstrated, oral history is a valuable resource to express what would otherwise remain silent. Oral testimonies are simply another text to be interpreted, along with letters, memoirs, and official documents.

Finally, to the issue of power. It is crucial for Jewish historians to explore the representation of women as well as their status in all periods of history, both to incorporate women into Jewish history and to analyze the cultural values and norms of Jewish communities in different times and places. Let me suggest some questions that come to mind in considering the modern period. What role did the status of women play in efforts at religious reform in the nineteenth and twentieth centuries? We know that the German Reform synods of the mid-nineteenth century dutifully expressed concern for enhancing the status of women within the synagogue, but we do not know how that resolution was implemented at the grassroots level. What does the concern of acculturated Jewish men for the treatment of women within traditional Judaism tell us about their sense of Jewish identity in the modern Western world? How much dissent did women express about their public religious role? What roles have women played in general in the development of all varieties of modern Judaism and in the growth of Jewish educational, philanthropic, and cultural institutions? What kind of model of appropriate feminine behavior have those institutions conveyed to Jewish women at different times and in different societies?[39] What cultural tensions are expressed in changing gender roles? Finally, how did the growing professionalization of philanthropy and education affect women's opportunities to achieve positions of leadership?

Turning to secular Jewish movements, such as Zionism and Jewish socialism, we find a theoretical commitment to women's equality that clearly attracted some women to those movements. New research on women in the early years of the Zionist movement indicates, however, that the model of the *halutz,* the Zionist pioneer, was rooted in male standards and offered equality to women only if they met those standards.[40] Indeed, the model of the halutz was more masculine in terms of Western cultural ideals than was the image of the male in traditional Judaism. Zionism deprecated traditionally female qualities as well as female work. Moreover, women pioneers, who were considered less valuable than their male compatriots, encountered overt discrimination at the hands of Zionist agencies in access to jobs and financial assistance. In the socialist movements as well equality was limited in practice by assumptions about the sexual division of labor, both in the workplace and in the home. The efforts of women to achieve respect and positions of authority within these movements, as well as how the movements confronted the "woman question," merit further research.

There is one more issue of power to discuss: the power to define the parameters of the field. Jewish historians have generally lagged behind their colleagues in the general field of history—resisting, or remaining ignorant of, the theoretical advances that feminist scholarship brings to the discipline, including techniques of anthropological and literary analysis that erode the last shreds of historical positivism. It is no accident that many of the feminist scholars who have contributed to our understanding of Jewish women's experience have been trained as American or European historians, not as Jewish historians, and have come to the study of Jewish women from outside the field of Jewish history. The marginality of most scholars within the general discipline of Jewish history who work on the history of Jewish women and the continued (and indefensible) marginality of American Jewish history have served to rationalize the attitudes of indifference of many Jewish historians. Graduate students in Judaic studies have gotten the message: if you want to succeed in this field, do not write your dissertation on a woman's topic. Wait until you have tenure.

The resistance to feminist inquiry in the study of Jewish history is all the more ironic given the symmetry between the Jewish question and the woman question. The woman question is as important a prism for viewing Jewish culture and its assumptions as the Jewish question is for viewing Western culture and its assumptions—the latter point being an assertion we Jewish historians frequently make. Regrettably, we know far more about the Jewish question in general culture than we do about the woman question in Jewish culture. Yet there are many issues that call for an examination of the relation of gender and Jewish culture, for example: that in strongly antisemitic cultures, such as turn-of-the-century Germany and Austria, both antisemites and self-hating Jews depicted male Jews as weak and manipulative (that is, womanish) and dismissed Judaism as too gentle and feminine; that antisemites were, virtually without exception, antifeminist; that male Jewish writers of our own time have created some of the most repugnant stereotypes of Jewish women that exist.[41] Gender representations of every variety need to be examined as a means of exploring how Jews in modern times have understood the complexities and ambiguities of their identity and their accommodation to the larger society and of probing more deeply the role of "the Jew" in the culture and imagination of the modern West.

I have by no means fully assayed the dimensions of the challenge of feminist scholarship to modern Jewish history. As feminist scholarship continues to grow in methodological sophistication—and I should add that some of the most methodologically stimulating work is being done in this field—and as Jewish historians become more receptive to the challenge of that scholarship, the writing of Jewish history will be enriched in ways that we can now only begin to grasp.

Notes

1. For the development of feminist historical scholarship, see Gerda Lerner, *The Majority Finds Its Past* (Oxford: Oxford University Press, 1979), 3–14, 160–80; Joan Wallach Scott, *Gender and the Politics of History* (New York: Columbia University Press, 1988), 15–27; Jane Lewis, "Women, Lost and Found: The Impact of Feminism on History," in Dale Spender, ed., *Men's Studies Modified* (Oxford: Pergamon, 1981), 55–72. On the trends in feminist scholarship in anthropology, history, education, philosophy, and literature, see Ellen DuBois, Gail P. Kelly, Elizabeth L. Kennedy, Carolyn W. Korsmeyer, and Lillian S. Robinson, *Feminist Scholarship: Kindling in the Groves of Academe* (Urbana: University of Illinois Press, 1987), esp. 15–84.

2. Joan Kelly-Gadol, "Did Women Have a Renaissance?" in *Becoming Visible: Women in European History* (Boston: Houghton Mifflin, 1977), 139–63.

3. Michelle Zimbalist Rosaldo, "Woman, Culture, and Society: A Theoretical Overview," in Michelle Zimbalist Rosaldo and Louise Lamphere, eds., *Woman, Culture, and Society* (Stanford: Stanford University Press, 1974), 17–42. For another dichotomization, see Sherry Ortner, "Is Female to Male as Nature Is to Culture?" ibid., 67–87.

4. Scott, *Gender and the Politics of History,* 42.

5. On the uses of the objective-subjective division, see Dale Spender, introduction to *Men's Studies Modified,* 1–9.

6. *Jewish Women in Historical Perspective,* ed. Judith Baskin (Detroit: Wayne State University Press, 1991). Its dozen essays range from the biblical period to the twentieth century.

7. See Charlotte Baum, Paula Hyman, and Sonya Michel, *The Jewish Woman in America* (New York: Dial, 1976); on Henrietta Szold, see Joan Dash, *Summoned to Jerusalem* (New York: Harper and Row, 1979); on Anzia Yezierska, see Louise Levitas Henriksen, with Jo Ann Boydston, *Anzia Yezierska: A Writer's Life* (New Brunswick, N.J.: Rutgers University Press, 1988); on Jewish women labor activists, see Alice Kessler-Harris, "Organizing the Unorganizable: Three Jewish Women and Their Union," *Labor History* 17 (winter 1976): 5–23, rep. in Milton Cantor and Bruce Laurie, *Class, Sex, and the Woman Worker* (Westport, Conn.: Greenwood, 1977), 144–65; and "Where Are the Organized Women Workers?" *Feminist Studies* 3 (fall 1975): 92–110; on Lily Montagu, see Ellen Umansky, *Lily Montagu and the Advancement of Liberal Judaism: From Vision to Vocation* (New York: Edwin Mellen, 1983); on Jewish women activists in America, see June Sochen, *Consecrate Every Day: The Public Lives of Jewish American Women, 1880–1980* (Albany: SUNY Press, 1981).

8. On the major German Jewish women's organization, see Marion Kaplan, *The Jewish Feminist Movement in Germany: The Campaigns of the Jüdischer Frauenbund* (Westport, Conn.: Greenwood, 1979); on the National Council of Jewish Women, see Sue Levi Elwell, *The Founding and Early Programs of the National Council of Jewish Women: Study and Practice as Jewish Women's Religious Expression*, Ph.D. diss., Indiana University, 1982; and Faith Rogow, *Gone to Another Meeting: The National Council of Jewish Women, 1893–1993* (Tuscaloosa: University of Alabama Press, 1993).

9. Linda Gordon Kuzmack, *Woman's Cause: The Jewish Woman's Movement in England and the United States* (Columbus: Ohio State University Press, 1990).

10. In addition to the sources cited in n.7, see William Toll, *The Making of an Ethnic Middle Class: Portland Jewry over Four Generations* (Albany: SUNY Press, 1982), 55–64; Beth Wenger, "Jewish Women of the Club: The Changing Public Role of Atlanta's Jewish Women (1870–1930)," *American Jewish History* 76(3) (March 1987): 416–38; and Evelyn Bodek, "'Making Do': Jewish Women and Philanthropy," in Murray Friedman, ed., *Jewish Life in Philadelphia 1830–1940* (Philadelphia: ISHI Publications, 1983), 143–62.

11. Toll, *The Making of an Ethnic Middle Class*, 55–62; "The Female Life Cycle and the Measure of Jewish Social Change: Portland, Oregon, 1880–1930," *American Jewish History* 72(3) (March 1983): 331–32; and "A Quiet Revolution: Jewish Women's Clubs and the Widening Female Sphere, 1870–1920," *American Jewish Archives* 41 (spring/summer 1989): 7–26.

12. Rogow, *Gone to Another Meeting*, 40.

13. Baum, Hyman, and Michel, *The Jewish Woman in America*, 170–75; Kaplan, *The Jewish Feminist Movement*, 103–45; and Edward Bristow, *Prostitution and Prejudice: The Jewish Fight against White Slavery, 1870–1939* (New York: Schocken, 1983), 231–41, 249–72.

14. Marion Kaplan, *The Making of the Jewish Middle Class: Women, Family, and Identity in Imperial Germany* (New York: Oxford University Press, 1991).

15. Beth Wenger, "Jewish Women and Voluntarism: Beyond the Myth of Enablers," *American Jewish History* 79(1) (autumn 1989): 16–36.

16. An exception to this rule was Jacob Katz's pioneering analysis of the traditional Jewish family in Eastern Europe. See his "Marriage and Sexual Life among the Jews at the End of the Middle Ages," *Zion* 10 (1944): 21–54; "Family, Kinship, and Marriage among Ashkenazim in the Sixteenth to Seventeenth Centuries," *Jewish Journal of Sociology* 1 (1959): 4–22; and *Tradition and Crisis: Jewish Society at the End of the Middle Ages* (New York: Schocken, 1961), 135–56.

17. On immigrant Jewish social mobility with attention to gender, see Thomas Kessner, *The Golden Door* (New York: Oxford University Press, 1977). On the role of women as participants in immigrant Jewish loan societies, see Shelly Tenenbaum, *A Credit to Their Community: Jewish Loan Societies in the United States, 1880–1945* (Detroit: Wayne State University Press, 1993); on immigrant women's lives, with a focus on the domestic, see Sydney Stahl Weinberg, *The World of Our Mothers* (Chapel Hill: University of North Carolina Press, 1988). See also Norma Fain Pratt, "Culture and Radical Politics: Yiddish Women Writers, 1890–1940," *American Jewish History* 70(1) (Sept. 1980): 68–90.

18. For an exploration of the importance of this intersection, see my "Culture and Gender: Women in the Immigrant Jewish Community," in David Berger, ed., *The Legacy of Jewish Migration: 1881 and Its Impact* (Brooklyn: Social Science Monographs–Brooklyn University Press, 1983), 157–68.

19. Elizabeth Ewen, *Immigrant Women in the Land of Dollars: Life and Culture on the Lower East Side, 1890–1925* (New York: Monthly Review Press, 1985); Judith E. Smith, *Family Connections: A History of Italian and Jewish Immigrant Lives in Providence, Rhode Island, 1900– 1940* (Albany: SUNY Press, 1985).

20. Susan A. Glenn, *Daughters of the Shtetl: Life and Labor in the Immigrant Generation* (Ithaca: Cornell University Press, 1990).

21. Mark Zborowski and Elizabeth Herzog, *Life Is with People: The Jewish Little-Town of Eastern Europe* (New York: International Universities Press, 1952).

22. A recent contribution to our understanding of an aspect of traditional Jewish culture and its impact on all family members is Immanuel Etkes, "Marriage and Torah Study among the *Lomdim* in Lithuania in the Nineteenth Century," in David Kraemer, ed., *The Jewish Family: Metaphor and Memory* (New York: Oxford University Press, 1989), 153–78.

23. See, e.g., the classic works of Jacob Katz, *Out of the Ghetto: The Social Background of Jewish Emancipation, 1770–1870* (Cambridge: Harvard University Press, 1973); and Michael A. Meyer, *The Origins of the Modern Jew* (Detroit: Wayne State University Press, 1967).

24. Deborah Hertz, *Jewish High Society in Old Regime Berlin* (New Haven: Yale University Press, 1988). For earlier analyses of the salon Jewesses, see Meyer, *The Origins of the Modern Jew*, 85–114; and Katz, *Out of the Ghetto*, 120–21.

25. Marion Kaplan, *The Making of the Jewish Middle Class;* "Tradition and Transition: The Acculturation, Assimilation and Integration of Jews in Imperial Germany—A Gender Analysis," *Leo Baeck Institute Yearbook* 27 (1982): 3–35; "For Love or Money: The Marriage Strategies of Jews in Imperial Germany," *Leo Baeck Institute Yearbook* 28 (1983): 263–300; and "Priestess and Hausfrau: Women and Tradition in the German-Jewish Family," in Steven M. Cohen and Paula E. Hyman, eds., *The Jewish Family: Myths and Reality* (New York: Holmes and Meier, 1986), 62–81.

26. Andrew Ritchie Heinze, *Adapting to Abundance: Jewish Immigrants, Mass Consumption, and the Search for American Identity* (New York: Columbia University Press, 1990), esp. 105– 17.

27. Barbara Kirshenblatt-Gimblett, "Kitchen Judaism," in Susan L. Braunstein and Jenna Weissman Joselit, eds., *Getting Comfortable in New York: The American Jewish Home, 1880– 1950* (New York: Jewish Museum, 1990), 77–105.

28. See my "The Modern Jewish Family: Image and Reality," in Kraemer, *The Jewish Family*, 179–93; and Jenna Weissman Joselit, "'A Set Table: Jewish Domestic Culture in the New World, 1880–1950," in *Getting Comfortable in New York*, 50–68.

29. Baum, Hyman, and Michel, *The Jewish Woman in America*, 235–51; Gladys Rothbell, "The Jewish Mother: Social Construction of a Popular Image," in *The Jewish Family: Myths and Reality*, 118–38; Riv-Ellen Prell, "Rage and Representation: Jewish Gender Stereotypes in American Culture," in Faye Ginsburg and Anna Lowenhaupt Tsing, eds.,

Uncertain Terms: Negotiating Gender in American Culture (Boston: Beacon, 1990), 248–66; and Norma Fain Pratt, "Transitions in Judaism: The Jewish American Woman through the 1930s," *American Quarterly* 30(5) (winter 1978): 681–702.

30. Paula E. Hyman, "Immigrant Women and Consumer Protest: The New York City Kosher Meat Boycott of 1902," *American Jewish History* 70(1) (Sept. 1980): 91–105.

31. Barbara Myerhoff, *Number Our Days* (New York: Dutton, 1978), 4–5. On women's "domestic Judaism," see pp. 232–68.

32. Alice Kessler-Harris, "Organizing the Unorganizable," in *Class, Sex, and the Woman Worker,* 155.

33. Elinor Lerner, "Jewish Involvement in the New York City Woman Suffrage Movement," *American Jewish History* 70(4) (June 1981): 442–61; and her "Family Structure, Occupational Patterns, and Support for Women's Suffrage," in Judith Friedlander et al., eds., *Women in Culture and Politics* (Bloomington: Indiana University Press, 1986), 223–36.

34. Chava Weissler, "The Traditional Piety of Ashkenazic Women," in Arthur Green, ed., *Jewish Spirituality from the Sixteenth-Century Revival to the Present* (New York: Crossroad, 1987), 245–75; "Women in Paradise," *Tikkun* 2(2) (April–May 1987): 43–6, 117–20; "The Religion of Traditional Ashkenazic Women: Some Methodological Issues," *Association for Jewish Studies Review* 12(1) (spring 1987): 73–94; "'For Women and for Men Who Are Like Women': The Construction of Gender in Yiddish Devotional Literature," *Journal of Feminist Studies in Religion* 5(2) (fall 1989): 7–24.

35. Umansky, *Lily Montagu;* and "Spiritual Expressions: The Religious Lives of Twentieth Century American Jewish Women," in *Jewish Women in Historical Perspective,* 265–88; and "Piety, Persuasion and Friendship: Jewish Female Leadership in Modern Times," in Paula M. Cooey, Sharon A. Farmer, and Mary Ellen Ross, eds., *Embodied Love: Sensuality and Relationship as Feminist Values* (New York: Harper and Row, 1987), 189–206.

36. *Four Centuries of Jewish Women's Spirituality: A Sourcebook,* ed. Ellen Umansky and Dianne Ashton (Boston: Beacon, 1992).

37. Bonnie Smith, *Ladies of the Leisure Class: The Bourgeoises of Northern France in the Nineteenth Century* (Princeton: Princeton University Press, 1981), 93–122; Ann Douglas, *The Feminization of American Culture* (New York: Knopf, 1977).

38. Pamela Nadell, "The Beginnings of the Religious Emancipation of American Jewish Women," paper delivered at the Berkshire Conference of Women Historians, 8 June 1990; Jenna Weissman Joselit, *New York's Jewish Jews: The Orthodox Community in the Interwar Years* (Bloomington: Indiana University Press, 1990), 97–122.

39. See, e.g., Maxine S. Seller, "Defining Socialist Womanhood: The Women's Page of the *Jewish Daily Forward* in 1919," *American Jewish History* 76(4) (June 1987): 416–38; and Nancy B. Sinkoff, "Educating for 'Proper' Jewish Womanhood: A Case Study in Domesticity and Vocational Training, 1897–1926," *American Jewish History* 77(4) (June 1988): 572–99.

40. Deborah Bernstein, *The Struggle for Equality: Urban Women Workers in Pre-State Israeli Society* (New York: Praeger, 1987), and her edited *Pioneers and Homemakers: Jewish Women*

in Pre-State Israel (Albany: SUNY Press, 1992); and Dafna Izraeli, "The Zionist Women's Movement in Palestine, 1911–1927: A Sociological Analysis," *Signs* 7(1) (1981): 87–114. For important primary source material, see Rachel Katznelson Shazar [Rubashow], ed., and Maurice Samuel, trans., *The Plough Woman: Memoirs of the Pioneer Woman of Palestine* (New York: Herzl, [1932] 1975). On women in the Bund, see Baum, Hyman, and Michel, *The Jewish Woman in America*, 77–78, 87; and Harriet Davis-Kram, "The Story of the Sisters of the Bund," *Contemporary Jewry* 5 (fall/winter 1980): 27–43. On the masculine tropes in European Zionist ideology, see Michael Berkowitz, *Zionist Culture and West European Jewry before the First World War* (Cambridge: Cambridge University Press, 1993).

41. On the convergence of antisemitic and antifeminist attitudes, see Shulamith Volkov, "Antisemitism as a Cultural Code: Reflections on the History and Historiography of Antisemitism in Imperial Germany," *Leo Baeck Institute Yearbook* 23 (1978): 25–46; on Jewish self-hatred, see Sander Gilman, *Jewish Self-Hatred: Anti-Semitism and the Hidden Language of the Jews* (Baltimore: Johns Hopkins University Press, 1986), 200–201, 243–46, 267. I address these issues at greater length in *Gender and Assimilation: Roles and Representations of Women in Modern Jewish History* (Seattle: University of Washington Press). In press.

Toward a Feminist Sociology
of American Jews

In surveying the literature on the sociology of American Jews, one becomes immediately aware that the recent proliferation of feminist theory and research has had minimal impact on this field. Not only have most sociologists of American Jews largely ignored the distinctive nature of women's experiences, but many perpetuate women's invisibility by applying to all Jews research results based on studies of Jewish men. Only a small proportion of the literature addresses comparative questions based on gender, and even these few studies use gender as a variable rather than as an analytic category. The feminist insight that gender is a fundamental basis of all social life and relations has not yet permeated research in this subject. By ignoring the various ways in which gender hierarchies shape all aspects of Jewish society, sociologists have produced an incomplete and at times distorted picture of contemporary American Jewish life. The incorporation of gender analyses into research, concepts, and theories in this field would lead not only to the reconceptualization of existing paradigms but to the development of new ones.

To analyze the integration of women and gender in the sociology of American Jews, we conducted an extensive review of the literature guided by the following questions: Where do women appear in the literature and in what contexts? When is gender seen as a variable and when is it incorporated into the theoretical apparatus as a category of analysis? Who are the sociologists of American Jews, and what concerns are primary to them? Which paradigms and theories dominate the field, and how do they shape its research agenda, leading to the dominance of some issues and the invisibility of others?

To address these questions we analyzed sociological books

and articles that have been published in the past twenty years. We discovered that the first full-length sociological studies of Jewish women did not appear until 1991 and that many of the books published before then did not include gender analyses. We reviewed the many articles published in four specialty journals—*American Jewish Year Book, Contemporary Jewry, Jewish Journal of Sociology,* and *Jewish Social Studies*—and found that the majority did not include women. We also conducted a computer search for articles on Jews in general sociological journals. Our search located few articles on Jews in mainstream journals; most research on Jews appeared in specifically Jewish publications.

Why has the sociology of American Jews not yet incorporated an understanding of the salience of gender in all aspects of its research? We offer three explanations for this exclusion. One pertains to the small size of the field: there are few practitioners, only a small percentage are involved in training graduate students, and the dominance of the field by men has meant that women's experiences and concerns have not been central.

The second explanation focuses on the fact that the broader discipline of sociology has failed to incorporate gender as an analytic category in a way that would reconstruct scholarship in most subfields of the discipline.[1] In their now-famous essay, "The Missing Feminist Revolution in Sociology," Judith Stacey and Barrie Thorne assert that one reason feminist scholarship has not yet transformed the field is the dominance of quantitative studies, which tend to use gender as a variable rather than as an analytic category.[2] This approach ignores the obvious power divisions that underlie gender differences. The dominance of statistical approaches to the study of contemporary American Jews produces the same lack of gendered analyses. Unfortunately, even in the one area of sociology that has been revolutionized by the incorporation of feminist insights, the study of the family, the sociology of American Jews lags behind its parent discipline. In most research in this field, women are not yet seen as distinct actors with their own perspectives and priorities.

The general lack of gendered analyses in the sociology of American Jews is also due to a preoccupation with the effects of modernization on Jewish continuity. In the shadow of the Holocaust, when a third of world Jewry was murdered, it is not surprising that the issue of survival has become of monumental importance to American Jews, including sociologists of American Jewish life. *Look* magazine's provocative 1964 article "The Vanishing American Jew" sent shivers up the spines of American Jews and sparked serious discussion in academic circles.[3] The titles of two relatively recent books—*Jewish Continuity and Change: Emerging Patterns in America* by Calvin Goldscheider and *American Assimilation or Jewish Revival?* by sociologist Steven M. Cohen, two of the most influential contemporary sociologists of American Jews—reflect the centrality of the survivalist theme. Both explore the question, Does modernization weaken the Jewish community, threatening its survival, or do the changes brought about by modernization simply mean that new, vital forms of Jewish cohesion and expression have emerged?[4]

In our analysis and critique of the modernization paradigm, we make two distinct but related points. First, research in this model does not incorporate gender into the study of patterns of assimilation and cohesion—hence our understanding of the very nature and meaning of these concepts is limited. Second, although we recognize that questions about group survival and continuity are indeed important, their overwhelming dominance in the field results in a failure to explore other issues in American Jewish life and culture, such as women's experiences and the influence of gender. By developing a feminist critique of the existing field, we are led to new questions that challenge the existing paradigms and seek to reformulate as well as transcend them.

The Modernization Paradigm

Given that sociologists of American Jews have focused primarily on the question of ethnic and religious cohesion, the subfields that have emerged in the discipline—including studies of identity, family, economic roles, and religious observance—represent thematic ways of exploring issues of Jewish continuity. In this chapter we review research in these areas to assess their level of integration of women's experiences and gender as an analytic category. Our critical review follows the well-known feminist model that distinguishes various stages of development of feminist perspectives in a discipline: (1) the critique of the invisibility of women, (2) research that studies women's lives according to the concepts and paradigms developed in scholarship based on men (what feminist activist Charlotte Bunch refers to as "add women and stir"),[5] and (3) studies that employ gender as a basic analytic category and therefore lead to paradigm shifts in the discipline. In the second part of the chapter, we discuss the limitations of the modernization paradigm for providing knowledge about women's lives and show how research that begins with women's experiences leads to new thematic foci and analytic models.

Women's Invisibility

Within the various subfields of the sociology of American Jews, many scholars have contributed to women's invisibility by generalizing for all Jews studies based only on men and ignoring the salience of gender as a factor that affects all aspects of social life. For example, although feminist scholars have documented the importance of gender identity to a person's overall sense of self, social scientific studies of Jews generally failed to examine how gender shapes Jewish identity.[6] In 1989, the Wilstein Institute of Jewish Policy Studies hosted a major conference on Jewish identity and published the proceedings as *Jewish Identity in America*.[7] The goals of the conference were to reflect on the nature of Jewish identity, the methods for assessing and measuring it, and the possibilities for nurturing it in the American environment. None of the presentations, however, considered the impact of gender on the nature of Jewish identity. In the introduction to the volume, editors David Gordis and Yoav Ben-Horin acknowledge this gaping omission: "Perhaps the single clearest addition to a revised conference agenda would be that of the changing perceptions and roles of women in American Jewish life, a complex and dynamic process of potentially enormous significance, though as yet only partially understood, let alone worked out."[8] Although it is commendable that the editors recognized the omission, the invisibility of gender as a category of analysis in a social-scientific conference that took place as recently as 1989 is significant and attests to the field's continuing failure to incorporate feminist research and insights.

In the first article in the Wilstein volume, "Sociological Analysis of Jewish Identity," Bruce Phillips provides an overview of the major themes in sociological studies of Jewish identity, discussing how key studies have conceptualized and measured changes in Jewish identity, the usefulness of these measures, and new directions for future sociological work.[9] When they ignore gender differences, sociologists of American Judaism produce an incomplete, and sometimes even flawed, picture of how social change actually affects Jews. Gender is never mentioned as a variable that could have a meaningful impact on the experience and manifestation of Jewish identity. Although many of the measures Phillips outlined are likely to be different for men and women—friendship patterns, for example—the studies cited generally do not consider the effects of gender on such indices of Jewish identification.[10] Since friendship patterns are an important index of ethnic cohesion, further attention to women might uncover new dimensions of Jewish solidarity based on women's patterns of interpersonal relations.

Jewish identity has been extensively studied by Cohen. In his books *American Modernity and Jewish Identity* and *American Assimilation or Jewish Revival?* he uses data collected in Boston and New York, respectively, to analyze the relation of Jewish identity to social class, family trends, politics, generation, geographic mobility, and education.[11] He found that Jewish identification varies with age and stage in the life cycle. Younger single Jews tend to be less "Jewishly" identified than those who have married and have children. The choice of a marriage partner also affects Jewish identification: although intermarried Jews retain some forms of ritual practice, communal affiliation, or close friendship ties and say that they rear their children as Jews, they are less Jewishly involved than the in-married. Cohen's studies also show that though upward economic mobility erodes ritual practice, it also promotes institutional affiliation, which is another measure of ethnic identification. Unfortunately, Cohen rarely considers how these various factors might differentially affect women's and men's involvement in the Jewish community.

Political attitudes are another important index of ethnic solidarity: if Jews share a particular political perspective, such as liberalism, then the absence of "internal conflict" in this realm promotes cohesion.[12] However, despite political polls and research studies that demonstrate that political attitudes often vary by gender, social scientists who study American Jewish political behavior have repeatedly ignored gender as a category for analysis.[13]

For example, Cohen found high levels of liberal attitudes among American Jews. They are more likely than other Americans to support social welfare spending, quotas for disadvantaged minorities, the Equal Rights Amendment, gay rights, and government support for abortion.[14] Although he correlated these political attitudes with generation, age, education, income, and ritual observance, he did not provide a breakdown by gender. Similarly, in *Cosmopolitans and Parochials* Samuel Heilman and Cohen provide survey data about the attitudes of Orthodox Jews toward such social and political issues as premarital sex, homosexuality, abortion, the Equal Rights Amendment, affirmative action, the death penalty, and public aid to private schools. Yet they did not investigate possible gender differences on these issues. Even for a question that we would clearly expect to show some gender differences—whether "a wife should make her own decisions even if she disagrees with her husband"—the authors present their findings in terms of how a respondent's level of Orthodox observance shaped her or his responses, ignoring an opportunity to examine a significant aspect of Orthodox Jewish life—how men and women respond to the gender roles prescribed in the religion.[15] Their study cannot yield any insights into the important question of possible gender differences in Orthodoxy since they do not even report on the gender composition of their sample.

Social scientific concern with how well Judaism can withstand the forces of modernization and maintain high levels of ethnic and religious cohesion has promoted a great deal of research on religious observance among Jews. Scholars have found that most American Jews celebrate the High Holy Days, Hanukkah, and Passover. The majority of Jewish parents circumcise their sons, and a very large percentage of Jewish children celebrate a bar mitzvah or bat mitzvah. Other observances, such as lighting Sabbath candles, keeping kosher, and attending synagogue regularly, are practiced much less frequently.[16] Rarely do these studies report whether women were included in the sample. Thus they provide no way of assessing whether there are gender differences in the overall rates of religious observance or whether particular rituals are more likely to be practiced by members of one sex than the other.

Most of the sociological literature on Orthodox Jews does not compare women and men in terms of their belief in God, an important index of religious identification. In *Cosmopolitans and Parochials,* Heilman and Cohen asked respondents about their level of belief in God and presented their findings in terms of the locations of respondents on the Orthodox continuum. Ninety-seven percent of those who fell in the traditional category and 85 percent of those labeled centrists definitely believed in God.[17] Similarly, in Janet Aviad's study of newly Orthodox Jewish men and women studying in Israeli yeshivot (Jewish institutes of learning), she reported that two-thirds of her respondents stated that they believed in God.[18] But neither study differentiated the women's experiences from those of the men. Although we do not know the gender composition of the Heilman and Cohen sample, two-thirds of Aviad's subjects were male. It is possible, then, that this finding about belief in God pertains primarily only to Jewish men and not all Jews.

By failing to ask about how female and male attitudes, beliefs, and practices might differ, these major quantitative works on American Jewish life provide an incomplete picture of the effects of modernization on Jewish survival. This point is highlighted by Cohen in a section of *American Assimilation or Jewish Revival?* in which he does provide some gender comparisons. He shows that by failing to control for gender, studies measuring the effects of Jewish education on identity reached the counterintuitive conclusion that those who had absolutely no formal Jewish education scored higher on measures of Jewish identity than those who had considerable instruction. This finding makes sense only when one takes into account the fact that

Jewish women, including those from highly observant homes, generally have significantly less exposure to Jewish education than men do. Therefore, the correlation between education and identification is different for women than for men.[19]

Add Women and Stir

In contrast to studies measuring religious observance, political attitudes, and identity, in which women and gender are generally invisible, studies of the Jewish family and economic and educational attainment often do provide comparative data by gender. In these studies, however, gender is used as a variable rather than a category of analysis. This means that instead of developing theoretical models that take into account the gendered and therefore hierarchical organization of all social institutions, research questions simply compare women and men along discrete variables. Thus, these studies do not ask those critical questions of power differentials that would be central to a feminist analysis, nor do they explore women's experiences in a way that might lead to new concepts and paradigms.

Family

Because Jewish families are seen as central to Jewish continuity, sociologists of American Jewry have studied them extensively. From a social-psychological standpoint, families play a critical role in the transmission of ethnic and religious identity; from a demographic perspective, families are indispensable for procreation and hence numerical survival. Rising divorce rates, postponement of marriage, delayed childbearing, and intermarriage are central foci of research on American Jewish families. Whether or not these trends will lead Jews to have a sufficient number of children not only to replace them but to ensure ethnic survival is the subject of fierce debate.

That American Jews have followed the pattern of other Americans in experiencing rising divorce rates is of interest to social scientists who are concerned that the "breakdown" of the family might adversely affect Jewish continuity.[20] When researchers examine subgroup differences in the Jewish population, they find that the Orthodox are the least likely to divorce and native-born Reform Jews the most likely.[21] Thus, religious observance still has a negative effect on marital dissolution. In addition, Cohen and others have found that after controlling for social class, education, and other factors, Jews are less likely to divorce than their non-Jewish counterparts.[22] Thus, although Jews are adopting the general American pattern of a rising incidence of marital breakup, they have a relatively high rate of marital stability.

In *Jewish Continuity and Change*, Goldscheider provides comparative data on the divorce rates of Jewish women and men, as well as on their non-Jewish counterparts. Although the differences in the rates of divorce between Jewish females and males is small (3 percent versus 5 percent), as is the difference between Jewish and non-Jewish men (5 percent versus 7 percent), the disparities between Jewish and non-Jewish women are greater (3 percent versus 15 percent). Similarly, Jewish women experience a much slower rise than non-Jewish women in the proportion of those divorced.[23] Although Goldscheider offers these gender differences, he does not explore their implications for understanding gender differences in Jewish life.

Students of the American Jewish family have asked whether Jews are more likely than other groups to postpone marriage and childbearing, a trend that could have an impact on demographic continuity and hence ethnic survival. Both Cohen and Goldscheider found that the high rates of education, professionalism, urbanization, and cosmopolitanism among Jews do result in their postponement of marriage.[24] Delayed marriage, however, does not necessarily imply nonmarriage. In comparing women and men in terms of age at first marriage, Goldscheider found that for women, higher levels of educational attainment lead to delayed marriage, whereas for men higher income levels are correlated with later marriage.[25] The reasons for these differences are not explored, however. Further explication of these findings are therefore needed to understand the different contexts and circumstances of women's and men's lives.

Delayed marriage is a concern for Jewish demographers because it has important repercussions for fertility patterns.[26] On the basis of national and Boston data showing fertility patterns, Cohen asserts that Jewish couples are having fewer than the average 2.2 children needed for replacement.[27] In contrast, Goldscheider uses data based on women's projections of their expected family size to argue that Jewish parents will have a sufficient number of children for replacement. For Goldscheider, expected family size is a reliable measure for Jewish population growth since Jewish women "plan and attain their desired family size with extreme accuracy."[28]

Increasing rates of Jewish intermarriage are an obvious focus of social scientists concerned with Jewish continuity. Families headed by intermarried couples are far more common today than they were earlier in the century. The intermarriage rate jumped from 7 percent in the 1940s to 17 percent in the early 1960s to 32 percent by the early 1970s. During the late 1980s, more than half of all born Jews married spouses who were born Gentile.[29] Until recently, Jewish women married outside the faith less often than men, leading one sociologist to label them reluctant exogamists.[30] A 1974 study found that "for every Jewish woman who intermarries, between two and four Jewish men will do the same."[31] For Rela Geffen Monson, the fact that boys were able to fulfill parental expectations by achieving high occupational status, while for girls there was "only one way to do so—marry a nice Jewish professional and produce grandchildren," helped to account for the differential intermarriage rates.[32] By 1990, however, women's intermarriage rates had caught up with those of men.[33] Nevertheless, the rate of women who convert to Judaism upon marriage to a Jew far exceeds that of men who convert. According to the 1990 National Jewish Population Survey, two-thirds of "Jews by choice" are female.[34] Focusing nearly exclusively upon the implications of these findings for Jewish survival, researchers have failed to ask how gender differences in conversion rates might reflect power differentials between females and males. A feminist approach would greatly enhance our understanding of this phenomenon.

Economic Roles and Educational Attainment

Goldscheider's *Jewish Continuity and Change,* based on a 1975 Boston sample, is one of the few studies to analyze male and female economic roles systematically. He found that 40 percent of Jewish men living in Boston were in the professions, and 28 percent held managerial positions; among Jewish women who work outside the home, 49 percent were in professional and managerial jobs. The levels of professionalism of both Jewish men and women exceeded those of their non-Jewish counterparts. Similarly, only 10 percent of Jewish men and 7 percent of Jewish women in the sample could be classified as working-class, compared to half the non-Jewish men and one-third of the non-Jewish women.[35]

In terms of education, 62 percent of Boston's Jewish males and 48 percent of Jewish women graduated from college, while only a quarter of non-Jewish men and about 17 percent of non-Jewish women attained a comparable educational level. College attendance was nearly universal for young Jews; more than 90 percent of young men and 87 percent of young women attended college.[36] In a New Jersey sample, Jewish women aged twenty-five to thirty-four had completed bachelor's and master's degrees nearly as often as men but were far less likely to complete medical, dental, legal, or doctoral degrees. Men, even in the youngest age cohorts, were twice as likely as women to practice law. Although women in large cities on the East and West Coasts are moving into prestigious professional fields with relatively large salaries, women in the Midwest and smaller cities are still concentrated in the lower-paid fields of teaching and social work.[37] Compared to the total female population in 1970, Jewish women's median income was 50 percent higher.[38] Although researchers use these data to demonstrate Jewish distinctiveness, a factor that encourages cohesion, they do not explore the reasons for gender differences among Jews.

Sylvia Barack Fishman has done feminist scholarship a great service by synthesizing educational and occupational data about women from available community studies.[39] Fishman finds that Jewish women follow the general pattern of contemporary American women in having much higher rates of labor force participation than they did in the 1950s. In 1957, only 12 percent of Jewish women with children under six worked outside the home; today, the majority of Jewish mothers with small children resemble other mothers in working outside the home at least part time. Although ultra-Orthodox women almost always leave the labor force when their children are born, they often resume paid work once the children enter school. Fishman attributes these significant changes to the need for two incomes to maintain a middle-class standard of living, as well as to employment opportunities, job preparation, and social pressure. "Younger Jewish women are more likely than their mothers to have used their schooling to prepare for specific careers, and they are often less willing to let those careers lie fallow while they become full-time homemakers. Younger women are also more likely to be surrounded by peers who urge them to work, rather than to become homemakers."[40]

Although these comparative quantitative studies offer important statistical data, their explanatory powers are limited by the inclusion of gender only as a comparative variable rather than as an analytic category. A feminist perspective that highlights how women and men have differential access to economic and educational opportunities and to power in the Jewish and larger society would more profoundly explicate the gender differences found. These data call for a feminist analysis that focuses on such matters as occupational stereotyping, pay inequities, "tracking," and gender socialization to understand fully gender differences in Jewish educational and occupational attainment.

A Feminist Reconceptualization of Modernization

When gender is employed as an analytic category in the study of Jewish social life, researchers find that there are significant gender differences in the ways modernization affects Jews. The studies reviewed here suggest that women are more resistant than men to forces of assimilation. These findings call for a revision of the classic modernization paradigm, which has assumed that the forces of modernity affect Jewish men and women in the same way.

For example, Herbert Gans's study of Park Forest (1958), a postwar suburban community south of Chicago, explored the implications of the friendship patterns of Jewish women on their level of involvement in the Jewish community. "It seems clear that the women live a greater part of their life within the Jewish community, and are more concerned with matters relating to ethnic problems. In Park Forest, they inaugurated social contacts with other Jews, set up the informal Jewish community, and put some pressure both on the men and on the children to keep their social contacts within the ethnic group."[41]

Gans's findings support other research showing that women tend to be more involved than men in the "work of kinship"—the creation and maintenance of family and community ties.[42] This difference suggests that those who study ethnic continuity must attend to gender differences in order to formulate a more subtle theory of ethnic assimilation and cohesion, one that takes account of the different patterns of ethnic affiliation that might be found among women and men.

That women and men may have different agendas when they participate in Jewish communal life was another important finding of Gans's Park Forest study. When the members of the Jewish community proposed the establishment of a Sunday school, the male residents voted to create the Sunday school as part of a synagogue, while the women insisted that building a synagogue could wait and that all energy should focus on establishing the school. "The men who wanted a congregation were thinking of an adult Jewish community training its children through a congregational Sunday school for eventual membership in the adult Jewish group. The women represented the child-oriented conception; they wanted a school for the children."[43]

Another important locus of Jewish identity is involvement with Jewish organizations. Several studies show that women are much more likely to be members of Jewish organizations than are men.[44] For example, Barry Tuchfeld has explained that the extensive women's involvement in Jewish organizations he found in Knoxville—91 percent were active in Jewish organizations—was related to perceived social expectations and pressure. As one woman respondent said, "You'll be a social outcast if you don't belong to Hadassah."[45] Tuchfeld also found that women are much more likely than men to limit their volunteer activities to Jewish organizations—nearly twice as many women as men do not belong to any non-Jewish organizations. He suggests that since the home is the traditional locus of Jewish women's activities, they are less likely than men to have the sort of contacts in the larger society that would lead to membership in non-Jewish organizations and that men are more likely to have business attachments that require involvement in organizations with a diverse membership.[46] These different rates of participation in Jewish and non-Jewish organizations can have an important impact on women's and men's affiliation with the Jewish community.

The number of children at home and the rate of full-time labor force participation have little impact on Jewish women's communal involvement. For women working part time, their employment actually has a positive effect on voluntarism. In her 1990 study of Jewish women's voluntarism, Alice Goldstein concluded that "increasing feminism may make it desirable for women to participate in organizations that allow them to share in the community power structure. Career goals may encourage memberships as . . . entrees to networks that might otherwise be unavailable. And [having] fewer children at home may remove some of the demands on women's time and allow more time for volunteer activity."[47]

Attitudes toward Israel have also been seen as important indices of Jewish identification. When sociologist Jay Brodbar-Nemzer compared these attitudes by gender, he found that Jewish women are stauncher supporters of Israeli policy than men: women are less willing to criticize the Jewish state publicly (32 percent versus 44 percent) and less willing to return occupied territories after Israel is guaranteed peace (34 percent versus 49 percent). In light of research indicating that women tend to be more liberal than men, this finding is surprising.[48] Brodbar-Nemzer attempted to resolve this paradox by explaining that the "same underlying dynamic that predisposed women to be more dovish on global issues may have the opposite effect regarding Israel."[49] Just as women are dovish from a desire to prevent harm to those they care for, Jewish women might advocate a strong Israeli defense in order to prevent fellow Jews from being hurt.

Jewish women's support of Israel is also apparent in their rates of *aliyah* (immigration to Israel). In 1970, women constituted 60 percent of American Jews between the ages of 20 and 29 who moved to Israel. Furthermore, of those who made aliyah, women were more likely than men to remain.[50]

This evidence suggests that women may score higher than men on pro-Israelism, a measure of Jewish identity.

Given the basic distinctions between males and females in Jewish religious obligations, the paucity of data comparing their rates of religious observance is striking. The few available studies, ranging from analyses of college students to analyses of elderly Jews, find that women are actually the more religiously observant.[51] These studies corroborate the finding of historian Marion Kaplan that through their roles in the family, Jewish women in imperial Germany maintained Jewish traditions longer than their husbands did. Although most historians of the period report that "Jews" had integrated into the broader culture and assimilated, Kaplan found this to be a more accurate description of the men than of the women. She writes: "Religion waned more slowly among Jewish women. . . . First, they experienced less dissonance between religious practice and their daily routines than men. Their private world was more traditional than modern. . . . Second, Jewish women could exert some control in the privacy of family and home, whereas Jewish men faced obstacles to the performance of their religious duties resulting from business obligations and travel. . . . Third, popular ideology . . . encouraged female religiosity. . . . Finally, Jewish women considered it easier to consider themselves religious that did Jewish men."[52] By maintaining religious traditions in the home and extended kinship and community networks and by transmitting the culture to the next generation, Jewish women contributed significantly to the continuation of Jewish life.

The incorporation of women's experiences thus not only adds to our knowledge but calls for revising basic concepts and paradigms in the field. Some of the research findings summarized here strongly suggest that we can no longer conceive of modernization as a monolithic force affecting women and men in identical ways, since women exhibit higher levels of ritual observance, stronger support for Israel, higher levels of communal activity, and do more of the work of maintaining the kinship networks and friendship patterns of American Jews. The evidence reviewed in this chapter, as well as other historical and anthropological research, calls for a revision of the modernization paradigm to recognize the fundamental role of gender in shaping Jews' response to modernity.

Beyond Modernization

When we begin from the standpoint of women, we are led to an even more fundamental critique of the modernization paradigm—one that goes beyond the failure to incorporate gender as an analytic category. The dominance of this paradigm has led to a failure to ask meaningful questions about women's experiences, the role of gender in shaping all aspects of Jewish life, and the power hierarchies that result from the gender distinctions in Jewish religion and culture. By focusing nearly exclusively on issues of cohesion and assimilation, researchers have subordinated women's priorities and points of view to the question of ethnic survival. For example, in 1971, sociologist Marshall Sklare expressed his concerns that women's changing roles were leading to smaller families and hence threatening the survival of American Jewry.

> Traditionally the Jewish woman has seen herself as a maternal figure whose status derived from her role as mother and homemaker. Within the short space of a generation a decisive change took place. Instead of "living for her children" as the expression had it, the Jewish woman of the second generation "owed it to herself" to receive an education . . . to interest herself in organizational activity, to travel, and (for a much smaller group) to pursue an advanced degree and/or a career. . . . A new orientation to the role of motherhood was developed—to be the mother of a large family was to be a beast of burden, an animal yoked to the treadmill, a primitive.[53]

This analysis reveals that the obsession with "what is good for the Jews" can lead sociologists to ignore women's own perspectives of their lives and thus to distort understanding of the issues facing contemporary Jews. In fact, Sklare's fears concerning the dangers that women's educational and career advancements may pose for Jewish survival are not corroborated by empirical evidence. In his Boston study, Goldscheider found that the most educated Jewish women had the highest expectations for family size and that expected family size was slightly higher for working than for nonworking Jewish women.[54]

A decade later sociologist Chaim Waxman analyzed the effects of various contemporary changes in Jewish families on the cohesion of the community. He concluded that "nontraditional family forms are not able to provide a framework within which the individual would acquire a stable sense of *Jewish* identity and *Jewish* reality."[55] Waxman acknowledges that the institutions and culture of Jewish life do not readily absorb single-parent families, but he does not acknowledge that most single-parent households, Jewish and not, are headed by women. Waxman's concern with Jewish continuity pushes into the margin questions about the daily lives of single Jewish mothers, the economic pressures they face, and their acceptance, or lack of it, in the Jewish community.

In *America's Jews in Transition,* Waxman shows how Jewish organizations make it difficult for women to rise to leadership positions. His concern, however, is with the negative implications of that inequality for Jewish survival. If women are alienated, they will seek leadership roles outside their ethnic community.[56] A feminist perspective, in contrast, would not focus exclusively on Jewish continuity but instead would develop an analysis of the institutionalized inequality within the Jewish community. It would provide a framework for exploring the structural and ideological barriers to women's exclusion, for analyzing the macro- and micromechanisms through which this inequality is maintained, and for examining how discrimination hurts individual women.

The dominance of the modernization paradigm can lead to the subordination of women as individuals. Women come to be seen as agents who either maintain or thwart Jewish continuity. In contrast, when questions are asked from a woman's standpoint, new themes emerge in the study of Jewish life, leading to fresh concepts and more inclusive theories.

Making Gender Central
Religion

Much of what we know about Jewish women's experiences comes from qualitative studies of Orthodox Jews in which gender, not group survival, is central to the analysis. Since the division of gender roles is the sharpest in the Orthodox community, this group provides a ready resource for exploring the pivotal role of gender in shaping the religious life of Jews. In 1991 the first two book-length sociological studies of Jewish women were published, Debra Renee Kaufman's *Rachel's Daughters: Newly Orthodox Jewish Women* and Lynn Davidman's *Tradition in a Rootless World: Women Turn to Orthodox Judaism.*[57] Both books begin with the experiences of *ba'alot teshuvah* (Jewish women who were not brought up as Orthodox but decided to become Orthodox as adults) and explore how these women negotiate within traditional religious institutions in order to find a meaningful place for themselves. Both authors develop an analysis of the meaning of Orthodoxy from the point of view of women and the reasons contemporary secular women are attracted to it.

In her interview-based study of married *ba'alot teshuvah* who had been Orthodox for several years, Kaufman presents the women's perspectives on their role in Orthodoxy. Despite their acceptance of traditional roles, these women do not necessarily view themselves as second-class citizens of the Jewish community. Rather, they turn their "devalued status in the secular world into a high-status aspect that the Orthodox community confers."[58] Orthodoxy appealed to ba'alot teshuvah precisely because of its positive valuation of the feminine and the female in the context of the nuclear family. Kaufman concludes that there are strong similarities between ba'alot teshuvah and radical feminists since both groups participate in sex-segregated communities that celebrate gender differences.

Davidman, in her comparative ethnographic study of modern Orthodox and Lubavitch Hasidic communities, also found that clarity about gender roles was a primary attraction for the new recruits. Her findings suggest, however, that ba'alot teshuvah are not postfeminists; rather, they are attracted to Orthodoxy because they see it as a socially legitimate alternative to feminism. Instead of the feminist program of broader gender options, sexual liberation, an emphasis on careers, and acceptance of a variety of family patterns, Orthodox Judaism proposes clearly circumscribed gender norms, control of sexuality, assistance in finding a partner, and explicit guidelines for nuclear family life.

The two types of Orthodox communities—the modern Orthodox and the Lubavitch—differed greatly in their willingness to blend traditional conceptions with modern gender ideals. Davidman shows how these differences led to the attraction of different types of women to each setting. The Lubavitch Hasidic community, which prohibits premarital physical contact between women and men, publicly eschews birth control, and trivializes women's interest in professionalism, attracted relatively young women who were not yet established in careers or independent lives. In contrast, the modern Orthodox community offered a complex blend of the traditional and modern that attracted single, professionally established, independent adults, who nevertheless were seeking assistance in forming nuclear families.

These two studies, in which women are the primary focus, build on but also extend in a feminist direction an earlier book about newly Orthodox Jewish men and women, Herbert Danzger's *Returning to Tradition: The Contemporary Revival of Orthodox Judaism*.[59] Danzger reported that most of the newly Orthodox are women and that women are more likely than men to turn to a religious way of life out of a desire to have a family. He provides a gendered analysis of the routes by which women and men enter the world of Orthodoxy. Many of the men were religious seekers who ventured into yeshivot to seek deeper knowledge. The women were less likely to be on a spiritual quest; they tended to become Orthodox through synagogue programs and marriage.

Although Danzger's study offers important insights into gender differences, most of his research focuses on male yeshivot, so that his data base on women is therefore much scantier. For example, although Danzger had written of the diverse approaches to resocialization in female and male yeshivot, his chapter "Practices and Beliefs" deals with the daily routine of life in a male yeshiva without telling the reader explicitly that this is the male version of the institution.[60] This makes it difficult to discern at what point his discussion includes women and where it refers to men only.

A systematic comparison of the role of gender in the recruitment and resocialization of newly Orthodox women and men at the Lincoln Square Synagogue in Manhattan is provided in a recent article by Davidman and Arthur Greil.[61] Like Danzger, they found that male recruits were more likely to have been active seekers and to have found Orthodoxy on their own, while women were more likely to enter through personal contacts. They also found that although men emphasized ethical and workplace concerns in discussing the appeal of Orthodoxy, women stressed issues related to family and personal relations.

Davidman and Greil also found that these newly Orthodox men reported higher levels of belief in God than did ba'alot teshuvah at Lincoln Square. Twenty of the twenty-six men interviewed professed a belief in God, compared to fourteen of the twenty-five female interviewees. Thus, belief in God may well be gender-differentiated among Jews, as it is among Christians, albeit in the opposite direction: among Christians, women report higher levels of belief in God than men do.[62] One possible reason for this difference between Jews and Christians is that in Jewish law women are not obligated to pray every day, while men are required to pray three times daily. Belief in God may be generated and reproduced through the daily process of praying to Him. By making gender central to the study of Jewish beliefs, we can also see how Jews differ in the patterns found in the mainstream sociology of religion literature, which is largely based on studies of Christian or new religious movements.

When women are made the focus of sociological inquiry, new dimensions of Orthodox Jewish life can be revealed. In examining the impact of their observance of a distinctly women's ritual—*mikveh* (ritual bath)—on women's feelings about menstruation, Sheila Jubelirer Siegel introduced a new topic in the study of Orthodox Jewish life. She hypothesized that compared with nonmikveh users, mikveh users would experience more menstrual distress since they were considered unclean during their periods but would also have a more positive attitude toward menstruation since they have more familiarity with their bodies. In fact, her research found no significant differences between the two groups.[63] Further research is needed to explore how the performance of this intimate ritual affects the users' sense of themselves as women and their relation to Judaism.

Samuel Heilman's ethnographic study of contemporary Orthodox life, although focused largely on men's experiences, nevertheless provides a microanalysis of how gender inequality is structured into the very architecture and social organization of the synagogue he studied. The physical division of the synagogue into men's and women's sections (and the allocation of the larger section to men) means that women have fewer spots for socializing with others. The location of the women's section, at the rear of the synagogue behind the young boys who sit at the rear of the men's section, suggests that young boys have a higher status than adult women in the sanctuary. Women have less access to ritual objects, no vote in synagogue affairs, and no obligation to pay dues. When women signal men to be quiet during synagogue services, their pleas are ignored. In contrast, if women are talking, men will sometimes stop the service and wait for the noise to cease. Men are allowed to invade women's space—they can use the women's section when women are absent—but women rarely use areas such as the men's foyer when men are not around.[64]

In general, we know little about the religious life of non-Orthodox women, although survey research shows that Conservative and Reform congregations, like those of Christian churches, are largely made up of women.[65] We have detailed descriptions of the decisions made by institutional elites that have allowed women to participate in religious life (for example, to be counted as part of the minyan [religious quorum] and to be ordained as rabbis).[66] In her ethnographic study of Reform Jews, Frida Kerner Furman missed a valuable opportunity to explore whether or not prayer had different meanings for Reform women and men. Although most of her respondents did not mention spirituality as a motivating force for attending Sabbath services, many did discuss the importance of community. In light of research suggesting that God is more central to the religious identity of Orthodox Jewish men than women and that women are more community-oriented than men, a gendered analysis of Reform Judaism could have yielded interesting results.[67]

Similarly, Charles Liebman based his important study of Reconstructionism in American Judaism on an overwhelmingly male sample consisting of synagogue presidents and leaders of a secular male Jewish organization. Despite the absence of data on the religious beliefs and attitudes of women, he concluded that "American Jews may act like Reconstructionists, but they neither think nor talk like them." According to Pamela Nadell's feminist critique of Liebman, "because men are normative one can generalize about the behavior of the entire American Jewish community from an exclusively male sample."[68]

Family

As is true of investigators of other aspects of American Jewish life, family sociologists have generally studied Jewish families from the perspective of Jewish continuity. The research agenda produced by this concern does not lead to work that "seeks to advance the general conceptualization of the sociology of the family or frames its projects in terms of theoretically interesting questions."[69] For example, a focus on ethnic cohesion tends to highlight the factors that affect the stability of the Jewish family and its levels of affiliation with the organized Jewish community. Some of these studies nostalgically bemoan the loss of the traditional Jewish family, which is stereotypically portrayed as a warm, loving refuge from hostile external forces. Feminist analyses have shown that the family has been in many ways a locus of conflict. Under this lens, the gilded image of the wonderful Jewish family of old dissolves and we are left with the project of building interdisciplinary feminist research that analyzes the complexities and varieties of Jewish family life.

Within feminist sociology, the division of household labor is seen as an important index of power distribution. We know little about how Jews across denominations divide household chores, or how the various levels of ritual observance affect female and male attitudes toward the division of labor in the home. Many home-centered rituals, such as the Sabbath and holiday feasts, require considerable preparation. How does women's increased participation in the labor market affect the level and nature of ritual observance that takes place in the home?

Recent feminist literature, such as Arlie Hochschild's *The Second Shift*, argues that despite all the apparent changes in women's roles since the feminist revolution, real changes in women's lives have been minimal.[70] The double burden of working outside the home while still being primarily responsible for the home and children means that many women have even less leisure time than they did before they were "liberated." Egon Mayer has argued that modern technology has liberated even Orthodox Jewish women from the kitchen and has led to changing roles in Orthodox families.[71] However, feminist studies report that increased levels of technology have not reduced women's efforts in the home but have simply led to higher standards of efficiency and cleanliness.[72] We need to ask whether Jewish women think that modern appliances truly liberate them from the kitchen and that roles at home have changed. When women are made central to the analysis, researchers begin by closely examining the daily realities of women's lives. From this new research, sociologists of American Jewish life might inductively produce new concepts for studying the Jewish family and new theoretical models about what is significant.

For example, a feminist analysis would turn our attention to gender politics in Jewish families, a topic that is rarely examined. The available statistical data suggest some obvious power differentials. Women who marry Orthodox men tend to become Orthodox more often than do men who marry Orthodox women. Among intermarried couples, more non-Jewish women convert to Judaism than do non-Jewish men,[73] so that intermarried Jewish fathers are more likely than intermarried Jewish mothers to have children who identify themselves as Jews.[74] It would be interesting to explore in a microsociological way how couples make these decisions and through the decisions negotiate and manifest power in their relationship. A woman's standpoint would provide a model for analyzing the connection between these statistics and the ways in which gender is hierarchically structured into the larger Jewish community.

Power inequities are also manifested in research that shows that Jewish women are still much more likely than Jewish men to move from a community to accompany their spouses and less likely to move for a new job. In his analysis of why young people had left one community, Murray Frost found that 12 percent of men, compared to a third of women, migrated to accompany their spouses. A third of the young men compared to a fifth of women left for occupational reasons. The percentages of men and women who migrated to pursue an education, however, were nearly identical.[75]

A gender-sensitive examination of the various manifestations of women's inequality would also focus attention on the concentration of poverty among Jewish elderly and single-parent-headed households, two groups that have a higher proportion of women. Poverty within the Jewish community, as in the general community, has been feminized. The elderly are disproportionately represented in the low-income categories, and the elderly poor are more likely to be women. In Minneapolis, for example, of the over-sixty-five population in the 1980s, the median income of males was $16,800, while that of women was only $6,500.[76]

In addition to age, divorce drastically depresses women's income levels, but not men's. In Rochester, for example, annual household incomes of Jewish married men and women were almost equal in 1987. More than half of the divorced women, however, earned less than $20,000 a year, while none of the divorced men earned less than $30,000. In fact, the salaries of 44 percent of the divorced men fell between $40,000 and $74,000.[77] As divorce rates rise, this trend of income disparity is bound to continue.

Feminist students of the family highlight the variety of family forms that exist; a feminist analysis of contemporary Jewish life reveals that there is no one type of Jewish family. We encourage the development of research that examines the diverse familial experiences of such subgroups as new immigrants (such as Iranians, Israelis, and Russians), single mothers, elderly people, and gays and lesbians. Feminist scholarship highlights the variety of experiences that are found even within a single family: each family is experienced very differently by its various members, depending on their position by gender and age, and thus their status in the household hierarchy varies.[78]

Other new thematic areas would be opened by research in which women are the focus of inquiry, such as studies of the participation of Jewish women in social movements (Jewish and secular) and their mutually reinforcing involvement in the home and community. Historical research shows how Jewish women have moved fluidly between home and public life by becoming politically active about issues of great import to their lives.[79] Although there are not yet any studies of Jewish women's participation in the recent wave of the women's movement, nor any in-depth sociological research on the contemporary Jewish women's movement, Steven Cohen has provided an analysis of the origins and initial development of the Jewish feminist movement in the 1970s.[80] His research highlights how a group of New York women, committed to the seemingly contradictory ideals of feminism and Judaism, negotiated these tensions and carved out a movement for social change in American Judaism. Their experiences in the counterculture and in secular feminism, combined with their continued dedication to Judaism, led them to seek changes in Jewish religious and communal life and to integrate feminism and Judaism into their lives. As feminists, they have organized women's prayer groups and have fought for equality in Jewish law and for the right of women to become rabbis and cantors. Following the model of secular feminism, they have founded a variety of nonhierarchical grass-roots organizations and a journal, *Lilith,* to disseminate their views.[81]

Another example of women organizing to expand their roles in the Jewish community is provided by Shelly Tenenbaum in her sociohistorical study of immigrant Jewish credit networks. She found that early-twentieth-century Jewish women established women's Hebrew free loan societies and women's credit cooperatives in such diverse communities as South Bend (Indiana), Los Angeles, Hartford, and New York. As leaders of these economic facilities, Jewish women moved outside the private sphere and into the public realm of communal service. Tenenbaum's research illustrates that women have not been passive subjects of male exclusionary practices. Rather, in response to discriminatory policies, they have acted together to establish independent institutional networks. In doing so, they demonstrated how to build on their social networks and friendship patterns in establishing public institutions that meet their particular needs.[82]

The central insights of our feminist analysis of the sociology of American Jews have relevance for other disciplines in Jewish studies. In particular, we refer to new perspectives on the division between public and private spheres; a new sense of women as agents who act to shape their lives; insights into gender differences in religious experience; and the view of the family as a place where conflict and power struggles take place alongside more positive emotions. Each of these themes, which emerge when we ask questions in terms of women rather than ethnic continuity, can be explored from many perspectives across disciplines.

For example, sociological studies showing how Jewish women moved between domestic life and the public sphere echo the exploration of this theme in history, anthropology, the Bible, rabbinics, and literature. By analyzing the complex patterns of interaction between the private and public domains, feminist scholars reveal that the division between these spheres is more permeable than has been presumed. Similarly, feminist sociological scholarship that shows Jewish women as actors who shape their own and their families' lives is part of an emerging interdisciplinary picture of women as agents with their own means of accessing power at home and in their communities.

The theme of gender differences in religious experience emerges in contemporary sociological studies as well as in research in other fields. Feminist anthropologists, historians, folklorists, biblical scholars, and theologians have begun to explore how Judaism, a highly gender-differentiated religion, produces different forms of religious expression for women than for men. Insights from these various approaches can be combined to produce a model of how gender differences shape the nature of Jewish communities across time and space.

Although feminist research in many disciplines is producing new perspectives on Jewish families, there is an absence of feminist sociological scholarship in this area. Sociologists of American Jews should draw upon the emerging insights in the general discipline of sociology and in the Jewish studies fields of anthropology, history, and literary and film studies to develop new foci in the study of Jewish families. The task of developing interdisciplinary, gender-sensitive research on Jewish families is an exciting one. By beginning with themes that are central to an understanding of gender, feminist scholarship has the potential to build bridges between the humanities and the social sciences.

Notes

1. Dorothy Smith, "A Sociology for Women," in Julia Sherman and Evelyn Torten Beck, eds., *The Prism of Sex* (Madison: University of Wisconsin Press, 1980), 137–38; Margaret L. Anderson, *Thinking about Women: Sociological Perspectives on Sex and Gender,* 2d ed. (New York: Macmillan, 1988), 18; Dorothy E. Smith, "Sociological Theory: Methods of Writing Patriarchy," in Ruth A. Wallace, ed., *Feminism and Sociological Theory* (Newbury: Sage, 1989), 57; Jessie Bernard, "Re-Viewing the Impact of Women's Studies on Sociology," in Christie Farnham, ed., *The Impact of Feminist Research in the Academy* (Bloomington: Indiana University Press, 1987), 193–216; and Mary Jo Deegan, "Women and Sociology: 1890–1930," *Journal of History of Sociology* 1(1) (1978): 11–34.

2. Judith Stacey and Barrie Thorne, "The Missing Feminist Revolution in Sociology," *Social Problems* 32(4) (April 1985): 301–16.

3. Thomas B. Morgan, "The Vanishing American Jew," *Look,* 5 May 1964.

4. Calvin Goldscheider, *Jewish Continuity and Change: Emerging Patterns in America* (Bloomington: Indiana University Press, 1986); and Steven M. Cohen, *American Assimilation or Jewish Revival?* (Bloomington: Indiana University Press, 1988).

5. Charlotte Bunch, *Passionate Politics: Essays 1968–1986—Feminist Theory and Action* (New York: St. Martin's, 1987), 140.

6. J. Money and A. A. Erhardt, *Man, Woman, Boy and Girl: The Differentiation and Dimorphism of Gender and Identity from Conception to Maturity* (Baltimore: Johns Hopkins University Press, 1972); and Laurel W. Richardson, *The Dynamics of Sex and Gender* (Boston: Houghton Mifflin, 1981).

7. David M. Gordis and Yoav Ben-Horin, eds., *Jewish Identity in America* (Los Angeles: Wilstein Institute, 1991).

8. Ibid., vii. Similarly, Arnold Dashefsky and Harold Shapiro acknowledged that they had omitted women from their study *Ethnic Identification among American Jews: Socialization and Social Structure* (Lexington, Mass.: Lexington Books, 1974), 33.

9. Bruce Phillips, "Sociological Analysis of Jewish Identity," in Gordis and Ben-Horin, eds., *Jewish Identity,* 3–24.

10. For feminist analyses of how women differently create and maintain personal relationships, see Nancy Chodorow, *The Reproduction of Mothering: Psychoanalysis and the Sociology of Gender* (Berkeley: University of California Press, 1978); and Carol Gilligan, *In a Different Voice: Psychological Theory and Women's Development* (Cambridge: Harvard University Press, 1982).

11. Steven M. Cohen, *American Modernity and Jewish Identity* (New York: Tavistock, 1983); and idem, *American Assimilation.*

12. Calvin Goldscheider and Alan S. Zuckerman, *The Transformation of the Jews* (Chicago: University of Chicago Press, 1984), 187. For the importance of liberalism on Jewish identity, also see: Marshall Sklare and Joseph Greenblum, *Jewish Identity on the Suburban Frontier: A Study of Group Survival in the Open Society* (Chicago: University of Chicago Press, 1979); Charles S. Liebman and Steven M. Cohen, *Two Worlds of Judaism: The Israeli and American Experiences* (New Haven: Yale University Press, 1990); Annette Steigelfest, "Ethnic Mediation in Political Socialization: Concepts of Power and Legitimacy in the Orthodox Jewish Community," *Contemporary Jewry* 5(2) (fall/winter 1983): 53–70; Samuel C. Heilman and Steven M. Cohen, *Cosmopolitans and Parochials: Modern Orthodox Jews in America* (Chicago: University of Chicago Press, 1989); Seymour Martin Lipset and Earl Raab, "The American Jews, the 1984 Elections, and Beyond," *Tocqueville Review* 6(2) (1984): 401–19; and Cohen, *Jewish Identity.* For a general discussion of Jewish political behavior, see Peter Medding, "Towards a General Theory of Jewish Political Interests and Behavior," *Jewish Journal of Sociology* 19(2) (Dec. 1977): 115–44.

13. Women, e.g., were far less supportive than men of the use of force in the 1990 Gulf crisis. In a poll conducted by the *Boston Globe,* 73 percent of women as opposed to 50 percent of men agreed with the following statement: "The death of American soldiers is too high a price to pay in this Persian Gulf conflict," *Boston Globe,* 14 Dec. 1990.

14. Cohen, *Jewish Identity,* 139–49.

15. Heilman and Cohen, *Cosmopolitans and Parochials,* 170.

16. Cohen, *Jewish Identity*; Cohen, *American Assimilation*; and Liebman and Cohen, *Two Worlds of Judaism.*

17. Heilman and Cohen, *Cosmopolitans and Parochials,* 91.

18. Janet Aviad, *Return to Judaism* (Chicago: University of Chicago Press, 1983), 81.

19. Cohen, *American Assimilation,* 82–95. Similarly, when Alena Janet Strauss replicated and extended a previous study on Jewish identity by including gender, her findings differed from the original results. Both studies concluded that for men the father's religiosity was the most important variable, followed by friends' expectations, Jewish education, and activities with parents. For women, however, Strauss found that activities with parents were the most significant variable, followed by Jewish education, friends' expectations,

and father's religiosity. See Arnold Dashefsky and Howard M. Shapiro, *Ethnic Identification among American Jews,* 2d ed. (Lanham, Md.: University Press of America, 1992).

20. For statistical data on rising Jewish divorce rates, see: Sylvia Barack Fishman, "The Changing American Jewish Family in the '80s," *Contemporary Jewry* 9(2) (1988): 8.

21. William Shaffir, "Persistence and Change in the Hasidic Family," in Steven M. Cohen and Paula E. Hyman, eds., *The Jewish Family: Myths and Reality* (New York: Holmes and Meier, 1986), 193–94; Chaim I. Waxman, *America's Jews in Transition* (Philadelphia: Temple University Press, 1983), 163–64; Sidney Goldstein and Calvin Goldscheider, *Jewish Americans: Three Generations in a Jewish Community* (Englewood Cliffs, N.J.: Prentice-Hall, 1968), 112–13.

22. Cohen, *Jewish Identity,* 121. Also see Andrew Cherlin and Carin Celebuski, "Are Jewish Families Different? Some Evidence from the General Social Survey," *Journal of Marriage and the Family* 45 (Nov. 1983): 903–10; and Nathan Goldberg, "The Jewish Attitude toward Divorce," in Jacob Fried, ed., *Jews and Divorce* (New York: Ktav, 1968).

23. Goldscheider, *Jewish Continuity and Change,* 62.

24. Cohen, *Jewish Identity,* 116–17; and Goldscheider, *Jewish Continuity and Change,* 58–73.

25. Goldscheider, *Jewish Continuity and Change,* 71.

26. Sylvia Barack Fishman, "The Impact of Feminism on American Jewish Life," *American Jewish Year Book* 89 (1989): 18.

27. Cohen, *Jewish Identity,* 118. See also Sergio Della Pergola, "Patterns of American Jewish Fertility," *Demography* (Aug. 1980): 261–73.

28. Goldscheider, *Jewish Continuity and Change,* 94. See also Sidney Goldstein, "Completed and Expected Fertility in an American Jewish Community," *Jewish Social Studies* 33 (2-3) (April–July 1971): 212–27; and Ronald K. Watts, "Jewish Fertility Trends and Differentials: An Examination of Other Evidence from the Census of 1970," *Jewish Social Studies* 42(3-4) (summer–fall 1980): 293–312.

29. Egon Mayer, *Love and Tradition: Marriage between Jews and Christians* (New York: Plenum, 1985), 48; and Barry Kosmin, Sidney Goldstein, Joseph Waksberg, Nava Lerer, Ariella Keysar, and Jeffrey Scheckner, "Highlights of the CJF 1990 National Jewish Population Survey," Council of Jewish Federations, 13–14. These statistics include marriages in which the non-Jewish spouse converted to Judaism.

30. Rela Geffen Monson, "The Case of the Reluctant Exogamists: Jewish Women and Intermarriage," *Gratz College Annual of Jewish Studies* 5 (1976): 121–26.

31. Nathaniel S. Lehrman, "Intermarriage and Its Effects on Jewish Survival," in Gilbert S. Rosenthal, ed., *New Directions in the Jewish Family and Community"* (New York: Federation of Jewish Philanthropies of New York, 1974), 33. For statistics on gender differences and intermarriage during the 1970s and 1980s, see also Bernard Lazerwitz, "Intermarriage and Conversion: A Guide for Future Research, *Jewish Journal of Sociology* 13(1) (June 1971): 41–63; Bernard Lazerwitz, "Jewish-Christian Marriages and Conversions," *Jewish Social Studies* 43(1) (winter 1981): 31–46; Arnold Schwartz, "Intermarriage in the United States," *American Jewish Year Book* 1970: 101–21; Sidney Goldstein, "American Jewry, 1970: A Demographic Profile," *American Jewish Year Book, 1971,* 30; and Cohen, *American Assimilation,* 28.

32. Monson, "The Case of the Reluctant Exogamists: Jewish Women and Intermarriage," 123.

33. Kosmin et al., "Highlights," 9.

34. Ibid., 8; see also Lazerwitz, "Intermarriage and Conversion."

35. Goldscheider, *Jewish Continuity and Change,* 107–15, 119–34.

36. Ibid., 115–19, 131–32.

37. Fishman, "The Impact of Feminism," 21–27.

38. Goldstein, "American Jewry, 1970," 83.

39. Fishman, "The Impact of Feminism," 3–62.

40. Ibid., 27; and Fishman, "Changing American Jewish Family," 1–33. See also Israel Rubin, *Satmar: An Island in the City* (Chicago: Quadrangle, 1972).

41. Herbert J. Gans, "The Origin and Growth of a Jewish Community in the Suburbs: A Study of the Jews of Park Forest," in Marshall Sklare, ed., *The Jews: Social Patterns of an American Group* (Westport, Conn.: Greenwood, 1958), 233.

42. Micaela di Leonardo, "The Female World of Cards and Holidays: Women, Families and the Work of Kinship," *Signs: Journal of Women in Culture and Society* 12(3) (1987): 440–53.

43. Gans, "A Jewish Community in the Suburbs," 215.

44. Sidney Goldstein, "Jews on the Move: Implications for American Jewry and for Local Communities," *Jewish Journal of Sociology* 32(1) (June 1990): 5–30.

45. Barry S. Tuchfeld, "The 'Involuntary' Voluntary Organization: Social Control in a Southern University," *Contemporary Jewry* 3(1) (fall/winter 1976): 17–18.

46. Ibid.

47. Alice Goldstein, "New Roles, New Commitments? Jewish Women's Involvement in the Community's Organizational Structure," *Contemporary Jewry* (spring 1990): 72.

48. John E. Mueller, *War, Presidents and Public Opinion* (New York: Wiley, 1973); and "Women and Men: Is Realignment Under Way?" *Public Opinion* 5 (April/May 1982): 21–32.

49. Jay Y. Brodbar-Nemzer, "Sex Differences in Attitudes of American Jews toward Israel," *Contemporary Jewry* 8 (1987): 57.

50. Calvin Goldscheider, "American Aliyah/Sociological and Demographic Perspectives," in Marshall Sklare, ed., *The Jew in American Society* (New York: Behrman House, 1974), 364; and Arnold Dashefsky and Bernard Lazerwitz, "North American Migration to Israel: Stayers and Leavers," *Contemporary Jewry* 7 (1986): 43–63.

51. Abraham D. Lavender, "Studies of Jewish College Students: A Review and a Replication," *Jewish Social Studies* 39(1–2) (winter–spring 1977): 37–52; Harold S. Himmelfarb, "Agents of Religious Socialization among American Jews," *Sociological Quarterly* 20 (autumn 1979): 477–94; Teresa D. Marciano, "A Note on Phantom Triads: Family Coalitions and Religious Observance after Divorce," *Jewish Social Studies* 44(3–4) (summer–fall 1982): 315–22; Nava Lerer, Ariella Keysar, and Barry Kosmin, "The Meaning of Being a Jew in America: A Religious Identity," paper presented at the American Sociological Association Conference, Aug. 1991; and Allen Glicksman and Tanya Ko-

ropeckyj-Cox, "Aging and Ethnic Identity: The Case of the American Jewish Elderly," paper presented at the Association for Jewish Studies Conference, Dec. 1991. Recent Soviet Jewish immigrants, however, may deviate from this pattern. When Rita Simon and Julian Simon asked their Soviet respondents about their own religious behavior and whether they wanted their children to belong to Jewish organizations, live in Jewish neighborhoods, contribute to Jewish charities, and marry Jews, they did not find gender differences. Rita J. Simon and Julian L. Simon, "The Jewish Dimension among Recent Soviet Immigrants to the United States, *Jewish Social Studies* 44(3–4) (summer–fall 1982): 283–90.

52. Marion Kaplan, *The Making of the Jewish Middle Class: Women, Family, and Identity in Imperial Germany* (New York: Oxford University Press, 1991), 77.

53. Marshall Sklare, *America's Jews* (New York: Random House, 1971), 83. Sklare supports his argument by discussing how some second-generation women had a "narcissistic preoccupation with self" (p. 101n12).

54. Goldscheider, *Jewish Continuity and Change,* 100–102. See also Rela Geffen Monson, "Relieving the Overload: Implications of Role Conflict of Jewish Career Women for Jewish Communal Planning," paper prepared for the Third Sydney Hollander Memorial Conference, Los Angeles, 9 July 1991; and Sidney Goldstein, "Completed and Expected Fertility in an American Jewish Community," *Jewish Social Studies* 33(2–3) (April–July 1971): 212–27. Similarly, Jewish women who converted out of Judaism have significantly lower educational attainment rates than other Jewish women. See Kosmin, "Highlights," 11.

55. Chaim I. Waxman, "The Threadbare Canopy: The Vicissitudes of the Jewish Family in Modern American Society," in Marshall Sklare, ed., *American Jews: A Reader* (New York: Behrman House, 1983), 143.

56. Waxman, *America's Jews,* 221.

57. Debra Renee Kaufman, *Rachel's Daughters: Newly Orthodox Jewish Women* (New Brunswick: Rutgers University Press, 1991); and Lynn Davidman, *Tradition in a Rootless World: Women Turn to Orthodox Judaism* (Berkeley: University of California Press, 1991).

58. Kaufman, *Rachel's Daughters,* 89.

59. Herbert Danzger, *Returning to Tradition: The Contemporary Revival of Orthodox Judaism* (New Haven: Yale University Press, 1989).

60. Ibid., 277.

61. Lynn Davidman and Arthur L. Greil, "Gender and the Experience of Conversion: The Case of 'Returnees' to Modern Orthodox Judaism," *Sociology of Religion* 54(1) (spring 1993): 83–100.

62. Michael Argyle and Benjamin Beit Hallahmi, *The Social Psychology of Religion* (Boston: Routledge, 1975); David A. de Vaus, "Workforce Participation and Sex Differences in Church Attendance," *Review of Religious Research* 25 (1984): 247–56; and Hart M. Nelson, Neil H. Cheek, Jr., and Paul Au, "Gender Differences in Images of God," *Journal for the Scientific Study of Religion* 24 (1985): 396–402.

63. Sheila Jubelirer Siegel, "The Effect of Culture on How Women Experience Menstruation: Jewish Women and Mikveh," *Women and Health* 10(4) (winter 1985/1986): 63–74. For another study of Orthodox women's ritual behavior, see Blanche Frank, "The American Orthodox Jewish Housewife: A Generational Study of Ethnic Survival," *Contemporary Jewry* 5(2) (fall–winter 1980): 55–65. Frank highlighted the behavioral transformations that took place among Jewish housewives over three generations: third-generation Orthodox women were the most knowledgeable about religious life, second-generation women had the highest rates of communal involvement, and first-generation women were the most devout. Frank's research suggests, then, that religious behavior, like other aspects of ethnicity, is not a constant and that over generations religious erosion is not inevitable.

64. Samuel C. Heilman, *Synagogue Life: A Study in Symbolic Interaction* (Chicago: University of Chicago Press, 1973).

65. National Survey of the United Synagogue, 1950, as cited in Sklare, *Conservative Judaism: An American Religious Movement,* (New York: Schocken, 1972, rep. 1955), 88; and Bernard Lazerwitz and Michael Harrison, "American Denominations: A Social and Religious Profile," *American Sociological Review* 44 (Aug. 1979): 656–66.

66. For three excellent articles that describe the movement toward gender equality within Jewish religious life, see Jack Wertheimer, "Recent Trends in American Judaism," *American Jewish Year Book* (1989): 63–162; Ann Lapidus Lerner, "'Who Hast Not Made Me a Man': The Movement for Equal Rights for Women in American Jewry," *American Jewish Year Book* (1977): 3–38; and Fishman, "The Impact of Feminism."

67. Frida Kerner Furman, *Beyond Yiddishkeit* (Albany: SUNY Press, 1987). See also Gerald Showstack, *Suburban Communities: The Jewishness of American Reform Jews* (Atlanta: Scholars Press, 1988).

68. Charles S. Liebman, "Reconstructionism in American Jewish Life," *American Jewish Year Book* (1970): 83. To his credit, Liebman tried to include members of Hadassah (a Jewish women's organization) in his sample, but none of the women responded to his questionnaire. He should, however, have clearly specified that his research was not about all Jews but was limited to the experiences of Jewish men. Also see Pamela S. Nadell, "Rereading Charles S. Liebman: Questions from the Perspective of Women's History," *American Jewish History* 80(4) (summer 1991): 511.

69. Jay Brodbar-Nemzer, "The Study of the American Jewish Family and Family Theory," paper prepared for the National Council on Family Relations Theory and Methods Workshop, San Francisco, 16 Oct. 1984.

70. Arlie Hochschild, *The Second Shift* (Berkeley: University of California Press, 1989).

71. Egon Mayer, *From Suburb to Shtetl: The Jews of Boro Park* (Philadelphia: Temple University Press, 1979).

72. Susan Strasser, *Never Done: A History of American Housework* (New York: Pantheon, 1982); and Marjorie Devault, *Feeding the Family: The Social Organization of Caring and Gendered Work* (Chicago: University of Chicago Press, 1991).

73. Danzger, *Returning to Tradition,* 29, 236; Lazerwitz, "Intermarriage and Conversion," 41–63; and Kosmin et al., "Highlights," 8.

74. Mayer, *Love and Tradition,* 255.

75. Murray Frost, "Analysis of a Jewish Community's Out-Migration," *Jewish Social Studies* 44(3–4) (summer–fall 1982): 231–38. See also Sidney Goldstein, "Population Movement and Redistribution among American Jews," *Jewish Journal of Sociology* 24(1) (June 1982): 5–24.

76. Gary A. Tobin and Ingrid Lomfors, "The Feminization of Poverty among Jews," paper prepared for the Center for Modern Jewish Studies, Brandeis University, Nov. 1985, p. 26.

77. Fishman, "Changing American Jewish Family," 11. For a general discussion of the negative impact that divorce has on women's economic lives, see Lenore Weitzman, *The Divorce Revolution: The Unexpected Social and Economic Consequences for Women and Children* (New York: Free Press, 1985).

78. Jessie Bernard, *The Future of Marriage* (New York: Bantam, 1973).

79. See Paula Hyman's chapter in this volume.

80. Steven Martin Cohen, "American Jewish Feminism: A Study in Conflicts and Compromises," *American Behavioral Scientist* 23(4) (March/April 1980): 519–58.

81. See also Fishman, "The Impact of Feminism on American Jewish Life," 7–13; and Fishman, *A Breath of Life: Feminism in the American Jewish Community* (New York: Free Press, 1993).

82. Shelly Tenenbaum, *A Credit to Their Community: Jewish Loan Societies in the United States, 1880–1945* (Detroit: Wayne State University Press, 1993). For a feminist critique of the public-private dichotomy, see Karen V. Hansen, "Feminist Conceptions of Public and Private: A Critical Analysis," *Berkeley Journal of Sociology* 32 (1987): 105–28.

"She Perceives Her Work to Be Rewarding": Jewish Women in a Cross-Cultural Perspective

Anthropology has special methodological and theoretical contributions to make to the feminist critique of Jewish studies. Methodologically, anthropologists rely on participant-observation techniques, which enable them to hear the voices of people who are outside the literary elite. Theoretically, anthropology as the holistic and comparative science of humankind is singularly able to assess the incidence and implications of male dominance.[1] Indeed, scholars in other disciplines have turned to anthropological data to fill in the gaps in knowledge about Jewish women's lives and have drawn on anthropological theories of gender inequality to interpret historical and textual evidence.[2]

Anthropology as an academic discipline began to take form in the late nineteenth century, when, in order to build evolutionary models, scholars embraced the study of primitive societies. By the early twentieth century anthropologists realized that they needed to do field research, rather than rely on historical and anecdotal literature, to learn about the contemporary non-Western cultures that supposedly resembled the earliest forms of human social organization. Later-twentieth-century anthropology has largely rejected the evolutionary leaning of its founders, yet most anthropologists have continued to concentrate on small-scale societies that lend themselves to participant-observation study. That is why Jewish anthropology—including feminist Jewish anthropology—has tended to look at such closed societies as moshavim (cooperative agricultural villages), kibbutzim, senior citizen day centers, development towns in Israel, and ultra-Orthodox neighborhoods.

The quotation in the title is from Proverbs 31:7 *(Eshet Hayil).*

Jewish anthropology—the anthropological study of Jews and Judaism—is a relatively recent academic pursuit,[3] and the bulk of Jewish anthropological work has been carried out following the introduction of the feminist intellectual agenda into the academy. A surprisingly large number of Jewish anthropologists have integrated the study of women into their work.

In the following pages I have chosen to look closely at a number of anthropological studies that clearly and coherently address issues of gender and the experiences of Jewish women. Since many of the studies that I review are relatively unknown to scholars outside Israel, I hope that this article will serve to enhance the future work of scholars in a variety of Jewish studies disciplines who wish to know more about what flesh-and-blood Jewish women do, say, and think.

The overwhelmingly patriarchal nature of the formal Jewish tradition makes the task of developing a feminist critique seem almost too easy.[4] I do not hesitate to utter the global statement that any anthropological study of Jews that does not both clarify whether the Jews in question are male or female and address the implications of gender is poor anthropology. The time is long past when anthropologists can interview male "Huchipuchis" and then write a book entitled *The Religion of the "Huchipuchis,"* without adding the subtitle *"Huchipuchi" Religion as Described by Male Huchipuchis.* This point has been so well argued by feminist anthropologists[5] that in this chapter I need only add that in the Jewish case—given the emphasis placed by Judaism on gender as a cultural category—it is especially true. Although not all the studies reviewed here are self-consciously feminist, I would argue that because gender is so crucial a category in Jewish culture, studies that emphasize gender carry an implicit critique of those that do not.

Feminist scholars have excelled at reexamining accepted anthropological wisdom from the standpoint of women. For example, structural anthropologist Claude Lévi-Strauss treated marriage as an act of exchange: two groups of men exchange an *object,* which is woman. Feminists, however, have looked at marriage from the perspective of women who certainly do not see themselves as objects. Economic arrangements have also come under feminist scrutiny: feminist anthropologists have asked whether economic development affects men and women in the same way. Other feminist anthropologists have reassessed the informal information transaction networks of women (what sexist anthropology used to belittle and ignore as "gossip") and have questioned traditional conceptions of power and authority.[6] Unfortunately, religion has not yet received as detailed or subtle a feminist critique as have other cultural institutions.[7] I suspect that the greatest contributions of feminist Jewish anthropology will indeed concern issues of religious beliefs and rituals.

Literacy, Power, and Sexual Segregation

Preliminary questions are whether kibbutz anthropology, the anthropology of ultra-Orthodox neighborhoods in Jerusalem, American Jewish anthropology, Ethiopian Jewish anthropology, and so on are independent fields,[8] or whether there is an overarching methodological or theoretical rubric (or more than one) that meaningfully defines a subset of anthropology as Jewish anthropology. If such a rubric exists, is it meaningful to the feminist critique? One such rubric is the Jewish "great tradition." Anthropologist Robert Redfield has distinguished between little traditions, religious cultures growing out of local or nonliterate communities, and great traditions, whose bearers are a transregional literate elite.[9] Jews cross-culturally share a sacred, written symbol system: a great tradition. Because that system is so totally dominated by men, it raises particularly interesting questions for feminist anthropologists: how women in various cultural contexts maneuver and find meaning within and around the same patriarchal textual heritage.

To begin, it is useful to clarify the key constituent of the Jewish cultural construction of gender: differential access to the great tradition as expressed through ritualized literacy for men and illiteracy for women. In the Middle Eastern Jewish world of the tenth to thirteenth centuries, as revealed by the Cairo genizah, S. D. Goiten has contended that "piety in Judaism was paired with knowledge, namely [knowledge] of the holy scriptures and the 'oral' teachings derived from them. [As it is written,] 'An ignoramus cannot be pious.'"[10] Men were literate and women were illiterate. Thus, "The educational gap between male and female was the ultimate source and manifestation of the repression of womanhood in civilized societies."[11] In one of the earliest studies of Moroccan Jews, Milton Jacobs found that until the twentieth century there was no formal education available to Jewish women: girls learned about religion from their mothers. The religious life of women and girls was conducted at home, while boys went to synagogue and to school from age five or six. In general, girls and women were excluded from the public religious ceremonies of men.[12]

Literacy in the absolute sense of recognizing letters is not the real issue. Rather, the issue is access, or lack of access, to the social status and spiritual satisfaction that result from extensive opportunities for religious study. Vi-

mala Jayanti found that in modern times the ultra-Orthodox education of
girls is not directed toward religious knowledge (other than basic laws related
to women's sphere), but toward simple faith and *midot* (personality characteristics). The result is that "the ultimate sacred propositions women believe
in are somewhat vague and cryptic."[13] Tamar El-Or shows that in the contemporary ultra-Orthodox community women actually learn a great deal;
they go to school for many years and then to informal and formal lessons
for women in the evenings. The interesting question is, What do they learn?
"The current situation of women's education within the ultra-Orthodox
community, as it emerges from the data and from the contemporary Jewish
history of the 'society of learned men,' reveals a paradox. *The women are
taught to be ignorant.*"[14]

Feminist anthropologists have been attracted to the study of ultra-
Orthodox women, I suspect, because of the rigid sex roles that characterize
their communities.[15] Ultra-Orthodox men are expected to spend as much
time as possible in all male yeshivot (seminaries) from which women are
absolutely excluded. Ultra-Orthodox women are expected to facilitate
men's Torah study by wearing especially modest clothing, so as not to dis-
tract them, and working at paying jobs so that their husbands can dedicate
themselves to Torah study.[16]

Feminist anthropologists have written extensively about how to measure
gender status. Perhaps the most widely accepted statement is that in sexist
societies women are barred from making decisions about their own lives and
the lives of the community, whereas in egalitarian societies decision-making
powers are not a function of gender. In traditional Jewish societies decisions
that affect the group are often made by those individuals who demonstrate
exceptional proficiency at Torah learning. Except for a few unusual situations, Jewish women as a group have systematically been barred access to
Torah learning.

Institutionalized ignorance for women is part of a broader cultural picture
of sexual segregation. Based on the cross-cultural research of more than 150
societies, feminist anthropologist Peggy Sanday has argued that "whether or
not men and women mingle or are largely separated in everyday affairs plays
a crucial role in the rise of male dominance. Men and women must be
physically as well as conceptually separated in order for men to dominate
women."[17]

Jewish law demands that men and women be separate in many social
contexts. Frequently, this has meant that women are excluded from the
dominant modes of Jewish cultural expression. (It does not mean, however,

that women are oblivious to those modes.) Kurdish Jewish women and men, for example, used to be almost totally segregated throughout their lives: working, celebrating, and even eating separately (women eat after the men). In Kurdistan most synagogues had no women's sections, and few women attended synagogue at all.[18] The norms of sexual segregation were reinforced by strictly interpreted laws of menstrual purity. In Kurdistan, there were special houses for *niddot* and *yoldot* (menstruating and postpartum women). A menstruating woman would sit separately, eat alone with her own spoon and dishes, and avoid handing any objects to her husband. In general men did not take anything from a woman's hand in order to maintain their own purity.[19]

Yemeni Jewish women rarely left their houses and had no real public life. They were excluded from the cultic and religious practices of the men. According to Nina Dubler Katz, women did not even *hear* men's music. Instead, they created their own "second world" of fantasy, storytelling, and singing. Katz has discovered that Yemeni Jewish men and women have different traditional songs. Men's are developmental and antiphonal with no accompaniment or definite rhythm. Women's are repetitive, rhythmic, are accompanied by a drum or other instrument, and are never truly antiphonal. The men sing fixed religious texts based on liturgical *taamim* (standardized melodies), in Hebrew or Aramaic. The women sing improvised words about secular themes in Arabic.[20]

In all three of the preceding examples sexual segregation is a two-edged sword: it cuts women off from important and culturally esteemed spiritual venues, but it also means that women have some level of autonomy in developing their own perspectives, constructing their own value system, managing their own resources, and forging their own rituals. In the following sections I look more closely at each of these points.

The Female Perspective

Roger Keesing has shown that gender inequality often means that men are conversant only with their own (male) traditions. Women, however, may have a separate female tradition at the same time that they are as "committed to . . . [the] dominant ideologies, mystifications, and celestializations as men are."[21] The implications of this statement are crucial for understanding the cultural experience of Jewish women: historically, Jewish women have been cognizant of the highly patriarchal Jewish great tradition, dedicated to preserving the great tradition, yet simultaneously critical and even subversive of that tradition. Jewish women have developed a bifurcated cultural experience.

That Jewish women see the world from a female perspective—a perspective that diverges from the official, or male, perspective—is the clearest theme that has emerged from feminist Jewish anthropology. Most anthropologists who have studied Jewish women have in some way referred to women's "alternative reality," women's "subculture," or women's second world.

Lisa Gilad provides several examples of differing female and male perspectives. Yemeni men in a development town in Israel, where Gilad carried out fieldwork, reminisce about how in Yemen "a woman was respected like a precious candle for she was the light of the home. This was the reason for her seclusion in it, for like a precious candle, a woman had to be protected." Unlike men, women "regard their past in Yemen with ambivalence. They lament the lack of simplicity in the present lifestyle in Israel, but they believe that in Yemen they were 'slaves' (rather than 'candles') and lacked 'cultured' learning."[22]

In a very different sort of study Riv-Ellen Prell has analyzed how men and women perceived women's participation in an American *havurah* (egalitarian prayer group) in the 1970s. Prell observed that "their differences indicated that interiorization of prayer required different experiences for men and women. If that was the case, then community, one of their prayer constituents, was not the same for men and women."[23] Men and women had different explanations for why women did not actively participate in leadership roles in the havurah: the men claimed it was because women were less educated in Jewish matters; the women claimed it was because they felt that silence was expected of them as women. "There were occasions when they [women in the havurah] felt like outsiders to the Judaism they felt was important to their own identity. That outsider status must have only been heightened by their need to assume traditional activities and symbols that had been associated with men."[24]

As a result of differences in perspective—which, as I have suggested, reflect sexual segregation and women's systematic exclusion from Torah learning—women have forged their own ways of evaluating their actions; they have constructed their own, gender-linked value systems. Jane Atkinson has argued that "the existence of an ideological assertion [regarding gender equality or inequality] in a culture is no predictor of the way in which social actors experience that assertion."[25] In a study of a Jewish senior citizen day center in California (frequented mostly by women), Barbara Myerhoff found that the old people there, like other "socially disdained groups have to find their own standards [for] generating internal codes for taking each other's measure. Only by doing so can they avoid the devastating consequences of judging themselves in the terms used by people who disdain them, in whose system they will always amount for nothing."[26] Myerhoff's analysis is relevant for Jewish women cross-culturally. Excluded from male systems of prestige, Jewish women have other ways of striving to be moral beings.

Among Yemeni Jews, for example, "rewards for good mothering in the immigrant generation are bestowed by other mothers, especially in terms of respect for those who are self-sacrificing. On countless occasions, I heard women praising other women for being excellent mothers while working outside the home. Efficiency has become a prized attribute."[27]

My research among elderly Kurdish women in Jerusalem exposes a religious gender gap. When they talked about righteous women, they tended to emphasize moral behavior in the realm of interpersonal relations—the model of a religious woman was one who prepared food for hungry beggars. In discussing saintly men, they stressed proper observance of religious rituals (in particular, prayer and study) and even commented that a man can be religious yet behave in an immoral manner. It is significant that when I solicited hypothetical descriptions, their description of a religious *human being* overlapped with that of a religious *woman* and not of a religious *man*. For these women, female religious modes are normative.[28]

Women's Rituals

According to Israeli anthropologist A. Brauer, "It is difficult to see in what the Judaism of Kurdish women is expressed, aside from the external observance of religious rules."[29] Anthropologists believe that through rituals people express their hopes, fears, dreams, values, conflicts, and existential dilemmas. Yet the rituals of Jewish women, rituals that for the most part are not required by Jewish law, have often been either invisible to anthropologists or dismissed as mere superstition. In the following section, I tease out the hopes, fears, values, and beliefs that are expressed in the rituals of Jewish women.

Lucy Garnet was the first anthropologist to notice that Jewish men and women in Turkey behaved differently on Jewish holidays.[30] On Purim, for example, men but not women would get drunk.

Maurie Sacks has shown how contemporary Orthodox American women use food rituals—an exchange of festive Purim treats *(mishloah manot)*—as tools for shaping community self-definition, setting values, and creating social networks. The women Sacks studied see their Jewish community as a network of reciprocal aid, which takes the form of emotional support and material assistance (errand running, childcare, car pooling, sick care, and help at times of bereavement). It is these networks of relation and reciprocity that from a female perspective define community. Women's rituals are what underscore and reinforce this view of community.

Sacks's work also shows a surprising power among Orthodox women to change Jewish tradition (not to break Jewish law, but to modify customs). The women she studied came up with the innovative idea of computerized lists and random exchanges of mishloah manot, rather than personally delivering the treats to a few friends or neighbors. This was done on their own, without rabbinical guidance.[31]

It is no coincidence that Sacks's fieldwork highlights food rituals. Joelle Bahloul has shown that among Algerian Jews living in France, men perform the public food rituals (blessing the bread and wine on Friday night), but women are the experts and guardians of the customs: the mother orchestrates and directs domestic ceremonies, and the father is but an actor.[32]

Through their involvement in daily food preparation, many Jewish women have used food to express and dramatize themes and values that are important to them. In my study of elderly Kurdish Jewish women I found that often they describe Jewish identity, traditions, laws, and holidays in terms of feeding others. Many of their foods embody potent Jewish symbols, and the rituals of food preparation imbue their everyday domestic work with holiness. The women perceive cooking to be far more than a preliminary chore that must be done in order to have a festive holiday meal. On the contrary, they treat food preparation as a meaningful sacred act in and of itself.[33]

Brauer has described the communal rituals of Jewish women in Kurdistan. Tu b'Shvat (the festival of the new calendrical year for trees) was a fertility holiday for women, and women's rituals connected their own fate to the fate of trees. If it rained or snowed, the women would say that the trees had dipped in the *mikveh*, or ritual bath (a good sign). They planted raisins and candies around the trees to increase their fertility and that of the trees. Barren women hugged trees in the middle of the night so that the tree's pregnancy would pass to them.[34] Fertility is certainly a theme in the great tradition of Tu b'Shvat. What Kurdish women did was to elaborate on this theme by performing additional rituals that spoke to their concerns.

Brauer records a ritual, called *simhat herayon,* for a woman's first pregnancy. Female friends and kin took the mother-to-be to her parent's house, where female relatives sewed baby clothes. Women played drums, sang, and danced. Numerous rules (not to eat sour food, to be careful with fingernail parings) and amulets (such as colored threads, copper, and snakeskin) protected the pregnant woman and baby. Many rituals and amulets also protected the *yoledet* (postpartum woman), who was seen as particularly vulnerable to evil spirits. Amulets have been stressed by everyone who has studied Kurdish Jews, and women have been especially involved with amulets.[35] Similarly, in regard to Persian Jews, C. Rice has noted that women made pilgrimages to holy shrines and put charms (such as blue beads and buttons) on their children's clothing.[36] The sewing of amulets, circumcision clothing, and shrouds has been a holy activity for many Jewish women.[37] I stress again the overlap between the sacred and the profane in many of the ritual activities of women.

A feminist interpretation of fertility and child health rituals acknowledges the social reality of women's lives. We know that high birth rates coupled with high infant and maternal mortality rates have been the reality for most Jewish women cross-culturally. Fear for the health and well-being of children (especially babies) and concern for the lives of pregnant, birthing, and postpartum women have been the most dramatic and most frequent themes in the ritual lives of Jewish women. Recognizing the frequency of infant and maternal death and the grief felt by mothers and other family members who have lost loved ones helps us to understand the many seemingly superstitious or magical rituals performed by women.

Family Relations

Cross-culturally, the rituals of Jewish women tend to have a great deal to do with family relations. In Kurdish Jewish life, for example, family conflict and cooperation were matters of physical and cultural survival—matters in which women were very active. Many of the ceremonies that established relations of mutual obligations between families or that expressed conflicts of interests, were carried out by women.[38]

Family relations are a critical arena in which Jewish men and women have tended to see matters from different perspectives. Feminist anthropology has made important contributions to the study of kinship. Prefeminist anthropology often treated the domestic realm as a given. Intrafamilial affairs were assumed to be basically uniform, whereas political, economic, and religious institutions were expected to vary cross-culturally and thus to warrant careful scrutiny. Prefeminist anthropologists presumed to know what happened inside the family. Feminist anthropologists, in contrast, have devoted much attention to the content of family roles, dynamics, relations, and functions.[39]

A feminist critique of Jewish anthropology must respond to the idealized depictions of the Jewish family—the wonderful Jewish family that has been responsible for the survival of the Jewish people.[40] From a feminist perspective, things look a bit different. Here is a traditional Kurdish Jewish wedding song, sung to a bride, that expresses how a young bride feels at being abruptly separated from her natal family and sent to live with the family of her husband:

> You will cry enough, sleep more tonight
> Tomorrow you are going
> Say good-bye to your sister-in-law
> And your three brothers
> As much as you cry, it won't help you
> You are going
> Why are you running to the mountains?
> The bridegroom's parents are taking you
> Don't hide yourself, it won't help you
> To hide yourself in the mountains
> Come and go, it is best for you
> Why are you standing against the wall crying?
> Go with the parents of the groom
> That will be best for you
> They take her and go.[41]

Gilad quotes a Yemeni woman informant's description of family life: "Yes, there are preferences for sons over daughters in Yemeni families! And how! I felt this when I married and my parents gave me nothing, but they gave money to my brothers. When my brothers married, my parents helped them to buy apartments. Even though I worked for them as a girl, they did not think I needed help. They said, 'That is it, you are married, go!' "[42]

Ethnographers have described the elaborate wedding rituals of Kurdish Jews.[43] In my fieldwork among Kurdish women who had come to Israel at the beginning of the twentieth century, I found an almost total disinterest in recalling their wedding festivities. Yet, they clearly remembered resenting their parents for not allowing them to attend school (so they would be free to help with housework) and for forcing them to marry older men they did not like.[44]

The fact of often less-than-idyllic relations between husbands and wives has been used by Rahel Wasserfall to interpret women's behavior surrounding the laws of menstrual impurity. During her fieldwork on a Moroccan moshav in Israel, Wasserfall found that some of her informants related to *niddah* (menstrual taboos) not as pollution, but as a bargaining tool in their relations with their husbands. She shows how both men and women use the rules and rituals of niddah and mikveh to maneuver power relations in their marriage. She quotes informants who told her that although the status of Moroccan women is generally very low, through niddah and mikveh they have some power to manipulate their husbands. The man waits impatiently for the woman to dip in the bath, and she can postpone dipping if she chooses. The women believe that men need them sexually and that they can serve that need while manipulating their husbands in other domains, such as in the distribution of resources and family decisions. Wasserfall suggests that this is one of the reasons that Moroccan women are so attached to niddah and mikveh.[45]

In a classic study of preclass societies, Karen Sacks has argued that the status of a woman as wife is far less enviable than the status of a woman as sister. Whereas sisters have a direct relation to production (they belong to the lineage that owns the means of production), wives work for their husbands' lineages but do not own what they themselves produce.[46] The interesting point for feminist analysis is that the same woman is simultaneously both wife and sister—she is a wife in her husband's family and a sister in her own—a point often lost when kinship is studied solely from the perspective of men.

According to Sacks, as a woman ages and becomes the mother of adults, her status improves in her husband's family: she now controls the productive labor of others. Sacks's insight helps us to integrate studies that document the low position of Jewish wives with studies that document the power of Jewish mothers. Jewish women in Kurdistan married very young and were passed from father to husband before they were mature enough to make decisions and express opinions.[47] Donna Shai, however, has claimed that mothers had great power in the family. A mother of grown children could, for example, oppose potential brides and grooms by quarreling with the prospective in-laws.[48] Despite their identification with patriarchal families and their exclusion from formal channels of power, women nonetheless maintained a sense of their own interests and priorities and developed techniques that sometimes resulted in their attaining their goals.

Jane Collier, Michelle Rosaldo, and Sylvia Yanagisako have urged anthropologists to look at families not as concrete "things" that fulfill concrete "needs," but as ideological constructs.[49] The relevance of their approach to Jewish anthropology is clear: Jewish families take form within (and in reaction to) the Jewish great tradition that legislates, idealizes, ritualizes, and mystifies highly gender-specific family relations. Yet perhaps the greatest lesson to be learned from a feminist analysis of Jewish families is that there is no such thing as *the* Jewish family. In *various* cultural situations "the Jewish family" has been monogamous (Europe), polygynous (Asia), patrilocal (North Africa), matrilocal (among some Eastern European Jews), and neo-local (United States). The implications of these kinship arrangements are highly significant both in assessing gender relations and in understanding the life experiences of specific Jewish women.

Modernization

The theme of women and development has been extensively treated by feminist anthropologists. Most current research stresses that with the breakup of extended families and the introduction of wage labor, women often lose the power that derived from their traditional social and economic expertise, as well as the cooperation and solidarity that kin- and village-based female support networks provided.[50]

An overview of the effects of modernization from the perspective of Jewish women presents a rather different picture than the one painted by most feminist anthropologists. Gilad's work is notable for discerning that women's experiences are dynamic, that the move from Yemen to Israel affected women in complex ways, and that women of different ages and social classes view their lives and opportunities differently. The move from the peasant economy and extended family of Yemen to a market economy and nuclear family in Israel had both positive and negative implications for women.

Gilad shows that among Israeli Yemeni families, wives often feel that they make equal contributions to the family's welfare, but husbands still consider wives to be subordinate to them. In addition, "Many women claim that they were 'subordinated' [their term] by their natal families; they say that they resented the pressure put on them to work during or after elementary or secondary school rather than continue to study. It seems that the early 'emancipation' of women into the labor market in Israel was really a form of exploitation by the traditional family structure, which prevented their further education by putting them to work as wage earners for their brothers' education."[51] Young Yemeni women, however, feel that any disadvantages they suffered were overridden by their being freed from the domination of their mothers-in-law. (Unfortunately, Gilad did not report on how older women who had achieved the status and power that accompanied the mother-in-law role feel about the move to Israel.)

Gilad found that many poorly educated Yemeni women who work in Israel as domestics, childminders, and office cleaners (for low salaries and low status in the wider society) feel that entering the labor market has liberated them (their term). They feel that their situation is better than it was in Yemen and better than that of other Middle Eastern Jewish and non-Jewish women in Israel who do not work in paid employment. Significantly, their husbands do not agree with this assessment. Yemeni men perceive the move to Israel as having caused a decline in their employment status; in Yemen many Jewish men were independent, albeit impoverished, artisans; in Israel they are wage laborers.

Rita Simon has looked at sex and generational roles among ultra-Orthodox Jews. She found that women far more than men embrace modern, secular Israeli culture. Sons even more than their fathers demand orthodoxy and isolation from the larger society; daughters and mothers express greater interest in and lesser insulation from the larger society. Women's social and economic roles in the ultra-Orthodox community mean that women cannot be as cut off from Israeli society as the men; the institutional structure of the ultra-Orthodox community serves to isolate boys and men more than girls and women. Simon found, for example, that more than half the women (mothers and daughters) speak Hebrew among themselves and outside the home, while their menfolk speak only Yiddish; men reserve Hebrew for sacred texts. One of the questions she asked her older informants was, "If you had a chance to live your life over again, what aspects of it would you live the same and what aspects would you live differently?" Seventy-five percent of the men said that they would have devoted more of their lives to prayer and religious study and been more isolated from day-to-day activities. For those women who would have wanted things to be different, they all wanted an easier, more comfortable life.[52]

Modernization has had a complex impact on the religious world of Jewish women. Formal education for girls has meant that male cultural modes are more available to them, often at the expense of traditional female cultural modes. As I explained earlier, many of the most important ritual constellations of Jewish women have traditionally involved fertility, childbirth, and the health of their children. In modern societies these are matters for physicians, not for female ritual experts. Still, the pluralism and cultural diversity that characterize modern societies have meant that Jewish women have other religious options available to them. In a study I conducted of contemporary childbirth rituals in Jerusalem, I found that many women performed both secular rituals (learned in Lamaze-style childbirth education classes) and religious rituals, including religious rituals that originated in ethnic groups other than their own.[53]

Understanding that women's and men's experiences of family and modernization differ is crucially important to applied anthropologists who study cultures in order to make public policy recommendations. Shalva Weil, for example, has found that although single-parent families are rather rare among Israelis, among Ethiopian immigrants as many as one-third of all families are headed by a single parent, usually the mother: "The research revealed that despite the idealization of Jewish family life in Ethiopia by observers, it appears that the frequency of divorcees, young widows, and abandoned women was high."[54] In Ethiopia, divorced, widowed, and abandoned women would return to the protection of their natal families. The move to the modern Israeli market economy, in which individuals are tied to jobs that are often situated at a distance from the homes of their natal families, has created particular problems for Ethiopian women.

Gender Differences

In the preceding sections I have documented how the life experiences of men and women differ and how those differences lead to gender-specific attitudes and views on diverse issues. I turn now to Israeli kibbutzim to address a question that is the bread and butter of anthropology: To what extent are men's and women's differing life experiences biologically determined universals, and to what extent are they a by-product of cultural patterns and conditioning?[55]

One could perhaps argue that the study of kibbutzim is not really *Jewish* anthropology but rather *Israeli* anthropology (as, for example, the studies of Israeli Arabs or Druze) and that the issues addressed in other studies of Jewish women (such as sexual segregation and maneuvering within the great tradition) are irrelevant to the experience of kibbutz women. It is significant, however, that the most interesting experiment of sexual equality in our times has been among Jews.

I have emphasized how women's perspectives differ from men's. Again, kibbutzim provide a classic example. From an androcentric perspective, the kibbutz is the perfect egalitarian (classless) society. From a gynocentric perspective, kibbutzim are highly sexist, with rigid sexual divisions of labor, a higher status accorded to male jobs, and disproportionate numbers of men in leadership positions.

Kibbutzim have been more thoroughly studied than other cultural settings relevant to Jewish women. Although early films, novels, and some scholarly studies portrayed gender relations on the kibbutz as egalitarian (the self-sufficient kibbutz woman laboring in the fields with a rifle slung over her shoulder), sociologists and anthropologists have shown this portrayal to be inaccurate.[56]

The first generation of studies of kibbutz gender roles assumed that kibbutzim had started out as egalitarian societies, but that women had opted for more traditional sex roles. Sociobiologists Lionel Tiger and Joseph Shepher, for instance, argued that among most birds and mammals, including humans, females invest more time and energy in parenting than do males. This is the cause of the sexual division of labor: involved with their children, women have to forgo investment in nonfamilial tasks. The researchers contended that kibbutz women who opted for increased involvement with childcare, at the cost of decreased economic and political involvement, were acting out the basic "biogrammar" of the human species. These kibbutz women were opting to act against the ideology of gender equality with which they had been socialized as children, against the economic interests of the kibbutz, and against even the wishes of the kibbutz men.[57]

The second generation of kibbutz gender studies has delved more thoroughly into the historical record and found that kibbutzim had in fact never strived for gender equality. Joseph Blasi shows that gender equality never received the infrastructural support that other revolutionary ideals (such as economic equality) had received. Marilyn Safir emphasizes that the early *kvutzot* (predecessors of kibbutzim) so thoroughly discouraged women from joining that in many there were only one or two women. These women were seen as economically less productive than men and were relegated to domestic chores. Once children were born, the kvutzot and kibbutzim did address the issue of how women could work and still look after their children. Yet the solution was that all women (including single and childless women) should participate in childrearing—not that men should share in the task: "We have not found evidence which suggests that in the formative years of the kibbutz movements there was equality—both men and women accepted prejudicial ideas about their own and each other's abilities."[58]

In short, kibbutzim have not provided an untainted test case for "nature or nurture." The well-documented gender inequality in contemporary kibbutzim reflects the cultural mind-set of the early pioneers—a mind-set that was grounded in the same unegalitarian notions of gender that have informed Jewish societies in Europe and the Middle East for hundreds of years.

Directions for Future Research

As in many other disciplines (see Paula Hyman's chapter in this volume), feminist anthropology began with the realization that much of our data, even that which purported to describe comprehensively all aspects of particular cultures, have excluded women's experiences. The first stage of feminist anthropology has been to accumulate information about women's lives cross-culturally. To a great extent, feminist Jewish anthropology has not moved far beyond that stage. In this chapter I have attempted to push our thinking a bit farther.

Henrietta Moore has suggested that the next stage of feminist anthropology needs to "come to terms with the real differences between women, as opposed to contenting itself with demonstrations of the variety of women's experiences, situations and activities worldwide."[59] Future studies of Jewish women should look more carefully at differences related to age, class, and marital status. A hundred years ago Lucy Garnet found that among the Jews of Turkey women of different marital statuses behaved differently: unmarried women did not go to synagogue, whereas married women would usually go on Shabbat and festivals and hold out their arms and kiss when the Torah was raised up. My fieldwork has shown that cooking for the Sabbath means something different to overworked mothers who cook three meals a day for large families than it does to elderly grandmothers whose descendants regard them as ritual experts. Menstrual taboos undoubtedly have different meanings for women forced into arranged marriages than for women who can choose to marry for love. I have no doubt that the Jewish family, as perceived by a young, in-marrying daughter-in-law, is not the Jewish family perceived by an established, successful grandmother who heads a large, extended family.[60] We know that Jewish women of almost all ethnic groups have been active in charity. It would be naive to think that charity means the same thing to the givers as it does to the receivers. All of Jewish life is different to a poor, illiterate woman than it is to a middle-class, literate one.

A second issue for future study is to what extent Jewish women resemble non-Jewish women of the same time and place. Harvey Goldberg has begun to deal with this question, showing, for example, that among North African Jews the husband-wife unit is emphasized, while among Arabs the patrilineal clan (brothers, uncles, and cousins) is the focal kinship unit.[61] It would be interesting to know how this difference is experienced by women and how it is experienced by men.

Several of the ideas to emerge from the feminist critique of Jewish anthropology should be of interest to feminist anthropology as a whole, and I would like to see Jewish anthropologists make their contribution to feminist anthropology more explicit. In particular, feminist Jewish anthropologists have excelled at contrasting androcentric and gynocentric views of religion. Many of the themes that prevail in the religious lives of Jewish women have also been documented for other populations of women. Concern over child death, the ritual manipulation of food, and domestically oriented religious activities characterize women's religious modes in many cultures.[62] Insights from feminist Jewish anthropology could surely shed light on other cultural situations.

Finally, Jewish feminists have a crucial contribution to make to applied anthropology. Many feminist academics have rightly refused to acknowledge traditional boundaries between the "ivory tower" and the "real world." Feminist Jewish anthropological fieldwork should address such issues as the high rate of abortion coupled with the low use of birth control among Russian women immigrants to Israel,[63] inheritance conflicts between widows and sons in a number of Jewish subcultures, and the role of women in the Israeli army.

Conclusion

The task of feminist critique in anthropology is not only to discover female forms of cultural expression, but also honestly and articulately to treat them as equally important as the more well-known (and to western academics, more similar) male ways. Issues of ethnographic distance are particularly poignant for Jewish feminist anthropologists, who research Others (such as Ethiopians, Kurds, kibbutznikim, and old people) who are simultaneously Self (Jewish women).

Not all the discoveries that we, as educated, western feminist anthropologists, make about Jewish women are pleasant or comfortable. When I began my fieldwork among Kurdish women I was, on some level of consciousness, searching for an alternative to the patriarchal Judaism of great tradition texts. (Unlike most of the Jewish feminists I had met in Israel, I was not interested in studying the Bible, the Talmud, or other texts that I believed reflected male interests and experiences.) What I found was women who revered those texts—even though they themselves could not read a single word of them. At a later stage of analysis I came to understand that they treated those texts as charms or talismans to ward off misfortune from their children and grandchildren. Not only had these women allowed themselves to be mystified by male literacy, I thought, but their so-called authentic female spirituality boiled down to nothing more than a slew of magical incantations! It is only in the past few years, as I have nursed my own children through illnesses, injuries, and emotional hurts, that I have begun—just begun—to respect traditional women's religiosity, which has more to do with love, death, and human relations than with abstract theological concepts.

Notes

1. Stacey and Thorne argue that "the transformation of the core domain assumptions of the discipline [anthropology] has been more radical than in any other field. And the conceptual breakthroughs have achieved greater acceptance by many of the prominent scholars in the field." Judith Stacey and Barrie Thorne, "The Missing Feminist Revolution in Sociology," *Social Problems* 32(4) (1985): 301–16 (esp. 305).

2. Biblical scholar Phyllis Bird, e.g., has used contemporary ethnographic studies of Iranian and Moroccan Muslim and Kurdish Jewish women to analyze women's role in the Israelite cultus. Phyllis Bird, "The Place of Women in the Israelite Cultus, in Paul Hanson, Patrick Miller, and Sean McBride, eds., *Ancient Israelite Religion: Essays in Honor of Frank M. Cross* (Philadelphia: Fortress, 1987), 397–419.

3. See Harvey E. Goldberg, "Anthropology and the Study of Traditional Jewish Societies," *AJS Review* 15(1) (1993): 1–22.

4. See, e.g., Judith Plaskow's chapter in this book. Some feminist and nonfeminist Jewish thinkers believe that normative Judaism is less patriarchal than the great traditions of surrounding cultures. Other writers show that the position of women in Judaism has changed over the centuries. Although I would certainly agree (at least to some extent) with both of these positions, I strongly assert that the Jewish great tradition—an inherently textual tradition—has been, and for the most part continues to be, male-dominated.

5. See Shirley Ardener, "The Representation of Women in Academic Models," in Leela Dube, Eleanor Leacock, and Shirley Ardener, ed., *Visibility and Power: Essays on Women in Society and Development* (Delhi: Oxford University Press, 1986), 3–14.

6. Rosaldo and Lamphere's anthology remains the best introduction to feminist perspectives in anthropology. Michelle Z. Rosaldo and Louise Lamphere, eds., *Woman, Culture, and Society* (Stanford: Stanford University Press, 1974).

7. This is most likely linked to the overlap between feminist and Marxist anthropology. Marxist analysis is far more meaningful in dealing with economic and political matters than it is in dealing with religion (see Strathern's paper on feminism and anthropology).

Anthropologists of religion have to a large extent been locked into a structuralist approach that stresses myths and symbols rather than ritual actors (see, e.g., Ortner's work on women and nature, and men and culture). Marilyn Strathern, "An Awkward Relationship: The Case of Feminism and Anthropology," *Signs* 12(2) (1987): 276–92; Sherry B. Ortner, "Is Female to Male as Nature Is to Culture?" in Michelle Rosaldo and Louise Lamphere, eds., *Woman, Culture, and Society* (Stanford: Stanford University Press, 1974), 67–88.

8. It is clear that Jews have lived with a variety of political, economic, and kinship systems that have no necessary relation to the fact of Jewishness or Judaism.

9. Robert Redfield, *Peasant Society and Culture* (Chicago: University of Chicago Press, 1956).

10. S. D. Goiten, *A Mediterranean Society*, vol. 3, *The Family* (Berkeley: University of California Press, 1978), 353.

11. Ibid., 356.

12. Milton Jacobs, *A Study of Cultural Stability and Change: The Moroccan Jewess* (Washington, D.C.: Catholic University of America Press, 1956).

13. Vimala Jayanti, *Women in Mea Shearim* (M.A. thesis, Hebrew University, 1982), 104.

14. Tamar El-Or, "Educated and Ignorant: The Paradox of Knowledge among Ultra-Orthodox Jewish Women," paper given at the Israel-Canada Conference for the Social Scientific Study of Judaism (Toronto, 1990), p. 14 (emphasis in original).

15. Ultra-Orthodox Jews not only believe in God and the sanctity of Jewish law (as do all Orthodox Jews) but also follow a total life-style that rejects modern, secular, and western ways, a life-style that often revolves around a charismatic leader. There are several neighborhoods in Israel that are populated solely by the ultra-Orthodox, lending themselves to anthropological participant-observation methodology.

16. See Rhonda Berger-Sofer, *Pious Women: A Study of Women's Roles in a Hasidic and Pious Community: Mea She'arim,* Ph.D diss., Rutgers University (1979); also see Jayanti, *Women in Mea Shearim.*

17. Sanday goes on to argue that the origins of sexual segregation lie in a people's perception of the environment as hostile the origins of sexual integration lie in a people's perception of the environment as a partner rather than as an opponent. She also connects the presence of male dominance with a mythology of a masculine creator god. Peggy Sanday, *Female Power and Male Dominance: On the Origins of Sexual Inequality* (Cambridge: Cambridge University Press, 1981), esp. p. 7.

18. Those few who did were very old and sat either in the courtyard or veiled in the men's section.

19. A. Brauer was the first scholar to investigate systematically and write about the cultural experience of Kurdish Jewish men and women. His comprehensive reconstruction of Jewish life in Kurdistan, *Jews of Kurdistan* (Jerusalem: HaMaarav, 1947, in Hebrew), contains a gold mine of information about Jewish women.

20. Linda Dubler Katz, "Culturally Determined Dichotomy in the Musical Practice of the

Yemenite Jews," paper given at the American Anthropological Association Seventieth Annual Meeting (1971), esp. pp. 9–10.

21. Roger M. Keesing, "Kwaio Women Speak: The Micropolitics of Autobiography in a Solomon Island Society," *American Anthropologist* 18(1) (1985): 27–39 (esp. p. 27).

22. Lisa Gilad, *Ginger and Salt: Yemeni Jewish Women in an Israeli Town* (Boulder: Westview, 1989), 16; see also Esther Schely-Newman's work on North African Jewish women's narratives, "The Woman Was Shot: A Communal Tale," *Journal of American Folklore* 106 (1993): 285–303.

23. Riv-Ellen Prell, *Prayer and Community: The Havura in American Judaism* (Detroit: Wayne State University Press, 1989), 278.

24. Ibid., 283.

25. Jane Monnig Atkinson, "Anthropology," *Signs* 8(2) (1982): 236–58 (esp. p. 248).

26. Barbara Myerhoff, *Number Our Days* (New York: Dutton, 1979), 142.

27. Gilad, *Ginger and Salt,* 128.

28. Susan Starr Sered, *Women as Ritual Experts* (New York: Oxford University Press, 1992).

29. Brauer, *Jews of Kurdistan,* 148.

30. Garnet was the earliest western observer to write about the culture of Jewish women of the East. She spent time among the women of Turkey and wrote an extensive (yet rather anecdotal) account of the folkways of Jewish women. Lucy Garnet, *The Women of Turkey and Their Folklore* (London: David Nutt, 1893).

31. Maurie Sacks, "Computing Community at Purim," *Journal of American Folklore* 102 (1989): 275–91.

32. Joelle Bahloul, *La Culte de la Table Dresse: Rites et Traditions de la Table Juive Algeriènne* (Paris: A.-M. Metailie, 1983), esp. pp. 263–4.

33. Sered, *Women as Ritual Experts,* 1992.

34. Brauer, *Jews of Kurdistan,* 274–5.

35. Israel Museum, *Jews of Kurdistan: Lifestyle, Tradition, and Art* (1981).

36. C. Rice, *Persian Women and Their Ways* (London: Seely, 1923).

37. Laurence D. Loeb, "Religious Imperatives and Women's Behavior in Two Middle Eastern Jewish Communities," paper presented at the American Anthropological Association Annual Meeting (San Francisco, 1992).

38. Donna Shai, "Family Conflict and Cooperation in Folksongs of Kurdish Jews," paper presented at the International Conference on Jewish Communities in Muslim Lands (Jerusalem: Hebrew University, n.d.).

39. Micaela di Leonardo, *The Varieties of Ethnic Experience: Kinship, Class, and Gender among California Italian-Americans* (Ithaca: Cornell University Press, 1984).

40. See, e.g., Blu Greenberg, *On Women and Judaism: A View from Tradition* (Philadelphia: Jewish Publication Society of America, 1981).

41. Donna Shai, "Wedding Customs among Kurdish Jews in (Zakho) Kurdistan and in (Jerusalem) Israel," *Folklore Research Center Studies* 4 (1974): 279. Shai's translation.

42. Gilad, *Ginger and Salt,* 59.

43. See, e.g., Brauer, *Jews of Kurdistan,* 1947.

44. Sered, *Women as Ritual Experts,* 1992.

45. Rahel Wasserfall, "Bargaining for Gender Identity: Love, Sex and Money on an Israeli Moshav," *Ethnology* 29(4) (1990): 327–40.

46. Karen Sacks, *Sisters and Wives: The Past and Future of Sexual Equality* (Westport, Conn.: Greenwood, 1979).

47. D. Weintraub and M. Shapiro, "The Traditional Family in Israel in the Process of Change: Crisis and Continuity," *British Journal of Sociology* 19 (1968): 284–99.

48. Shai, "Family Conflict" (n.d.), p. 8.

49. Jane Collier, Michelle Rosaldo, and Sylvia Yanagisako, "Is There a Family? New Anthropological Views," in Barrie Thorne and Marilyn Yalom, eds., *Rethinking the Family* (New York: Longman, 1982), 25–39.

50. Esther Boserup, *Women's Role in Economic Development* (London: Allen and Unwin, 1970); Mona Etienne and Eleanor Leacock, *Women and Colonization, Anthropological Perspectives* (New York: Praeger, 1980).

51. Gilad, *Ginger and Salt,* 66.

52. Rita Simon, *Continuity and Change* (Cambridge: Cambridge University Press, 1978), 117.

53. Susan Sered, "Religious Rituals and Secular Ritual: Interpenetrating Models of Childbirth in a Modern, Israeli Context," *Sociology of Religion* 54(1) (1993): 101–14.

54. Shalva Weil, *Ethiopian One-Parent Families in Israel* (Jerusalem: Hebrew University, NCJW Research Institute for Innovation in Education, 1991), 9.

55. Anthropologists interested in gender have argued both sides of the question. One side contends that western constructs prevent us from seeing egalitarian gender relations in unfamiliar contexts, and that privatized ownership has been the real cause of sexual asymmetry in previously egalitarian cultures. The other side asserts that biological sexual differences always lead to some sort of socially constituted gender differences.

56. Yonina Talmon-Garber, "Sex-Role Differentiation in an Egalitarian Society," in *Sexual Equality: The Israeli Kibbutz Tests the Theories,* ed. Michal Palgi, Joseph Blasi, Menahem Rosner, and Marilyn Safir, pp. 8–26 (Norwood, Penn.: Norwood, Kibbutz Studies Book Series, 1983); Judith Buber Agassi, "Theories of Gender Equality: Lessons from the Israeli Kibbutz," *Gender and Society* 3(2) (1989): 160–86.

57. Lionel Tiger and Joseph Shepher, "Conclusions from Women in the Kibbutz Research," in Palgi et al., *Sexual Equality,* 27–44; Melford Spiro, "Gender and Culture: Kibbutz Women Revisited," ibid., 57–68.

58. Joseph Blasi, "A Critique of *Gender and Culture: Kibbutz Women Revisited,*" ibid., 91–99; Marilyn Safir, "The Kibbutz: An Experiment in Social and Sexual Equality? An Historical Perspective," ibid., 100–29 (esp. p. 128).

59. Henrietta Moore, *Feminism and Anthropology* (Cambridge: Polity, 1988), 11.

60. Atkinson ("Anthropology," 252) reviews studies of Gusii, Australian, Taiwanese, Sarakatsani, and Hausa women that highlight this point.

61. Harvey E. Goldberg, "Family and Community in Sephardic North Africa: Historical and Anthropological Perspective," in David Kraemer, ed., *The Jewish Family: Metaphor and Meaning* (New York: Oxford University Press, 1989), 133–51.

62. See, e.g., Cornelius Ouwehand, *Hateruma: Socio-Religious Aspects of a South-Ryukyan Island* (Leiden: E. J. Brill, 1985); Jack M. Potter, "Cantonese Shamanism," in Arthur Wolf, ed., *Religion and Ritual in Chinese Society* (Stanford: Stanford University Press, 1974); Lucy Rushton, "Doves and Magpies: Village Women in the Greek Orthodox Church," in Pat Holden, ed., *Women's Religious Experiences* (London: Croom Helm, 1983).

63. Delilah Amir, "Abortion Committees: Educating and Controlling Women," in Clarisse Feinman, ed., *The Criminalization of a Woman's Body* (Newton, N.J.: Haworth, 1991).

Sleeping with the Other:
The Problem of Gender in
American-Jewish Literature

In the past few decades, American Jewish writing has gar-
nered great critical attention, much of it accolades, as well
as enthusiastic popular support. According to Theodore
Gross, writing in 1973, American Jewish writing was "the
most important literary expression in our time."[1] Although
critics worried that the Jewish novel might have run its
course since its major themes (variously described as cultural
dislocation, alienation, and marginality) were no longer
sharply relevant to the lives of modern Jewry, most agreed
that Jewish literature had had an enormous effect on American letters.[2]

Despite the prominence of American Jewish writing in
the contemporary period and the considerable body of criticism that has developed around it, until recently relatively
few scholars have addressed a key issue that is virtually om-
nipresent in this field—the theme of gender. If American
Jewish writing owed its popularity to the coincidence of
traditional Jewish angst (the angst of survival in the modern
world, the simultaneity of dislocation and assimilation) with
that of most other Americans, who were also caught in the
vise of modernization, then understanding the sexual and
gendered representations of that angst would seem to be
requisite.

The ubiquity of the shiksa as a character in American
Jewish novels and of intermarriage as a theme is only one
indication of the importance of gendered messages in Jewish
literature. As Frederic Cople Jaher suggests, fictional interfaith couplings reveal "momentous issues of group and self
survival and betrayal, of balancing anxieties and ambitions,
of reconciling religious and national loyalties, and of bridg-
ing past and present."[3] Jaher, who uses only the works of

male authors in his examination of this problem, comments that the theme of the shiksa in both popular and high culture has received scant attention.[4]

Jewish women authors have also used interfaith romance as a central theme. Anzia Yezierska's troubled real-life romance with John Dewey was the template for many of her short stories and novels, as Mary Dearborn's *Love in the Promised Land: The Story of Anzia Yezierska and John Dewey* reminds us. Their liaison is also the subject of a new novel by Norma Rosen.[5] Authors as varied as Elizabeth Stern, Fannie Hurst, and Tess Slesinger have used intermarriage as a theme in their writings.

In recent years, an increasing number of scholars, most of them women, have begun to turn their attention to the work of Jewish women writers as they explore questions involving what critic Nancy K. Miller has called the "sex-gender system" in literature. Feminism has provided these scholars with the "fundamental understanding that the deployment of the universal is inherently, if paradoxically, partial and political," as Miller notes.[6] To remedy this problem, feminist scholars have been conducting a broad-based effort of reconstruction and rediscovery that has taken them through several stages of literary analysis. According to Elaine Showalter, these have involved first, "exposing the misogyny of literary practice"; second, discovering that women writers have a "literature of their own"; and third, rethinking the conceptual basis of the discipline itself.[7] Although these approaches have called up many different, and often conflicting, feminist analyses, a common denominator has been the focus on reconstituting the canon through the study of women's writings.

"What does it mean to read and write as a woman within the institution that authorizes most reading and writing?" Miller asks.[8] The answer, as critics Sandra Gilbert and Susan Gubar observe, requires attention to both the biographical and textual aspects of women's work. Because the concepts "male" and "female" have always had an impact on human experience, they argue that it is essential to analyze how the lives of writers and the texts they create are embodied in "the materiality and mythology of history, which has almost always been gendered."[9] In contrast to French feminist theory, Anglo-American theorists like Gilbert, Gubar, and Showalter have focused on how literature represents the social and historical realities of women's oppression and their resistance to oppression, as well as how sexual differences are constructed through language.[10]

Contemporary feminist scholars have emphasized gender differences in reading as well as in authorship. Miller is one of several recent critics who have seen woman's reading as "politics," a crucial organizing center, which according to Wai-chee Dimock is a "site of contestation" and a "site of celebration . . . a site from which to construct an alternative canon."[11] What is at stake, argues Judith Fetterly, is the control of textuality: when their experiences can be read into texts, women will refuse the role of the Other "without reciprocity," as now exists in men's writing.[12]

Such readings take us beyond the bounds of conventional literary and psychoanalytic frameworks, Marianne Hirsch notes. If, for example, they allow for the voices of both mothers and daughters, fashioning a "double voice" that yields a "multiple female consciousness," then reading as well as writing can become a "re-vision."[13] Employing these and other strategies that revise (or resist) the convention that defines the feminine only in relation to the masculine, women readers and authors engage in feminist acts and define a feminist poetics, according to Nancy Miller.[14]

The feminist literary project has come relatively late to Jewish scholarship. Thanks, however, to *Studies in American Jewish Literature,* which has devoted several complete issues and an increasing number of articles to women writers and female subjects, and thanks to many individual authors, the concerns I have outlined are moving more rapidly to the center of the field. Until this happens more regularly, the full implications of the gendered content of literary texts and the historical experience of readers and writers will remain elusive.

An example of this unrealized vision comes in the 1987 study *After the Revolution,* an analysis of the American Jewish imagination by Mark Shechner. In the introduction, Shechner notes that many of his students, particularly Jewish women, deeply disliked, and in fact were "repulsed" by, the "character and conduct" displayed in works they had read for a course on the American Jewish novel. As Shechner explains, "They just did not like Roth's Alex Portnoy and Peter Tarnopol, nor did they care much for Bellow's Joseph in *Dangling Man* or Moses Herzog; they did not warm to Malamud's Morris Bober and Frank Alpine and felt a special kind of sexual distaste for Helen Bober." After some further examples of the students' displeasure, Shechner notes that they gained support from Vivian Gornick's essay, "Why Do These Men Hate Women?" which appeared at that time in the *Village Voice.* Although Shechner accuses Gornick of misreading some scenes from the novels and charging Jewish authors "with virtually every crime known to women," he acknowledges that her accusations, although exaggerated, are not readily dismissed. Admitting that the Jewish novel was by no means the "unalloyed contribution to the moral enrichment of mankind" that some observers had made it, Shechner launches into describing the main subject of his book: the "tumultuous" and "polemical" quality of Jewish literature that resulted from the "conversion" of the major Jewish intellectuals from "politics to therapy"—from the political to the personal— after midcentury.[15]

The main outlines of Shechner's acute analysis need not concern us here. What is relevant, perhaps, is that he has defined the trajectory of the Jewish imagination to exclude not only several important male writers but practically all female ones. Although Saul Bellow, Norman Mailer, and Philip Roth are included—along with Sigmund Freud, Allen Ginsberg, Wilhelm Reich, Isaac Rosenfeld, and Lionel Trilling—Hortense Calisher, Bernard Malamud, Tillie Olsen, Cynthia Ozick, Grace Paley, Henry Roth, Muriel Rukeyser, Jo Sinclair, Tess Slesinger, and many more are out. Shechner does not ask why noteworthy women writers did not take the same journey that he believes most of the prominent male writers did. Nor does he return to the problem posed at the book's outset: Why were the Jewish women students, in particular, so "repelled" and "appalled" by the fiction they had read? If readers' reactions are influenced by their gender identity and attitudes, should we not conclude that the works themselves require analysis specifically around issues of gender?

If the clue given by Shechner's students is taken up, issues of gender must be considered as fundamental to understanding the imaginations of Jewish literati, both male and female. The portrayal of Jewish (as well as Gentile) women, their relations with Jewish men, and the more general relation of what is considered feminine or masculine are topics that a gendered analysis of American Jewish literature must include. Caught in the struggle between tradition and modernity, between family and community and the demands of self, the characters in much Jewish literature (particularly in works penned by men) deploy a sexual battleground to achieve a resolution to their dilemmas. Achieving selfhood is depicted in gendered terms; for Roth, Bellow, and Mailer, the quest was for a self-sufficient manhood. For Yezierska, Olsen, Paley and other female writers, the goal was female independence, an independence expressed in relation to family and communal responsibilities.

Sexual politics involve the depiction of intra- and interfaith romances, masculine and feminine character, the competing realms of family and the world, and the bedroom as battleground—private and public—and thus serve as an important lens with which to examine larger meanings of the Jewish experience in America. Mother-daughter relations, especially those that give voice to maternal as well as filial experience, are another crucial indicator of the workings of the sex and gender system in literature, one that does not posit concepts of women only in relation to men. The importance of the reader's and the writer's experience in engaging multiple meanings of texts must also be taken into account.

If recent scholarly writings and presentations at conferences are indicative, these subjects are becoming increasingly important to American Jewish literary criticism. Moving beyond the stage of exposing misogyny to the dual tasks of exploring women's writings and probing the conceptualizations of gender difference, a growing number of critics are fruitfully adapting the categories of analysis set forth by feminist theorists.

American Jewish literature offers especially rich material for the latest phase of feminist criticism, which critic Teresa de Lauretis has articulated as one based on an "eccentric subject"—a subject who embodies the many paradoxes of identity and difference that characterize recent feminist writing. Theorists like de Lauretis, interested in differences between women (though not in the sense of binary opposition of woman versus man), describe subjectivity itself as multiple and fluid, shifting across "variable axes of difference," as they seek to redefine questions of marginality and displacement in literature and society.[16] The eccentric subject, who may be "lesbian, *mestiza*," or any "Inappropriate/d Other" (in Trin T. Minh-ha's words), lives in a "conceptual and experiential space carved out of the social field, a space of contradictions, in the here and now, that needs to be affirmed but not resolved." It is a space in which the subject affirms "'I am like you' while pointing insistently to the difference; and . . . unsettling every definition of otherness arrived at."[17]

Because Jewish women, like mestizas and lesbians, often occupied a space on the cultural borders of gender, ethnicity, and nationality, the attempt to define literary politics that focus on the subject-author-reader as simultaneously identical and different is particularly relevant. Analysis of the varied, contradictory, and multiple contexts of female and male selfhood expressed in American Jewish writing can add immensely to the ongoing reconceptualization of feminist critical theory while illuminating American Jewish literary history.

A Gendered Analysis of American Jewish Literature: Exploratory Themes

Although not all critics agree that there exists a specific American Jewish literature, defined by a particular, unvarying "Jewish" style, sensibility, and substance, most have in fact located diverse representations of an ethnic,

Jewish fiction over the generations.[18] Contexts, milieus, and characters have changed, but the dilemmas of ethnicity—the problem of living within, among, and yet outside mainstream America—have been continuous for Jewish writers since the early twentieth century. Writers of the immigrant generation, their depression era proletarian-conscious successors, and the "breakthrough," mainstream writers of the late 1940s and 1950s each examined the disjunction between their own "modern" sensibilities and the overbearing pieties of the past and present.

The quest for identity that arose from such disjunctions has been a prominent theme both of Jewish novels of acculturation and of those of social criticism, two dominant twentieth-century forms of American Jewish fiction. Each of these conflicts may be interpreted from a gendered lens, since the dominant writers of each era (usually male) have often depicted main themes—whether the struggle for material success, power, or love, or the exploration of identity itself—as deeply connected to male-female relations or the expression of masculine and feminine selfhood.

As June Sochen and other feminist critics have pointed out, questions of identity and ethnicity for female writers have been "multilayered" and in many respects different from those for male writers.[19] In creating themselves as authors, Jewish women have first had to defy tradition, religious and secular, in different ways than men. The struggles they experienced in becoming artists parallel many of their characters' conflicts as they express desires for independence that run counter to traditional responsibilities. In telling their stories, they illuminate realities of Jewish women's lives that derive from the common Jewish heritage but that are specific to female experience. Writing about the self and family, community and tradition, history and destiny, women writers offer a special window on the experiences of being Jewish in America.

The Immigrant Period

One of the female authors most often cited by critics for her authentic portrayals of Jewish life is Anzia Yezierska (1880–1969). The first Eastern European woman writer to achieve literary prominence in fiction, Yezierska has been called the "most significant Jewish writer of the twenties"[20] In her stories, collected in the 1919 anthology *Hungry Hearts* (purchased for screen adaptation by Samuel Goldwyn), and in several novels of the 1920s, including *Bread Givers,* which received critical acclaim, she dramatized the struggle of immigrant Jews to become Americanized. Although many of her protagonists leave the poverty and despair of the ghetto behind them, this triumph is mitigated by the loneliness they find when they have abandoned the community and values to which they have been bred.

Yezierska herself had been a "ghetto Cinderella," plucked out of the poverty of her first writing years when Goldwyn discovered her work and brought it to national attention. By 1930, some years after she had left Hollywood in disgust, her stories of immigrant life no longer attracted either a popular or a critical audience. Impoverished and neglected, she joined the Works Progress Administration (WPA) Writers Project in 1937 and spent several unhappy years afterward in a small town in Vermont, trying, unsuccessfully, to write. Although her 1950 autobiography, *Red Ribbon on a White Horse,* was favorably reviewed, she spent most of her remaining years lonely and forgotten. Not until the women's movement of the late 1960s, and especially the reissuance of her works by historian Alice Kessler-Harris, did Yezierska come to the attention of a wide public.

In her important introductions to Yezierska's novel *Bread Givers* and *The Open Cage,* a collection of her short stories, Kessler-Harris cites themes that Yezierska shared with other immigrant novelists—"poverty, Americanization, family tensions, the ambiguity of success." Yet she explains that the author's depiction of women's experiences of immigration distinguished her work from that of fellow writers, usually men, who portrayed women as "manipulative and overly protective mothers, or dependent wives made fearful by their helplessness." In contrast to these portraits were Yezierska's "independent and self-willed women," struggling to survive yet scarred by their pain and sacrifices. These images, as well as the conflict Yezierska experienced between her ambition as a writer and the gendered expectations of her family and community, are explored in *Anzia Yezierska: A Writer's Life,* by Louise Levitas Henriksen, Yezierska's daughter and a journalist in her own right. Carol Schoen's literary biography *Anzia Yezierska* contrasts the maturity of the writer's later works with less professional early works. Both emphasize Yezierska's painful struggle to consecrate herself to the craft of writing, however high the cost.[21]

Since Yezierska's rediscovery, many other critics have focused on her dramatic portrayals of women's struggles for autonomy. Louis Harap, for example, cites Yezierska's "merciless exposure of male supremacism in the orthodox home" as one of her four major themes; he observes that romantic love, usually with a "higher" Gentile, is another.[22] In a chapter on Yezierska in *The New Covenant: Jewish Writers and the American Idea,* Sam B. Girgus also notes Yezierska's "passionate feminist consciousness," which he believes made her interpretation of the new covenant (the Jewish idea of the American way) different from that of the male writers he analyzes in the book. Yezierska's notion of selfhood and success, for example, so critical to American Way writers, was marked not by wealth and status, but by "individual fulfillment and social progress."[23]

Feminist scholars have elaborated several interpretative strategies for elucidating the gendered meanings of Yezierska's work.[24] In "Art, Gender, and the Jewish Tradition in Yezierska's *Red Ribbon on a White Horse* and Potok's *My Name Is Asher Lev,*" Shelly Regenbaum compares the efforts of the books' protagonists, both "outcast artists," to develop their art in the face of family and community rejection. Regenbaum suggests that whereas Asher Lev is able to develop a strong sense of identity as a Jewish man and as an artist, Yezierska must sacrifice her writing in order to become reconciled with the Jewish tradition.[25] Still the "punishing patriarch" in her memory, Yezierska's father finally succeeds in silencing the writer's voice. The tranquillity she achieves in *Red Ribbon,* says Regenbaum, does not reflect self-reliance; rather, it is a "state of narcotic bliss, gained at a terrible loss, for Anzia has killed the artist in her."[26] In Regenbaum's view, the difference between Asher Lev's successful rebellion against family dictates and Yezierska's tragic one is that he is a male with "prestige, responsibility, potential and actual power," who could take an active role in society, while Yezierska could be perceived as only a "wife and mother." Asher, secure in his manhood, questions others' definitions of him and never allows the Orthodox community's rejection of his art to interfere with his own positive masculinity, while Yezierska does not challenge her father's definition of her as a queer woman (because unmarried) and a violent threat to the community because of her "masculine" vocation. The confusions of identity that result from this judgment ultimately weaken her commitment to her art and her power to write.[27] Although there are some pitfalls in contrasting Chaim Potok's work of fiction to Yezierska's autobiographical novel, her method can serve as a model for the comparative analysis of Jewish literature based on gender differences.

Rose Kamel also addresses Yezierska's struggles to become an artist and the undermining of her talent and self-worth by her father. Focusing on the writer's narrative style, Kamel suggests that Yezierska's lack of confidence, engendered by her father's hostility, undermined the authority of her authorship and led to the lack of self-detachment, which Kamel feels weakens her prose. Only in a few portraits, like her character Hanneh Breineh, does Yezierska move from "self-consciousness to otherness" to create a necessary narrative distance. Informing Kamel's analysis of narrative style is an acute reading of Yezierska's gendered characters—paternal (when Jewish, they are patriarchal and domineering, though sometimes saintly; when New England Yankees, they are benevolent, though distant) and maternal (resourceful and strong).[28]

Ellen Golub's intriguing article, "Eat Your Heart Out: The Fiction of Anzia Yezierska," points to the importance of orality in Yezierska's work. She notes that in fiction, with such titles as "The Fat of the Land," *Bread Givers,* and *Hungry Hearts,* Yezierska uses metaphors of hunger and eating to express the immigrant's "balked desire" to belong to America, a hunger that cannot be sated. Golub's contribution to the understanding of the interaction between gender and ethnic fiction is to connect Yezierska's use of these themes to libidinal messages regarding the mother-child interaction—the getting and giving of food—and to highlight the poignancy of Yezierska's untrusting, unhappy heroines, fleeing the patriarchy of Old World Judaism but unable to sustain relations in the New World. According to Golub, Judaism is "a stale relic from which Yezierska's women flee," a world "controlled by men: a few ineffective immigrants, servile and flaccid; neglectful husbands and fathers, piously observant of other-worldly concerns; tyrannical brutes—matchmakers, landlords, fathers, and moneylenders—who hypocritically torment, deceive, and deny all those in their greedy power."[29] Women, however, are portrayed differently. Golub sees the mother in *Bread Givers,* for example, as a significant landmark in American Jewish literature: "The first real portrait drawn of the Jewish mother in America," this mother is "virtuous" because "unlike her husband," she is the "one who feeds."[30] Critic Sonya Michel, the author of one of the earliest treatises on Jewish mothers and daughters in American literature, agrees that the portrayal of the immigrant mother in *Bread Givers* was marked by respect and tolerance, a far cry from the sentimental encomiums to "My Yiddish Momme," written by men.[31] As we shall see, the Jewish mother's desire to feed her family, also depicted by a later generation of male writers, becomes detached from the benevolent meanings ascribed by Yezierska.[32]

In *Pocahontas's Daughters: Gender and Ethnicity in American Culture,* Dearborn uses Pocahontas's marriage as a trope for fiction about the ethnic woman. The marriage of an ethnic woman to a "pure" American is doomed to failure, Dearborn suggests, for it represents both a sense of selfhood unavailable to women and relations of power in which women participate only as victims. The futility and contradictions of intermarriage as a symbol for ethnic women find their fullest expression, says Dearborn, in the life and work of Yezierska.[33]

Another writer of the immigrant period whose work is important to the study of gender in American Jewish literature is Mary Antin, the author of *The Promised Land,* an autobiographical memoir published in 1912. Several critics have pointed to the fact that because autobiography exists as both history and literature, it has been an especially rich mode for ethnic and minority expression, for Jews and women in particular as well as for blacks.[34] In writing on American Jewish autobiography, Steven J. Rubin cites two female authors, Yezierska and Antin, as exemplars of Jewish writers' use of the autobiographical format to explore personal and group identity, to link their lives to an "entire social process."[35]

The Promised Land, called one of the "first great works" of American-Jewish literature by such critics as Allen Guttmann, is commonly seen as the classic story of "assimilation, transformation and hope"—the immigrant's version of Ben Franklin's optimistic story of freedom and progress.[36] A dissenter to the usually admiring appraisal of *The Promised Land* as an assimilationist epic is Sarah Blacher Cohen, who has angrily called the book a "breach of promise" as a model of Jewish-American literature by a Jewish-American woman.[37] Cohen's denunciation derives from her view that Antin speaks as a completely assimilated American who has given up her Judaism entirely. She is a "cheerleader" for American secularism who never comes to terms with her own religious or cultural past. Cohen notes that although Antin writes of the discriminatory treatment accorded girls in the European shtetl, she never challenges it; "the voice of the Jewish girl from Polotzk" is never heard.[38] She compares *The Promised Land,* moreover, to some of the "recent disappointing novels" by American-Jewish women writers whom she believes are "every bit as *gentile*" as Antin in their ignorance of the spiritual dimensions of Judaism.[39]

Steven Rubin offers a more nuanced reading. Rubin emphasizes Antin's celebration of American possibilities but also finds a nostalgic longing for the past, a "time of familial warmth, of meaningful ceremony, of childhood happiness, of love and of caring," in spite of the restrictions it held for Jews.[40] Rubin notes Antin's powerful descriptions of women's inferior role in Polotzk, where she grew up, though he feels that she did indeed challenge women's confinement even before she left Russia. Yet his argument that Antin's narrative is more complex than the naive, optimistic account of acculturation that critics usually take it as being does not develop the gendered meanings that he cites as partial evidence. For, in fact, Antin's celebration of her own spiritual rebirth in America is tempered by her admission that for her mother and older sister, Frieda, life continued much as before. Although Antin was free to fashion her own life in America, the other women in her family remained like the "treadmill horses" they had been in the shtetl, caught in a round of ceaseless, thankless labor.[41] She is aware of this "injustice" but accepts her relatives' sacrifices on her behalf. Her father's economic failures in the New World, along with his insistence that his more pious wife abandon her religious faith—an insistence he took with "manly haste" to ensure the family's Americanization—are further indications that Antin recognized, and regretted, the continuation of patriarchal forms in America.[42] Antin's narrative abounds with examples of tensions between her parents over issues of religious practice and the family's disintegration in America. Despite her insistence on her own successful adaptation, these clues suggest that her continuing concern over the issues of women's place within the home, and within Judaism, tempered her enthusiasm for American life. Along with her short stories and later articles, which also reveal her awareness of gender discrimination, they suggest a more cautious approach to *The Promised Land* as a classic myth of acculturation.[43]

Another window on the connection between acculturation and gender is afforded by the work of Abraham Cahan—especially the short stories collected in *Yekl and the Imported Bridegroom* and *The Rise of David Levinsky,* the "classic, if not the greatest, novel of the Jewish immigrant experience in America."[44] As Jules Chametzky has pointed out, Cahan offers a rich gallery of women, "not a sentimentalized figure among them: they work, dance, think (or don't), read (or don't), act, do, love, renounce—in short are figures in their own right, neither to be condescended to nor mythicized."[45]

Usually regarded as an expression of the bitter fruits of assimilation, Cahan's fiction presents many examples of gender conflict as well as generational conflict, a theme that has only begun to be explored by critics. Susan Kress notes, for example, that in Cahan's work, the ambivalence of immigrants about assimilation is mirrored in the attitudes of the characters (especially women) toward marriage.[46] Kress believes that although Cahan does not offer "strikingly bold" female protagonists, he frequently presents women's perspective. Kress suggests that Cahan sees marriage—the primary option for immigrant women—as merely an "arrangement" of economic convenience, a trap that means "conversion to the life of the husband and death of the self." The dilemma of Cahan's women is that "to marry is to risk absorption in the identity of another; not to marry is to risk displacement."[47]

Although I believe Kress is right, Cahan's ambivalence about assimilation is shown not only in his portrayal of marriage as confinement, as she suggests, but in its possibilities for mutuality. In "A Sweatshop Romance" and "A Ghetto Wedding," for example, despite the probability of unhappy economic futures, a young woman and man who work together in their shops will become more equal in marriage than was possible in the Old World. Cahan's stories show the dark side of immigrant adjustment to urban America, but the modern women he writes about offer hope that the new generation might find greater success in America than in the Old World. Cahan's portrayals of love, marriage, and divorce offer a complex panorama of the younger generation's reaction to the challenges of modern America.[48]

American Jewish Literature: The 1930s and 1940s

The 1930s and 1940s represented a transition period in American Jewish literature. As David Martin Fine suggests, Jewish writers of this period built on the foundation of immigrant experience to establish a "Jewish literary and moral sensibility that would reach full maturity in the post–World War II 'Breakthrough' of the Jewish writer as essential American."[49] In their narratives of ghetto childhoods and proletarian novels of awakening and conversion, they explored those sources of pain that characterized second-generation Jewry—generational conflict, political estrangement, and discontinuity with tradition.

Writing convincingly of the national scene—poverty, displacement, and protest—by depicting their own experiences, authors made the depression a pathway to a majoritarian Jewish literature.[50] As Harap and others have pointed out, Jewish writers played a major role in the development of proletarian literature and were disproportionately represented in literary positions of influence throughout the decade.[51] The period saw the publication of several lasting Jewish novels, particularly Michael Gold's *Jews without Money* (1930), Henry Roth's *Call It Sleep* (1934), and Meyer Levin's *Old Bunch* (1937). Yet most critics agree that by the mid-1940s, the amount of Jewish material in fiction by Jewish writers had declined significantly. As they grew more assimilated to American life, Jewish writers dealt less with questions of Jewish identity, heritage, and tradition.

In analyzing these trends, critics have not focused on gender as an illustrative theme as much as they had in studies of the earlier, immigrant period. Yet as is suggested by Beverly Gray Bienstock's article "The Changing Image of the Jewish Mother," transformations of gendered images of men and women reflected larger shifts in the social worlds of American Jews. Tracing the evolution of the literary image of the first-generation Jewish mother from the strong but sentimentalized "Yiddishe Momma" characteristic of Sholem Asch's *The Mother* or Samuel Raphaelson's drama *The Jazz Singer* (both 1925) to the more negative depression era image of an aggressive, materialistic matriarch, seen especially in Clifford Odets' play *Awake and Sing!* and Jerome Weidman's popular novel *I Can Get It for You Wholesale* (1957), Bienstock suggests that the 1930s Jewish mother came to embody "all that is wrong with America."[52] As portrayed by writer-sons who were the heirs of their immigrant fathers' failures and the repository of their mothers' hopes for the future, the 1930s Jewish mother "inspires her son to become a model of successful assimilation by pursing monetary goals." Though her intentions are good, "leading her sons to worship at the altar of Mammon" is a sin that the writer-sons cannot forgive.[53]

Although the bullying, authoritarian father in *Call It Sleep* is not weak in the usual sense, Bienstock argues that he may be viewed as acting out of "a sense of disorientation common to immigrant males" and that the novel follows a pattern that began to emerge in the 1930s—that of writers' expressing the psychological danger of drawing too close to mothers.[54] The unapologetic exaltation of the Jewish mother etched in Gold's popular proletarian fiction *Jews without Money* became increasingly rare.

Though their works are less well known than those of their male colleagues, Jewish women writers also wrote novels of acculturation and social protest in the depression and in the 1940s.[55] Their works explore problems of family conflict and sexual and Jewish identity, providing special insight into how women experienced these dilemmas. For example, Leane Zugsmith's *Time to Remember* (1937) and her story "Room in the World" depict the reactions of a young, radical woman striker and the wife of an unemployed worker, respectively, to the bitter hardships of the depression. Both show women as family members deeply caught in the social ferment of the time.

Jewish women writers also examined gendered subjects not broached by men. Tess Slesinger's "Miss Flinders," about a married woman's abortion, appeared in *Story* magazine in 1932, perhaps the first time a general circulation magazine addressed the issue of abortion.[56] Responding to requests that she expand the story, Slesinger wrote the critically acclaimed novel *The Unpossessed*, published in 1934. This novel and her short stories, collected in *Time: The Present* (1935), reveal a strikingly modern sensibility critical of the sexual and emotional exploitation of women by male radicals and expressive of female experiences of love, marriage, sexuality, and childbearing. A writer for the *Menorah Journal,* the chief outlet for left-leaning Jewish intellectuals in the late 1920s and early 1930s, Slesinger married Herbert Solow, its assistant editor, in 1928 and was closely associated with the "New York Intellectuals" (among them Eliot Cohen, Clifton Fadiman, Philip Rahv, and Trilling), whom she satirizes in *The Unpossessed.* Her depiction of the emotional pain suffered by the wife of a radical leftist reflects her view of the *Menorah Journal*'s interlocking treatment of women and politics. The story was based on Slesinger's own abortion, which her husband had demanded.

Another example of the relation between gender and literary politics is afforded by the work and reputation of the poet Muriel Rukeyser. Rukeyser came to critical attention when she won the Yale Younger Poets Prize in 1935, when she was twenty-one, for her volume *Theory of Flight.* The Spanish Civil War, which she had covered as a journalist, had made a profound impression on her. What followed was an outburst of poetry about resisting authoritarianism. Later in the decade she contributed to several periodicals dedicated to dramatizing the lives of the working class or to poetry and fiction that addressed world events. In the 1940s, which saw the triumph of analytic and New Criticism in the academy and the conversion of formerly radical Jewish writers to apolitical modes, Rukeyser continued in "the dauntless spirit of the thirties," as her biographer, Louise Kertesz, has noted, flaunting the standards of the day.[57]

Although Rukeyser was invited to become poetry editor of the *Partisan Review,* the literary successor to the *Menorah Journal,* she refused, a decision that perhaps led to a malicious unsigned attack by the *Partisan Review* editors on her poem *Wake Island,* Rukeyser's first response to the nation's involvement in World War II, published in 1942. The editorial on Rukeyser had the "baldly sexist title," as Kertesz notes, "Grandeur and Misery of a Poster Girl." As for the piece itself, Kertesz writes that "it would be difficult to find a comment with more malice and distortion on any modern writer in a major publication. . . . [It was] replete with innuendoes, personal abuse, and sexism."[58]

Slesinger's sensitivity to the sexism of the mostly Jewish New York intellectuals, evidenced in the attack on Rukeyser, suggests a further dimension to the study of gender and Jewish literature. The more prominent these writers became in the nation's cultural elite, the less tolerant they seemed to be of the human needs and differing opinions of the women in their circle. Rukeyser, in particular, offered a real alternative to the diminishing political commitment of Jewish male intellectuals. Her conviction that poetry and literature should be reciprocal with social action continued to the end of her life, and she became deeply involved in the women's movement, the civil rights movement, and in protests against the Vietnam War (for which she was frequently jailed). Even as most intellectuals of this period continued to dissociate political life from personal life, as Shechner forcefully argues, Rukeyser insisted that "in facing history, we look at each other," that the public and the private were intimately connected. As many male writers and critics moved farther from their Jewishness in the 1940s and 1950s, Rukeyser moved closer to hers. She wrote: "My themes and the use I have made of them have depended on my life as a poet, as a woman, as an American, and as a Jew. I don't know what part of that is Jewish; I know I have tried to integrate these four aspects, and to solve my work and my personality in terms of all four. . . . To live as poet, woman, American and Jew—this chalks in my position. If the four come together in one person, each strengthens the others."[59]

Jewish Writing in the Mainstream: The 1950s and 1960s

It is widely held that Jewish writing came fully of age in the 1950s. Moving beyond the limited frameworks of immigrant, acculturation, and social protest novels, writers like Bellow, Malamud, and Philip Roth responded to themes of marginality and suffering and the quest for "identity and meaning in a dehumanized and irrational age" that affected all Americans.[60] The Jewish experience of alienation became a universal metaphor for the condition of modern society, and Jewish literature reflected the knowledge that continuous uncertainty—"the unpredictable, the unanticipated and the unfathomable . . . adversity, trouble, grief and sorrow . . . are the normal conditions of life."[61]

Although most depression era writers had sought broad social and cultural solutions to the anxieties of their age, postwar Jewish intellectuals were much more likely to turn inward, focusing on personal questions of identity, responsibility, and trust. In so doing, they posed new challenges to old stereotypes of ethnic, national, and sexual identity. Yet as Bellow, Mailer, Malamud, Roth, and others created new types of heroes who discovered new ways of being men in the modern world, they were far less innovative in their portraits of women. A trickle of criticism came from critics at the time who objected to these writers' portrayal of sexual aggressiveness and their stereotyping or neglect of women; over the years, such criticism has increased mightily. Although some scholars have argued that these writers may be more sympathetic to their female characters than at first appears, few go so far as to suggest that their works reveal important truths about women. "Bellow often views the new woman sympathetically but perhaps not seriously enough," writes Daniel Fuchs; "Could the central character in a Bellow novel ever be a woman?"[62]

Critics have objected to the negative portrayals of Jewish mothers in the works of leading Jewish male writers. "Too well we know the Jewish mother our male writers have given us, the all-engulfing nurturer who devours the very soul with every spoonful of hot chicken soup she gives, whose every shakerful of salt contains a curse," writes Erika Duncan in a typical comment.[63] The caricature of the Jewish mother in Bruce Jay Friedman's *Mother's Kisses* (1964) is, according to Bienstock, a "supremely bitter example of the writer-son looking back in anger and responding with venom."[64]

But it was Philip Roth's *Portnoy's Complaint* (1969), called a comic masterpiece by many critics, that drew the greatest ire. To Marya Mannes, Roth's treatment of women was "abominable" and Portnoy was "the most disagreeable bastard who ever lived."[65] Sophie Portnoy—in Bienstock's words, "a domineering, castrating, enticing, meddling, and thoroughly maddening monster"—dominated the novel, refusing to allow its hero, her son, a life of his own. Yet although Bienstock acknowledges that Roth played for laughs in ridiculing Mrs. Portnoy, she sees the novel not only as a caricature of Jewish mothers but as a "brilliant study of the male mentality."[66]

Some critics have emphasized the role of the shiksa rather than the mother in *Portnoy's Complaint*. Girgus suggests that through the shiksa motif, Roth relates sexuality to culture: embodying America, the Gentile women in the book represent Portnoy's deepest desires to "rediscover" and claim America for his own, demonstrating a "Jewish version" of a classical literary theme. For Girgus, Roth's struggle to establish himself both as a Jewish writer and as a man appears as a latter-day version of Yezierska's deep struggle to find her identity and freedom as a woman writer and a Jew. "Perhaps no other modern American writer has done so much to challenge old stereotypes and concepts about masculinity," Girgus believes.[67] Girgus paints Roth as a pioneer of female as well as male sexual freedom and identity. In Roth's novel *When She Was Good* (1968), Girgus notes, "Becoming a man and achieving true sexual and personal liberation require a culture of freedom for women as well."[68] Girgus suggests that readers ought to rethink popular notions about Roth's sexism, a view also espoused by Barbara Frey Waxman.[69]

Whether or not a sexist label is applied, it is unlikely that most female readers recognized their own stories in the works of Roth or Bellow (and certainly not in Mailer's). Grace Paley began her career after what she termed "that long period of very masculine writing" that followed World War II to write about the ordinary lives of women and children. In an interview, Paley spoke of the "big difference" that separates her from Bellow and Roth, writers whose work she admires but that she thinks is "distorted": "[It is] nice to see the sexual feeling [in their work]," she said, "but I knew it wasn't written for me at all."[70] Although Paley felt Bellow's stories to be beautifully written, she was bothered that "there were no women in it." "The guys had a woman or there was an aunt that everybody loved or an aunt that everybody hated. Whatever. But the wives were terrible."[71]

Paley worried that perhaps her subject was trivial, but she became increasingly confident that the lives of the "bunch of women" who interested her—PTA women and the like—"were common and important."[72] "As a woman," Paley has said, "I'm trying to restore something to the scales, so that the woman can be seen," not as she had been, as a sexual object, or a victim, but in her full strength. "How strong they were" was what interested Paley in women's lives in the first place.[73] "Unless *we* tell about *our* lives, those stories [of male writers] can't be listened to. You can't hear half the truth. But as long as we *women* are being read, then I can accept *them*."[74]

As male Jewish writers broke through to the mainstream with fiction about the angst of marginal men, such Jewish women writers as Olsen, Paley, and Sinclair spoke for the silenced voices of women and children. In her first novel, *Wasteland,* which won the prestigious $10,000 Harper Prize in 1946, Sinclair explored the crisis of identity experienced by John Brown (born Jacob Braunowitz), who changes his name to conceal his Jewish origins. Sinclair presents a realistic portrait of a second-generation Jew struggling to come to terms with the ghetto heritage of his parents, which he must reject, as he searches for more enduring meanings of Jewish life and ritual. Speaking in Jake's voice, the author draws an equally sympathetic portrait of Debby, a lesbian who has had to confront the perils of her own sexual nonconformity. In showing how a Jew or a lesbian stood outside the cultural mainstream in America in the early 1940s, Sinclair pioneered comparisons of sexual and ethnic difference.

In a second innovative novel, *The Changelings* (1955), Sinclair assumes the voice of Judith Vincent, a teen gang leader known as Vincent who shrugs off both gender and ethnic stereotypes. Dismayed by the crude racism of her family and community, she intervenes when one of the neighbors attacks a black man who inquires about housing. Vincent's friendship with Clara, a black girl as tough and spirited as herself, opens up the possibility that people of the young generation, the changelings of the title, can come together without their elders' prejudices. Sinclair's frank examination of black-Jewish relations links questions of race to those of class and gender. It is the economic insecurity of her characters that fuels their ethnocentrism and desperate fear of change. The men of Vincent's neighborhood feel cheated by their failure to realize the American dream. In turn, they cheat on their wives, bully their children, and turn to unlawful means to solve the "problem" of black intrusion. Although Sinclair's work has attracted almost no scholarly review, her strong female characters and special attention to the question of the relation of Jewish identity to sexual, class, and racial difference merit attention from those interested in gender and ethnicity.[75]

"Tell Me a Riddle," the title story of Olsen's 1961 collection, tells the tale of Eva, an older working-class woman who refuses her husband's entreaties to go with him to a retirement home, arguing that after years of raising her children and "being with others," she wanted time for herself. Though Eva is an atheist, she reaches back to her past to recover what she considers to be the spiritual essence of Judaism—its messianic mission and its concern for a wider humanity. On her deathbed, Eva recalls the dreams of her revolutionary youth in Czarist Russia, when, as a socialist orator and organizer, she talked "not of family but beyond . . . of humankind." As she recaptured the zeal and commitment of her girlhood, the anger she felt at sacrificing her own identity to her family dissipates.

Joining self-assertion with interdependence, Olsen's vision is a strongly feminist one. When women live only through their families, she suggests, they are denied their individuality and any possibility for a larger connection to humankind. For Olsen, this vision is also a Jewish one, drawn from her Jewish socialist background. As she explained in an interview, this background, which she calls *Yiddishkeit,* taught her "knowledge and experience of injustice, of discrimination, of oppression, of genocide and of the need to act against them forever and whenever they appear," as well as "an absolute belief in the potentiality of human beings." As she says, "What is Yiddish in me . . . is inextricable from what is woman in me, from woman who is mother."[76]

The link that Olsen makes between Jewish tradition and mothering, reflected in several short stories, especially "I Stand Here Ironing," and in her novel *Yonnondio: From the Thirties* (1974), creates a portrait of Jewish family life that differs from those created by male authors. As Elaine Orr observes in a recent critical study of Olsen's work, the powerful description of Jewish home life that Henry Roth offers in *Call It Sleep* "is still a boy's perspective, that is, the perspective of one who will leave home. Similarly, a writer like Alfred Kazin, lovingly describing his mother, is able to romanticize the sound of her sewing machine because he did not and would not sit for hours at such a machine."[77] Orr notes that Olsen's perspective was dictated by the combination of her sex and working-class background; other commentators have described the importance of Jewish ideals in this mix.[78]

Paley's four collections of short stories explore the lives of women and children as seen especially through her leading character, Faith Darwin, a divorced, middle-class, activist mother of two who is deeply involved in raising her children, devoted to her neighbors and friends, and urgently committed to the betterment of her local, national, and international community.[79] As Faith matures during the course of Paley's several collections, she moves out from her domestic role to become a social activist, accepting the burden of responsibility inherited from her Jewish ancestors. To be truly American, she learns, is not merely a matter of unflinching optimism, but also one of commitment to others.

That Paley's characters are rarely defined separately from communities and that this attachment to community is an aspect of Jewish ideology have been observed by several critics—among them Victoria Aarons, Bonnie Lyons, and Dena Mandel.[80] Because of their ties to tightly bound communities, Paley's women characters, who control most of the stories, are optimists who can both invent themselves anew and connect to others through the power of their stories and their actions. As Aarons points out, to be "in the hands of strangers," as one of Paley's characters admits, is a metaphor for the absence of community that Paley abhors: the marginalized position of outsider, alienated to varying degrees from self and others.[81] Through their friendships and their roles as mothers and social activists—in short, their emphasis on "caring and responsibility"—Paley's characters avoid the stressful, isolating subjectivity that troubles so many protagonists of Jewish male writers of these times. Paley's celebration of the women of her stories, the "little people" who though lacking in power and influence attempt to lead "morally aware and engaged lives," offers an alternative expression of the Jewish accommodation to modernity.[82]

Lyons claims that Paley's portrayal of *menshlichkayt* ("a readiness to live for ideals beyond the clamor of self," as Irving Howe once defined it) is a "generally androgynous ideal," fitting for both men and women though expressed differently by each. But Lyons notes that though all protagonists in contemporary American-Jewish literature struggle toward menshlichkayt, the values of menshlichkayt are directly opposed to traditional American ideals of manliness, which stress toughness, self-sufficiency, and physical and sexual aggressiveness.[83] She suggests that a central tension in Philip Roth's work is the conflict between the two ideals. Scholars would do well to follow the lead Lyons offers by investigating the connections between menshlichkayt and masculinity in the work of male Jewish authors.

Gender and the Holocaust

Most critical scholarship devoted to the Holocaust rarely treats questions of gender difference; such scholarship usually focuses on writings by male victims or survivors under the assumption that these writings reflect universal experience. But as Marlene E. Heinemann notes in her arresting book *Gender and Destiny: Women Writers and the Holocaust* (1986), such an assumption is false. Important aspects of the Holocaust experience (such as sexual assault, maternity, and fertility) were unique to women and are represented differently in literature written by women. For this reason, Holocaust memoirs and fiction need to be regarded from the prism of gender. Although Heinemann acknowledges that to regard the Holocaust merely as an attack on femininity may seem an "intolerably sexist narrowing of perspective for a historical cataclysm," she argues that such emphasis can bring into sharper focus the experiences of particular women and of the sex collectively; it can also suggest universal aspects of the Holocaust.[84] Her analysis of six texts by women, published between 1957 and 1980, reveals the special suffering of women in their roles as mothers.[85] The grotesque choices women were forced to make between their children and their own deaths, the experience of rape, the frequency of amenorrhea, the strong friendships between women prisoners, as well as their heroic acts of resistance to save their children, are depicted in women's memoirs and in fiction about women—for example Susan Fromberg Schaeffer's closely researched, panoramic *Anya,* which focuses on a mother-daughter relation.[86] Although Heinemann does not include short fiction in her analysis, stories by women writers also depict the special meaning of the Holocaust for mothers and daughters. Cynthia Ozick's "Shawl," about a shawl that helps the main character, Rosa, nurse her baby in a concentration camp, combines the supernatural and realistic in a portrait of the totality of a mother's love for a child and her helplessness in the face of Nazi brutality. Ozick's powerful sequel to this story, "Rosa," explores the traumatic effects of her daughter's murder on Rosa many years later.[87]

Opening Holocaust critical studies to the subject of gender can be a two-way street, Heinemann hopes, for in addition to adding the unique experiences of women to existing male-oriented analyses, it can modify feminist theories of behavior and personality based on less extreme situations. She argues, for example, that female survivors' bold presentations of self may differ in important ways from the self-effacing narrative models suggested by feminist scholars as a general type.[88]

Directions in American-Jewish Literature:
1970 to the Present

Over the past two decades, critics have repeatedly expressed the concern that contemporary American Jewish writing is losing its vitality. According to Ted Solotaroff, Jewish writers who were no longer camped on some "fertile bicultural margin" could not vividly employ themes of acculturation or marginality. For Solotaroff, the possibility of recapturing "the Jewish edge" in fiction lay in the work of Ozick and such younger writers as Allegra Goodman, Daphne Merkin, and Nessa Rapoport, each "drawn to the dialogue between Judaism and modernism under the impact of feminism, the sexual revolution and the Holocaust."[89]

Solotaroff's comment points to several important trends in contemporary literature concerning the relation between gender and Jewish expression. Since the early 1970s, a new group of writers has emerged that writes from a sense of positive identification with Jewish tradition, history, and legend. The most important member of this group is Ozick. Highlighting the centrality of Jewish experience to modern life by focusing on the religious rather than the sociological dimensions of Jewish identity and culture, Ozick also writes prominently of the relation of women to Judaism. Though she chafes at being called a woman writer, Ozick identifies herself as a "classical feminist" who champions "justice and aspiration made universal," but not as someone who has a special female sensibility.[90] In several articles and stories, she protests Judaism's discrimination against women. In her three "Puttermesser" fictions, she creates a remarkable heroine, Ruth Puttermesser, an unconventional, ambitious intellectual who identifies with the spiritual traditions of her ancestors yet puts them to specifically feminist use.[91] Like Ozick, Norma Rosen uses female characters and issues involving relations between the sexes to illuminate Jewish experience.[92] The new generation of women writers whom Solotaroff predicts may help to rescue American Jewish writing from a downward spiral is following the path pioneered by

Ozick and Rosen in their focus on the tension between secular and spiritual values, specifically as seen by women.

As they have explored these issues, some of these writers have focused on another set of tensions—those between Israel and North America. Anne Roiphe's *Lovingkindness* (1987), a novel about an assimilated mother's coming to terms with her daughter's turn to Orthodoxy, and Nessa Rapoport's *Preparing for Sabbath* (1981), about a young Canadian woman's spiritual quest, each have characters that journey between Israel and North America as they seek spiritual comfort. The relation between Americans and Israel offers another promising site for exploring the intersections between Jewish identity and gender in the modern world.[93]

In addition to these novels, Jewish women writers are exploring their Jewishness today in ways that are more emphatically secular and feminist. Influenced by the women's movement, these writers have given new expression to the main theme that characterized the work of their forebears—the conflict between heritage and individuality. Often they have cried out against their cultural and spiritual rootlessness and their lack of knowledge and connections to tradition. They have been especially concerned with understanding their roles as mothers and as daughters, the relations between them, and the ties that bind families, generations, and the Jewish people. Even in emphasizing these bonds, however, they have staked new claims to the authority of the female voice and female experience.

Separation and reconciliation of Jewish daughters and parents are the themes of much of this literature. Kim Chernin's poignant memoir, *In My Mother's House* (1983), like Gornick's *Fierce Attachments* (1987), explicitly confronts the antagonisms between her powerful mother and herself. Lynne Sharon Schwartz's *Leaving Brooklyn* (1989), a tour de force of autobiographical fiction, describes the distance between her own generation, hungry for experience and connections, and her parents' desire for conformity and their historical amnesia.

In seeking to recover and understand the influences of heritage, American Jewish women writers point to the risks and pleasures ahead for mothers and daughters who want to create new relations to each other and to Judaism. Roiphe's memoir, *Generation without Memory* (1981), which examines her family's assimilation to Christian America and the beginnings of her own "ethnic return," was followed by *Lovingkindness*. Another mother seeking her daughter and trying to understand not only their own lives but their relation to Jewish female tradition is the subject of *Her Mothers* (1975) by E. M. Broner. Like this work, Broner's *A Weave of Women* (1978) experiments with language, form, and character to present a new kind of group, different from the individual: narratives of Jewish women seeking to empower their lives. Chernin's spiritual meditation, *Reinventing Eve* (1983), connects the author's feminism with Jewish and Christian sacred writings and Holocaust women's narratives. Recognizing her own "Goddess hunger" as a desire for empowerment connected with tradition, she tries to know "God as a woman" and "re-invents" Eve as a mother-figure and Goddess. Meredith Tax's historical novels *Rivington Street* (1984) and *Union Square* (1988) and Tema Nason's fictional autobiography of Ethel Rosenberg, *Ethel* (1990), also reflect the imaginative attempts of Jewish women writers to recreate Jewish heroines whose stories have been denied or distorted in the past. Lesléa Newman in *A Letter to Harvey Milk* (1988) and *In Every Laugh a Tear* (1992), Judith Katz in *Running Fiercely toward a High Thin Sound* (1992), and Melanie Kaye/Kantrowitz in *My Jewish Face and Other Stories* (1990) portray the variety of lesbian life and its meaning for Jewish identity.[94]

Finally, Johanna Kaplan's *O My America!* (1980) points to the confluence of themes of mother-daughter relations, gender identity, and problems of acculturation in contemporary Jewish writing. The story is about an American studies intellectual, Ezra Slavin, his several wives, and many affairs. This arresting novel has been interpreted by critics like Girgus as precisely representing "the relationship of the American idea to the Jewish experience": Slavin is a lover of women and of America.[95] A different, feminist, reading comes from C. Beth Burch, who argues that *O My America!* when viewed as the story of Merry Slavin, Ezra's daughter, is one that "rejects the patriarchy and claims no less than the entire country—'my America'—as female domain. . . . The novel is more a celebration of femaleness in the shadows of a waning patriarchy than a memorial to a great American man." Burch claims that "it is also an assertion of the independence of women, especially of Jewish women."[96] The multiple readings of the novel suggest its richness as a text that explores the connection of gender to ethnicity.

In connecting feminism to Judaism, contemporary life to history, and daughters to mothers and past generations of Jewish experience, the recent writings I have discussed offer a rich vein of analysis for the study of the relations between gender and Jewish identity. As feminist critics have noted, Jewish women writers have generally challenged conventional depictions of Jewish life, particularly family and sexual relations. In a pioneering article published in 1976, Sonya Michel noted that the theme of reconciliation between mothers and daughters in much of the fiction of Jewish women writers suggests that despite pressures of assimilation, conflict between generations is neither inevitable nor irreparable.[97] Writing a decade later, Ruth Adler analyzed the images of Jewish mothers presented by American Jewish women writers, finding a common portrait of an overworked, harried "victim of circumstance" that deeply conflicted with the stereotypical overly solicitous mother presented by Jewish male writers. Daughters in this fiction regarded mothers with compassion and understanding, even when their needs went unmet. Evelyn Avery also depicts Jewish mothers as sources of emotional strength and family ties. In an analysis of changing images of women in American Jewish literature over several generations, Sylvia Barack Fishman emphasized the prevalence of strong, opinionated, intelligent, and active women. From immigrant portrayals to midcentury mothers and daughters to contemporary "soldier women," these women shaped their own destinies and influenced those about them.[98]

Some contemporary critics allege that Jewish women writers not only overturn outworn content but also offer new textual forms that embody alternative visions of ritual and meaning. Claire Satlof argues, for example, that by creating a new literary synthesis between spirituality and secular, physical modernity, Jewish women writers have moved beyond the realistic "mainstream of the Bellow-Roth-Malamud tradition" toward what Ozick has termed liturgical fiction, a recasting of Jewish ritual and tradition as text. Satlof believes that Jewish feminist fiction is a "form of rebellion, usurpation or re-visioning" and that its texts serve as "actual agents of change" by realigning and revaluing the realms of ritual and history."[99] Janet Burstein persuasively observes that women's writings about problems of gender relations within the family and community simultaneously reveal an intense "quarrel with God," a probing of the spiritual meanings of Jewish tradition that remains continuously fresh and vital. Most recently, Nessa Rapoport suggests that the influence of Torah, Talmud, and other Jewish texts on the literary creativity of contemporary writers, especially women, marks the arrival of a new, "culturally confident" stage in the history of American Jewish literature that can support the "ongoing flowering of Jewish letters in America."[100]

As the fine work of these and other recent critics suggests, contemporary American Jewish women writers' portrayals of the male and female, of sexual and familial relations, and of other concerns of gender have been inextricably linked to a female literary tradition and to the actual experiences of Jewish women as wives, mothers, workers, and friends.[101] They have portrayed Jewish women as occupying a common space with other American women, but they have also depicted their particular experiences and sensibilities, showing why American Jewish women are indeed "eccentric subjects," similar and different. To connect Jewish female ethnicity fully with the sexual and spiritual expressions of generations of American Jewish male writers who have pleased or affronted readers with their explorations of Americanized masculinity remains a crucial next task in the study of gender in American Jewish literature. The development, finally, of a comparative perspective that places this analysis within the framework of gender studies in other ethnic literatures would allow readers to assess what makes this literature both especially Jewish and peculiarly American.

Notes

1. Theodore Gross, ed., *The Literature of American Jews* (New York: Free Press, 1973).
2. See, e.g., Allen Guttman, *The Jewish Writer in America: Assimilation and the Crisis of Identity* (New York: Oxford University Press, 1971), 180. In *The World of Our Fathers* (Harcourt, Brace Jovanovich, 1976), Irving Howe suggests that the central cultural experience of American Jewish writers is "tradition as discontinuity," since these novelists, writing in English, had to dissociate themselves from Yiddish culture. Among general studies of American Jewish literature, see Charles Angoff and Meyer Levin, *The Rise of American Jewish Literature* (New York: Simon and Schuster, 1970); Robert Alter, *After the Tradition: Essays on Modern Jewish Writing* (New York: Dutton, 1969); Lewis Fried, ed., *Handbook of American Jewish Literature* (New York: Greenwood, 1988); Louis Harap's several studies: *The Image of the Jew in American Literature from Early Republic to Mass Immigration* (Philadelphia: Jewish Publication Society of America, 1954), *Creative Awakening: The Jewish Presence in Twentieth-Century American Literature, 1900–1940s* (Westport, Conn.: Greenwood, 1987); *In the Mainstream: The Jewish Presence in Twentieth-Century American Literature, 1950s-1980s* (Westport, Conn.: Greenwood, 1987); and *Dramatic Encounters: The Jewish Presence in Twentieth-Century American Drama, Poetry and Humor and the Black-Jewish Literary Relationship* (Westport, Conn.: Greenwood, 1987); Irving Malin, ed., *Contemporary American-Jewish Literature: Critical Essays* (Bloomington: Indiana University Press, 1974); Sanford Pinsker, *The Schlemiel as Metaphor: Studies in the Yiddish and American Jewish Novelists* (Athens: Ohio University Press, 1969); Daniel Walden, ed., *On Being Jewish: American Jewish Writers from Cahan to Bellow* (Greenwich, Conn.: Fawcett, 1974). Daniel Walden, ed., *Twentieth-Century American-Jewish Fiction Writers*, vol. 28 of *Dictionary of Literary Biography* (Detroit: Gale, 1984), is an important source. See also Irving Howe, introduction to *Jewish-American Stories*, ed. Howe (New York: New American Library, 1977); Irving Malin and Irwin Stark, introduction to *Breakthrough: A Treasury of Contemporary American-Jewish Literature*, ed. Malin and Stark (New York: McGraw Hill, 1964); Ted Solotaroff, "American Jewish Writers: On Edge Once More," *New York Times,*

18 Dec. 1988; and Mark Shechner, "Jewish Writers," in Daniel Hoffman, ed., *Harvard Guide to Contemporary American Writing* (Cambridge: Harvard University Press, 1979).

3. Frederick Cople Jaher, "The Quest for the Ultimate *Shiksa,*" *American Quarterly* 35 (winter 1983): 519.

4. Ibid. One of the first authors to consider the shiksa figure as a trope to explore the ramifications of assimilation in Jewish (male) fiction of the 1920s and 1930s was Leslie Fiedler. See Fiedler, "Genesis: The American-Jewish Novel through the Twenties," *Midstream* 4 (summer 1958): 570–86. Also see Guttmann, *The Jewish Writer,* 57–64. The theme of intermarriage in American Jewish fiction has been used more recently by Sam B. Girgus in *The New Covenant: Jewish Writers and the American Idea* (Chapel Hill: University of North Carolina Press, 1984), 19; and Mary V. Dearborn, *Pocahontas's Daughters: Gender and Ethnicity in American Culture* (New York: Oxford University Press, 1986), chaps. 5 and 6.

5. Mary V. Dearborn, *Love in the Promised Land: The Story of Anzia Yezierska and John Dewey* (New York: Free Press, 1988); Norma Rosen, *John and Anzia: An American Romance* (New York: Dutton, 1989); *Anzia Yezierska: A Writer's Life* (New Brunswick, N.J.: Rutgers University Press, 1988), written by Yezierska's daughter, Louise Levitas Henriksen, provides valuable information about the Dewey-Yezierska affair and its fictional incorporations.

6. Nancy K. Miller, "Changing the Subject: Authorship, Writing, and the Reader," in Teresa de Lauretis, ed., *Feminist Studies/Critical Studies* (Bloomington: Indiana University Press, 1986), 115.

7. Elaine Showalter, ed. *The New Feminist Criticism: Essays on Women, Literature, and Theory* (New York: Pantheon, 1985), 5–8.

8. Miller, "Changing the Subject," 112.

9. Sandra M. Gilbert and Susan Gubar, *No Man's Land: The Place of the Woman Writer in the Twentieth Century,* vol. 2, *Sexchanges* (New Haven: Yale University Press, 1989), xv. Other important works of feminist literary theory include Gayle Greene and Coppelia Kahn, eds., *Making a Difference: Feminist Literary Criticism* (London: Methuen, 1985); Toril Moi, *Sexual/Textual Politics* (London: Methuen, 1985); Marjorie Pryse and Hortense J. Spillers, eds., *Conjuring: Black Women, Fiction and Literary Tradition* (Bloomington: Indiana University Press, 1985); Judith Newton and Deborah Rosenfelt, eds., *Feminist Criticism and Social Change: Sex, Class, and Race in Literature and Culture* (New York: Methuen, 1985); Shari Benstock, ed., *Feminist Issues in Literary Scholarship* (Bloomington: Indiana University Press, 1987).

10. For a useful examination of the differences between Anglo-American and French feminism, see June Howard, "Feminist Differings: Recent Surveys of Feminist Literary Theory and Criticism," *Feminist Studies* 14 (spring 1988): 167–90.

11. Miller, "Changing the Subject," 107; Wai-Chee Dimock, "Feminism, New Historicism, and the Reader," *American Literature* 63 (Dec. 1991): 602.

12. Judith Fetterly, "Reading about Reading: 'A Jury of Her Peers,' 'The Murders in the Rue Morgue,' and 'The Yellow Wallpaper,'" in Elizabeth A. Flynn and Patrocinio P.

Schweickart, eds., *Gender and Reading: Essays on Readers, Texts, and Contexts* (Baltimore: John Hopkins University Press, 1986), xviii. Other useful studies of reading are Janice Radway, *Reading the Romance: Women, Patriarchy, and Popular Literature* (Chapel Hill: University of North Carolina Press, 1984); Louise Rosenblatt, *The Reader, the Text, the Poem: The Transactional Theory of Literary Work* (Carbondale: Southern Illinois University Press, 1978); and Annette Kolodny, "A Map for Rereading: Or, Gender and the Interpretation of Literary Texts," *New Literary History* 11 (1980): 451–67.

13. Marianne Hirsch, *The Mother/Daughter Plot: Narrative, Psychoanalysis, Feminism* (Bloomington: Indiana University Press, 1989), 159–61.

14. Miller, "Changing the Subject."

15. Mark Shechner, *After the Revolution: Studies in the Contemporary Jewish Imagination* (Bloomington: Indiana University Press, 1987), 1–13. Also see Vivian Gornick, "Why Do These Men Hate Women?" in her collection, *Essays in Feminism* (New York: Harper and Row, 1978), 189–99.

16. Teresa de Lauretis, "Eccentric Subjects: Feminist Theory and Historical Consciousness," *Feminist Studies* 16 (spring 1990): 115–50.

17. Ibid., 144–45.

18. There are almost as many opinions of the definition of "Jewish writing" as there are critics. Frequently cited criteria include Jewish origins; collective tradition, memory, or culture (including laws, language, customs, and food); a feeling for ambiguity and irony; dissociation from tradition; family themes; location, place, or neighborhood; and use of language or inflection. Although some critics maintain that authentic Jewish fiction must reflect an engagement with recognizable Judaic tradition, laws, texts, or values, I prefer a looser standard that incorporates a range of identity issues involving both the individual Jewish-American and the collectivity. For examples of the multiple definitions of Jewish writing, see Irving Howe's introduction to *Jewish American Stories;* "What Is Jewish in Jewish Literature? A Symposium with Israeli Writers" (Cambridge: Harvard University, 1993); Leslie Fiedler, *Fiedler on the Roof: Essays on Literature and Jewish Identity* (Boston: David R. Godine, 1991); and Aharon Appelfeld, "The Artist as Jewish Writer," in Asher Z. Milbauer and Donald G. Watson, eds., *Reading Philip Roth* (New York: St. Martin's, 1988), 13–16.

19. June Sochen, "Identities within Identity: Thoughts on Jewish American Women Writers," *Studies in American Jewish Literature* 3 (1983): 6–10.

20. See David Martin Fine, "In the Beginning: American Jewish Fiction, 1880–1930," in Fried, *Handbook,* 28.

21. Alice Kessler-Harris, introduction to Yezierska's *Bread Givers: A Novel* (New York: Persea, 1975), xv, xvi. Also see her introduction to *The Open Cage: An Anzia Yezierska Collection* (New York: Persea, 1979), v–xiii; Levitas Henriksen, *Anzia Yezierska;* Carol B. Schoen, *Anzia Yezierska* (Boston: Twayne, 1982).

22. Harap, *Creative Awakening,* 48.

23. Girgus, *The New Covenant.*

24. For useful summaries of contemporary critical opinion, see Charlotte Goodman, "Anzia

Yezierska," in *Dictionary of Literary Biography* 28:332–35; "Anzia Yezierska," *Contemporary Literary Criticism* 46:44–49.

25. Shelly Regenbaum, "Art Gender, and the Jewish Tradition in Yezierska's *Red Ribbon on a White Horse* and Potok's *My Name Is Asher Lev*," *Studies in American Jewish Literature* 7 (1988): 55–66.

26. Ibid., 65.

27. Ibid., 58.

28. Rose Kamel, "'Anzia Yezierska, Get Out of Your Own Way': Selfhood and Otherness in the Autobiographical Fiction of Anzia Yezierska," *Studies in American Jewish Literature,* 3 (1983): 40–50. In the same volume, Susan Hersch Sachs's "Anzia Yezierska: 'Her Words Dance with a Thousand Colors'" (pp. 62–67), notes that Yezierska achieved a dramatic, vivid, depiction of immigrant life by her sometimes contradictory, exaggerated prose.

29. Ellen Golub, "Eat Your Heart Out: The Fiction of Anzia Yezierska," in *Studies in American Jewish Literature* 3 (1983): 51–61.

30. Ibid., 56. Several other critics have noted the theme of hunger, though not as extensively as Golub. See Fine, "In the Beginning," 20.

31. Sonya Michel, "Mothers and Daughters in American Jewish Literature: The Rotted Cord," in Elizabeth Koltun, ed., *The Jewish Woman: New Perspectives* (New York: Schocken, 1976), 272–82.

32. Evelyn Avery notes that the self-sacrificing mother in *Bread Givers* (and in Mary Antin's *Promised Land*) has parallels in contemporary works by Jewish women writers, citing Helen Yglesias, *Family Feeling,* and Joanna Kaplan, *O My America,* and argues that these works form a continuum in Jewish writing. See "Oh My 'Mishpocha'! Some Jewish Women Writers from Antin to Kaplan View the Family," *Studies in American Jewish Literature* 5 (1986): 45.

33. Dearborn, *Pocahontas's Daughters,* 122. Dearborn explores this theme in Yezierska's own life in *Love in the Promised Land.*

34. See, e.g., Steven J. Rubin, "Style and Meaning in Mary Antin's *The Promised Land*: A Reevaluation," *Studies in American Jewish Literature* 5 (1986): 35–43.

35. Steven J. Rubin, "American Jewish Autobiography: 1912 to the Present," in Fried, *Handbook,* 287.

36. Rubin, "Style and Meaning in Mary Antin's *The Promised Land,* 36. Richard Tuerk, "The Youngest of America's Children in *The Promised Land*," in *Studies in American Jewish Literature,* 5 (1986), 29–34, also sees the book as a sentimental assimilationist tale, though he notes that Americanization is "not an unmixed blessing" for the Antin family (p. 32).

37. See Sarah Blacher Cohen, "Mary Antin's *The Promised Land: A Breach of Promise*," joint issue of *Yiddish* 3 (fall 1977), and *Studies in American Jewish Literature* 3 (winter 1977–78): 28–35.

38. Ibid., 32–33.

39. Ibid., 34–35. Although as condemnatory as Cohen, Mary Dearborn also sees *The Promised*

Land as an expression of the values of the dominant culture, without any "mediating, alternative voice" (*Pocahontas's Daughters*, 42).

40. Rubin, "American Jewish Autobiography," 290.

41. Antin, *The Promised Land*, 96, 201–2.

42. Ibid., 246–47.

43. See, e.g., "Malinke's Atonement," in Joyce Antler, ed., *America and I: Short Stories by American Jewish Women Writers* (Boston: Beacon, 1990).

44. Jules Chametzky, "The Assimilation of the American Jewish Writer," in *Our Decentralized Literature* (Amherst: University of Massachusetts Press, 1986), 48, 62. Irving Howe, in *The World of Our Fathers* (New York: Harcourt, Brace, Jovanovich, 1976), 525, calls *The Rise of David Levinsky* a "minor masterpiece of genre realism."

45. Chametzky, "Immigrant Fiction as Cultural Mediation," originally published in *Modern Jewish Studies Annual* 5 (fall 1984): 14–21, rep. in *Our Decentralized Literature*, 64. Also see Chametzky, *From the Ghetto: The Fiction of Abraham Cahan* (Amherst: University of Massachusetts Press, 1977), esp. 113–14.

46. Susan Kress, "Women and Marriage in Abraham Cahan's Fiction," *Studies in American Jewish Literature* 3 (1983): 26–39.

47. Ibid., 36.

48. Several critics have noted the portrayal of new women in immigrant fiction, both in Yiddish and English. See, e.g., Carole Kessner, "Ghetto Intellectuals and the 'New Woman,'" *Yiddish* 2 (winter/spring 1976): 23–31. For a discussion of radical Jewish women writing in Yiddish, see Norma Fain Pratt, "Culture and Radical Politics: Yiddish Women Writers in America, 1890–1940," in Lois Scharf and Joan M. Jensen, eds., *Decades of Discontent: The Women's Movement, 1920–1940* (Westport, Conn.: Greenwood, 1983).

49. Fine, "In the Beginning," 31.

50. Lewis Fried, "American Jewish Fiction, 1930–1945," in Fried, *Handbook*, 36, 41, 19.

51. Harap, *Creative Awakening*, 90–92.

52. B. G. Bienstock, "The Changing Image of the American Jewish Mother," in V. Tufte and B. Meyerhoff, eds., *Changing Image of the Family* (New Haven: Yale University Press, 1979), 180. Jules Zanger also describes the transition of the Jewish mother from the turn of the century to the depression and beyond. See his "On Not Making it in America," *American Studies* (1977): 39–48.

53. Bienstock, "The Changing Image," 182.

54. Ibid.

55. One of the few critics to discuss these women's works is Louis Harap. See his discussion of Zugsmith's *Time to Remember* and Sinclair's *Wasteland* in *Creative Awakening*, 99, 162–63.

56. Similar material on Schlesinger, Sinclair, and Olsen (pp. 21–22, 28–30) appears in the introduction to Antler, *America and I*.

57. Louise Kertesz, *The Poetic Vision of Muriel Rukeyser* (Baton Rouge: Louisiana State University Press, 1980), 175.

58. Kertesz, *The Poetic Vision of Muriel Rukeyser*, 179–80.
59. Adrienne Rich, "Muriel Rukeyser, 1913–1978: "Poet . . . Woman . . . American . . . Jew,'" in *Bridges* 1 (spring 1990): 28–29. Rukeyser's article "Under Forty," originally appeared in "Under Forty: A Symposium on American Literature and the Younger Generation of American Jews," in *The Contemporary Jewish Record* (American Jewish Committee, 1944).
60. Abraham Chapman, introduction to *Jewish-American Literature: An Anthology of Fiction, Prose, Poetry, Autobiography and Criticism* (New York: New American Library, 1974), xxviii, cited in Richard Tuerk, "Jewish-American Literature," in Robert J. di Pietro and Edward Ifkovic, eds., *Ethnic Perspectives in American Literature: Selected Essays on the European Contribution* (New York: Modern Language Association of America, 1983), 152.
61. Chapman, xvii, also cited in Tuerk, 152. On Jewish literature during this period, see Bonnie K. Lyons, "American Jewish Fiction since 1945," in Fried, *Handbook*, 60–89.
62. Daniel Fuchs, *Saul Bellow: Vision and Revision* (Durham: University of North Carolina Press, 1984), 26. Leslie Fiedler is one of a number of critics to find Bellow's work lacking in vivid female characters. "Where women are introduced, they appear as nympholeptic fantasies, peculiarly unconvincing": Fiedler, *Love and Death in the American Novel* (New York: Stein and Day, 1967), 363. The point is disputed in two articles in *Studies in American Jewish Literature* 3 (1977–78): Ada Aharoni, "Women in Saul Bellow's Novels," 99–111, and Alan Chavkin, "The Feminism of *The Dean's December*," 113–26. In the same issue, Barbara Koenig Quart discusses Malamud's weak portrayal of women characters in "Women in Bernard Malamud's Fiction," pp. 138–48. Also see Daniel Fuchs's "Malamud's *Dublin's Lives*: A Jewish Writer and the Sexual Ethic," *Studies in American Jewish Literature* 7 (1988): 205–12. Evelyn Torton Beck has written on "I. B. Singer's Misogyny," in *Lilith* 6 (1980).
63. Erika Duncan, "The Hungry Jewish Mother," in Susannah Heschel, ed., *On Being a Jewish Feminist* (New York: Schocken, 1983), 27–29.
64. Bienstock, "The Changing Image," 188.
65. Marya Mannes, "A Dissent," *Saturday Review* 22 (Feb. 1969): 39, in Bernard F. Rogers, Jr., *Philip Roth: A Bibliography* (Metuchen, N.J.: J. L. Scarecrow, 1984, 2d ed.), 76–77. In *After the Revolution*, Mark Shechner calls *Portnoy's Complaint* a "particularly combative book," which, he says, makes students ("the women in particular") uncomfortable (p. 203).
66. Bienstock, "The Changing Image," 189. In "Sophie Portnoy and 'The Opossum's Death': American Sexism and Jewish Anti-Gentilism," *Studies in American Jewish Literature* 3 (1977–78): 166–78, Barry Gross argues that *Portnoy's Complaint* was not so much sexist as a complaint against "being Jewish," embodied by Portnoy's mother. For other treatments of the mother-son relationship in *Portnoy's Complaint*, see Melvin J. Friedman, "Jewish Mothers and Sons," *Tempest* 2 (1970): 33; Jack Ludwig, "Sons and Lovers," *Partisan Review* 36 (1969): 524–34; Therese Pol, "The Jewish Mama Market," *Nation* 10 March 1969.
67. Girgus, *The New Covenant*, 118.

68. Sam B. Girgus, "Between *Goodbye Columbus* and *Portnoy:* Becoming a Man and Writer in Roth's Feminist 'Family Romance,'" *Studies in American Jewish Literature* 8 (1989): 153.

69. See Barbara Frey Waxman, "Jewish American Princesses, Their Mothers, and Feminist Psychology: A Rereading of Roth's 'Goodbye Columbus,'" *Studies in American Jewish Literature* 7 (1988): 90–104.

70. Neal D. Isaacs, *Grace Paley: A Study of the Short Fiction* (Boston: G. K. Hall/Twayne Series, 1990), 113.

71. Ibid.

72. Ibid., 119–20.

73. Ibid., 136.

74. Ibid., 113.

75. One of the few studies of Jo Sinclair is Elisabeth Sandberg's doctoral diss., "Jo Sinclair: Towards a Critical Biography," University of Massachusetts, 1985.

76. Interview with Naomi Rubin, May 1983, in Bonnie K. Lyons, "Tillie Olsen: The Writer as a Jewish Woman," *Studies in American Jewish Literature* 5 (1986): 91.

77. Elaine Neil Orr, *Tillie Olsen and a Feminist Spiritual Vision* (Jackson: University Press of Mississippi, 1987), 32.

78. In addition to Lyons's article "Tillie Olsen," see Deborah Rosenfelt, "From the Thirties: Tillie Olsen and the Radical Tradition," in Judith Newton and Deborah Rosenfelt, eds., *Feminist Criticism and Social Change,* pp. 216–48 (New York: Methuen, 1985).

79. In addition to her first volume, she is the author of *Enormous Changes at the Last Minute* (New York: Farrar, Straus & Giroux, 1974), *Later the Same Day* (New York: Farrar, Straus & Giroux, 1985), and *Long Walks and Intimate Talks* (New York: Feminist Press at the City University of New York, 1991).

80. See Dena Mandel, "Keeping Up with Faith: Grace Paley's Sturdy American Jewess," *Studies in American Jewish Literature* 3 (1983): 85–98; Minako Baba, "Faith Darwin as Writer-Heroine: A Study of Grace Paley's Short Stories," *Studies in American Jewish Literature* 7 (1988): 40–55; Bonnie Lyons, "Grace Paley's Jewish Miniatures," *Studies in American Jewish Literature* 8 (1989): 26–33; Victoria Aarons, "Talking Lives: Storytelling and Renewal in Grace Paley's Short Fiction," *Studies in American Jewish Literature* 9 (1990): 20–35; Gloria L. Cronin, "Melodramas of Beset Womanhood: Resistance, Subversion, and Survival in the Fiction of Grace Paley," *Studies in American Jewish Literature* 11 (1992): 140–49.

81. Aarons, "Talking Lives," 24.

82. Cited in Lyons, "Grace Paley's Jewish Miniatures," 32.

83. Lyons, "American-Jewish Fiction since 1945," 66; Paul Breines discusses a "tough Jew" masculine image depicted in popular "Rambowitz" novels by such authors as Leon Uris and Gloria Goldreich. See *Tough Jews: Political Fantasies and the Moral Dilemma of American Jewry* (New York: Basic Books, 1990).

84. Marlene E. Heinemann, *Gender and Destiny: Women Writers and the Holocaust* (Westport, Conn.: Greenwood, 1986), 34.

85. The texts are Gerda Klein, *All But My Life* (New York: Hill and Wang, 1957); Charlotte

Delbo, *None of Us Will Return* (New York: Grove, 1968); Judith Dribben, *A Girl Called Judith Strick* (New York: Cowles Book Company, 1970); Susan Fromberg Schaeffer, *Anya* (New York: Macmillan, 1974); Fania Fénelon, *Playing for Time* (New York: Atheneum, 1976); and Livia Bitton Jackson, *Elli* (New York: Times Books, 1980).

86. Schaeffer's *Anya* is also discussed in detail in Dorothy Seidman Bilik's *Immigrant-Survivors: Post-Holocaust Consciousness in Recent Jewish American Fiction* (Middletown, Conn.: Wesleyan University Press, 1981); and Alan Berger's *Crisis and Covenant: The Holocaust in American Jewish Fiction* (Albany: SUNY Press, 1985). Berger comments that *Anya* is the only novel in his study that concerns the relation between survivor and child during and after the Holocaust (p. 119)

87. See, e.g., Marjorie Sandor, "The Gittel"; Rebecca Goldstein, "The Legacy of Raizel Kaidish: A Story," and Cynthia Ozick, "The Shawl," in Antler, *America and I;* Cynthia Ozick's *The Shawl* (New York: Alfred Knopf, 1989) also contains "Rosa."

88. Heinemann, *Gender and Destiny,* 76–77. Although it does not include fiction, *Different Voices: Women and the Holocaust* (ed. Carol Rittner and John K. Roth [New York: Paragon House, 1993]), offers a powerful collection of survivors' testimonies and scholarly articles concerning women's experiences of the Holocaust. Also see recent articles by Susanne Klingenstein ("Destructive Intimacy: The Shoah between Mother and Daughter in Fictions by Cynthia Ozick, Norma Rosen, and Rebecca Goldstein") and S. Lillian Kremer ("Holocaust-wrought Women: Portraits by Four American Writers") in *Studies in American Jewish Literature* 11 (1992).

89. Solotaroff, "American-Jewish Writers on Edge Once More," 1. Dorothy Seidman Bilik suggests that the appearance of many new novels about the Holocaust denies the assertion that Jewish writing has entered a period of decline. See her book, *Immigrant Survivors.* For an account of other recent changes in the literary expression of American Jewish identity, see Sanford E. Marovitz, "Images of America in American Jewish Fiction," in Fried, *Handbook,* 315–56.

90. Ozick, "Literature and the Politics of Sex: A Dissent," in *Art & Ardor* (New York: Knopf, 1983), 288.

91. See the articles "The Hole/Birth Catalogue" and "Justice to Feminism," in *Art & Ardor,* and "Ruth," in Ozick's collection *Metaphor & Memory* (New York: Knopf, 1989). Also see "Notes toward Finding the Right Question," *Lilith* 6 (1979); and "Torah as the Matrix for Feminism," *Lilith* 12–13 (winter/spring 1985): 47–48. "Puttermesser: Her Work History, Her Ancestry, Her Afterlife," and "Puttermesser and Xanthippe," are in *Leviathan: Five Fictions* (New York: Knopf, 1982); also see "Puttermesser Paired," *New Yorker,* 8 Oct. 1970. Ozick has received much critical attention in recent years. *Studies in American Jewish Literature,* vol. 6 (1987), includes a dozen articles titled "The World of Cynthia Ozick"; other important studies include Harold Bloom, ed., *Modern Critical Views: Cynthia Ozick* (New York: Chelsea House, 1986); Lawrence S. Friedman, *Understanding Cynthia Ozick* (Columbia: University of South Carolina Press, 1991); Vera Emuna Kielsky, *Inevitable Exiles: Cynthia Ozick's View of the Precariousness of Jewish Exis-*

tence in a Gentile Society (New York: P. Lang, 1989); and Sanford Pinsker, *The Uncompromising Fiction of Cynthia Ozick* (Columbia: University of Missouri Press, 1986).

92. See *Touching Evil*, Rosen's 1969 novel about two women whose lives change after watching the Eichmann hearings on television; *At the Center* (1982), a novel about a daughter who finds her way back to Hasidism by working in an abortion clinic after her parents, Holocaust survivors, are murdered in Brooklyn; her most recent work, *John and Anzia: An American Romance;* and a recent collection of articles, *Accidents of Influence: Writing as a Woman and a Jew in America* (Albany: SUNY Press, 1992).

93. The theme is also used in Philip Roth's *Counterlife* (New York: Penguin, 1986).

94. *Nice Jewish Girls: A Lesbian Anthology,* ed. Evelyn Torton Beck (Boston: Beacon, 1982), is a pioneering collection of poems and essays; *The Tribe of Dina: A Jewish Women's Anthology,* ed. Melanie Kaye/Kantrowitz *(sic)* and Irena Klepfisz (Boston: Beacon, 1986), includes some fiction. Of related interest are Klepfisz's *A Few Words in the Mother Tongue: Poems Selected and New, 1971–1990* (Portand, Ore.: Eighth Mountain Press, 1990), and *Dreams of an Insomniac: Jewish Feminist Essays, Speeches, and Diatribes* (ibid.); and *Twice Blessed: On Being Lesbian, Gay, and Jewish,* ed. Christie Balka and Andy Rose (Boston: Beacon, 1989).

95. See, e.g., Girgus, *The New Covenant,* 6–9, 13, 20.

96. C. Beth Burch, "Johanna Kaplan's *O My America! The Jewish Female Claim to America,"* *Studies in American Jewish Literature* 9 (1990): 38–39.

97. Sonya Michel, "Mothers and Daughters," 281.

98. Ruth Adler, "Mothers and Daughters: The Jewish Mother as Seen by American Jewish Women Writers," *Yiddish* 6 (1987): 87–92; Evelyn Avery, "Oh My 'Mishpocha'!" 45; see the introductory text in Sylvia Barack Fishman, ed., *Follow My Footprints: Changing Images of Women in American Jewish Fiction* (Hanover, N.H.: University of New England Press, 1992).

99. Claire R. Satlof, "History, Fiction and the Tradition: Creating a Jewish Feminist Poetic," in Heschel, *On Being a Jewish Feminist,* 193.

100. Janet Burstein, "Jewish-American Women's Literature: The Long Quarrel with God," *Studies in American Jewish Literature* 8 (1989): 9–25; see Rapoport's introduction in Ted Solotaroff and Nessa Rapoport, eds., *Writing Our Way Home: Contemporary Stories by American Jewish Writers* (New York: Schocken Books, 1992), xxviii–xxx.

101. Avery, "Oh My 'Mishpocha'!"

Modern Hebrew Literature:
The Impact of Feminist Research

The field of modern Hebrew literature has come belatedly to include feminist criticism and gender studies. Although these approaches have flourished over the past twenty years in English and other literatures, parallel work in Hebrew has taken on momentum only since the mid-1980s. Compared to the voluminous publications informed by feminist thinking in other areas of literary study, only a handful of books and articles have appeared that deal with modern Hebrew writing. In recent years, however, interest has been rising among scholars, critics, and writers both in Israel and America. Several conferences have also helped to foster dialogue on these topics.[1] It is primarily women who have taken the initiative to open up this area of inquiry, but men have made significant contributions in research and in supporting publications and meetings.

The awakening to feminist and gender criticism, though delayed, is not without its positive aspects. Belatedness has allowed scholarship in the field of modern Hebrew literature to recapitulate quickly major trajectories of feminist thinking developed elsewhere. Consequently, the work that has been done displays much diversity. Hebraists have had the opportunity to critique a range of feminist literary approaches and theories while applying and adapting those ideas and methods to their own field. These circumstances often result in both an energetic and sophisticated production of work. Part of the reason feminist criticism bears so much promise and potential is its diversity. Far from a uniform creed, it has fostered varied modes of dealing with literary texts.

To begin with, feminist criticism has opened new areas of thematic inquiry. While documenting the stereotypes, omissions, and misperceptions of women in a wide variety of texts, it has also called attention to depictions of women, dimensions of women's lives, and women's roles previously neglected in critical studies (including such topics as mother-daughter relations, female adolescence, women's experiences during wartime, and female eroticism).[2] Insights from disciplines outside literature have enhanced many such thematic studies. In particular, feminist revisions of psychoanalytic theory have proved indispensable for the rereadings of many texts and for understanding how culture constructs gender;[3] ideas about the importance of the preoedipal mother-child relation have had an especially influential impact.[4] These approaches ascribe new importance to the earliest bonds between mothers and children, postulating that the preoedipal realm affects gender definitions and the child's psychic and emotional growth throughout life. This understanding is key in interpretations of narratives that deal with personal development, regressive states, the assignment of gender identification, challenges to gender boundaries, and the questioning or rejection of social values associated with entrance into the patriarchal culture by the oedipal passage. Studies that examine the construction of masculinity as well as femininity move beyond the basic concerns of feminist criticism with women's lives and experiences. Yet they emerge out of, enhance, and enlarge feminist theory and so form an integral whole with it, meriting consideration together with it under the wider rubric of gender studies.

A similar expansion of concerns has evolved from feminist explorations of language. Observations from feminist sociolinguistics have helped to illuminate the treatment of women's speech and expression in literary texts.[5] As they clarify power relations and assertions of authority through verbal exchange, these approaches address issues of central importance to the literary portrayals of women that deal with patterns of dominance, vulnerability, and shifting social roles. Additional insights have come from feminist revisions of history, religion, philosophy, and other fields.

Some feminist critical approaches have focused specifically on women writers: on styles and genres prevalent in the writing of women, on the psychodynamics of female creativity, and on canon formation.[6] Interest in canonization has encompassed both the recovery of women writers long neglected and the debate about why certain writers have been excluded from the ranks of the recognized and the celebrated. In one of its most engaging forms, this kind of criticism traces the interconnections of female literary traditions. Much of the work in this category might fall under the rubrics of history of literature or sociology of reading and entails assessments of who wrote what for whom and when and what the reception of the audience was.

Although all these issues are important for Hebrew literature as well as for other national literatures, some take on a special acuteness for modern Hebrew literature. To assess the impact of feminist efforts in this field it is useful first to review the features that make this literature of particular interest from the feminist perspective. It is then possible to sketch an overview of work already accomplished and to consider future research directions.

Gender and Hebrew Literature

Hebrew literature poses particular challenges and rewards for feminist inquiry because of the exceptional history of the Hebrew language and because of the changing roles of women in Jewish life over the past hundred years.

Language and Gender

For centuries, traditional Jewish culture maintained an internal bilingualism marked by gender differences. Hebrew, the holy tongue—*leshon hakodesh*—was the province of men alone. The study of sacred texts, a male imperative, was forbidden to women. The realm of women was that of the daily vernacular. So, for example, in Europe, Yiddish became known in some ways as a woman's language.[7] Toward the end of the nineteenth century Hebrew underwent a remarkable transformation into a secular modern language, and this dramatic evolution began to dismantle earlier gender divisions. Women could and did learn modern Hebrew. Still, the previous division continued to exert an influence. It was a learned elite who led the revival of Hebrew, and they drew on an erudite foundation in classical texts to fashion a modern literature. One of the consequences was that Hebrew belles lettres, until recently, was heavily populated by male voices, which meant that women in Hebrew texts were imagined primarily through the filter of men's perceptions. Similarly, the dilemma of women writers searching out precursors is aggravated in the case of Hebrew and prompts various basic questions. Have women writers relied on traditional sources of special appeal to females, or have they had recourse to a general cultural idiom? How have women managed to grapple with not just the language, but also the literary conventions and social biases created by the singular medium in which they work?

In the early generations after modern Hebrew literature was opened to female scrutiny, most women still lacked the background in sacred sources that made erudite literary conventions accessible to men. Since these were the dominant, respected literary modes, to write in another fashion was simply not to write respectable literature. Consequently, even those women born into Hebrew as a native spoken language were at a disadvantage. Everyday Hebrew did not equip them to be serious writers—that is, to be *taken seriously* as writers. Today, more women than ever are mastering classical texts and skills once reserved for men, yet the legacy of the linguistic differential in Hebrew is still notable. For example, contemporary women can never read S. Y. Abramovitch (known by the pen name Mendele the Bookseller) with the same assumptions the author's original readers held in the nineteenth century. The same, of course, holds true for contemporary men, but for them Mendele's status as an indispensable precursor has been secure for many generations. Women looking for forerunners cannot identify in the same way. It is not just that Abramovitch's frequent misogynistic comments distance women from him. More important is the absence of literary foremothers who might have modeled their narratives after his. Because of the gap in time since Abramovitch's era, women's writing in Hebrew will never absorb his influence in the same way as men's writing has.

Similar matters of continuity impinge on the practice of criticism and so on the voices that help determine the canon. Few women scholars have tackled the Mendele narratives. It was not women who established this author's revered status, and it is intriguing to consider how gender might affect authoritative interpretation: what might have been Abramovitch's stature had women been the judges of his greatness? My intent is not to dispute his genius—certainly not to question his importance as a founding figure of the rebirth of Hebrew culture—but to wonder how the discussion of his work might have been widened, might have achieved different emphases, or might have responded to different interests, had his readership included more members of the opposite sex. The issue applies also to the present; where are the great female commentators on Mendele even now?

Issues of Gender: Public and Private Realms

In addition to these questions, which derive from linguistic circumstances, Hebrew literature poses special challenges because it emerges during a period of enormous upheaval in Jewish social, political, and religious life. Secularization, Zionism in its various guises, protracted military conflicts, mass migrations—all have had a profound effect on the definitions of women's roles and, by extension, on their representation in literature and their experience as writers. This circumstance has given rise to a series of prominent thematic concerns that are shaped by matters of gender. To mention but a few: women's relation to rabbinic law as religious authority has changed under the pressures of modernization; the changing expectations of women who leave the protection of a traditional environment for new worlds that offer political and sexual unknowns; and the woman pioneer and the woman soldier in Zionist history and ideology.

Several feminist issues take on special resonance in the field of Hebrew literature, since in this corpus an emphasis on peoplehood as opposed to private matters prevails. Hebrew writing has been intensely concerned with collective issues such as a national cultural rebirth and the struggle for independence. The great names have achieved their revered status because of their attention to these issues. The classic example is that of Hayim Nahman Bialik, acclaimed as national poet in the period of the Hebrew Revival (1890–1920). Although he is now recognized for his vast production of personal lyrics, he was celebrated in his own day for the elements of protest and prophecy in his poetry—such as his angry response to the Kishinev pogroms of 1903, his expression of Zionist yearnings, and his richly ambivalent portrayals of the Study House tradition in decline. Recent writers, such as Amos Oz, A. B. Yehoshua, and Aharon Appelfeld have also received much recognition as spokespeople for national concerns or as commentators on collective dilemmas.

In this context two feminist issues arise. First: in modern Hebrew literature many male authors use female figures to symbolize collective crises, thus eliciting vexed questions about stereotyping, for they recall a long tradition in which women served as embodiments of the Jews as a people. (Examples include the desolate widow of Lamentations, the personification of Zion as a beloved woman in medieval poetry, and modern attempts to write psychohistories of Zionism.) Many recent texts run the risk of projecting male perceptions or preoccupations onto women within an allegorical framework.

The second, converse, issue that arises is the treatment of women as individuals. Has Hebrew literature recognized experiences particular to women? In Western literature the canon has commonly dismissed writing by and about women as narrow or thematically trivial. This judgment and the texts it disavows often reflect the exclusion of women from public activity that has been part of social reality in Jewish life as elsewhere. Feminist criticism naturally must ask how female predicaments as a theme have fared within the Hebrew corpus, why women's voices have emerged more in lyric poetry than in fiction or drama, and what has been the relative prestige and status of these genres.

While celebrating the insights promised by a feminist critical apparatus, I hasten to issue a caveat. The social history that sets this literature apart, a literature that poses specific gender problems and so invites feminist scrutiny, also defies glib generalizations from feminist theory developed in other cultural contexts. Though Hebrew literature was inaccessible to women at the turn of the century because of the language obstacle, the male literary establishment at that time was exceptionally welcoming to women writers. As part of the renascence of Hebrew as the Jewish national language (in Europe and in Palestine, late in the nineteenth century and in the first decades of the twentieth), authors were highly self-conscious about the absence of women from their ranks. They lavished attention on the few who could cross the gender barrier.

Devorah Baron, a writer of prose fiction (1887–1956), presents an outstanding example. A rabbi's daughter, she learned Hebrew at home as a child by listening in on the lessons her father gave to young boys. Armed with this linguistic skill, she turned to composing fiction and became a literary phenomenon from the very beginning of her career, at age 16. Male writers, editors, and critics showered her work with accolades and waxed enthusiastic about the appearance of that curiosity, a woman author of Hebrew. The small number of female writers in these early decades, then, is not solely the result of misogyny or bias. Nonetheless, the picture becomes more complicated in view of the fact that expectations of feminine modesty did temper male openness to women writers. Baron's readers encouraged her creativity but urged her not to broach certain topics or to express herself too freely. Altogether, the tensions and contradictions that marked the introduction of women writers to Hebrew defy simplistic analyses or claims of discrimination.

Feminist Approaches to Modern Hebrew Literature: An Overview

Critics in the field of Hebrew literature have begun to address all these issues. They have opened up new thematic areas of inquiry and discussion on subjects that previously received little attention. Part of that effort has resulted in expanding the scope of the canon—not in the sense of redefining a restrictively authoritative corpus of texts and deeming these alone to be worthy of study, but rather in the sense of "enlarging the literary map."[8] That is to say, feminist approaches have occasioned a shift in emphasis about which themes, which texts, and which authors merit consideration, and this new perspective can lead to incisive analysis as it leads to a more comprehensive understanding of the forces that have shaped Hebrew literary discourse and the *literary polysystem*. The term is Even Zohar's and refers to the diverse genres, some elitist and some popular, and the varieties of diction, some high and some low, that constitute the whole of literary production in a language.[9] As it charts what has been left out as well as what has been included in the canon, as it examines the movement of conventions from the margins to the center of the literary world (and vice versa), the wider reading fostered by gender studies allows a new assessment of the ebb and flow of writing that has contributed to the resurgence of Hebrew culture in this century.

These critical moves are of clear merit for literary historians. A valuable complementary effort is that of investigating the history of criticism itself. It is useful to analyze how critics and how authors of intellectual history have reacted to women writers and so have helped to establish norms for Hebrew culture in the past hundred years. Some scholars have taken steps in this direction. A crucial aspect of their enterprise has been not just to document literary values but to deconstruct those patterns, to set in relief and question their assumptions, and to challenge the ideas by which the (predominantly male) literary world has judged itself, society, and women's part in both. Through thematic as well as literary historical studies, critics have begun to examine the definitions of gender in Hebrew culture, particularly in Israeli society, and in the social revolutions and movements for national renewal of the past century.

As I shift now to a more specific review of current work, I do not intend to comment in depth on individual studies. My aim, instead, is to outline clusters of material that have attracted attention and so to track some of the first questions on which feminist criticism has concentrated in the field of Hebrew. By setting up the following categories I run a distinct risk of lumping diverse works together indiscriminately. The critics in each group would disagree about many things; their work has most often been the result of independent efforts and not the product of a coordinated debate among scholars. Consequently, each study has its own focus, its own virtues, and its own shortcomings. Nonetheless, these categories usefully point to a number of issues that have generated discussion and raise questions of far-reaching implications for the field as a whole.

Stereotypes and Images of Women

As has been the pattern in other literatures, in the field of Hebrew pioneering work has also turned to images of women and to exposés of stereotypes in the literary depiction of females. In *Eve's Journey* Nehama Aschkenasy considers images of women in a broad canvas of modern and ancient texts.[10] She finds that female characters fall into four main categories: demonic figures, maternal figures, victims of oppression, and tricksters or others who triumph over oppression. Within these general categories Aschkenasy brings special attention to Jewish contexts (for example, by highlighting religious themes with a Jewish cast). She writes about the plight of the *agunah* (the abandoned wife), divorce dictated by rabbinical courts, and infertility as those themes surface in the fiction and poetry of S. Y. Agnon, Baron, M. Y. Berdichewsky, Y. L. Gordon, and others.[11]

Also central to Aschkenasy's book are portrayals of women in Israel, particularly at times of war. This latter topic is Esther Fuchs's point of departure in a number of articles and in her book *Israeli Mythogynies*.[12] Fuchs looks at representations of women in writing by men, concentrating on fiction by Yehoshua and Oz. She then considers women's voices speaking back against male preconceptions, particularly in the fiction of Amalia Kahana-Carmon. The primary claim is that Israeli literature by men often projects onto females those values that the authors condemn in society as a whole: materialism and disloyalty. In this way men use women as symbols to express disappointment when Israel fails to realize the idealistic dreams of its founders. Kahana-Carmon's fiction, in contrast, represents women as individuals endowed with intentionality and rich inner lives, even though that complexity and inner richness is often unappreciated by the men around them.[13]

Hamutal Bar Yosef has also concentrated on examining stereotypes in modern Hebrew literature.[14] Her approach differs from others in its emphasis on genre and period. Bar Yosef focuses on tracing the development of female stereotypes in various literary movements—especially Romanticism, Decadence, and Symbolism—and then documents how Hebrew writing has absorbed and transformed these European literary models and their views of women.

A Female Literary Tradition in Hebrew

As in other literatures, women authors long neglected and texts once disregarded are now gaining attention. For example, Yaffa Berlowitz has anthologized selected writings by women who were among the first wave of Jewish pioneers in Palestine in the nineteenth century.[15] Another example: Nurith Govrin's study of Baron investigates her early stories, stories that were never anthologized and that were therefore largely forgotten.[16] Although such an excavation of texts is intrinsically interesting for students of Baron, it may also make the case for the value of gender as a category of analysis in literary biography—that is, as a tool to help explain shifts within an author's career. Of most interest in this particular case is a pattern of development within Baron's writing—a renunciation of protest and a move away from self-disclosure—that finds significant parallels in the work of other women writers. Uncovering a phenomenon approached from various angles by several critics, Govrin's study can be read as a corroboration of the theory that ambivalence about self-expression has had a major impact on women's literary production in Hebrew.

To begin with Baron: Govrin shows that this author's early texts touched on topics that, at the time of their writing, were dangerous or unduly bold for a woman to discuss. These topics included rebellion, bitterness, and passionate sexuality; the later texts, the well-known ones, turn from such matters. Similarly, although the early stories also offer personal anecdotes, many of which bear a resemblance to incidents in the author's life, the later stories have shed this feature. Instead, the canonical narratives favor a collective perspective while downplaying personal emotion. Take the story "Genizah." This tale features a little girl who wants to add the *tkhines* book to other volumes destined for the genizah. The genizah is a storage area within the synagogue that is reserved for sacred texts that have worn out but, according to Jewish law, may not be discarded or destroyed. The tkhines, supplicatory prayers for women written in Yiddish, may not enter there. Govrin points out that the early version of Baron's story (1913) constitutes a protest against the patriarchal order and, specifically, against the father and the brother who obstruct the little girl's plan to honor the women's prayers. The second version of Baron's story (anthologized in 1950) calls attention to the cyclicality of life, burial, and rebirth. Focusing on the ceremony of the genizah itself and not on the girl's feelings of anger, this tale takes on an emphasis that is more mythic than personal or familial.

According to Hamutal Bar Yosef, a similar progression marked the work of the later poet, Zelda (1914–84).[17] Zelda also shifted from early self-revelation toward a style that exhibits restraint, freedom from pathos, and an inclination toward universality. Her first works, from the 1930s, emphasize erotic longing, worries about infertility, fears of death without personal fulfillment, and hints of tension in relations with her mother. All these topics constitute a kind of taboo in Zelda's mature poetry, that is, the work that was published in book form after 1967 and that has gained her most public recognition. Tellingly, Zelda did not publish many of her youthful pieces.

Zelda's inclination to lessen or hide the intimate elements of her writing involves a move from prose to poetry. Her early work took the form of lyrical prose written without vocalization *(nikud)*, rhyme, or short lines. Pressures toward modesty seem to have been decisive factors in the poetry of this religiously observant woman from a Hassidic family, and so it is not surprising that she developed her art through short lyric verse rather than along the lines of the realistic autobiographical novel. This point merits special consideration, though, as Zelda's choice of form clearly implicates the question of genre into this debate about gender.

For both these writers, then, canonical status or widespread acceptance in Hebrew literature has gone hand in hand with a reining in of protest and self-display. Several reasons suggest themselves: overt pressure from editors or rejection from readers; a fatigue, increasing with age, that comes from doing battle with existing norms; self-censorship in response to traditional values; a maturity that aims for universals rather than self-reflection. It remains a desideratum for future discussion to try to pinpoint the causes.

That task takes on importance in view of the fact that the retreat from intimacy is common to a number of women writers. Bar Yosef does not directly discuss female literary tradition in Hebrew; her book is a monograph devoted to explicating Zelda's favorite themes and metaphors, her prosody, and her biographical background. Nonetheless, Bar Yosef's observations serve as a good point of departure for the consideration of women's writing as a tradition in Hebrew. Like Zelda, other women who have sought self-expression also feared it as humiliating disclosure. According to articles by Miriam Glazer and Lily Rattok,[18] one of the major identifying qualities of women's poetry in Israel has been the adoption of a private, poetic *I,* as opposed to the more public or collective stance of male poets. At the same time, the argument goes, this poetic *I* is wary of revealing too much.

Compatible ideas also underlie Dan Miron's extended discussion of the "founding mothers"—Rahel, Esther Raab, Elisheva, and Yocheved Bat Miriam—in his analysis of the social and literary forces that converged to allow women entrance into Hebrew poetry in the 1920s and not earlier.[19] Poetry of that decade features an oscillation between outspokenness and its opposite, an evasion of grandeur and ambitious vistas. Miron ascribes this mixture of qualities to the peculiar receptiveness that Hebrew literature offered women after the period of the Second Aliyah (1906–17). Thanks to an influx of Russian Jewish immigrants to Palestine at that time, the social climate of the Jewish community, the Yishuv, opened to imported revolutionary ideals—including egalitarianism and a reassessment of women's freedoms. In addition, many of the newcomers were not learned scholars trained in the tradition of the yeshiva. The Bialikean norms of Hebrew poetics relaxed in the effort to welcome these immigrants, and this move had the additional effect of removing a once formidable barrier to women's participation in writing. At the same time, women writers were still burdened with expectations of refinement and modesty that permitted their work to be neither too complex, too hardened, nor too revolutionary. The result was a series of complex negotiations with audacity.

Yael Feldman's work on "camouflaged autobiography" finds evidence of ambivalence about self-disclosure in the fiction of much more recent authors, such as Shulamit Hareven, Kahana-Carmon, and Shulamit Lapid.[20] Feldman argues that their writing, too, is marked by tensions between an urge for self-revelation and a desire not to show too much. In this case, the result is an evasion of personal detail plus a submerging of self in stories about earlier periods of history and communal events. Because they are reticent to challenge the status quo of today's Israel, where feminism is still widely unpopular, the women writers project concerns with women's rights anachronistically back to a distant time frame. With its emphasis on the choice of fictional format for expressing feminist ideas, Feldman's research confirms the importance of the ongoing debate on gender and genre.

Gender Boundaries

Yet another kind of camouflage has attracted feminist criticism: women writers who attempt to inhabit the consciousness of men by developing male narrators or by focusing primarily on the inner lives of male characters. Sonia Grober has discussed this narrative strategy in connection with Kahana-Carmon's fiction, in particular, the short story "First Axioms."[21] There, a protagonist-narrator aspires to a career as a writer and attempts to elucidate the principles that animate his art. Grober claims that the character's main preoccupations, especially his sense of displacement and exclusion from a literary tradition, resemble those of many women authors. Moreover, she argues, it makes sense to read this story against the background of Virginia Woolf's *A Room of One's Own*. She concludes that Israeli audiences by and large have not been alert to these points, because of their unfamiliarity with feminist theory.

Now, why did Kahana-Carmon create a male character to present her ideas? In this discussion, Grober does not speculate about reasons, but it is likely that putting ideas about art into the mouth of a male writer will ensure that readers take the points made more seriously. It is clearly attractive at times for a woman writer to adopt the mask of a male character as spokesperson for her thoughts. In view of these matters, larger, related questions arise: when, how, with what effects, and with what difficulties have women authors represented the consciousness of men? Insofar as it is the business of fiction to imagine the private thoughts of others, is it a challenge, an obstacle, an escape, a solution, or a matter of indifference to cross gender boundaries when imagining the inner life or the perspectives of another?

The converse situation, which has elicited considerably more discussion, is how men have imagined the voices of women by turning to female narrators or to other representations of women's consciousness. There were strides in this direction even before feminist inquiry per se, as in a 1971 article by Arnold Band comparing Oz's *My Michael* and Agnon's *In the Prime of Her Life*.[22] More recent work returns to this topic informed by an awareness of debate on sexual politics, feminist sociolinguistics, and Julia Kristeva's notions of the semiotic and preoedipal relations. See, for example, Fuchs's commentary on Oz and Yehoshua; my readings of Aharon Appelfeld's *Tzili* and *In The Prime of Her Life;*[23] and the distinctive readings of that same Agnon text by Ruth Ginsburg and Efrat Golan.[24] These studies provide evidence that a male author's attempt to speak through a female persona does not necessarily mean that he champions woman's self-expression—at least, not unequivocally. Instead, ventriloquism of this sort may make for versatility in terms of dramatic plot development or the deployment of symbolism. By the same token, it may curtail or enhance certain narrative prerogatives. Because there are things a female voice is not allowed to say or is permitted to say only indirectly, the way a woman tells a tale may differ from that of a man. A resulting emphasis on the suppression of voice may strengthen a thematic attention to silence, to repressed desires, or to inadequacies and defects of character.

Part of what makes this phenomenon interesting and distinct within Hebrew literature is that attention to the powerlessness of women and the silencing or muting of female voice becomes a way to express a variety of attitudes toward the power and powerlessness of Jews. Dull-witted Tzili stands in her muteness as an emblem of Jewish incomprehension about the Holocaust, suggesting the inability or unwillingness of Jews to foresee the disaster before it hit them. Yehoshua's elderly character, Veducha, in her incoherent ramblings, symbolizes a worn-out Zionist ideology. Agnon's Tirzah, in her wavering efforts at vocal self-assertion, enhances thematic attention to the rebirth of Hebrew and to doubts about whether that ancient tongue will succeed at reasserting itself as a modern language.

A particularly complex case of ventriloquism is that studied by Miron:[25] Uri Nissan Gnessin's appropriation of a poem written in Russian by Celia Dropkin (later renowned for her Yiddish poetry). Gnessin translated this poem into Hebrew and incorporated it into one of his short stories (published in the early twentieth century). Without acknowledging Dropkin, Gnessin presents the poem as the creation of one of his female characters. The episode merits close consideration, in part as an anecdote of literary-political relations between the sexes. In addition, and most important, the transformations wrought by the male author as he translates this poem reveal much about the poetic norms of the era and about the male biases in Hebrew letters at the time. The pose Gnessin adopted (of a man creating woman's poetry) while actually appropriating and deforming a woman's poem, blurs gender categories or scrambles the borders between them. The contrast between his poem and the original puts into relief some of the prevalent literary conventions of the time, suggesting why these were foreign to women and why they inhibited or delayed the entrance of women into Hebrew poetry.

The speaker in each version of the poem is a woman abandoned by her lover. Miron explains that Dropkin's poetic *I* voices murderous rage at being abandoned, but Gnessin's speaker adds metaphor, vocabulary, and a series of rhetorical moves that cast the absent lover as a wanderer doomed to exile. This change not only enlarges the role of the man but glorifies it, associating him with the fate of the Jews as a people in exile. Evoking connections between the man's destiny and collective grief or hardship, the Gnessin poem romanticizes the hero and justifies his inattention to the woman. The allusions and the poetic devices that make this message possible follow the standards of Bialik's poetics. They draw heavily on those elements of sacred learning that were still largely unavailable to women at the turn of the century and that defined a poem as serious poetry. Dropkin's unconventional, iconoclastic poem, because it is so different, makes these norms and biases much clearer by contrast. It is her voice from the margins that proves instrumental in illuminating the dominant assumptions and values of the period.

Poststructuralist feminist approaches, such as those explored by Anne Golomb Hoffman, provide yet another mode of examining male norms by homing in on the dissolution of ordinary gender categories.[26] Concentrating on the breakdown of male-female oppositions as a theme in the fiction of Agnon, Yehoshua, and Yaakov Shabtai, Hoffman has employed psychoanalytic understandings to examine the construction of gender and challenges to it—in a personal and national dimension—in the Israeli context. She identifies how these authors highlight themes (such as regression to the gender confusion of a preoedipal infantile sexuality and stalled oedipal passages) and incorporate them into their depiction of collective crisis. In the case of Yehoshua and Shabtai, at issue are moments of national withdrawal from the entrenched position of certainties about a macho, warrior ethos. In the case of Agnon, primary attention goes to moments of disintegration in western intellectual culture.

The Collective and the Personal in the Representation of Women

Whether dealing with stereotypes, a feminine tradition, or gender boundaries, all the research I have outlined hinges on a fundamental issue: the relation between private and collective matters in literary texts. In diverse ways critics have returned time and again to the basic knotty problem that a woman's sphere of experience has been different from that of men. Hers, moreover, has often been considered secondary to his. Several individuals have addressed this issue explicitly. For pathbreaking articles on the topic by one of Israel's major writers, see Kahana-Carmon's articles, which ask how to regard women's writing without making it subordinate to the male domain.[27] Elaborating on a series of metaphors, Kahana-Carmon builds the case that women's domain has been distinct but no less significant than men's; to judge women's writing by the existing norms of literary criticism is to force their work into a procrustean bed. Much as a dolphin would misapprehend the insights of a jellyfish, she writes, or much as human beings would fail to perceive the high-pitched song of a bat that eludes their range of hearing, literary critics have measured women's writing in Hebrew by inadequate means and so declared that writing itself to be inadequate.[28]

Karen Alkalay-Gut's views on women and war also turn to matters of the collective and the personal, claiming a basis in sociology.[29] This critic argues that women have become increasingly active in protest movements in Israel since 1982 and so are increasingly active as poets of war and antiwar stances. Lesley Hazelton's book *Israeli Women* (1977), although it was published some years ago, remains useful as a polemical survey of troublesome issues.[30] It is not a work of literary criticism per se; it is a work of popular sociology, but it refers frequently to poems and other literary texts to illustrate key points and to challenge fundamental myths about women's equality in Israeli society.

Directions for Future Research

The possibilities for future research can certainly accommodate more work in many of the areas I have reviewed here. A new application of similar ideas would prove enlightening in rereading many authors. Such efforts would do well to include more commentary on cinema and theater along with poetry, fiction, and autobiography. In addition, achieving recognition of the breadth and potential for gender studies remains an essential goal. At stake here is neither a narrow agenda nor a monolithic ideology, but a wide-ranging set of questions that have fostered diverse attitudes and critical enterprises.

Above all, it would be desirable to pursue comparative approaches to literature in Hebrew, Yiddish, and other languages in which Jews have written. There exist in these literatures many shared themes useful for comparison, such as the Holocaust and the relation of women to sacred study. Similarly of interest are women writers' statements of their ars poetica or their visions of the connections between female identity and poetic craft.[31] I am imagining, for instance, a dialogue between Anne Lapidus Lerner's reading of Esther Raab's "Shirat Isha" (*A Woman's Song,* 1969) and Kathryn Hellerstein's interpretation of Kadya Molodowsky's "Froyen-Lider" (*Women-Poems,* 1927).[32] Both these poets are centrally concerned with a widely assumed opposition between women's social roles and poetry and between reproductivity and creativity. Both aim to undo the opposition by reconciling art with Jewish understandings of womanhood. And, in the process, both revise or re-vision prayer as they examine Jewish tradition in relation to the female body. Molodowsky draws on the tkhines and the shm'a to fashion a new kind of prayer; Raab inverts the Eighteen Benedictions to assert what a blessing it is to have been born female. Though Raab's poem comes from a much later date than Molodowsky's, her poetic work first appeared in print in the 1920s, as did "Froyen-Lider." Tracing the treatment of gender, the body, and tradition throughout Raab's and Molodowsky's careers would be a step toward charting the changing visions of these issues over the course of the twentieth century.

Another attractive area for comparisons is the question of how women have sought out precursors by conjuring foremothers and rewriting biblical tales. Yocheved Bat Miriam's "Miriam," as discussed by Ilana Pardes, invites a comparison with English verse or verse in other languages that retells the stories of female figures from the Bible.[33] An analysis of such texts in tandem might indicate which characters have had the greatest appeal and served as role models for Jewish women across linguistic and cultural boundaries, and which have exerted power only at specific times and places. As part of the general discussion about why and how Hebrew authors have retold classical stories—including tales of female characters as reinvented by men—this approach could and should be integrated directly into teaching curricula, and not relegated to one side as "women's studies."

Finally, Hebrew as a modern secular literature is still a relatively young phenomenon. Consequently, feminist insights may prove influential not only in studying the past, but in intervening at a comparatively early, formative stage of the literature. At the conference "Gender and Text: Feminist Criticism and Modern Jewish Literature" (1990), Israeli novelist Ruth Almog remarked that as a result of the conference meetings, she had taken an interest for the first time in Yiddish writing by women.[34] She also said that the conference discussion gave her pause for relection as well as new ideas for the fiction she was currently composing. In such ways as these, feminist criticism may affect the direction Hebrew poetry and fiction will take in the years to come.

Notes

1. The conference "Woman in American and Israeli Literature and the Arts" was held at Tel Aviv University in March 1989; sessions included modern Hebrew literature and cinema, feminist approaches to biblical and rabbinic texts, folklore, and contemporary Hebrew linguistics. Another conference, "Gender and Text: Feminist Criticism and Modern Jewish Literature," took place at the Jewish Theological Seminary of America in June 1990 and was devoted specifically to modern Hebrew and Yiddish literature. For an annotated bibliography of feminist research in modern Hebrew belles lettres see the volume that emerged from this conference: *Gender and Text in Modern Hebrew and Yiddish Literature,* Naomi B. Sokoloff, Anne Lapidus Lerner, and Anita Norich, eds. (New York: Jewish Theological Seminary of America, 1992).

   The works cited in this chapter include only published titles. In a rapidly changing field, this list is bound to become outdated. Considerable work is in progress by many scholars, including Marcia Falk, Regine Friedman, Zilla Goodman, Haya Hoffman, Ilana Kochen, Tirsa Kubler, Yosefa Loshitzky, Anat Zanger-Shpatz, and Wendy Zierler. Since this volume went to press, the following publications have appeared: Michael Gluzman, "The Exclusion of Women from Hebrew Literary History," *Prooftexts* 11(1) (1991): 259–78; Naomi Seidman, "'It Is You I Speak from within Me': David Fogel's Poetics of the Feminine Voice," *Prooftexts* 13(1) (1993): 87–102; and a special issue of *Modern Hebrew Literature* (6 [1991]), devoted to women's writing in the 1980s. There has been an outpouring of new fiction and poetry by women in the past decade, and the reviews and remarks in this journal cover some of these new voices, such as Orly Castel-Bloom, Batya Gur, and Hannah Bat Shahar. Gershon Shaked discusses the question of whether there is a woman's literature in Israel in his book *Sifrut az, k'an, ve'akshav* (Literature Then, Here and Now) (Tel Aviv: Zmora Bitan, 1993), 70–77.

A special impetus for feminist criticism has come from the North American context and among Israelis of Anglo-American background. In North America that momentum comes in part from contact with a more vigorous and widespread women's movement in Israel today, although cooperation between Israel and America has been good, including the translation of essays from Hebrew to English and vice versa, participation in conferences, and a shared readership.

2. Toril Moi presents a useful overview and critique of such approaches in *Sexual/Textual Politics* (London: Methuen, 1983), 19–49. This book provides an excellent general introduction to feminist literary criticism, in both its Anglo-American and French varieties. Moi also includes a substantive bibliography and a guide to further reading.

3. A fine sample of this line of research is available in Shirley Nelson Garner, Clair Kahane, and Madelon Sprengnether, eds., *The (M)other Tongue: Essays in Feminist Psychoanalytic Interpretation* (Ithaca: Cornell University Press, 1985); Katherine Dalsimer, *Female Adolescence: Psychoanalytic Reflections on Literature* (New Haven: Yale University Press, 1986); Alice Jardine, *Gynesis: Configurations of Woman and Modernity* (Ithaca: Cornell University Press, 1985); and Kaja Silverman, *The Subject of Semiotics* (New York: Oxford University Press, 1983).

4. Cited especially frequently are Dorothy Dinnerstein, *The Mermaid and the Minotaur: Sexual Arrangements and Human Malaise* (New York: Harper and Row, 1976); Nancy Chodorow, *The Reproduction of Mothering: Psychoanalysis and the Sociology of Gender* (Berkeley: University of California Press, 1978); and Julia Kristeva, *Desire in Language: A Semiotic Approach to Literature and Art,* ed. Leon Roudiez and trans. Alice Jardine, Thomas Gora, and Leon Roudiez (Oxford: Blackwell, 1980).

5. For a range of applications, see Sally McConnell-Ginet, Ruth Borker, and Nelly Furman, eds., *Women and Language in Literature and Society* (New York: Praeger, 1980).

6. For an overview of major issues, an informative collection of essays, and an extensive bibliography, see Elaine Showalter, ed., *The New Feminist Criticism* (New York: Pantheon, 1985). Of particular interest are Showalter's own articles in this anthology, "Toward a Feminist Poetics," pp. 125–43, and "Feminist Criticism in the Wilderness," pp. 243–76.

7. Anita Norich's essay, "Jewish Literatures and Feminist Criticism: An Introduction," discusses the connections between Hebrew and Yiddish and some of the feminist issues these two literatures raise. In Sokoloff, Lerner, and Norich, *Gender and Text,* 1–16.

8. I borrow the phrase from Alan Mintz's closing comments at the "Gender and Text" conference.

9. "Polysystem Studies," *Poetics Today* 11(1) (1990).

10. *Eve's Journey: Feminine Images in Hebraic Literary Tradition* (Philadelphia: Jewish Publication Society, 1986).

11. For more on these issues, see Anne Lapidus Lerner's work on Esther Raab, "Lost Childhood in Eastern European Hebrew Literature," in David Kraemer, ed., *The Jewish Family: Metaphor and Memory* (New York: Oxford University Press, 1990). For stereotypes of women in a single-author study, see Tova Cohen's work on Mapu: "Beyn elilah lelilit: Hagiborah baromans shel Mapu" (Between Idol and Lilith: The Heroine in the Romance of Mapu), in her book *Yesharim, utsevu'im, elilot veliliot: 'Iyunim bitsirot Mapu* (Tel Aviv: Papyrus, 1991).

12. See, e.g., the following by Esther Fuchs: "Casualties of Patriarchal Double Standards: Old Women in the Fiction of A. B. Yehoshua," *South Central Bulletin* 43(4) (1984): 107–9; "The Beast Within: Women in Amos Oz' Early Fiction," *Modern Judaism* 4(3) (1984): 311–21; "The Sleepy Wife: A Feminist Consideration of A. B. Yehoshua's Fiction," *Hebrew Annual Review* 8 (1984): 71–81; "The Representation of Biblical Women in Israeli Narrative Fiction: Some Transformations and Continuities," in Mark H. Gelber, ed., *Identity and Ethos: A Festschrift for Sol Liptzin,* pp. 361–74 (New York: P. Lang, 1986); "Images of Love and War in Contemporary Israeli Fiction: Toward a Feminist Re-Vision," *Modern Judaism* 6(2) (1986): 190–96, rev. and rep. as "Love and War in Israeli Fiction," in Helen M. Cooper, Adrienne Auslander Munich, and Susan Merill Squier, eds., *Arms and the Woman: War, Gender, and Literary Representation* (Chapel Hill: North Carolina Press, 1990); *Israeli Mythogynies: Women in Contemporary Hebrew Fiction* (Albany: SUNY Press, 1987); "Amalia Kahana-Carmon and Contemporary Hebrew Women's Fiction," *Signs: A Journal of Women in Culture and Society* 13(2) (1988): 299–310; "Amalia Kahana-Carmon and *Moon in the Valley of Ajalon,*" *Prooftexts* 8(1) (1988), 129–41.

13. For a more extensive discussion and a critique of these two books by Esther Fuchs and Nehama Aschkenasy, see Naomi Sokoloff, "Feminist Criticism and Modern Hebrew Literature," *Prooftexts* 8(1) (1988): 143–56.

14. "Decadence and the Concept of Femininity in Bialik's Poetry," in Sokoloff, Lerner, and Norich, *Gender and Text,* pp. 145–70.

15. *Sifrut nashim benot ha'aliyah harishonah* (Literature of the Early Women Pioneers) (Tel Aviv: Tarmil, 1984).

16. *Hamahatsit harishonah: Devorah Baron, hayeha vitsiratah* (The First Half: Devorah Baron, Her Life and Work) (Jerusalem: Mossad Bialik, 1988).

17. *'Al shirat Zelda* (On Zelda's Poetry) (Tel Aviv: Hakibbuts Hameuchad, 1988).

18. Myra (Miriam) Glazer, introduction to *Burning Air and a Clear Mind: Contemporary Israeli Woman Poets* (Athens: Ohio University Press, 1979); Lily Rattok, "Deyokan ha'isha kimshoreret Yisra'elit" (Portrait of a Woman as an Israeli Poet), *Moznayim* (May 1988): 56–62.

19. *Imahot meyasdot, ahayot horgot* (Stepsisters, Founding Mothers: The Emergence of the First Hebrew Poetesses and Other Essays) (Jerusalem: Hakibbuts Hameuchad, 1991). A portion of this work appears in English as "Why Was There No Women's Poetry in Hebrew Before 1920?" in Sokoloff, Lerner, and Norich, *Gender and Text,* 65–92.

20. Feldman's titles include: "Roman histori o 'otobiografiah' bemasekha? 'Al 'Gei'oni' uvney mino besiporet akhshavit" (Historical Novels or Masked Autobiographies? On Gei'oni

and Its Genre in Contemporary Fiction), *Siman Kri'ah* 19 (1986): 208–13; "Inadvertent Feminism: The Image of Frontier Women in Contemporary Israeli Literature," *Modern Hebrew Literature* 10(3–4) (1985): 34–37; "Gender in/Difference in Contemporary Hebrew Fictional Autobiography," *Biography* 11(3) (1988): 189–209; "Feminism under Siege: The Vicarious Self of Israeli Women Writers," *Prooftexts* 10(3) (1990):493–514; "Ideology and Self-Representation of Women in Israeli Literature," in Janice Morgan and Colette Hall, eds., *Redefining Autobiography in Twentieth-Century Women's Fiction,* pp. 281–301 (New York: Garland, 1991); and "Androginiut bamatsor: Hafeminism haselektivi shel Shulamit Hareven" (Androgyny under Siege: The Selective Feminism of Shulamit Hareven), *Siman Kri'ah* 23 (1991).

21. "First Axioms: A Writer's Attempt at Self-Definition," *Modern Hebrew Literature* 13(3–4): 10–14.

22. "Hamesaper habilti meheyman beMicha'el sheli uvidmi yameha" (The Unreliable Narrator in *My Michael* and *In the Prime of Her Life*), *Hasifrut* 3 (1971): 30–47.

23. "Tzili: Female Adolescence and the Holocaust in the Fiction of Aharon Appelfeld," in Sokoloff, Lerner, and Norich, *Gender and Text,* 171–94; and "Narrative Ventriloquism and Muted Feminine Voice: Agnon's *In the Prime of Her Life,*" *Prooftexts* 9(3) (1989): 115–37.

24. Ruth Ginsburg, "Bidmi yamehah metah Tirtsah: O, yafah at re'ayati keTirtsah navah kirushalayim ayumah kenidgalot" (And Tirzah Died in the Prime of Her Life, or, Thou Art Beautiful, O My Love, as Tirzah, Comely as Jerusalem, Terrible as an Army with Banners), *Dapim lemehkar besifrut* 7 (1992); and Efrat Golan, "Kri'ah feministit shel 'bidmi yamehah' " (A Feminist Reading of *In the Prime of Her Life*), *'Alei siah* 27/28 (1990): 81–92.

25. See *Imahot meyasdot,* esp. 72–85, and "Why Was There No Woman's Poetry?" 1992.

26. "Gender, Writing, and Culture: Shira," in *Between Exile and Return: S. Y. Agnon and the Drama of Writing,* pp. 149–76 (Albany: SUNY Press, 1991); "Constructing Masculinity in Yaakov Shabtai's Past Continuous," *Prooftexts* 11(2) (1991): 279–95; and "Oedipal Narrative and Its Discontents: A. B. Yehoshua's *Molkho* (Five Seasons)," in Sokoloff, Lerner, and Norich, *Gender and Text,* 195–216.

27. Kahana-Carmon's essays include "Lihyot isha soferet" (To Be a Woman Writer), *Yedi'ot aharonot* (4 April 1984): 20–21; "Lehitbazbez'al hatsedadi" (To Be Wasted on the Peripheral), *Yedi'ot aharonot* (15 Sept. 1985); "Ishto shel Brenner rokhevet shuv" (Brenner's Wife Rides Again), *Moznayim* 59(4) (1985): 13; "Hi kotevet dey nehmad aval'al shebiyarkhatayim" (She Writes Rather Well, but . . .), *Yedi'ot aharonot* (2 May 1988); "Shirat ha'atalefim beme'ofam" (The Song of the Bats in Flight), *Moznayim* (Nov.–Dec., 1989): 3–7l; and "The Song of the Bats in Flight," in Sokoloff, Lerner, and Norich, *Gender and Text,* 235–49.

28. The accusation of triviality leveled at women's writing is a question that likewise preoccupies the novelist Ruth Almog, and it is one that she addresses in connection with her own artistic vision. See her comments in "Feminism and Hebrew Literature: A Personal Approach," in Sokoloff, Lerner, and Norich, *Gender and Text,* 227–34.

29. See, e.g., "Poetry by Women in Israel and the War in Lebanon," *World Literature Today* (winter 1989): 19–25.

30. *Israeli Women: The Reality behind the Myths* (New York: Simon and Schuster, 1977).

31. Women's poetics and intellectual life as a theme are a topic of interest for Rivka Elinav, "The World of the Intellectual Heroine: A Comparative Study of the Prose Writings of Elisheva Bikhovsky and Leah Goldberg," Ph.D. diss., Jewish Theological Seminary of America, 1990.

32. Anne Lapidus Lerner, "'A Woman's Song': The Poetry of Esther Raab," in Sokoloff, Lerner, and Norich, *Gender and Text*, 17–38; Kathryn Hellerstein, "'A Word for My Blood: A Reading of Kadya Molodowsky's 'Froyen-Lider,' " *AJS Review* 13:47–79.

33. See Pardes's "Yocheved Bat Miriam: The Poetic Strength of a Matronym," in Sokoloff, Lerner, and Norich, *Gender and Text*, 39–64. For a selection of verse in English that deals with biblical female figures, see the following from the collection *Voices within the Ark*, ed. Howard Schwartz and Anthony Rudolf (New York: Avon, 1980): Chana Bloch, "Paradise," pp. 423–24; Kim Chernin, "Eve's Birth," p. 443; Elaine Dallman, "From the Dust," pp. 443–44; Rose Drachler, "Zippora Returns to Moses at Rephidim," p. 448; Marcia Falk, "Shulamit in her Dreams," p. 454; Shirley Kaufman "Leah," p. 785; Linda Zisquit, "Rachel's Lament," pp. 675–76.

34. Almog wrote up some of these impressions in her literary column in *Ha'arets*, 6 July 1990.

Jews, Gender, American Cinema

Contemporary scholars have challenged conventional thinking about ethnicity, race, and gender. Many now argue that
none of these is a natural category; rather, they are culturally,
politically, and socially constructed.[1] Along with class and
sexual preference, race, ethnicity, and gender have come to
be seen as identities that are not biologically determined, but
fluid and changing. Though specific social groups carry their
own histories, apparent continuities of behaviors or traits are
now construed not as fixed essences but as bundles or layers
of contingent attributes and roles that have emerged—indeed, are often actively negotiated—within changing social
configurations. As Stuart Hall has put it, writing about black
identity, " 'black' is essentially a politically and culturally
constructed category, which cannot be grounded in a set of
fixed trans-cultural or transcendental racial categories and
which therefore has no guarantees in Nature."[2] The same
might be said for Jewish, female, and male.

Although theories of identity construction have been part
of contemporary feminist scholarship since its inception in
the late 1960s, such thinking has entered the scholarship on
race and ethnicity more recently. Despite similarities in their
conceptualizations of the origins of social identities, theories
of gender, on the one hand, and those of race and ethnicity,
on the other, have evolved more or less independently.
Feminist scholars have continuously attempted to analyze

I would like to thank Ramona Curry, David Desser, Maurice Fried-
berg, Larry Grossberg, Seth Koven, Elizabeth Klein Shapiro, Michael
Shapiro, and the editors for their many helpful suggestions. Members
of the audience at a screening of *How Mosha Came Back* at Temple
Sinai, Champaign, Illinois, offered important insights into the film. I
am grateful to Sharon Rivo and the staff at the National Jewish Film
Center at Brandeis University for providing me the opportunity to
screen many of the films discussed here.

intersections between gender and other "planes of social difference,"[3] but scholars of race and ethnicity have paid less attention to the ways in which racial and ethnic identities are inflected by gender (though they usually do consider class as significant). Many studies, in fact, implicitly assume that the universal representative of a given racial or ethnic category is "the male." Yet just as gender identities are always specified by race, ethnicity, and class, so ethnic identities are also always *gendered.* Moreover, individuals respond to such representations on the basis of gender. Viewed from both inside and outside their own social groupings, individuals are seen not simply as Jewish (or Italian or Japanese), but as Jewish *women* or *men.*[4] Gender thus becomes a constitutive element of racial and ethnic identity.[5]

To understand the construction of identities, scholars must analyze the political, cultural, and social processes through which they are produced. Such projects are inherently interdisciplinary, involving (at the very least) history, anthropology, psychology, and all types of cultural studies. This last is crucial; again, quoting Hall, "How things are represented and the 'machineries' and regimes of representation in a culture . . . play a *constitutive,* and not merely a reflexive, after-the-event role [in the construction of identity]. This gives questions of culture and ideology, and the scenarios of representation—subjectivity, identity, politics—a formative, not merely an expressive, place in the constitution of social and political life.'"[6] Cultural studies are, then, key to the making of ethnic identities—of *all* identities, for that matter.

How *culture* is defined—what it consists of—varies from one society to another and over time, but for the purpose of studying identity formation, it should be construed as broadly as possible. Those whose identity is at stake come into contact with many different forms of culture, and it is through the conjunction of such forms—high and low, material and performed, ritual and spontaneous—that identity is formed.[7] Since the nineteenth century (and even earlier in some societies), the artifacts of popular and then mass cultures have become increasingly significant elements in the mixture; these, then, merit close analysis.

In Jewish cultural studies, as in the other areas of Jewish studies discussed in this volume, attention to gender will advance our understanding of the issues at hand. In this chapter I propose a feminist approach to culture in general, using illustrations drawn from only one of the cultural media implicated in the formation of modern Jewish ethnicity: film. One reason for this choice is that the relation between gender and ethnicity is usually most explicit in cultural representations that take visual and narrative form. In visual terms, ethnicity is almost always marked by gender, so much so that it is difficult to conceive of ethnicity without gender.

Until recently, the subject of cinema has been a minor one in Jewish studies. This is surprising, since linkages between film and the Jewish community, particularly in the United States, are numerous. From the time of its origins around the turn of the century, Jewish immigrants from Eastern Europe figured significantly in the American film industry, both as members of the public streaming into urban nickelodeons and movie palaces, and as the producers, directors, and actors who built Hollywood.[8] The immigrant generation and those that succeeded it have received a great deal of attention from historians, social scientists, and literary analysts working in Jewish studies. But film has been relatively neglected. Only within the past decade or so have scholars begun to examine the place of Jews in cinema—as creators, subject matter, and audiences.[9]

As a newly developed intellectual area, Jewish cinema studies might be expected to open itself to the current trends in theory and methodology emerging in film studies generally. This has not been the case, however, particularly with regard to gender-based approaches. For more than a decade, feminist theory has been making important advances in cinema studies, yet it has had little impact on film scholars concerned with Jewish issues. The handful of books and articles that constitute Jewish cinema studies have paid only scant attention to issues of gender.[10] By the same token, it should be noted, despite the evident overlap between the growth of the Jewish community and that of the American film industry, few scholars outside Jewish studies have taken into account the Jewish background of so many Hollywood producers, directors, and actors, or the relation between their work and the presence (or absence) of Jewish themes in American films.[11] As with many aspects of Jewish history and culture, these issues tend to be studied separately, either by themselves or subsumed under the general rubric of ethnicity and film.[12]

The resulting ghettoization of Jewish film studies has not only contributed to its isolation but also limited the explanatory powers of mainstream theory. Recently, however, as calls for multiculturalism have intensified, both mainstream and feminist cinema scholars have begun to incorporate the categories of race and ethnicity (including Jewish ethnicity) into their analytic apparatus.[13] In Jewish studies, however, few film scholars have reciprocated by approaching their subject at the level of sophistication that has become the norm in mainstream cinema studies. Most continue to examine "Jewish" films in isolation from those treating other ethnic groups, and almost all persist in ignoring the importance of gender.

Yet both mainstream and Jewish cinema studies potentially have much to say about the questions that have concerned Jewish studies for decades. Scholars in that field, working on the understanding that identities are forged through interactions between Jews and other social groups, have paid close attention to processes of assimilation and acculturation and the maintenance or erosion of Jewish identity over time. In the twentieth century, film (along with mass culture generally) has become a significant factor in these processes because of its influence on public opinion and popular consciousness. To understand how Jews have come to see themselves and be seen by others, Jewish studies should develop an analysis of the cultural mechanisms through which self-identities and gender and ethnic identities are constructed. The task of Jewish cinema studies, as one aspect of this project, is to examine filmic representations of Jews and Jewish life[14] and attempt to explain the relation between these representations and the perceptions and responses of various audiences, both Jewish and Gentile, female and male.[15]

I focus in this chapter on one topic within Jewish film studies: American film and the construction of American-Jewish identity. There is not space here to provide an exhaustive analysis of the role of American film in the production of Jewish identities. Rather, I offer several examples to illustrate the enriched understandings that can result from the approach I am suggesting.[16] Though my examples are historically specific, the approach can readily be applied to other times and places.

My examination of film and Jewish identity begins with early American cinema and moves quickly through several later periods in order to map some of the permutations of gender and ethnicity in American film and their implications for identity formation. Film analyst David Desser has mounted a compelling argument for studying ethnicity during the silent era (from about 1900 to 1927), when Jewish immigration to the United States was at its height and issues of ethnic conflict salient:

> Ethnicity was a fact of American life, as was racism, sexism, and other forms of bigotry and discrimination. The question of unifying these cultural variations, of erasing differences, constituted a "cinematic dream," one obviously aligned to the American Dream, the American mythos of the melting pot. . . . It can be argued that this cinematic dream during the silent era provides a privileged site for understanding

how the discourse of the melting pot was structured into the American psyche, and how the contradictions and repressions of the myth can similarly be isolated.[17]

Film becomes, for Desser, the collective dream of a particular society. It is difficult to interpret such a dream, however, because there is no single, unitary dreamer, but rather a multiple, fragmented unconscious already fissured by ethnicity, gender, and other dimensions of difference.[18] Nevertheless, by attending to subject positions within specific film texts, one can begin to see how ethnicities and genders produce one another (and create social hierarchies) within specific cultural systems.

We must go further, however, to understand how a specific cultural text comes to play a constitutive role in the construction of identity. We can probably never assess the impact of a specific film (or any other text) on an unspecified, undifferentiated audience, but we can strive to understand it as one discourse among many in a reconstructed historical context. This is the approach implicitly proposed by film analyst Ramona Curry, who asserts that the "meanings of any given text arise not predominantly in readers' experience of its construction but in their discursive interactions with it in the context of myriad associated texts."[19] With its emphasis on discursive contexts, Curry's approach calls for historical as well as textual analysis. It also reminds us that films must not be studied in isolation from other sociocultural texts.

Curry and other contemporary interpreters of popular culture stress that audiences are not passively manipulated by cultural texts but rather actively draw meanings from them. Some contend that audiences turn to the media for help in working through common problems, that melodramas, for example, "model" problems and solutions for viewers. Writing about television, sociologist and critic Ella Taylor notes, "Like all storytelling, television speaks to our collective worries. . . . Television comments upon and orders, rather than reflects, experience, highlighting public concerns and cultural shifts."[20] To understand how texts might function in this way, they must, once again, be placed in a broader context.

This leads us to consider the proper subject matter of Jewish cinema studies. To date, most of the books and articles in this field have taken as their primary task the locating, describing, and analyzing of films in which identifiably Jewish characters appear or those in which Jewish issues figure into the plot.[21] Applied conservatively to American commercial production since its inception, this definition turns up more than five hundred studio films, most of them feature-length.[22] Yet such a definition, even with its vast yield, might still be too narrow to accomplish the task of explaining cinema's role in the construction of Jewish ethnicity.

This is because the definition restricts the study of film to *explicit* content, assuming that Jews and their life, society, and culture are being discussed or referred to *only* when they appear directly on the screen. As film analyst Ella Shohat notes, however, "Ethnicity and race inhere in virtually all films, not only in those where ethnic issues appear on the 'epidermic' surface of the text. . . . Ethnicity is culturally ubiquitous."[23] Shohat goes on to explain that ethnicity is present even in its absence, simply by virtue of its being excluded or marginalized in films that take the experience of the dominant or mainstream group (assumed, erroneously, to be "nonethnic") as universal. In other words, silence on the issue of ethnicity cannot be taken as unproblematic or without consequence, particularly for the ethnic groups whose presence and experience are being effaced. With regard specifically to Jewish ethnicity, examples of silencing are legion; one of the most obvious would be the unselfconscious presentation of Christmas as an "American" holiday in film after film.[24]

There is another argument for broadening the selection of films to be examined. Ethnic groups do not restrict their filmgoing to only those in which they are represented, nor do ethnically specific films attract audiences only from the groups they portray. Historians have found, for example, that in the urban immigrant communities formed in the early decades of this century, movies were the most popular form of public entertainment, and audiences, particularly women, flocked to all sorts of films, in part to learn about American ways and culture.[25] To assess the powers of early movies in Americanization and in the construction of a hierarchy of ethnicities in American culture, we should examine comparatively a wide array of films. For later decades, other mass media, especially television, should be included.[26]

Following this line of reasoning, we would have to expand considerably the purview of American Jewish cinema studies in order to understand the representation of Jews and Jewish life. For a study of the cultural construction of Jewish identity during a particular period, we might select only the films screened widely during that period, but *not* only those that explicitly presented Jewish characters or themes. Our study should also include *noncinematic* texts and discourses concerning ethnicity (or other relevant issues) that circulated at the same time, as well as refer to the general historical climate.

Although the selection of films should be broadened, the notion of audience should be narrowed—that is, specified as closely as possible. Audiences are differentiated not only by ethnicity and gender, but also by other planes of social difference; these factors filter audience responses to films and mediate the impact of films on subsequent identity development. But even when the composition of an audience can be narrowly specified, we cannot predict how messages about gender and ethnicity will be received by reference to film images alone. Though films continuously emit both explicit and implicit messages about the relation between ethnicity and gender, for most audience members they are not the exclusive source of such information.

It is, nevertheless, tempting to read image as effect, for in no medium is the gender of ethnicity as immediately evident as it is (and was) in film. On the screen, "ethnicity" is always embodied in palpable actors playing identifiably male and female characters. Except in cases of extreme exaggeration, viewers would be more likely to recognize a character's sex before (or at least simultaneously with) her or his ethnicity. And very often in early films, ethnicity itself was denoted precisely by the degree of proximity between the gender identity of the "ethnic" character and that of the ideal American man or woman.

The significance of such positionings would not be lost on ethnic viewers concerned about their own social location. The perception of the appropriateness of ethnic gender identities—of the fit between minoritarian and majoritarian gender roles and traits—often provides strong motivation for assimilation. Immigrants struggle for acceptance in American society because they feel themselves to be outsiders not only in cultural, economic, and religious terms, but also by virtue of their gender identities. Jewish immigrants were no exception. The East European Jews who came to the United States during the period of massive immigration around the turn of the century were concerned about appropriate gender behavior, and this has continued to be an issue for successive generations of American Jews as their ethnic identities have undergone renegotiation and rearticulation throughout the course of twentieth-century history.[27]

It has by now become almost a truism that the gender roles dictated by East European Jewish culture were virtually the opposite of those being prescribed for American men and women at the time of immigration.[28] The ideal Jewish man was a scholar who carried himself with a gentle, reflective mien, while his female counterpart was to serve not only as domestic helpmate but also as breadwinner, with a strong, no-nonsense personality to match. Turn-of-the-century American gender ideals, however, called for assertive, rough-and-ready men and docile, ladylike, family-oriented women.[29] For many immigrants, both male and female, repudiation of their East European sex roles and a "conversion" to American gender styles became part and parcel of assimilation.[30]

Ghetto culture teemed with messages about appropriate "American" gender traits, compelling immigrants to be self-conscious about an aspect of their identities they may previously have taken for granted. Fashion, social rituals, schools, clubs, recreational facilities—all emitted blatant cues. Columns like the *Jewish Daily Forward*'s *"Bintel Brief"* advised male and female readers how to behave in specific situations; short stories and novels provided more elaborate scenarios.[31] Relevant texts and forms of experience also lay outside the bounds of what is conventionally defined as culture. Historian Susan Glenn, for example, has pointed to the " 'idioms' of occupational sex-typing" that governed the assignment of Jewish immigrants to jobs in the garment industry during the early decades of this century.[32] Occupational discourses concerning the gender appropriateness of specific tasks would have played off more typically cultural encodings of gender traits.

It is difficult to determine exactly how and to what extent these texts affected their immigrant audiences. When the same message emerged from a variety of sources, its authority would, of course, become amplified. But the conditions of reception also filtered messages. Screen images of Jews might have had a more powerful effect on their immigrant audiences than written texts because they were disseminated and received *in public.* Thus Jewish viewers would have been aware that the representations they were seeing were also available to Gentile audiences. Depending upon whether or not these representations were flattering, such images could be a source of either pride or embarrassment and might affect subsequent behavior accordingly.

Dramas of gender appear frequently in early films about American Jewish life, as immigrants are depicted in confrontation with American gender ideals.[33] In discussions of the cinema of this period, analysts have examined to some extent the struggles of Jewish women with American notions of womanhood,[34] but the ordeals of men and the construction of a new gender system have largely been ignored.[35] Thus I turn first to these issues.

The comic short *How Mosha Came Back* (Crystal, 1914) turns precisely on the issue of masculinity. The film draws its humor from the incongruity between Jewish Mosha's slight build and his aspirations to become a prize-fighter. Egged on by his girlfriend, he challenges an overpowering Irish opponent whose muscular body more closely approximates the American ideal. The film provides many cues to the ethnicity of the two men, including names, clothing, plot, and references to physical strength (stereotypically more for Irish male characters, less for Jewish ones, in the cinema of this period).[36] The ethnicity of the girlfriend is indeterminate; she may well be a native-born American. This indeterminacy in itself drives the ethnic and gender dynamics of the film. For Mosha to succeed with the woman, he must prove himself the equal of a "real American man" by displaying his prowess in the ring.[37] Mosha manages to defeat the Irish Goliath, not by calling on hidden reserves of superior strength, but by drugging his opponent.

The film is framed as a daydream—Mosha's daydream. Curiously, even his unconscious does not allow him to play the hero. First, the dream suggests that he can win only by trickery, a stereotypically Jewish form of behavior. Then it reveals his cheapness (another stereotypical trait), as he steals the tip his girlfriend leaves after paying for their victory dinner. The dream is not, of course, really Mosha's, but that of the filmmaker.[38] For our purposes here, what is most significant is not the anti-Semitism itself, blatant though it is, but the gendered dimensions of it. The Jewish man is defined by his lack of (American-style) masculinity. What is more, he is depicted as being unable to overcome this deficit because of inherent character flaws.

Over the decades, the theme of prizefighting reappears in such films about American-Jewish life as the features *His People* (Universal, 1925) and *Body and Soul* (United Artists, 1947). Though the linkage with masculinity is not always as obvious as it is in *Mosha,* concern with gender identity cannot be ignored as a subtext in these later movies. One might argue that the recurrence merely reflects one of the realities of Jewish immigrant life: during the early part of the century a number of Jewish men made names for themselves in the American ring.[39] This fact in itself, however, needs to be explained. Prizefighting, if one was successful at it, was a lucrative occupation, but also one that brought young Jewish men into direct conflict with some of the deepest-held values of their culture.[40] As sports scholar Jeffrey Sammons puts it, "In eastern Europe parents had taught their children that moderation, goal orientation, intellect, and the cherishing of traditional values were legitimate 'Jewish' characteristics, but preoccupation with the body, sensuality, rashness, and ruthless force were deemed 'un-Jewish,' or goyish."[41]

Though Jewish men found many occupational avenues constricted, they did have alternatives to boxing that were less likely to provoke parental wrath or communal disapproval. Why, then, did they pursue the sport? Because, beyond money (and even that was not guaranteed), prizefighting seemed to hold out rewards that made it eminently worthwhile for male Jewish youths to defy their elders. According to Sammons, "Avoidance of violence was an admirable trait among Jews but was often misconstrued as weakness and cowardice by an American society born in bloody revolution, expanded through violence, and defended by force. . . . Discriminated against at all levels of society and ridiculed for their appearance, language, and manner, some Jews turned to boxing as a way to earn respect, a sense of belonging."[42] Sammons's analysis is astute, but he fails to specify that he is talking only about men. Thus he misses the point that these young Jews were also seeking acceptance as American *males.*

His People, produced during the heyday of Jewish prizefighting, touches on all these issues. The film contrasts the filial behavior of Morris and Sammy, the sons of David Cominsky, a poor but proud peddler. Cominsky favors "the intelligent one," Morris, who aspires to the law. But Morris, scrambling for uptown success, disavows his ghetto background, even to the point of claiming that he is an orphan. Though Sammy remains loyal and hardworking, he earns only his father's scorn because he has chosen to make his living as a "box fighter." Only after Morris's heedless deception has been exposed does Cominsky recognize the sacrifices Sammy has made for his family. The old father grudgingly admits, "In this country even box fighting can be a success."

Most analysts interpret such films (as well as novels and other works from the immigrant period) as texts of cultural conflict, since they depict the identity crises of characters caught up in the tensions between tradition and assimilation. Read in the light of feminist theory, however, these texts reveal the underlying gender dilemma that permeated cultural tensions and actually constituted the identity crises themselves. At stake in *His People* is the issue of reconciling American occupational success with Jewish male gender ideals.

Early in the film, a neighbor berates Cominsky for allowing a customer to bargain him down with a tale of woe. "Shmoos!" says the neighbor. "That woman's got more money than both of us—you're too soft-hearted, too easy!" When it turns out that the customer was indeed lying about her hardship, Cominsky's compassion is made to look like naïveté. Clearly Jewish men with traits like his cannot succeed in America.[43] But neither, it turns out, can men who behave like Morris—men who are willing to repudiate family and cultural birthright simply to get ahead. With its closing reconciliation, *His People* implies that a Jewish man can embrace American masculinity—even become a prizefighter—and still honor traditional Jewish values. As the narrative builds to a paean of assimilation, the seemingly intractable opposition between two sets of gender ideals yields to a synthesis dominated by the American way of manhood, albeit tempered by filial deference and family loyalty. Sammy the prizefighter has found the formula for a new, American-Jewish style of masculinity.[44]

The texts of popular culture produced during the immigrant period and in later decades dramatize not only the formation of individual ethnic identities but also negotiations for power among ethnic groups (including white Anglo-Saxon Americans). Here again, feminist analysis reveals the gender dimensions of ethnicity. Ethnic hierarchies are forged in interactions and confrontations that often assume the dynamics of sexuality and gender. That is, ethnic politics frequently take the form of sexual politics.[45] This is particularly true in film because the screen favors representations of sexual (as opposed to more baldly political) exchanges. Once again ethnicity and gender appear to be so closely fused that it is difficult to disaggregate them.

The sexual situation that lends itself most readily to cultural explorations of early-twentieth-century Jewish-American relations is interreligious (or cross-ethnic) romance and marriage. Intermarriage—or the threat of it— appears frequently in Jewish-American novels and films, for it sets off powerful familial dramas.[46] Orthodox Jewish law dictates that when a child marries outside the faith, the family treat her or him as dead and go through a period of ritual mourning. In observant families, the intermarriage of a child in the prime of his or her life thus represents a tragic loss (for both parents and child).[47] Whether or not the exogamous Jew is considered to be dead, his or her ties to the community are inevitably weakened if not entirely broken.[48] Thus intermarriage also came to be seen as a threat to the continued existence of American Jewry.

On the surface in films of intermarriage, we have an instance of the familiar clash between old and new, tradition versus the pull of America. On a deeper level, the gender dynamics of intermarriage stand revealed. Particularly during the immigrant period, but even later, intermarriage came to symbolize a preference for the majoritarian culture, as embodied in the desire for sexual and marital union with "the other" and consequent rejection of one's own people.[49]

In the early years, exogamy typically occurred between Jewish men and Gentile women, though the overall rate for both sexes was low.[50] Jewish women were thus more likely to experience a sense of rejection as Jewish men rushed to assimilate through intermarriage.[51] Abraham Cahan depicts just such a situation in his early novella, *Yekl: A Tale of the Ghetto* (1896), in which an ambitious young immigrant casts off his traditional wife for one who, although also Jewish, looks more American.[52]

Although Cahan's story reflected the predominant trend, early films about intermarriage were characterized by a curious displacement and denial of reality; most presented Jewish women marrying Gentile men. One might speculate that for male Jewish filmmakers, these narratives constituted gestures of propitiation. As a marginal group, they were offering up their women in order to gain acceptance in the mainstream. Such an interpretation appears plausible in light of the sexual dynamics surrounding the position of Jewish women in American culture in the period before East European immigration. Literary critic Leslie Fiedler was one of the first analysts to point to the ambiguous, if not negative, connotations of the female Jewish image in nineteenth-century American fiction. Particularly in texts that (implicitly or explicitly) took the position of the Gentile man, Jewish women appeared as "forbidden exotics—dark, alien types whom the hero . . . is not permitted to marry—for lurking behind and beside them is the Jewish villain, the Smiler with a Knife. In the deepest American imagination, the Jewish male . . . is an embodiment of evil . . . but the female is postulated as desirable."[53] In the eyes of Gentile men, according to Fiedler's schema, Jewish women could easily fall victim to a double standard that categorized them as sexual but not marriageable, while Gentile women were seen as less sexually attractive but more appropriate as marriage partners.

In the films of the immigrant period, Jewish women continued to be depicted as attractive to Gentile men, though in contrast to earlier literary images, they were not necessarily portrayed as being inherently or actively seductive. Rather, they were pursued by Gentile men who found them desirable—"Virginal Jewesses" (as Patricia Erens has dubbed them), continually put upon to defend their virtue. The fact that they now became suitable candidates for exogamy neutralized their seductiveness, although at the cost of alienation from the Jewish community.[54]

In later, highly successful films, such as *The Jazz Singer* (Warner Brothers, 1927) and *Abie's Irish Rose* (Paramount, 1928) (both based on Broadway hits), it is the Jewish men who are more likely to intermarry. These films are significant for the extent to which they neutralize the negative religious aspects of intermarriage by presenting it as the golden route to assimilation or, at the least, a form of bland, utopian pluralism.[55] In *Abie,* it is even condoned by a rabbi.[56] Moreover, though in this film both marriage partners are initially disowned by their parents, their families become reconciled to one another upon the birth of twins Patrick and Rebecca. In *The Jazz Singer,* Jack Robin (Al Jolson) has alienated his Orthodox father by abandoning a career as a cantor to become a popular performer. After his father's death, his mother comes to the theater to watch him perform and to meet his Gentile bride. His marriage is presented as simply one more aspect of his success and acceptance by an all-American audience.

In the mood of mutual congratulation and celebration that characterizes the endings of both these films, there is of course no mention of the Jewish women Abie and Jack *might* have married. The impact of intermarriage on Jewish *women* is decisively silenced. Yet by ignoring this dimension of intermarriage, such films were in fact confirming on a cultural level the social repudiation of Jewish women and the traditional gender ideals they represented.

Intermarriage readily slipped into the realm of male privilege in the later films, which not only condoned intermarriage but also featured Jews who were readily following the American way of courtship, which relegates women to a passive role.[57] Thus intermarriage began to appear as a relatively unproblematic way for Jewish *men* to move rapidly into American society. It almost seemed foolish for a Jewish man to marry within his faith, since he would be foregoing a free ticket to success as an American.[58] For women, such an option was seldom even considered.

The neutralization of intermarriage was necessary if Jews were to be included in the cinematic celebration of the American success story.[59] Even so, Jewish characters appeared in this story only briefly. By the mid-1930s, American cinema had undergone what film historians refer to as de-Semitization, and Jewish characters, situations, and identifiably Jewish actors and actresses all but disappeared.[60]

Film historians tend to ignore the gender aspects of de-Semitization, but once again, they were central to the process. On one level, the virtual erasure of Jews from the screen was gender-neutral; it affected men and women equally. Throughout the first three decades of American filmmaking, Jewish characters and situations appeared frequently, though few identifiably Jewish men or women became stars. In the silents, Theda Bara achieved fame by changing her name (Theodosia Goodman) and playing conspicuously non-Jewish roles, ranging from an Arab temptress to the Madonna.[61] Al Jolson was allowed to be visibly Jewish in *The Jazz Singer* since the plot turned on his repudiation of his father's orthodoxy. Though his identity is altered in the course of what turns out to be a triumphant narrative of assimilation, he remains in some sense "Jewish." Eddie Cantor, however, had to become completely de-Semitized as he moved from the vaudeville stage to Hollywood to star in the film *Whoopee.*[62] Significantly, neither Jolson nor Cantor ever achieved the status of matinee idol.[63]

Jews remained cinematically invisible from the mid-1930s to the 1960s, when stars like Barbra Streisand and Woody Allen began to appear.[64] The period of invisibility was also (and not coincidentally) the very time when Hollywood films and stars were at the apex of their influence on American values,[65] particularly in the areas of gender and sexuality.[66] The absence of Jews (as well as most other identifiable "ethnics") from the screen meant that Jewish ethnicity and notions of sexuality and gender were almost entirely de-coupled. This did not mean that ethnicity no longer mattered in issues of gender, but rather that Jews, like other recognizable ethnics (read non-WASP's), did not qualify. Male and female both, Jews were, in a sense, given the choice between being without ethnicity or without gender.

When ethnicity did return to the screen, the relation between Jews and gender once again appeared as an issue, and once again, it was presented primarily from the male point of view. To a large extent Woody Allen's screen persona was built on the highly problematic nature of Jewish male sexuality, and this theme also turned up in non-Allen films like *Portnoy's Complaint* (Warner Brothers, 1972). Although Portnoy's neurosis remains unresolved, the Allen persona usually manages to get the girl by stumbling on a combination of wit, vulnerability, and sensitivity. Many Allen characters find their own worst enemies in themselves, but they also implicitly criticize the machismo of the typical American male. Among the generation of filmgoers who came of age with feminism, Allen's films have always found a warm reception. Indeed, it might be argued that his screen persona helped to shape a new set of standards for postfeminist American masculinity.[67]

During these same years, only a few films centered on female characters, and most either picked up on earlier negative portrayals of Jewish women or introduced new ones. Films like *Sheila Levine Is Dead and Living in New York* (Paramount, 1975) and *The Heartbreak Kid* reproduced—this time for comic effect—the presumably self-evident notion that Jewish women were simply unsuitable as wives. Other movies, borrowing from contemporary fiction, presented and then built up the stereotype of the Jewish-American princess. The series that began with *Marjorie Morningstar* (Warner Brothers, 1958) and continued with *Goodbye, Columbus* (Paramount, 1969) was not broken until Goldie Hawn joined the army and became Private Benjamin in her eponymous film (Warner Brothers, 1980).[68]

Private Benjamin was an expression of the influence of feminism on film-making about Jews. This wave also brought to the screen films as diverse in budget (if not in impulse) as Joan Micklin Silver's modest *Hester Street* (Midwest Film, 1975), based on Cahan's *Yekl,* and Barbra Streisand's elaborate version of an Isaac Bashevis Singer story, *Yentl* (United Artists, 1983). These texts not only presented more positive Jewish female characters but also questioned the gender system that had produced inequality for so long. *Yentl* is the story of a young woman who masquerades as a man in order to circumvent the Orthodox tradition that bars women from pursuing scholarship. Though Streisand's shtetl looks more like suburbia, she does manage to dramatize the injustice of a centuries-old custom.[69] *Hester Street,* filmed in black and white to evoke the flavor of the New York ghetto at the turn of the century, nevertheless gives Cahan's original story a feminist gloss. Yekl gets his comeuppance for behaving cavalierly when his first wife appears to be better off without him, and his second wife turns out to be an aggressive, domineering woman who gives him no peace.[70]

Both *Hester Street* and *Private Benjamin* criticize Jewish men from the perspective of Jewish women. At first glance *Dirty Dancing* (Vestron Pictures, 1987) appears to take a similar position, but further analysis indicates that the film's point of view is really a double one: the position of the Jewish woman becomes conflated with and ultimately effaced by that of the male-dominated American gender system.

It is the summer of 1963 and "Baby" (Jennifer Grey) Houseman is spending her final weeks before going off to Mount Holyoke with her family at a Jewish resort in the Catskills. In these surroundings—legendary grounds for matchmaking—Baby's parents fully expect her to take her pick from the corps of waiters and busboys, all handsome Jewish men recruited from Yale and Harvard and slated for professional careers. The resort owner even offers his own nephew, Neil, a student at Cornell Hotel School. But the independent-minded Baby snubs the Ivy League in favor of Johnny (Patrick Swayze), the muscular but monosyllabic dance instructor from "the other side of the tracks."

More than religion or ethnicity, class threatens to keep these two apart. In a curious reversal of so many earlier films, Jews—both Baby and her family, as well as the entire social stratum that constitutes the resort's clientele and most of its staff—are presented as the "insiders," while the working class, represented by Johnny, are "the other." But Johnny refuses to be "othered."

At first he tries to maintain his distance from Baby, taunting her for being oblivious to her own class privilege and his marginality. Baby acknowledges her failings but is not easily put off. Equilibrium is temporarily established when they reach the dance floor, where Johnny is the expert. Through lessons in dirty dancing, Baby simultaneously discovers her own sensuality and crosses the class line into "real life."[71] But Johnny also learns from Baby— about the value of persistence, trust, and hope. Eventually he claims that she has taught him "about the kind of person I want to be."

Playing in and around the film's central focus on romance and mutual *bildung* is the issue of ethnicity and gender. Though Baby is identified as Jewish through her family and the situation, she is not stereotypically so. Despite the conjunction of class and ethnicity in her background, the film avoids slotting her as a Jewish-American princess by making frequent references to her commitment to "turning the world into a better place." (Her sister, by contrast, fits the stereotype perfectly.) Although Johnny's working-class background is stressed repeatedly, his ethnic origins remain vague. (His last name is Castle—he might even be Jewish, were it not for the assumption that Jews are usually middle-class, an assumption the film does nothing to disturb.) Neil and the waiters, however, are clearly marked as being Jewish.

Using these male characters, the film sets up a series of correlations between ethnicity, class, masculinity, and sexuality. Neil is portrayed as crass, insensitive, and self-important. He has learned to treat every form of human pleasure as a commodity; as a result, he is "out of touch" with his own body.[72] Attempting to demonstrate the cha-cha to Baby, he makes a foolish contrast to the smooth and sensuous Johnny, who, though being paid to dance, manages to avoid being turned into a commodity himself. Waiter Robby Gold, "headed for Yale Medical School," matches Johnny for looks and sex appeal but lacks his moral fiber.

Thus, despite their superficial credentials, the two Jewish men do not have what it takes to win Baby. Only Johnny cares enough to learn her real name, Frances ("a very grown-up name," he says). In the finale he announces it publicly, signaling her passage from infancy to adulthood, and then acknowledges their relationship by leading her onto the dance floor, where they are joined by the entire population of the resort—guests and staff alike—in dirty dancing.

Like *Abie's Irish Rose* and *The Jazz Singer* before it, *Dirty Dancing* neutralizes intermarriage, or, in this case, the modern equivalent, cross-class or cross-ethnic romance. But unlike its predecessors, *Dirty Dancing* does not present the union between Frances and Johnny as a route to upward mobility for the Jewish partner (though it might well serve that purpose for the Gentile one). Ironically, it is Baby's elevated social position that now seems to be keeping her on the margins of what she perceives to be the "authentic" America. She does not need the alliance with Johnny to achieve success in any conventional material or social sense, but rather so that she can fulfill herself as a person, both sexually and politically (by helping to bring about social unity and peace).

On this level the relationship between Frances and Johnny appears to be equal. If anything, she has the upper hand, since it is her idealism that finds expression in the social composition of the final scene. Yet it is *his* mode of expression—dancing—that is, after all, the reigning metaphor of the film. His brief tribute to her character ("She taught me who I want to be") fades wanly as an extended scene of high-spirited and energetic dancing closes out the movie.

And Johnny, not Frances, ultimately determines the standard by which masculinity is to be measured. Though it is through her eyes that Neil's and Robby's flaws are revealed, it is Johnny who takes the lead (in all senses) on the dance floor and comes to stand as the signifier of true masculinity. Notably, Johnny's physicality and honest simplicity link him to traditional American manhood, while Robby's duplicity and Neil's clumsiness (shades of Mosha) are stereotypically Jewish traits. The implication is that none of the young Jewish men in the film could "partner" Frances adequately.

To be sure, Johnny's masculinity is in the postfeminist style of the eighties: he is sensitive as well as sexual. But his masculinity is still strong enough to outweigh the disadvantages of class, allowing him to emerge as a kind of populist hero. Even Frances's father (a doctor!) winds up apologizing to Johnny for misreading his character and implicitly accepts him as his daughter's lover. Baby, in the process, is trafficked from her father to Johnny, losing whatever modicum of autonomy she has managed to acquire. As the couple dances together, the camera limns her loss of independence with close-ups of Frances's feet matching Johnny's, her body bending back under his.

Thus a film that begins by presenting a nonstereotypical young Jewish woman ends up by giving us a stereotypical American girl, a relatively anonymous young woman whose most notable quality is her ability to "follow" her male partner. What started out as an exploration of the relation between ethnicity and gender from the position of a Jewish-feminist critique ends up caricaturing Jewish masculinity from the position of American manhood.

My examples can only begin to suggest the ways in which gender and ethnicity are implicated in forming the identity of American Jews. As cultural analyst Larry Grossberg has put it, "It seems that gender and ethnicity have to be thought of as continuously rearticulating each other, not only in specific historical contexts, but also in the context of specific struggles."[73]

I have focused on the cultural elements of such processes, but that does not mean that the analysis of identity formation should be limited to cultural studies. Indeed, the questions raised by examining Jews, gender, and American cinema spill over onto Jewish studies as a whole. Scholars who are willing to work across disciplines can address more fruitfully such issues as the linkages between gender and ethnicity and the role of culture in identity formation. Moreover, as scholars of mainstream cinema recognize that such issues also concern them, questions of ethnicity and film will shift from the margins to the center of their work, just as gender already has. In this way we can move toward a greater understanding of how the politics of gender and ethnicity reinforce each other. This will happen only by breaking down the artificial and obstreperous barriers that now divide fields and disciplines that are (if they would only realize it!) embarked on common quests.

Notes

1. The feminist scholars advancing this argument are too numerous to mention. Among scholars of ethnicity, one of the first to articulate this view was Werner Sollors in his controversial book *Beyond Ethnicity: Consent and Descent in American Culture* (New York: Oxford University Press, 1986).

2. Stuart Hall, "New Ethnicities," in *Black Film, British Cinema*, ICA Document 7 (London: Institute for Contemporary Arts, 1988), 28 (emphasis in original).

3. The term is Larry Grossberg's (pers. comm. to author, Oct. 1991). Two interesting recent examples of feminist scholarship deal with race, ethnicity, and homosexuality: Tomas Almaguer, "Chicano Men: A Cartography of Homosexual Identity and Behavior," and Ekua Omosupe, "Black/Lesbian/Bulldagger," both in *Differences* 3 (summer 1991).

4. Eve Kosofsky Sedgwick has pointed out that "the study of sexuality is not coextensive with the study of gender"; that is, the categories *male* and *female* carry an implicit heterosexist bias and are too crude to capture the nuances of differences that mark individual (sexual) identities; see *Epistemology of the Closet* (Berkeley: University California Press, 1990), 27. While accepting Sedgwick's stipulation, I use these categories here not only for the sake of efficiency but also because I think a binary gender system still generates a fundamental dynamic of power within American society. Sedgwick alerts us to the fallacy of assimilating homosexual categories into the heterosexual binary; that is, e.g., *gay male* is not the inversion of *male*—is not *female*—but lies along a different axis of distinction.

Nevertheless, popular culture, in assigning Jewish men stereotypical homosexual traits, was simultaneously (and, arguably, *primarily*) coding them as *nonmasculine* (by American standards). For a useful discussion of this phenomenon, see David Desser, "The Cinematic Melting Pot: Ethnicity, Jews, and Psychoanalysis," in Lester D. Friedman, ed., *Unspeakable Images: Ethnicity and the American Cinema* (Urbana: University of Illinois Press, 1991), 390–91.

5. Here I differ somewhat from Mary V. Dearborn, who implies that gender and ethnicity should be considered as parallel or analogous categories, such that gender—i.e., femininity—with its implications of marginality and oppression, can even be taken as a metaphor for ethnicity. See *Pocahontas's Daughters: Gender and Ethnicity in American Culture* (New York: Oxford University Press, 1986). I maintain that the two categories cannot really be separated, even into the two terms of a trope.

6. Hall, "New Ethnicities," 27 (emphasis in original).

7. My definition here is far broader than, for example, that adopted by Glenda Abramson as editor of *The Blackwell Companion to Jewish Culture* (Oxford, U.K.: Blackwell Reference, 1989). Using a "Renaissance definition" of culture as "the cultivation of fine arts and the humanities," she focuses on literature, language, music, the performing and visual arts, philosophy, and the humanities (see preface, xii). Though the volume does include essays on arts not strictly considered "fine" such as food, humor, folklore, and popular music, as well as film, it makes only passing reference to radio, television, vaudeville, street life, domestic rituals, and other categories that I consider critical. Much creative work on Jewish culture has been done by the anthropologist Barbara Kirshenblatt-Gimblett; see *Traditional Storytelling in the Toronto Jewish Community: A Study in Performance and Creativity in an Immigrant Culture* (Ph.D. diss., Indiana University, 1972), and her essay "Kitchen Judaism" in *Getting Comfortable in New York: The American Jewish Home, 1880–1950* (New York: Jewish Museum, 1990).

8. Neal Gabler, *An Empire of Their Own: How the Jews Invented Hollywood* (New York: Crown, 1988).

9. For general overviews of the literature in the field, see Frank Manchel, *Film Study: An Analytical Bibliography* (Cranbury, N.J.: Associated University Presses, 1990), 818–51; and Allen L. Woll and Randall M. Miller, *Ethnic and Racial Images in American Film and Television* (New York: Garland, 1987), chap. 10. In-depth analysis and detailed historical background on American Jewish films can be found in Lester Friedman, *Hollywood's Image of the Jew* (New York: Ungar, 1982); Patricia Erens, *The Jew in American Cinema* (Bloomington: Indiana University Press, 1984); and David Desser, *American Jewish Filmmakers: Traditions and Trends* (Urbana: University of Illinois Press, 1993), all of which include useful filmographies. See also Stuart Fox, comp., *Jewish Films in the United States: A Comprehensive Survey and Descriptive Filmography* (Boston: G. K. Hall, 1976).

10. One major exception is Erens, *Jew in American Cinema*. Although excellent in many respects, the book is limited by Erens's reliance on a typological method that dichotomizes the sexes but does not readily allow for gender analysis. Moreover, since Erens is interested in content rather than the role of film in the formation of ethnic identity, she pays little

attention to audiences or to the gendered aspects of audience responses to films. In the introduction to her recent edited volume, *Issues in Feminist Film Criticism* (Bloomington: Indiana University Press, 1990), Erens calls for further research on gender, ethnicity, and film, including "a more diversified theory of female spectatorship" (xxiii). Another exception is Desser, "Cinematic Melting Pot." Desser is sensitive to gender issues, particularly the construction of masculinity. Yet, he relies heavily on a psychoanalytic approach, which can sometimes be problematic, as I discuss later here.

11. Here the exceptions are Gabler, *Empire of Their Own,* and David Desser, *In Search of a Tradition: American Jewish Filmmakers and the Jewish Experience* (Urbana: University of Illinois Press, 1992).

12. See, e.g., Woll and Miller, *Ethnic and Racial Images,* and an earlier volume edited by Miller, *Ethnic Images in American Film and Television* (Philadelphia: Balch Institute, 1978). The special issue of *Quarterly Review of Film and Video* on race, gender, and cinema (13 [1–3] [1991]), as well as Friedman's recent anthology *Unspeakable Images,* also fall in this category, but both collections contain a number of excellent essays that incorporate and advance contemporary film theory. Other racial and ethnic cinemas are also often studied in isolation; see, e.g., Thomas Cripps, *Slow Fade to Black* (New York: Oxford University Press, 1977), and *Making Movies Black* (New York: Oxford University Press, 1993); and Chon Noriega, ed., *Chicanos and Film* (New York: Garland, 1992).

13. See, e.g., the essays by Jane Gaines, "Women and Representation: Can We Enjoy Alternative Pleasure?" and "White Privilege and Looking Relations: Race and Gender in Feminist Film Theory," and by Teresa de Lauretis, "Rethinking Women's Cinema: Aesthetics and Feminist Theory," in Erens, *Issues.* In other areas of feminist theory and women's studies, such as history and literature, issues of race and ethnicity have a longer track record.

14. For the most part, popular media represent Jewish life as a form of ethnicity rather than as a religion, although occasionally specific religious tenets and values, such as the ban on intermarriage, take on dramatic power.

15. This approach assumes that cultural representations are by no means transparent, but rather highly mediated versions of reality and therefore not in themselves reliable markers of reality or behavior either past or present.

16. These illustrations are necessarily somewhat truncated and by no means fulfill the requirements of the approach I outline, particularly with regard to historical comprehensiveness.

17. Desser, "Cinematic Melting Pot," 383.

18. For a discussion of audience differentiation for another (relevant) medium, see Andrea Press, *Women Watching Television: Gender, Class, and Generation in the American TV Experience* (Philadelphia: University of Pennsylvania Press, 1991).

19. Ramona Curry, "Madonna from Marilyn to Marlene—Pastiche and/or Parody?" *Journal of Film and Video* 42(2) (summer 1990): 16.

20. Ella Taylor, *Prime Time Families: Television Culture in Postwar America* (Berkeley: University of California Press, 1989), 3; see also Press, *Women Watching Television.*

21. This is the stated goal of Erens (in *Jew in American Cinema),* as well as Friedman (in *Hollywood's Image).* For an exhaustive compendium of films that fall into this category, see Stuart Fox, *Jewish Films in the United States: A Comprehensive Survey and Descriptive Filmography* (Boston: G. K. Hall, 1976). See also filmographies in the Erens and Friedman volumes.

22. For the period from about 1903 to 1920 Fox and most other film historians include "short" films, since few full-length features were being produced at that time. Stuart Samuels, an early commentator, complained that during the first half of the twentieth century, "the image of Jews was almost invisible on the screen" (Samuels, "The Evolutionary Image of Jews in American Films," in Miller, *Ethnic Images,* 23). But Lester Friedman notes, "Between 1900 and 1929 alone, approximately 230 films featured clearly discernible Jewish characters—a figure far surpassing the number of films featuring other ethnic types" (*Hollywood's Image,* 9).

23. Ella Shohat, "Ethnicities-in-Relation: Toward a Multicultural Reading of American Cinema," in Friedman, ed., *Unspeakable Images,* 215.

24. The absence of specifically Jewish characters and themes in films produced and/or created by Jews presents an unusual puzzle. David Desser argues that Jewish writers and composers have actually *displaced* their concerns about Jewish life, and particularly about anti-Semitism, by presenting them in other guises. In creating films and plays like *Porgy and Bess* and *Brigadoon,* Jewish artists dealt with issues of racism and ethnicity but did not actually mention Jews. See "Performing Arts, Jews in," in Abramson, *Blackwell's Companion,* 582–5.

25. Early movies were not only inexpensive and convenient, but because they were silent, readily accessible to non-English-speaking or illiterate viewers who could probably follow the plot without reading the intertitles. See Desser, "Performing Arts," 580; Elizabeth Ewen, *Immigrant Women in the Land of Dollars: Life and Culture on the Lower East Side, 1890–1925* (New York: Monthly Review Press, 1985), chap. 12; and Kathy Peiss, *Cheap Amusements: Working Women and Leisure in Turn-of-the-Century New York* (Philadelphia: Temple University Press, 1986), chap. 6. Both Ewen and Peiss emphasize the cross-over values that immigrants absorbed from these movies. See also Douglas Gomery, *Shared Pleasures: A History of Movie Presentation in the United States* (Madison: University of Wisconsin Press, 1992), chap. 2.

26. To specify the composition of audiences, especially during later decades, market research studies conducted by various branches of the culture industry itself may prove useful. See also Hortense Powdermaker's study of Hollywood in the 1940s, *Hollywood: The Dream Factory* (Boston: Little, Brown, 1950).

27. See Charlotte Baum, Paula Hyman, and Sonya Michel, *The Jewish Woman in America* (New York: Dial, 1976), chaps. 7–8. Though the problem of gender identity affects both men and women, scholars have until recently focused primarily on shifting ideals for women. This is partly the result of women's studies, which early on began to problematize female identity and theorize it as a social construction, and partly due, again, to the assumption on the part of nonfeminist scholars that male identity and masculinity are

universal (and therefore *not* changeable social constructions). Following the lead of women's studies, some scholars have begun to problematize masculine identity; see Harry Brod, ed., *The Making of Masculinities: The New Men's Studies* (Boston: Allen and Unwin, 1987); and Mark C. Carnes and Clyde Griffen, *Meanings for Manhood: Constructions of Masculinity in Victorian America* (Chicago: University of Chicago Press, 1990). Brod has another volume devoted exclusively to Jewish masculinity: *A Mensch among Men: Explorations in Jewish Masculinity* (Freedom, Calif.: Crossing Press, 1988). In *Tough Jews: Political Fantasies and the Moral Dilemma of American Jewry* (New York: Basic Books, 1990), Paul Breines also examines the problem of Jewish male identity, but he fails to analyze masculinity in relation to femininity, as part of a system of gender, and thus implicitly re-privileges male experience and renders female experience invisible.

28. The focus here is on cultural *prescriptions,* not actual behavior, which may or may not have conformed to them.

29. See Baum, Hyman, and Michel, *Jewish Woman,* chap. 7. For male ideals in particular, see Joe L. Dubbert, "Progressivism and the Masculinity Crisis," in Elizabeth Pleck and Joseph Pleck, eds., *The American Man* (Englewood Cliffs, N.J.: Prentice-Hall, 1980); and Michael S. Kimmel, "The Contemporary 'Crisis' of Masculinity in Historical Perspective," in Brod, *Making of Masculinities,* esp. 137–53. Dubbert and Kimmel explain that the so-called crisis in masculinity began in the mid-nineteenth century as a result of "the twin forces of industrialization and the spread of political democracy" (p. 138). This resulted in a renewed emphasis on presumed masculine traits. Not all men and women followed the prescriptions, of course; the "new woman," for example, challenged the female model (see Carroll Smith-Rosenberg, "The New Woman as Androgyne: Social Disorder and Gender Crisis, 1870–1936," in *Disorderly Conduct: Visions of Gender in Victorian America* [New York: Oxford University Press, 1985]). From the 1910s on, American social observers bemoaned a perceived loss of patriarchal power within the family and blamed a variety of social ills on what was seen as an inverted gender hierarchy.

30. The emphasis on adhering to "traditional" American gender roles within Jewish communities stemmed less from perceptions of gender crisis and social disorder than from a desire for assimilation. The desire of male Jews to emulate the American ideal of masculinity may well have been overdetermined. Desser points out that Jewish men were frequently associated with homosexuality in late nineteenth-century European culture. To the extent that they were aware of this, Jewish men may have had added motivation to appear masculine in a conventional (American) sense. See Desser, "Cinematic Melting Pot," 391. See also the introduction to Sedgwick, *Epistemology;* and Sander Gilman, *Jewish Self-Hatred* (Baltimore: Johns Hopkins University Press, 1989). On American male gender ideals, see Kevin White, *The First Sexual Revolution: The Emergence of Male Heterosexuality in Modern America* (New York: New York University Press, 1993), chap. 5.

31. See Baum, Hyman, and Michel, *Jewish Woman,* chap. 7. For the texts of sample letters, see Isaac Metzker, ed., *A Bintel Brief* (Garden City, N.Y.: Doubleday, 1971).

32. Susan A. Glenn, *Daughters of the Shtetl: Life and Labor in the Immigrant Generation* (Ithaca: Cornell University Press, 1990), 114. Glenn attributes the term *idioms of occupational sex* *typing* to Ruth Milkman in *Gender at Work: The Dynamics of Job Segregation by Sex during World War II* (Urbana: University of Illinois Press, 1987).

33. Many rare early Jewish-American and Yiddish films have been restored and are being distributed by the National Center for Jewish Film, Brandeis University, Waltham, Massachusetts.

34. See, e.g., Erens, *Jew in American Cinema.*

35. The examination of masculinity in film is just beginning. A pioneering collection is Steven Cohan and Ina Rae Hark, eds., *Screening the Male: Exploring Masculinities in Hollywood Cinema* (New York: Routledge, 1993), which deals primarily with more recent cinema, and, to the extent that it deals with race and ethnicity, ignores Jewish identity.

36. See Tom Gunning, "Outsiders as Insiders: Jews and the History of American Silent Film" (Waltham, Mass.: National Center for Jewish Film, Brandeis University, n.d.), 11. As noted earlier, the stereotyping of Jewish men as effeminate was not particular to American culture of this period but had deep roots in European iconography (see n.29).

37. Similar issues are at stake in the 1987 film *Dirty Dancing,* discussed later here.

38. Little is known about the production of this film, whether it was made by a Jewish or non-Jewish filmmaker, and so on. The pervasive anti-Semitism, however, suggests that it was made either by a Gentile expressing the rampant nativism of her or his day, or by a rather self-deprecating, self-hating Jew. For a somewhat different interpretation of this film, see Friedman, *Hollywood's Image,* 23.

39. In *Beyond the Ring: The Role of Boxing in American Society* (Urbana: University of Illinois Press, 1988), Jeffrey T. Sammons notes that "by 1928 there were more prominent Jewish boxers than there were boxers from any other single ethnic or racial group" (p. 92). See also Steven Reiss, "A Fighting Chance: The Jewish-American Boxing Experience, 1890–1940," *American Jewish History* 74 (1985): 223–53.

40. According to Sammons, prizefighting offered members of struggling immigrant groups an avenue of upward mobility; "the succession had gone from Irish to Jewish and would pass on to Italians, to blacks, and to Latins" (*Beyong the Ring,* 92). For a discussion of Irish and other immigrant fighters in the nineteenth century, see Elliott J. Gorn, *The Manly Art: Bare-Knuckle Prize Fighting in America* (Ithaca: Cornell University Press, 1986), chaps. 1 and 5.

41. Sammons, *Beyond the Ring,* 91.

42. Ibid. For insights into the motivation of several Jewish boxers from the twenties, see the first-hand accounts of Charley Phil Rosenberg, Mushy Callahan, and Jackie Fields in Peter Heller, *"In This Corner . . . !" Forty World Champions Tell Their Stories* (New York: Simon and Schuster, 1973).

43. The fact that both the neighbor and the customer are women further underscores Cominsky's weakness and "inappropriate" male traits.

44. For an interesting discussion of how a small amount of surrender can actually strengthen male power, see Christopher Newfield, "The Politics of Male Suffering: Masochism and Hegemony in the American Renaissance," *Differences* 1(3) (fall 1989): 55–87.

45. African-American history provides one of the most striking examples of such dynamics

at work. During slavery and after, the sexual exploitation of African-American women by white American men served not only as an end in itself, but also as a means of establishing and reinforcing the domination of white over black. See Deborah Gray White, *Ar'n't I a Woman? Female Slaves in the Plantation South* (New York: Norton, 1985); and Elizabeth Fox-Genovese, *Within the Plantation Household: Black and White Women in the Old South* (Chapel Hill: University North Carolina Press, 1988), esp. chap. 6. For African-American women's responses, see Hazel Carby, *Reconstructing Womanhood: The Emergence of the Afro-American Woman Novelist* (New York: Oxford University Press, 1987), chap. 1; and Darlene Clark Hine, "Rape and the Inner Lives of Black Women in the Middle West: Preliminary Thoughts on the Culture of Dissemblance," *Signs* 14(1) (summer 1989): 912–20. For a discussion of sexual-political domination in another context, see Ann Laura Stoler, "Carnal Knowledge and Imperial Power: Gender, Race, and Morality in Colonial Asia," in Micaela di Leonardo, ed., *Gender at the Crossroads: Feminist Anthropology in the Post-Modern Era* (Berkeley: University of California Press, 1991), 51–101.

46. See Friedman, *Hollywood's Image,* esp. chap. 1. The dramatic potential of intermarriage is underscored by the fact that its frequency in films, especially during the 1910s, was far greater than it was in the Jewish community; according to Erens, between 1908 and 1912 the rate was only 1.17 percent—"scarcely higher than that of intermarriage between Negroes and Whites" (*Jew in American Cinema,* 48).

47. This, of course, is the theme of the famous Sholem Aleichem story "Tevye," on which the Broadway play and Hollywood film *Fiddler on the Roof* were based. Though both the stage and screen versions of the story were criticized for softening or prettifying it, the essential tragedy of intermarriage remains unmitigated (see Friedman, *Hollywood's Image,* 240–42; and Erens, *Jew in American Cinema,* 153). A Yiddish film version, *Tevya* (Globe, 1939), was closer in spirit to the original story.

48. This was especially true for exogamous men, whose children would not be considered Jewish under religious law.

49. See, e.g., the film *The Heartbreak Kid* (20th Century-Fox, 1972).

50. See n.41.

51. On Jewish men's persistent desire for Gentile women, see Baum, Hyman, and Michel, *Jewish Woman,* 222–7; and Fredric Jaher, "The Quest for the Ultimate *Shikse,*" *American Quarterly* 35(5) (winter 1983): 518–42.

52. Abraham Cahan, *Yekl: A Tale of the New York Ghetto* (New York: Appleton, 1896). The modern film version of this story, Joan Micklin Silver's *Hester Street* (Midwest Film, 1975), is discussed below.

53. Leslie Fiedler, *Love and Death in the American Novel* (New York: Criterion, 1960), 251; quoted in Erens, *Jew in American Cinema,* 64. See also Fiedler, *The Return of the Vanishing American* (New York: Stein and Day, 1968); and Kristin Herzog, *Women, Ethnics, and Exotic: Images of Power in Mid-Nineteenth Century Fiction* (Knoxville: University of Tennessee Press, 1983).

54. See Erens, *Jew in American Cinema,* 56, 63–64. It would be worth considering the extent

to which these "innocent victims" are meant to stand for the entire Jewish community, which is being made to suffer by American prejudice and injustice when their only goal is assimilation.

55. *Abie's Irish Rose* was the last in a series of 1920s Irish-Jewish films, most of which portrayed congenial relations between the two groups; see Erens, *Jew in American Cinema*, 81–82.

56. See Erens, *Jew in American Cinema*, 106–7.

57. In the East European tradition, both men *and* women were passive throughout the process by which matchmakers (often female) and parents arranged marriages for them.

58. In fiction, however, intermarriage and cross-ethnic or religious romance continued to appear problematic for decades to come; see Baum, Hyman, and Michel, *Jewish Woman*, 222–27.

59. It is probably not coincidental that the marital patterns of the Jewish Hollywood moguls followed a similar pattern. Many divorced the Jewish wives of their youth to marry younger Gentile women. See Gabler, *Empire of Their Own*, chaps. 7, 10. As Gabler comments, "Here, life not only imitated art. Here, among the Hollywood Jews, life became art itself" (p. 249).

60. See Erens, *Jew in American Cinema*, 149–50.

61. See Kevin Brownlow, *Hollywood: The Pioneers* (New York: Knopf, 1979), 160–61.

62. For a fascinating description of this process, see Henry Jenkins III, "Shall We Make It for New York or for Distribution?" Eddie Cantor, *Whoopee*, and "Regional Resistance to the Talkies," *Cinema Journal* 29(3) (spring 1990): 32–52.

63. Even Rudolph Valentino had to overcome ethnic barriers to become the "Great Lover of the Silver Screen" since "Latin types" were not especially popular when he began his screen career. Latin men, however, were not associated with a lack of conventional masculinity, as Jews were. See Brownlow, *Hollywood*, 184–86; Miriam Hansen, "Pleasure, Ambivalence, Identification: Valentino and Female Spectatorship," *Cinema Journal* 25 (summer 1986), 6–32; and Gilman, *Jewish Self-Hatred.*

64. Not surprisingly, American Jews rushed to embrace Marilyn Monroe—the ultimate sex symbol—as one of their own when she converted to Judaism at the time of her marriage to Arthur Miller. See Darryl Lyman, *Great Jews on Stage and Screen* (Middle Village, N.Y.: Jonathan David, 1987), 157–60. It is interesting to speculate about whether Monroe would have become such a remarkable phenomenon had she been identified as a Jew from the outset.

65. See Robert Sklar, *Movie-Made America: A Social History of American Movies* (New York: Random House, 1975), pt. 3. For a discussion of the impact of film on popular consciousness, see Andrea Walsh, *Women's Film and Female Experience, 1940–1950* (New York: Praeger, 1984), introduction.

66. See Elaine Tyler May, *Homeward Bound: American Families in the Cold War Era* (New York: Basic, 1988), 41–47, 60–67.

67. It remains to be seen what effect recent revelations about his personal life will have on the reception of his films.

68. See Erens's discussion of the stereotype and these films in *Jew in American Cinema*, 205–6, 273–76, and 371.

69. Notably, Singer distanced himself from the film version of his tale. He was more interested in exploring the ironic and erotic dimensions of the situation than making a feminist point. These aspects of masquerade are not, of course, incompatible; see Mary Ann Doane, *Femmes Fatales: Feminism, Film Theory, Psychoanalysis* (New York: Routledge, 1991), chaps. 1–2.

70. For a more detailed discussion of this film, see Sonya Michel, "'Yekl' and *Hester Street*: Was Assimilation Really Good for the Jews?" *Literature/Film Quarterly* 5 (1977): 142–46.

71. The embodiment of sensuality in a working-class character who sparks a sexual awakening in his or her lover is not new; consider such famous examples as D. H. Lawrence's *Lady Chatterly's Lover* and E. M. Forster's *Maurice*.

72. My thanks to Seth Koven for sharing with me his insights into the relation between Jewish masculinity and commoditization.

73. Grossberg, pers. comm.

Contributors and Editors

JOYCE ANTLER teaches American studies at Brandeis University, where for many years she directed the Women's Studies Program

LYNN DAVIDMAN is associate professor of Judaic studies and sociology at Brown University

TIKVA FRYMER-KENSKY is director of biblical studies for the Reconstructionist Rabbinical College

JUDITH HAUPTMAN is an associate professor of Talmud at the Jewish Theological Seminary of America

PAULA E. HYMAN is the Lucy Moses Professor of Modern Jewish History at Yale University

SONYA MICHEL teaches the history of women, men, and gender at the University of Illinois at Urbana-Champaign

JUDITH PLASKOW is professor of religious studies at Manhattan College

SUSAN STARR SERED is a senior lecturer in anthropology at Bar-Ilan University in Israel

NAOMI SOKOLOFF is associate professor of Hebrew at the University of Washington, Seattle

SHELLY TENENBAUM is associate professor of sociology and Jewish studies at Clark University

HAVA TIROSH-ROTHSCHILD is an associate professor of religious studies at Indiana University, Bloomington

Index